Embedded Systems Dictionary

*Jack Ganssle and
Michael Barr*

CMP**Books**

San Francisco, CA • New York, NY • Lawrence, KS

Published by CMP Books
an imprint of CMP Media LLC
Main office: 600 Harrison Street, San Francisco, CA 94107 USA
Tel: 415-947-6615; fax: 415-947-6015
Editorial office: 1601 West 23rd Street, Suite 200, Lawrence, KS 66046 USA
www.cmpbooks.com
email: books@cmp.com

The programs in this book are presented for instructional value. The programs have been carefully tested, but are not guaranteed for any particular purpose. The publisher does not offer any warranties and does not guarantee the accuracy, adequacy, or completeness of any information herein and is not responsible for any errors or omissions. The publisher assumes no liability for damages resulting from the use of the information in this book or for any infringement of the intellectual property rights of third parties that would result from the use of this information.

Editor:	Rita Sooby
Layout design & production:	Justin Fulmer
Managing editor:	Michelle O'Neal
Cover art design:	Damien Castaneda

Distributed to the book trade in the U.S. by:
Publishers Group West
1700 Fourth Street
Berkeley, CA 94710
1-800-788-3123

Distributed in Canada by:
Jaguar Book Group
100 Armstrong Avenue
Georgetown, Ontario M6K 3E7 Canada
905-877-4483

For individual orders and for information on special discounts for quantity orders, please contact:
CMP Books Distribution Center, 6600 Silacci Way, Gilroy, CA 95020
Tel: 1-800-500-6875 or 408-848-3854; fax: 408-848-5784
email: cmp@rushorder.com; Web: www.cmpbooks.com

Library of Congress Cataloging-in-Publication Data
Ganssle, Jack G.
Embedded systems dictionary / Jack Ganssle and Michael Barr.
    p. cm.
  ISBN 1-57820-120-9
    1. Embedded computer systems--Dictionaries. I. Barr, Michael, 1971-
II. Title.
TK7895.E42G38 2003
004.16'03--dc21

ISBN: 1-57820-120-9

CMP**Books**

Transferred to Digital Printing 2009

Dedication

For Marybeth –Jack Ganssle

For Teju –Michael Barr

Reviewer's Comments

"An indispensable guide for anyone who needs to understand the terminology and buzzwords that embedded developers throw around."

—Stuart Ball, Seagate Technologies; author, *Embedded Microprocessor Systems: Real World Design* and *Analog Interfacing to Embedded Microprocessors*

"A dictionary that covers the territory and then some—software, hardware, organizations, people, standards—in a manner that is sometimes irreverent but never irrelevant. This is a technical dictionary that is fun to read."

—Benjamin M. Brosgol, senior technical staff member, Ada Core Technologies

"This book is a must for hardware engineers, software engineers, and students alike. It is comprehensive—encompassing not just commonly-used phrases, but esoteric terms from a variety of fields and disciplines. The definitions give not just meaning, but relevant background information. This book is a much-overdue addition to the growing world of embedded systems development."

—John Catsoulis, author, *Designing Embedded Hardware*

"Every engineering professional should have a copy of this dictionary on their desk. It is both a powerful, quick reference guide, and a valuable educational tool. Jack and Michael have done a tremendous service to the technical community by capturing all this knowledge in one, easy-to-use manual. My copy was dog-eared after the first day!"

—Bill Gatliff, freelance embedded consultant

"This comprehensive reference will quickly become a strategic ally of both engineers and managers."

—Andrew Girson, CEO, InHand Electronics, Inc.

"This is an incredible piece of work and a must-have book for every seasoned professional and newbie to Embedded Systems. I never realized how many words and definitions are part of our discipline. I even learned a few new terms such as 'kibibit' and 'kibibyte.' Definitions are very clearly described and some are even accompanied by practical examples. Once in a while, you will spot a few tidbits of humor which are characteristic of the authors (see 'lone guru,' 'spaghetti code,' and 'X-Acto-Knife'). You can be sure that I'll have this book on my shelf and will reference it on a regular basis. My compliments to the authors."

> — Jean J. Labrosse, author, *MicroC/OS-II: The Real-Time Operating System* and *Embedded Systems Building Blocks*

"We have electrical dictionaries, we have computer science encyclopedias, and of course, we have the Net, but until now, in what single tome could you look up 'ARP,' 'bit banger,' and 'ZIF socket'? The embedded systems engineer has to work in a highly versatile manner and deal with a multitude of disciplines—each with their own lingo and acronyms. Ganssle and Barr have captured this breadth by not only including the obvious dictionary terms, but also the venerable product names of the embedded world such as 'Intel x86' and 'MAX232.'"

> —Christopher D. Leidigh, director of embedded networking and technology, American Power Conversion

"The Embedded Systems Dictionary is an excellent, and much needed, resource for not only the real-time embedded engineer, but also for the greater computer science and engineering communities."

> —Kevin M. Obenland, Ph.D., director of systems architecture, Science Applications International Corporation

"Countless times in my career did I wish for a book like this…. It is the first book we recommend to all our students."

> —Olaf Pfeiffer, tutor and co-founder of Embedded Systems Academy

"The Embedded Systems Dictionary is a valuable desktop reference to the confusing plethora of terms that are thrown around and not really defined anywhere. Jack Ganssle and Michael Barr's book will find a place on my desktop!"

> —Bruce Powel Douglass, Ph.D., chief evangelist, I-Logix

Foreword

In his 18th century *Dictionary*, Dr. Samuel Johnson defined *Tory* as "one who adheres to the ancient constitution of the state and the apostolical hierarchy of the Church of England." On the other hand, he defined *Whig* simply as "a faction." While Dr. Johnson's *Dictionary* was an important contribution to the English language, the distinction he drew in defining two opposing political parties vividly demonstrates that compiling a dictionary is not a mechanical process. The final document will reflect the knowledge and biases of the authors.

A dictionary presents some particular design challenges. It must be accessible to readers from diverse backgrounds. It must lucidly communicate a definition in the fewest possible number of words. It must be comprehensive and accurate. Creating a dictionary that meets these demands is a daunting task.

A technical dictionary only adds to the challenge. Compiling a dictionary focused on technology has the increased burden of having to communicate to readers with varying comprehension of the technology, an audience that is likely to extend from engineers to students to marketers. How much can the authors take for granted? An early dictionary compiler defined *mouse* as "an animal well known," which assumes perhaps more prior knowledge than can be justified.

My experience in test-and-measurement and medical imaging industries, coupled with work on hardware, software, and test publications has taught me that the vocabulary used to describe a technology may differ markedly between companies. The group of people who share a common technical vocabulary is smaller than one might think, which, I might add, makes the proliferation of acronyms especially egregious.

Developing a common vocabulary in the context of embedded systems is made more difficult by the breadth of the field. Moreover, since embedded systems development spans both hardware and software, a dictionary must address both disciplines. In the introduction to this dictionary, the authors note that "virtually every electronic device designed and manufactured today is an embedded system." That fact does not imply that all embedded systems were created equal. The definition applies over products ranging from a simple remote control to the avionics in a Boeing 777.

To my mind, Michael Barr and Jack Ganssle are ideal candidates for the task of compiling an embedded systems dictionary. Because they have spent years as working engineers and have taught and written about technology, they bring to this project the unique combination of a deep understanding of embedded systems technology and a sensitivity to the nuances of language. Their engineering experience gives them the knowledge and discipline that compiling such a dictionary demands, and the years they have spent writing and teaching about technology have given them the ability to marshal information and present it cogently.

This remarkable dictionary represents the fruits of their labors. As you page through it, you'll find not only descriptions of terminology that are clear, readable, and occasionally amusing, but you'll also learn quite a bit about the history of computing. It's a worthy addition to your bookshelf.

Lindsey Vereen
Editorial Director, *Embedded Systems Programming*
CMP Media LLC

Preface

Of the 6.2 billion processors manufactured in 2002, less than 2% became the brains of new PCs, Macs, and Unix workstations. The other 6.1 billion went into embedded systems. The essence of every modern electronic device, from toys to traffic lights to nuclear power plant controllers, these processors help run factories, manage weapon systems, and enable worldwide communication and the flow of information, products, and people.

Embedded processors span the range from simple 4-bit microcontrollers like those at the heart of a greeting card or children's toy, to powerful custom 128-bit microprocessors and specialized DSPs and network processors. Some of the products that include these chips run a short assembly program from ROM with no operating system; many more run real-time operating systems and complex multithreaded C or C++ programs; and it's also increasingly common to find variants of desktop-lite operating systems based on Linux and Windows controlling more powerful devices that are still clearly embedded systems.

Virtually every electronic device designed and manufactured today is an embedded system, and virtually no first-world person is untouched by this technology. In fact, once you start looking for them, we're sure you can quickly find a few dozen embedded systems in your home and at least a few on your person. Yet despite their ubiquity remarkably few non-engineers have heard the word "embedded" used in this context. Fewer still could tell you which of the embedded systems they own or use are also real-time systems.

Though the use of embedded processors is now a practice more than three decades old, there's been no previous attempt to gather all its vocabulary in one place and clarify the meanings and usage of individual terms. This dictionary provides the precise definitions needed to use embedded systems terminology properly.

Intended Audience

As we compiled the terms and definitions in this dictionary, we had in mind a variety of readers from different backgrounds. There were first, of course, the many hardware and software engineers who envision, design, implement, and test embedded real-time systems.

Though we have both spent many years working in this field, we were ourselves shocked to discover just how many terms there were. The field is broad and encompasses hardware, software, debugging, mathematics, algorithms, control, real-time, and many other aspects. New terms enter the field regularly, particularly with the pace of technological advance continuing to increase.

No one of us (even the authors of this dictionary) can know all the meanings of so many terms off the top of our heads. And certainly no engineer cares to be stumped—especially in front of a boss or a peer—by a word whose meaning we don't know or can't quite remember. We've compiled this dictionary to help organize all that data for you. Your mind is better able to think clearly when it is uncluttered with memorized facts, formulas, and definitions; we've included such technical details throughout the book for your easy reference.

Secondly, this book is for managers who run individual development projects, VPs who run engineering divisions, and corporate executives. We recognize that the acronyms and techie terms used by your staffs can be baffling at times; sometimes it even seems they use them specifically to confuse you. So that this doesn't lead to miscommunication or misinformed decisions, we suggest keeping a copy of this dictionary nearby. It will help thwart the usual torrent of developer-speak gibberish—and to keep you up to date with the latest advances in the technology inside your products. We've begun each definition with a concise accessible sentence, so that you can quickly grasp what the term is about without getting bogged down in the details.

There are also the many administrative support folks, sales and marketing staff, and technical writers who must work with the engineers and organize the reams of documentation they produce. You'll need this reference to check spelling and meanings of the words the engineers themselves have chosen. It'll also help you learn to use the terms correctly in a sales presentation or requirements discussion. And that will give you more confidence to know when to ask important questions and when to just let the engineers babble on. We've included tons of cross-references between entries and the expansion of every acronym with your needs in mind.

Finally, those who edit or publish technology books, newsletters, trade magazines, newspapers, and websites may find this a helpful guide to term spelling, usage, and meaning. The editors of *Embedded Systems Programming* magazine and **Embedded.com** have adopted this dictionary as a de facto editorial style guide.

In short, there's something here for everyone.

Organization of this Book

We begin each definition with the part of speech and, where it's not obvious, standard pronunciation. The first sentence is a concise statement of that term's meaning. We follow the concise definition with any abbreviations, alternative terms or, in the case of an acronym for example, expansions. For the sales and marketing folks and managers this may be all that they really need.

Part of Speech Key

abbr.	abbreviation or acronym
adj.	adjective
adv.	adverb
cmd.	command
fn.	function
lit.	literal
N.	proper noun
n.	common noun
num.	part number
pre.	prefix
res.	reserved word
sym.	symbol
v.	verb

For the engineers and technical writers, though, far more depth follows. Definitions of key terms are almost encyclopedic in their length, and those and many others include helpful diagrams, schematics, figures, equations, and code listings. There are even tips for further reading where appropriate sources exist. And everything is cross-referenced to the nth degree.

Sure, you could just leave this on your shelf as a dusty reference tool, picking it up only on those occasions when you encounter an unknown term or acronym. But we recommend paging through the terms occasionally. You'll definitely learn a lot that way, even if you're an old embedded hand. Let the cross references lead you down interesting paths, and enjoy the fun definitions when you find them.

Updates

This is the first of what we hope will be many editions of this dictionary. So we intend to add new terms and patch bugs in our existing definitions regularly. In this we solicit your help. Those of you who would like to sign up for e-mail news updates can send a blank e-mail to esdictionary@news.cmpbooks.com. Furthermore, if you would like to contribute to the effort by reporting any errors you spot in this edition or any terms we've overlooked, please e-mail us at dictionary@ganssle.com.

Beware, though, that our time is limited and that we may not always be able to respond to all e-mails directly; likewise we may not always agree with your interpretations. You can be sure, though, that your suggestions and inputs will be taken into account when we prepare the next edition. Please do not suggest the addition of proprietary or company-specific acronyms or terms. We're striving to set the standard across the embedded real-time systems industry as a whole.

We have, by the way, discovered that some terms have multiple, somewhat conflicting uses. You may disagree with some of our choices on spelling or interpretation. Rest assured that, where such conflicts exist, we've scoured other reference books, libraries, and the web in pursuit of the best possible solution. In cases where a word is commonly spelled or used in different ways (e.g., Is 1,024 bytes 1 KB, 1 kB, or 1 KiB?) we've adopted popular international standards where they exist, or studied usage frequencies and trusted sources where they don't. In the end sometimes we made a judgment call based on our combined experiences

We hope that, over time, the choices we've made here will help resolve conflicting usage and standardize the vocabulary of embedded systems.

Acknowledgments

We'd both like to offer a very special thank you to Robert Ward, who was the inspiration for this work, its constant guide, and a mentor to us both. And thanks too, Robert, for creating the phenomenal database and web-based authoring and editing tools we used to build this book.

CMP Books' production staff did a great job of turning our bits into pages. Thanks to Rita Sooby, in particular, for editing our 4,500 plus entries and pointing out their many initial shortcomings and inconsistencies. Thanks also to Justin Fulmer for managing the art and layout.

Stuart Ball, Kevin Banks, Sean Beatty, Tim Behne, Jeremy Bentham, Ben Brosgol, Christopher Brown, John Canosa, Bruce Powel Douglass, Brad Eckert, Lewin Edwards, Phil Ekstrom, Bill Gatliff, David Hinerman, Nigel Jones, David Kalinsky, Roee Kalinsky, Mark Kohler, Markus Levy, Russel Massey, Don Morgan, Niall Murphy, Don Rowe, Dan Saks, Miro Samek, Dan Simon, Jason Steinhorn, Dave Stewart, Steve Stolper, Dan Sweeney, and Tim Wescott contributed their wording or knowledge in one form or another. We thank them for helping make this dictionary both broader and deeper than the authors' expertise alone would otherwise allow.

Michael also wishes to thank Nitin Madnani, who was an intern at Netrino when we started this project and did some background research.

Jack Ganssle
Baltimore, Maryland

Michael Barr
Annapolis, Maryland

# #

\# (pound) 1. *n.* A spare key on a phone's tiny keypad. In that capacity, often used as a data delimiter ("Enter your account number followed by the pound sign."). *See also* dual-tone multiple frequency.

2. *n.* An abbreviation for the English-system unit of weight that's also abbreviated "lb".

`#define` (pound define) *res.* In C and C++, a preprocessor command used to define constants and macros.

`#include` (pound include) *res.* In C and C++, a preprocessor command that incorporates the named file that follows at the current location of the current source file, prior to compilation of the current file.

`#pragma` (pragma) *res.* In C and C++, a preprocessor command used to invoke compiler-specific functionality.

`!` (not) *res.* The logical-NOT operator in C and various related languages. In C and C++, `!foo` is 0 if `foo` is nonzero; 1 if `foo` is 0.

`^` (ex or) *res.* The bitwise-XOR operator in C and various related languages.

`|` (or) *res.* The bitwise-OR operator in C and various related languages. The `|` operator is easily confused with the `||` operator. However, their behavior is in fact very different. `0x55 | 0x0F` performs a binary OR resulting in `0x5F`. `0x55 || 0x0F` performs a logical OR that says true (nonzero) OR true, therefore true. Beware that the compiler won't warn you if you choose the wrong one.

`||` (or) *res.* The logical-OR operator in C and various related languages. Often confused with `|`.

`~` (not) 1. *res.* The unary bitwise-NOT operator in C and various related languages. Sometimes confused with the logical NOT operator `!`, though their functions are very different. Make sure you use the right one; your compiler won't know to warn you of the error.

EXAMPLE: If 16-bit `x` is `0x0123`, `~x` is `0xFEDC`; `!x` is 0 (Boolean false).

2. *symb.* A prefix used on schematic diagrams and in logic equations to indicate active low signals.

`%` (mod) 1. *res.* The modular division operator in C, C++, and Java. The result of `a % b`, where `a` and `b` are both integers, is the integer remainder of `a` divided by `b`. The result is, by definition, between 0 and `b−1`.

2. *n.* Percentage.

`&` (and) 1. *res.* The bitwise-AND operator in C and various related languages. The `&` operator is easily confused with the `&&` operator. However, their behavior is in fact very different. `0x55 & 0x0F` performs a bitwise-AND resulting in `0x05`. `0x55 && 0x0F` performs a logical-AND resulting in true, since both are non-zero. Beware; the compiler won't warn you if you choose the wrong one.

2. *res.* In another context, the unary address-of operator in C and C+. The `&` is interpreted as an address-of operator when it precedes the name of a variable in a statement like `p = &a` or `&b + sizeof(b)`.

3. *res.* In the declaration of a variable, an & preceding a variable's name tags it a reference type in C++.

&& (and) *res.* The logical-AND operator in C and various related languages. Often confused with &.

> (greater than) *res.* The greater than operator in C and various related languages. If a is greater than b, the test a > b is true.

>> (right shift) *res.* The right-shift operator in C and various related languages. Shifting an integer right by n bits is equivalent to dividing its value by 2^n. Any bits shifted out the right end are discarded. In C and C++, the bits shifted in from the left depend on the type of the operand: if it is unsigned, 0s are always shifted in from the left; if it is signed, however, it is up to the implementer (of the compiler) to decide whether the sign bit in the MSb position is duplicated or 0s are shifted in. In Java, this situation was corrected, and the >> operator always handles signed operands portably; a second >>> operator is used to explicitly ignore the sign bit during right shifts.

EXAMPLE: If variable uint8_t x contains the value 01010101b, the result of x >> 1 will be 00101010b.

>>> (unsigned right shift) *res.* Right-shift with zero extension. In Java, there are separate signed and unsigned right-shift operators. This is the unsigned one, which does not copy the sign bit into the uppermost bit as the pattern is shifted to the right. Instead, 0s are shifted in from that end. *See also* >>.

< (less than) *res.* The less-than operator in C and various related languages. If a is less than b, the test a < b is true.

<< (left shift) *res.* The left-shift operator in C and various related languages. Shifting an integer left by n bits is equivalent to multiplying its value by 2^n. However, be forewarned that it could result in

an overflow. Any bits shifted out the left end are discarded; 0s are shifted in from the right.

μA (microamp) *abbr. See* microamp.

μC/OS (micro-kos) *N.* A real-time operating system for small microcontrollers. Derived from a two-part expository article in *Embedded Systems Programming* in May–June 1992, this little RTOS took on a life of its own with the publication of a book-length treatment of the subject by creator Jean Labrosse. Now in the operating system's second release (μC/OS-II), the revised book includes complete source code and explanations of everything it does.

μCLinux *See* uClinux.

μF (microfarad) *abbr. See* microfarad.

μs (microsecond) *abbr. See* microsecond.

μV (microvolt) *abbr. See* microvolt.

π (pie) *n.* A mathematical constant representing the relationship between a circle's diameter and circumference. Approximately equal to 3.141592653589.

USAGE: Programmers often overspecify π when defining it in their programs. Even with double-precision data types, specifying the value to more than 16 decimal digits is a waste of effort. The following listing shows an appropriate C/C++ declaration.

This declaration for π is precise enough for most applications.
```
const double pi = 3.1415926;
```

* 1. *res.* In C and various related languages, an operator used to declare a variable or parameter of pointer type.

EXAMPLE: To declare a pointer p to integer x:
```
int * p = &x;
```

2. *res.* In C and various related languages, an operator used to dereference a pointer.

EXAMPLE: If pointer p points to integer x, you can read and write x via *p.

3. *n.* A spare key on a phone's tiny keypad. As in, "To disable call waiting, dial ★70, then the number." *See also* dual-tone multiple frequency.

++ (plus plus) *res.* The increment operator in C and various related languages. *See also* preincrement, postincrement.

– – (minus minus) *res.* The decrement operator in C and various related languages. *See also* predecrement, postdecrement.

.bss *See* BSS segment.

.data *See* data segment.

.HEX *See* Intel Hex format.

.text *See* text segment.

1-Wire *N.* A low-cost bidirectional serial communications bus requiring just a single wire to implement. Developed by Dallas Semiconductor, 1-Wire is an asynchronous, half-duplex, single-master component bus. 1-Wire minimizes device pin count by using extra on-chip circuitry to enable each 1-Wire component to communicate serially (over a single shared connection) with other 1-Wire devices. Compatible serial EEPROMs, A/D converters, temperature sensors, and other compatible devices are available. Electrical features include low data rates (about 16 kbps, max), flexible voltage and timing requirements, long maximum distances (up to 1,000 feet), and optional parasitic powering of slaves. Each 1-Wire device has a unique 48-bit serial number, so multiple slaves can share the same bus. *See also* I²C, SPI.

HISTORY: The 1-Wire protocol was invented by Dallas Semiconductor, which holds a related patent.

FURTHER READING: Willey, H. Michael. "One Cheap Network Topology," *Embedded Systems Programming,* January 2001.

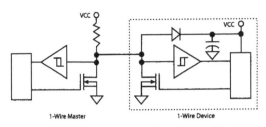

A representation of the circuitry used to connect 1-Wire devices.

100Base-T (hundred base tee) *abbr.* The most popular and cost-effective interface circuitry for Fast Ethernet. Short for 100 Mbps, BASEband, Twisted pair. Though competitive Fast Ethernet interfaces over fiber and four-pair cable are defined and used, 100Base-T is popular because it's based on the successful 10Base-T standard.

10Base-T (ten base tee) *abbr.* An IEEE standard for sending information at 10 Mbps on ordinary unshielded twisted-pair cable. Short for 10 Mbps, BASEband, Twisted pair. The standard defines connector types (typically RJ-45), pin connections, voltage levels, and noise immunity requirements. *See also* 100Base-T.

USAGE: Often misused to mean any 10 Mbps Ethernet connection or connector. However, the standard for running Ethernet LANs over 10Base-T-compliant cables and connectors is actually distinct and part of IEEE 802.3.

1488 (fourteen eighty-eight) *num.* A now-obsolete driver chip for RS-232 circuits. The 1488, introduced by Motorola in the 1970s, converted TTL logic levels (0 to 5 V) to the plus/minus 15 V used by RS-232. No longer used because it required external power supplies to provide these levels; Maxim and others today produce driver chips that internally create the needed RS-232 levels.

1489 (fourteen eighty-nine) *num.* An obsolete chip used to receive RS-232 signals. A 1970s part originally from Motorola, the 1489 was a line receiver that translated the +/-15-V RS-232 levels to TTL signals. Now replaced by combined receiver/transmitter chips such as the MAX232 from Maxim.

16-bit 1. *adj.* Generally used to denote a processor that uses a data bus 2 bytes wide. Note that this always refers to the processor's data bus width; address buses are typically unrelated to CPU size. Confusing the issue more, many embedded processors have an internal data bus of one size, but an external bus of quite a different size. The 188, for instance, is 16 bits internally but has only eight external data lines.

2. *adj.* Any circuit or algorithm that operates on data 2 bytes wide. Examples include 16-bit counter/timers and 16-bit A/D converters.

186 (one eighty-six) *num.* A 16-bit processor from Intel. The 186 instruction set is virtually the same as the 8088/8086, but the part packs a number of on-board peripherals, such as timers, DMA controllers, and serial channels. The 186 is part of a family of CPUs from Intel aimed specifically at the embedded market.

HISTORY: The 8088/8086 were wildly successful in the PC market but struggled in the embedded space because of the extensive support circuits needed. The 186 and its 188 baby brother also were licensed to AMD and others, who created their own variants with the same instruction set but a different mix of on-board peripherals.

188 (one eighty-eight) *num.* A peer of the 186 with an 8-bit external data bus. The narrower bus reduces memory bandwidth (every 16-bit data transfer takes twice as long) but also reduces memory cost and the number of traces on the PCB. Highly integrated microcontroller versions of the 188 from Intel and AMD are popular in embedded designs.

1s complement *See* one's complement notation.

2s complement *See* two's complement notation.

3-dB *adj.* Represents halving the power of a signal. The decibel is $10 \log(P_1/P_2)$, where P_1 and P_2 are two power levels. If P_1 is the power of a frequency component input to a filter and P_2 the power output at that frequency, P_1/P_2 is 2. 10 log 2 is about 3, so this half-power point of the amplitude response will show as -3 dB of attenuation at that frequency.

Decibels are often used because the logarithmic scale compresses huge ranges of data to smaller, more manageable, values. For example, the human ear responds to inputs ranging from 10^{-16} to $10^{-4} W/cm^2$, a range of 1 trillion. Using logs compresses the range to 12.

32-bit 1. *adj.* Generally used to denote a processor that uses a data bus 4 bytes wide. Note that this always refers to the processor's data bus width. However, many 32-bit CPUs do use a 32-bit address bus as well. Confusing the issue more, many embedded processors have an internal data bus of one size, but an external bus of a different size. The 386EX, for instance, is 32 bits internally but has only 16 external data lines.

2. *adj.* Any circuit or algorithm that operates on data 4-bytes wide. Examples include 32-bit CRCs and 32-bit address buses.

386EX *n.* A microcontroller variant of the 80386 processor from Intel. Designed specifically for use in embedded systems, the 386EX processor included numerous on-chip peripherals. This part was a hermaphrodite, with a 32-bit internal data bus but only a 16-bit external bus.

4004 (four thousand four) *num.* The first microprocessor. Invented by Intel (a memory company at the time) in 1971, the 4004 was the world's first general-purpose microprocessor. A far cry from modern processors, the 4004 had a 12-bit instruction pointer, forty six 8-bit opcodes,

The world's first single-chip processor.

and sixteen 4-bit registers. The 4004 was a 16-pin DIP part, containing about 2,000 transistors. *See also* Busicom.

555 (five five five) *num.* An historically popular 8-pin integrated circuit that can be used to generate a one-shot pulse or periodic clock signal. Also called a 555 timer.

56000 *num.* A family of digital signal processors from Motorola.

68000 *num.* The first 16-bit microprocessor from Motorola. The first member of the 68k family. The 68000 is a 16-bit CPU with separate address and data buses, a single-phase clock, and no on-chip peripherals. The device offered a very orthogonal instruction set reminiscent of the PDP-11s. Its flat address space allowed programmers to address up to 16 MB of memory directly. *See also* 680x0.

HISTORY: Reputedly named for the number of transistors on the die, the 68000 was Motorola's attempt to create a PC processor for IBM. The 68000 was technically superior to the 8088/8086, which required cumbersome segmentation for addresses beyond 64 KB. Unable to produce the part on time, however, Motorola lost the PC business to Intel. Apple used the 68000 and later successors in the Mac.

680x0 *num.* The family of 68000-series processors comprising the 68010, 68020, 68030, 68040, and beyond. Also called the 68k family. The 680x0 family was the basis of the original Apple and Macintosh computers.

683xx *num.* Motorola's family of 68000-like microcontrollers targeted specifically at embedded systems. The 683xx family primarily comprises the CPU32 series of processors, which use essentially the 68000 instruction set. Each of the family members has a different mix of on-chip peripherals.

68k (sixty-eight kay) *abbr. See* 680x0.

68xx *num.* A family of 8- and 16-bit microcontrollers from Motorola. Family members include the 68HC05, 68HC11, and 68HC12.

6DOF (six doff) *n.* Able to move in either direction along three different axes, typically in the 3-D world. Short for Six Degrees Of Freedom.

EXAMPLE: A helicopter can move up or down, left or right, and forward or backward; thus, it is the quintessential example of the 6DOF capability.

7-segment display *n.* A device that displays all numbers and many letters and symbols via just seven linear segments. Most also have one or two decimal points. The LED version of an 7-segment display comes in both common anode and common cathode configurations, indicating whether each diode's anode or cathode is connected together. 7-segment LCD displays are also widely used.

There's no standard for driving LEDs. Some designers drive them directly from the processor's PIO pins, connecting each segment to an output pin. This uses more I/O pins but lets the programmer generate any of the possible characters. Others use a driver IC (e.g., 74HC4511), which accepts a 4-bit input, creates a character, amplifies the output, and drives the segments. These limit the possible characters that can be displayed.

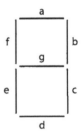

Layout of a 7-segment display.

To support multidigit displays, most vendors supply banked 7-segment displays, in which the anodes or cathodes are brought out individually to pins, and the other terminals—those connected to segments—are all tied together. This supports multiplexing of the display via dedicated hardware or smart software.

8-bit 1. *adj.* Generally used to denote a processor that uses a data bus 1 byte wide. Note that this always refers to the processor's data bus width. Typical 8-bit CPUs have 16 or 20 address lines.

2. *adj.* Any circuit or algorithm that operates on data 1-byte wide. Examples include 8-bit buffers and 8-bit D/A converters.

80/20 rule *n.* An approximate rule of thumb that states 20% of a domain accounts for 80% of the evil. Common 80/20 rules include performance—80% of the real-time issues will be in 20% of the code—bugs—20% of the code is responsible for 80% of the trouble—and work ethic—80% of the work in an organization is done by 20% of the people.

802.11 (eight oh two dot eleven) *N.* A popular wireless networking standard for LANs.

8051 (eighty fifty-one) *num.* An 8-bit microcontroller family. The original 8051 was designed in the late 1970s by Intel. Its many variants are still popular with embedded systems developers and are now available from multiple suppliers. Related chips include Siemens' 80C517, TI's TMS370, and the 80251.

80x86 (eighty ex eighty-six) *num.* The family of "Intel Architecture" processors. Abbreviated x86. Commonly used to refer to the processors used in PCs, from the early 8086 to the 80286, 80386, 80486, Pentium, and beyond.

8253 (eighty-two fifty-three) *num.* A programmable timer IC used in the early IBM PC and compatible computers.

8254 (eighty-two fifty-four) *num.* The programmable counter/timer chip used in the original IBM PC and still emulated to this day.

8259 (eighty-two fifty-nine) *num.* An obsolete interrupt controller IC designed for x86 systems. *See* 8259A.

8259A (eighty-two fifty-nine-A) *num.* The original interrupt controller IC designed for x86 systems. Created by Intel in conjunction with their 8088 processor, the 8259 and later the 8259A (which had better electrical and timing characteristics) allowed the single interrupt pin on the 8088 to handle eight external interrupts. Via cascading and nesting modes, the designer could combine multiple 8259As to support as many as 256 interrupts in an x86 system.

Currently, the 8259A is no longer available from Intel, though other vendors still make equivalent parts.

8N1 (as letters and numbers) *abbr.* A common flavor of serial communications that features 8 data bits, no parity, and 1 stop bit. Other specifications have the same format, with E and O indicating even and odd parity, respectively. This information is normally coupled with the number of data bits per second, such as 9600 bps or 57.6 kbps.

9s complement *n.* A way of encoding decimal numbers that simplifies logic circuits by replacing subtractions with additions. The 9s complement technique can be used to subtract decimal numbers on any machine that can add. Use a four-digit adder to compute $x - y$. Write $x - y$ as: $x - y = x + (9999 - y) + 1$ (Note that $9999 + 1 = 10000$ and the 10000 simply carries off the end of the four-digit adder.) Compute $9999 - y$ by replacing each 0 in y with a 9, each 1 with an 8, each 2 with a 7, and so on. The adder computes $x + (9999 - y)$. Increment the result to add the final 1.

EXAMPLE: Compute $7853 - 5678$.
The 9s complement of 5678 is 4321.
Add $7853 + 4321 + 1$ to get 2175.
The leftmost 1 overflows out of the four-digit adder.

; 1. *res.* The end-of-statement delimiter in C and various related languages.

2. *res.* A common choice of comment delimiter for assemblers.

An x86 assembly statement with trailing comment.

```
mov  ax, 100   ; comments follow semi-colons
```

a.out (eh dot out) *n*. An object file format output by some compilers and read by related linkers and loaders. *See also* ELF, COFF.

A/D (A-to-D) *abbr. See* A/D converter.

A/D converter *n*. A hardware device that reads an analog signal—typically a voltage—compares it to a reference signal, and converts the resulting percentage to a digital value. Short for analog-to-digital converter. The reference signal represents 100%. An n-bit A/D converter has a maximum value of $2^n - 1$ and a resolution of $V_{ref}/2^n$.

A/D converter, dual-slope *n*. A commonly used device to digitize an analog input that measures capacitor charge times. Dual-slope A/Ds charge a capacitor for a particular number of counts of a clock. The A/D then discharges the capacitor until the capacitor's voltage meets some reference level, while counting clock cycles.

Dual-slope A/Ds can be very accurate but are slow; worse, their conversion time varies depending on the input voltage.

A/D converter, flash *n*. A device that very quickly digitizes an analog input voltage. A flash converter compares the input to a number of reference sources in a single clock cycle. They're fast! But they use one comparator per input step (16 for a 4-bit A/D, 256 for 8 bits), so they are expensive for any but the smallest resolution applications. And they're power hogs too.

Here, flash means lightning quick, rather than having any similarity to flash memory technology.

A/D converter, single-slope *n*. A device that converts an analog input to its digital representation by measuring the time it takes to charge a capacitor up to some percentage of the input voltage. Single-slope converters are slow because of the capacitor charge time and are subject to errors from clock inaccuracies.

A/D converter, successive approximation *n*. A device that digitizes analog signals. Successive-approximation converters send the input signal to one input of a comparator; the other input goes to the output of a D/A. Smart logic adjusts the D/A's digital input to null the output of the comparator. When zero, the D/A's digital input is the digital representation of the A/D's analog input. In practice, the control logic first determines the MSb, then each successively lower bit.

Successive-approximation A/Ds require *n* comparison cycles to achieve *n*-bit resolution, so they are slower than other approaches. However, they are cheaper than some approaches (e.g., flash), and widely used in microcontrollers.

ABEL (like Cain's brother) *abbr*. A design language for creating the logic to be implemented in a simple programmable logic device. Short for Advanced Boolean Expression Language. Programs created with ABEL are compiled into the binary pattern necessary to create the PLD with a device programmer.

ABI (as letters) *abbr*. A binary-compatible platform for software. Short for Application Binary Interface. A typical ABI specifies the processor (and any other hardware requirements) and is OS specific. If all goes properly, a program written and compiled for a particular such platform will run on any other equivalent.

One of the nifty things about Java is that this kind of portability is available without recompiling and in an OS-agnostic way. That's the power of Java's generic hardware platform (Java virtual machine) and its processor-independent machine code (the bytecodes).

absolute address *n.* A memory or I/O reference that explicitly and without further translation will yield the data required. Processors generate a variety of addresses. The code might issue a "logical" address; the program might be relocatable so that it lives in any part of memory, issuing addresses relative to some offset. At some point, the CPU, via an MMU or other hardware, translates these intermediate addresses into an absolute physical address that goes to the memory array.

absolute value 1. *n.* The absolute value of a number is its magnitude stripped of sign. So, abs(4) and abs(-4) both equal 4. The result is always positive. The notation |x| is often used.

2. *n.* Occasionally used to denote the magnitude of a vector. Vectors have both magnitude and direction; the absolute value of a vector is just its magnitude.

abstraction *n.* A way of removing detail or simplifying a problem or concept. The entire history of computer tools is one of abstraction, of progressively removing detail from the programmer's domain. The earliest developers wrote binary code; assemblers abstracted that tedium from them. High-level languages further abstracted the machine implementation details from the programmers. Abstraction is an important part of decomposing problems. Assigning a driver routine to handle a complex hardware device isolates those details from the rest of the system.

AC (as letters) *abbr. See* alternating current.

acceleration *n.* The rate at which a moving body's velocity is changing. Acceleration, velocity, and position are all related by a simple calculus. Velocity is the rate of change of position; therefore, it is the derivative of position. Likewise, acceleration is the derivative of velocity or the second derivative of position. That is, $a = dv/dt$.

accumulator 1. *n.* A register inside a processor used as both one operand of, and the destination for, arithmetic and logical operations. Generally used to designate the only register on a processor that holds the result of an arithmetic or logical operation. The 8085 is a single-accumulator machine since essentially all math and logic happens with and to register A. The 68000 can do math on any general-purpose register, so one rarely speaks of it as having an accumulator.

2. *n.* The register, which can be a real register or a data structure in memory, that is used as one argument of, and the destination for, floating-point operations. Abbreviated FPA (Floating-Point Accumulator).

accuracy *n.* The repeatability of a data measurement. Accuracy is a measure of a signal's stability. Multiple readings of a highly accurate input yield identical or very close results. Often confused with precision.

ACK (rhymes with hack) *n.* An acknowledgment of some sort. On a network, the ACK can take the form of an entire packet or simply a 1-bit flag in the next data packet. The sender would typically set a retry timeout to occur if the ACK is not received within some required amount of time. Once the ACK is received, the timeout is canceled.

ACM (as letters) *abbr.* A nonprofit professional association serving the computer engineering community. Short for Association for Computing Machinery. The ACM has only about one-tenth the membership of the IEEE and publishes fewer journals. Rather than competing with IEEE as a whole, it largely competes head-to-head with IEEE's Computer Society, but both organizations publish noteworthy work, so most professionals and academics in computer engineering belong to both organizations.

FURTHER READING: http://www.acm.org

acquisition memory *n.* Where development tools store captured data. The term is most often used with logic analyzers and digital oscilloscopes, which suck in vast quantities of real-time data and store it in the acquisition memory for later review by the user. Acquisition memory is measured by its depth (how many words it can store) as well as width (the size of each word).

active filter *n.* A circuit using an op-amp that blocks signals depending on their frequency. Active filters either pass only a range of frequencies (called bandpass filters) or block a single narrow range of frequencies (notch filters). A typical use is any radio device (FM radio, cell phone, TV); a band-pass filter eliminates all stations other than the one the listener is tuned to.

HISTORY: Active filters require considerable electronics. Until recent years, they were difficult to construct, so all radio frequency devices were tuned circuits of capacitors and inductors. Take apart an old AM radio and you'll find that the tuning knob turns the plates of a capacitor, changing the resonant frequency of the simple LC circuit.

active high *adj.* Denotes a logic device or circuit where a logic 1 is a higher voltage than a logic 0.

active low *adj.* Denotes a logic device or circuit where a logic 1 is a lower voltage than a logic 0.

active object *n.* A state machine object endowed with its own thread of execution that communicates with other active objects by exchanging event instances. The most important characteristic of an active object is its opaque encapsulation shell, which strictly separates the internal structure of an active object from the external environment. The only objects capable of penetrating this shell, both from the outside and from the inside, are event instances. Active objects in the UML specification are the roots of threads of control in multitasking systems and engage one another asynchronously via events.

Ada *N.* An internationally standardized object-oriented programming language. Unlike C, Ada was originally developed (in the early 1980s) to meet the needs of embedded and real-time applications. The international standard was updated in 1995, and the resulting language was named Ada 95. Typical applications involve aircraft avionics, command and control, transportation systems, and other systems where reliability and performance are critical.

Ada can be used as a general-purpose programming language with built-in support for multitasking and hardware control or as an object-oriented programming language complete with all the trimmings.

HISTORY: The language is named for Charles Babbage's assistant, Ada Lovelace (1815–1852), who is considered the first programmer.

Ada 95 *N.* A 1995 update to the original Ada 83 language standard. The updated standard is formally known as *ISO/IEC 8652: Programming Languages—Ada.*

ADC (as letters) *abbr. See* A/D converter.

adder *n.* A hardware device that computes the sum of two numbers. In computer systems, adders only sum two numbers; in single-accumulator processors, one input is the accumulator, which is where the answer will be stored. Generally, the CPU's adder also accepts a "carry" input, which allows propagation of carries when summing numbers larger than can be expressed in one register. Although the logic for an adder is very simple, with larger register sizes, quite a bit of time is needed to propagate carries. Many processors use more sophisticated logic to "look ahead" to anticipate carry values.

address *n.* A location in memory or I/O space. Every memory cell and peripheral has a location specified uniquely by its address, rather like the way your postal address vectors your mail precisely to your house. In many computer systems, there are intermediate forms of addresses that might not correspond directly to a memory location, but each of these will be translated to one unique address before it's applied to the memory array.

address bus *n.* A set of wires connected to a processor and all of the peripherals with which it communicates, for the purpose of selecting a specific memory location or register within a particular peripheral. If the address bus contains n electrical lines, the processor can address up to 2^n unique locations. Address decoding logic between the processor and the devices connected to the bus select the proper device, typically based on the uppermost bits.

address decoder *n.* Hardware that selects a memory or I/O device based on the value on the address bus. When multiple memory or I/O devices connect to a single processor, an address decoder is needed to enable the correct chip for each access. At one time, these decoders were all separate ICs (e.g., 74LS138) that extracted information from high-order address lines. Today, many microcontrollers include a multitude of integrated chip-select outputs, which can be configured at boot time to properly enable external devices and memory as needed.

address latch enable *n.* A signal that, when asserted, tells external logic the bus contains address information. Abbreviated ALE. Conventional Von Neumann architecture processors have both a data and an address bus. On a microprocessor, though, pins are expensive, consume space, and are a source of reliability problems. To reduce pin counts, many processors multiplex both address

and data on the same pins. At the start of a cycle, the CPU supplies the address on these connections and asserts ALE. External logic must then strobe this address into a latch. Later in the cycle, ALE goes away and the bus transfers data information. ALE is the Intel nomenclature for this signal; other vendors use other names. *See also* address strobe.

address space *n.* The maximum amount of memory a processor can address. A CPU with 32 address lines has a 4-GB (2^{32}-byte) address space, though it is unlikely that much physical memory will actually be present.

address strobe *n.* A signal that, when asserted, tells external logic the bus contains address information. Abbreviated AS. Conventional Von Neumann architecture processors have both a data and an address bus. On a microprocessor, though, pins are expensive, space-consuming, and a source of reliability problems. To reduce pin counts, many processors multiplex both address and data on the same pins. At the start of a cycle, the CPU supplies the address on these connections and asserts AS. External logic must then strobe this address into a latch. Later in the cycle, AS goes away and the bus transfers data information. AS is the Motorola nomenclature for this signal; other vendors use other names. *See also* address latch enable.

addressing mode *n.* Any of a number of schemes used by a machine instruction to reference an argument. The term is used exclusively when working in machine or assembly language. *See also* register-indirect addressing, predecrement, postincrement, postdecrement, PC-relative addressing.

admission control *See* admittance control.

admittance control *n.* A possible feature of a real-time operating system that ensures all spawned threads will meet their deadlines. In order for such a system to work, each thread must be associated with a set of resource parameters describing its deadlines, periodicity, and worst-case execution time. Based on parameters like these, the RTOS might perform an RMA-style analysis to ensure that a new thread can meet all of its deadlines in the worst case, even as all of the threads previously admitted continue to meet their deadlines. If this guarantee cannot be met, an attempt to create a new thread will fail.

agile development *n.* A software development philosophy that values individuals and interactions over processes and tools, working software over comprehensive documentation, customer collaboration over contract negotiation, and responding to change over following a plan. Agile development is not a methodology; it embraces many different approaches, like XP, SCRUM, pragmatic programming, and others. Adherents of agile development believe that change is a basic fact of software engineering, so heavyweight processes that respond poorly to change are not appropriate.

ahead-of-time compiler *n.* A cross-compiler that takes Java source code or bytecodes as its input and produces native opcodes for a particular target processor as output. In practice, an ahead-of-time compiler for Java works just like a cross-compiler for C or C++. However, because Java programs are not normally compiled beyond bytecodes before they are downloaded to the target, this special terminology has been created.

For all practical purposes, compiled Java is equivalent to compiled C++ in both efficiency (the very same compiler back-ends and optimizers are typically used) and code size. Even precompiled and linked Java programs still require a small run-time environment consisting of the garbage collector and run-time checks. The GNU compiler for Java (gcj) is a Java front end for gcc.

Because it does not have access to the source code or resulting parse tree, a just-in-time compiler cannot achieve nearly the same level of optimization of the resulting code.

FURTHER READING: http://www.netrino.com/Articles/CompilingJava/

ALE (as letters) *abbr. See* address latch enable.

algebra *n.* A branch of mathematics in which symbols represent numbers or members of a specified set. Manipulating the symbols using defined rules results in generic equations that are true regardless of the actual numeric quantities involved. *See also* Boolean algebra.

algorithm *n.* A step-by-step problem-solving procedure, especially an established, recursive computational procedure for solving a problem in a finite number of steps.

HISTORY: Named after the Iranian mathematician Al-Khawarizmi.

aliasing 1. *n.* Allowing one memory location or register to be accessible at more than one address. Aliasing is a result of address decoding and often happens with peripheral control and status registers. For example, if an I/O device has just four byte-wide registers but is mapped into a 256-byte region of memory, aliasing will occur. In this case, the same four registers can be read or written at any of 16 different locations within that region.

2. *n.* An effect, because of undersampling, where a time-varying signal appears to be running at a much lower frequency than it really is. Aliasing is a common effect of using a digital oscilloscope to view fast waveforms, like clocks. If the scope's sampling rate is low, the perfect 20-MHz clock could appear to be oscillating at 10 kHz.

3. *n.* Different variables reference the same physical memory location. In languages that support pointers, it is common for a program to maintain multiple references to the same storage. Each of these references is an alias. Aliasing can create problems when optimizing compilers and pipelined processors because it becomes more difficult for them to identify and analyze data dependencies within the program.

alignment *n.* How bytes or bits fill a word or memory space larger than needed for the data. Typical uses include: left-aligned (bytes or bits fill the word from left to right), right-aligned (bytes or bits fill the word from right to left), byte-aligned (bits fill the word on 8-bit boundaries), and word-aligned (bytes or bits fill the word starting on even 16-bit increments).

alkaline battery *n.* Short for alkaline manganese, a type of nonrechargeable battery used for flashlights, cameras, and other consumer devices that need moderate power levels and easy replaceability. Alkaline batteries offer moderate cost, moderate energy density, and low impedance when discharged. Unfortunately, their voltage rapidly decreases as discharged, making power supply designs difficult in embedded applications.

Altera *N.* A billion-dollar-plus company that makes a variety of programmable logic ICs. Started in 1983, Altera created some of the earliest reprogrammable PLDs. Today, they produce components ranging from low-end PLDs to large programmable devices that even include on-chip microprocessors.

alternating current *n.* An electrical signal with a voltage that varies over time. Abbreviated AC. An AC signal varies, generally periodically, at a rate measured in hertz (Hz) and moves with excursions measured in volts (V). In practice, AC signals move between positive and negative levels in each cycle. Thus, a digital pulse stream in a TTL circuit, which moves between zero and a few volts, is rarely considered alternating current. Engineers typically view quickly moving signals as alternating current; a voltage that moves periodically but extremely slowly (on the order of many seconds or more) is usually direct current. The classic example of an AC signal is the voltage at a household outlet, which (in the U.S.) cycles at a 60-Hz rate.

alternator *n.* A device that converts mechanical motion to DC current. Alternators produce three-phase AC that is rectified by diodes to DC.

The term is sometimes used incorrectly in place of commutator.

ALU (as letters) *abbr. See* arithmetic logic unit.

AM (as letters) *abbr. See* amplitude modulation.

AMD *N.* A $4 billion dollar company that produces a variety of integrated circuits, including flash memory and processors. Founded in 1969 by the colorful Jerry Sanders and seven others, AMD is Intel's main competitor for CPUs in desktop computers. Although AMD once had a large embedded focus, that seems to have declined in recent years in favor of their PC business.

ammeter *n.* A piece of electrical test equipment that measures current.

amp (like guitar amp) *abbr. See* ampere.

amperage 1. *n.* The strength of an electric current. 2. *See* ampere.

ampere (amp-ear) *n.* A standard unit of electrical current. Abbreviated A. One ampere is 1 coulomb of electrical charge flowing past a point in 1 second. A car's starter might suck 300 A while cranking the engine. Your cell phone requires only milliamps. A high-end processor can draw as much as 100 A for very short periods of time, yet a little 8-bit 6805 might require only microamps, and so run for years from a couple of AA batteries.

Ampere's law *N.* An expression of the relationship between current and the magnetic field

$$\mathbf{B} \bullet \mathbf{l} = \mu i$$

where $\mathbf{B}$ is the magnetic field, $\mathbf{l}$ is the path, μ is the permeability constant (of the medium), and i is the amount of current. Ampere's law is one of the four basic equations of electromagnetics as codified by Maxwell. It says that the path integral around any (imaginary) closed path is equal to the current enclosed by the path multiplied by μ.

amplifier *n.* A device that boosts signal levels. *See also* track-and-hold amplifier, class D amplifier.

HISTORY: The invention of the vacuum tube, which is nothing more than an amplifier, started modern electronics. Transistors are modern versions of the tube and do nothing more than amplify a signal. A little bit of current at the base of a transistor modulates the much higher currents at the collector. Logic devices, whether implemented as transistors or as transistors disguised inside ICs, are high-gain amplifiers that yank wimpy, barely-in-spec signal levels to manly highs and lows.

amplifier, differential *n.* An electrical circuit that subtracts two input signals. Usually constructed from an op-amp and a few resistors, a differential amplifier takes two inputs, one to the op-amp's positive input and the other to the negative, and produces the analog difference at the op-amp's output.

amplifier, linear *n.* An analog circuit that multiplies an input by a constant value. Specifically, output = a × input + b, where a and b are constants. Op-amps form the basis of most linear amplifiers. A resistor in the feedback loop sets the amplifier's gain, which can be greater or less than 1.

amplifier, log *n.* A device that translates linear input signals to nonlinear logarithmic levels. The transfer function of a log amplifier is typically something like: *f*(input)= a log(input × b), where a and b are constants. Log amps serve many purposes; some analog engineers and other Luddites design circuits that compute results without the benefit of a processor because it's easy to compute roots and other complex functions using logs. Log amps also are often used to compress vast data ranges into smaller scales, which allows a low-resolution A/D converter to deal with a wide range of inputs.

amplifier, operational *n.* An extremely versatile amplifier that can be "programmed" using external circuits to transform an analog signal in almost any way. Abbreviated op-amp. These devices have open loop gains of 1 million or more. By placing components in the part's feedback loop, one can control the gain or even make the device amplify using a logarithmic transfer function. Op-amps generally have two inputs and one output and follow two golden rules: (1) the inputs draw no current and (2) with negative feedback, the output will do whatever is necessary to drive the difference between the inputs to zero. Typical applications include linear amps, log amps, summers (adders), comparators, differential amps, active rectifiers, and active filters. The op-amp is the basic unit of modern analog circuit design.

HISTORY: The earliest electronic computers were analog and were nothing more than a collection of hundreds of op-amps implemented with vacuum tubes. "Programmers" connected wires, capacitors, and resistors to patchboards to create their algorithm by building a circuit. It sounds crude, perhaps, but for some simulation problems—like computing ballistic trajectories—these yielded pretty good answers very quickly.

amplitude *n.* The size of a signal, usually in volts. A DC signal's amplitude is its voltage level. For AC, it's either the peak-to-peak size (the maximum extremes of voltage) or the RMS (root mean square) value.

amplitude distortion *n.* Corruption of a signal's voltage levels. Phase and frequency information might still be intact in an amplitude-distorted signal. Often caused by an overdriven amplifier.

amplitude modulation *n.* A way of sending information over a communications link by varying the signal's voltage over time. Abbreviated AM. A carrier, which is essentially a pure-tone broadcast at the AM transmitter's center frequency, is multiplied by the signal, be it voice, music, or even data. AM is the simplest of all modulation techniques, as well as the least efficient (since the carrier itself carries no information yet eats most of the energy broadcast). It is very susceptible to interference as well.

amplitude response *n.* The effect of a filter on the energy of a signal component passed through to the output. Also called magnitude response. The purpose of a filter is really to attenuate, or massively reduce the energy of, certain frequency ranges while allowing others to pass through virtually unchanged. A filter's transfer function shows how much frequency components in various ranges will be attenuated (or, sometimes, increased). *See also* phase response.

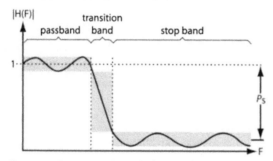

The amplitude response of a typical lowpass filter.

AMPS (just like current) *abbr.* The United States' analog cellular telephone network. Short for Analog Mobile Phone System.

analog *adj.* Describes data represented by a continuous range of values. The opposite of digital, in which all information is quantized. Analog is the way the world beyond the quantum level works. Part of the challenge of digital engineering is to convert noisy, inaccurate, and ugly real-world data to the pristine purity of 1s and 0s. The last ten years have seen a massive growth in digital signal processors, partly because they allow us to replace analog circuits with digital. Ultimately, the goal is to push the digital components all the way back to all systems' front ends—essentially connecting a

radio's antenna, for example, directly into a DSP input.

analog filter *n.* A filter that processes signals without converting them to a digital representation. Analog filters comprise analog components, such as resistors, capacitors, and inductors. Their use predates digital filters by many decades.

analog ground *n.* The common, zero-voltage, reference point in an analog circuit. Analog circuits are subject to noise, some of which is created by digital logic. Wise designers use at least two different grounds in their circuits: one for the logic and one for the analog. These grounds, then, are tied together at a single point. This reduces coupling of digital noise into the sensitive analog side.

analog multiplexer *n.* A device that selects one input from a number of analog inputs based on a binary value. Analog multiplexers typically have from two to eight analog inputs. A binary input code selects one of these, funneling the selected one to the output. Most analog multiplexers have a nonzero "on" resistance, so they are often placed in the feedback loop of an op-amp, which reduces the effective resistance almost to zero (it's divided by the op-amp's 10^6 or more open loop gain).

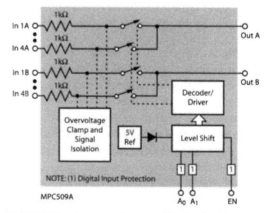

TI's MPC509A analog mux selects one of four analog inputs.

analog noise *n.* Generally, low-level distortion in a signal. Every analog signal will have some amount of erratic and unwanted random fluctuation. Noise comes from thermal sources (e.g., Johnson noise in a resistor or shot noise in a semiconductor device) and from coupling to other signals (e.g., a sensitive system might pick up radio or TV stations or digital transitions from elsewhere in the system). Just 1 or 2 mV of noise to a 16-bit A/D converter, scaled from 0 to 5 V, will generate more than a count of error. Analog designers minimize noise by carefully shielding their components, separating grounds, and adding filters. Firmware engineers further reduce noise levels of the digitized data by various algorithms, ranging from simple averaging to complex convolutions.

analog oscilloscope *n.* A now mostly obsolete device that displays waveforms of voltage versus time and does not first digitize the signal. Analog scopes directly amplify the incoming signal and apply it to plates of the CRT. *See also* digital storage oscilloscope.

The very popular Tektronix 545 analog oscilloscope.

analog switch *n.* An IC that selects one of several analog inputs. When dealing with multiple analog sources, it's usually cheaper to use an analog switch to direct each input to a single A/D converter than to employ multiple converters. The analog switch takes a number of analog inputs, passing just one that was selected by a digital code.

analog-to-digital converter *See* A/D converter.

analogue *See* analog.

AND *n.* The logical operation that results in a true result if and only if all of the inputs are true. Symbolically, a small, centered dot (•). A•B is the AND of inputs A and B. Put another way, the result of an AND operation is always false if any input is false.

AND gate *n.* A hardware device that computes the AND of two or more inputs. AND gates can exist as separate ICs (e.g., 74HCT08) or as terms used in more complex programmable parts, such as PALs, PLDs, and FPGAs.

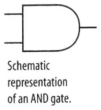
Schematic representation of an AND gate.

and-state *n.* Two or more states within a composite state that are simultaneously active. And-states offer a way to model independent aspects of an object's behavior. In UML statechart notation, they are separated by a dotted line. They are also called orthogonal regions. *See also* or-state.

angstrom *n.* A unit of measure equivalent to 10^{-10} meter. Often given as 10^{-8} cm. One angstrom is about the size of an iron atom—a very small size indeed. As semiconductor line widths shrink, the dimensions are not so many angstroms; 50-nm geometries, which will be available this decade, are 500 angstroms wide.

angular encoder *See* rotary encoder.

angular momentum *n.* The rotational equivalent of linear momentum. Mathematically, angular momentum is the vector product of a particle's linear momentum (which is mass times velocity) and the particle's position. Note that both terms are vectors, because position changes with time, and velocity includes both direction and speed components. Angular momentum is conserved, which is an expression of Newton's second law of motion: a body in motion stays in motion—the same motion—unless acted on by external forces.

anode *n.* The element of a semiconductor device that accepts electrons. In a diode, for example, current passes from the anode to the cathode. On a diode, the anode is the terminal not marked by a band.

ANSI (like antsy, without the t) *abbr.* A standards-setting body for the U.S. Short for American National Standards Institute.

FURTHER READING: http://www.ansi.org

ANSI C *See* ISO C.

antenna *n.* A device that receives or transmits electromagnetic energy. An antenna receives a signal by being present in the signal's electromagnetic field. The changing field induces electrical current flow in the antenna; electrons race up and down and are coupled to the rest of the receiver circuit. As such, they are inherently tuned circuits: the length of an antenna very much affects its ability to receive or transmit signals of a specific frequency.

anti-fuse *n.* One of the three processes used to build FPGAs. FPGAs are mostly SRAM-based, though a small number of flash-based devices exist as well. Anti-fuse is the third option—more common than flash but much less so than SRAM. Anti-fuse devices have a small insulating layer that is destroyed on programming, creating a connection.

Anti-fuse devices are one-time programmable. Once programmed, they cannot be modified, but they do retain their program when the power is off. Anti-fuse devices are programmed in a device programmer by either the end user or the factory or distributor.

antialiasing *n.* A graphical technique in which pixels are smoothed by adopting the average of the colors of pixels surrounding them.

antialiasing filter *n.* An analog lowpass filter that removes all frequencies above the Nyquist frequency (which is one half of the sampling rate). Typically used in data-acquisition circuits (like a digital scope), such a filter removes any high-fre-

quency components that might cause aliasing or erratic results from undersampling.

antistatic *adj.* Any of a series of components or tools used to remove static charges from parts and circuits. Modern semiconductor components have features that are so small—less than 100 nm in some cases—that any high voltage applied to their pins will likely destroy parts of the device. Static charges, accumulated by walking around a lab or even combing one's hair, can charge a human to thousands of volts. Various antistatic devices (wrist straps, foam, workstations) all discharge that potential before damaging circuits.

AOT (as letters) *abbr. See* ahead-of-time compiler.

aperiodic *adj.* Lacking periodicity; random. The term is most often used in the embedded context when scheduling periodic threads via RMA. The issue of what to do about aperiodic threads and interrupts inevitably arises in real-world systems. Aperiodic threads become ready to run on the occurrence of unpredictable events. *See also* sporadic.

EXAMPLE: The arrival of interrupts is often aperiodic.

aperiodic server *n.* A task that responds to events of an aperiodic nature.

API (as letters) *abbr.* A set of function calls that provide the interface to a software package. Short for Application Programming Interface.

EXAMPLE: POSIX and Win32 are the most popular operating-system APIs.

append *v.* To write data at the end of an open file, thus requiring additional storage space on the filesystem.

applet *n.* A stand-alone Java program.

USAGE: This term typically is used only on the desktop, where an applet is a Java class that specifically extends Applet and runs in a Java-enabled Web browser.

application benchmark *See* real-world benchmark.

application layer *n.* The protocol layer that manages the details of end-to-end communication within a particular application. Layer 5 of the OSI reference model. In a TCP/IP suite, applications such as telnet and FTP operate at the application layer. *See also* transport layer.

application software *n.* Software that is specific to a particular embedded system. Such application-specific code is generally built on a layered architecture of reusable components, such as a real-time operating system and network-protocol stack or other middleware. If there is no such architecture, then this term may not be used. The application software is unlikely to be reusable across embedded platforms, simply because each embedded system has a different application.

application-specific integrated circuit *n.* A piece of custom-designed hardware in a mass-produced chip. Abbreviated ASIC.

approximation *n.* An algorithm that computes, to some imperfect level of precision, the value of a function. Certain trig, square root, and other functions are slow or difficult to compute. Compiler-provided run-time packages include approximation routines for these functions, which almost always use polynomials or ratios of polynomials to return a result. Developing these approximating routines is a delicate business; there's a trade-off between precision and execution time.

ar *See* binutils.

architecture *n.* The general design of an embedded system or of a processor used in such a system. The system or CPU architecture typically determines the bus size, memory configuration, and bus type (Harvard, etc.). When applied to a processor, it designates RISC or CISC, MMU or not, and many other parameters.

ARCnet (arc net) *n.* An obsolete standard for communications between computers. Has since been supplanted by Ethernet. ARCnet was a 2.5-Mbps LAN originally developed by Datapoint. ARCnet used a modified token-passing protocol.

argc *lit.* The name typically used for the number of command-line arguments passed to a C/C++ program:

```
int main(int argc, char * argv[])
```

Note that the name argc is wholly arbitrary and can be changed by the programmer.

argument *See* parameter.

argument, immediate *n.* A parameter used by an instruction that is included as part of the instruction. Instructions could require data from registers, memory, I/O, or other sources. Immediate arguments are encoded directly into the instruction itself.

EXAMPLE: In the Z80 instruction LD BC,0x1234, the 16-bit value 0x1234 is encoded into the instruction itself. An assembler would generate a 3-byte opcode: 01 34 12 (hex).

argv *lit.* The name typically used for the array of string command-line arguments passed to a C/C++ program:

```
int main(int argc, char * argv[])
```

Note that the name argv is wholly arbitrary and can be changed by the programmer.

Ariane 5 *N.* An infamous European rocket (made by Aerospatiale) that demonstrates the flawed principle of redundancy based on duplicated software. Unlike hardware subsystems, which either work or fail and can be made more reliable through duplication, software is either right or wrong in its logic. If software fails once, it will fail again given the same inputs; merely duplicating the code does not add redundancy.

In the case of Ariane 5, some code borrowed from the successful Ariane 4 design experienced an overflow during flight. Recognizing the overflow, the primary controller shut itself down and the secondary controller took over. Unfortunately, the secondary controller experienced the very same overflow condition and shut down as well. The rocket self-destructed in midair, taking some very expensive cargo with it. *See also* Therac-25.

arithmetic logic unit *n.* The part of a processor that executes arithmetic and logical operations. Abbreviated ALU. The ALU generally takes a pair of input values, an input carry, and a control signal. The control signal tells it how to combine the values and carry to produce an output result. In addition to the numerical or logical result, one or more output signals, like an output carry, are typically generated. Depending on the architecture of the processor, the input values can come from a combination of accumulators and memory locations.

arithmetic overflow *n.* An error that occurs when the result of a mathematical operation is too large to store into the intended variable. Integer and fixed-point data types have limited range. For example, an 8-bit unsigned value can hold values 0 to 255. If the result is larger than 255, attempts to store it in a variable of that size will not produce reliable results. A result less than 0 would also produce an arithmetic overflow (not an underflow!).

Unless the range of the input values is well known at design time and can be guaranteed at run time, the result of all operations should be checked to ensure an overflow does not occur. If an overflow does occur, it must be handled in some safe way before the result is used. The designers of Ariane 5 learned about proper overflow handling the hard way.

arithmetic underflow *n.* An error that occurs when the result of a mathematical operation is too small to be stored. For example, no integer data type can store a value less than 1. All of the data after the decimal point will be lost if that result is stored in an integer. The integer will simply contain 0 (or possibly 1). *See also* arithmetic overflow.

ARM (like your arm) *abbr.* A 32-bit RISC processor widely used in low-power embedded applications. Short for Advanced RISC Machine.

HISTORY: The ARM design was started in 1983 as a project at Acorn Computer Group. After being refused access to the upcoming Intel 80286 for newer generations of their computer line, they responded by starting up a team to design and build a new CPU. When launched in 1985, the chip was the first commercial RISC processor.

DEC later licensed the design and produced the StrongARM. This work was later passed to Intel as part of a patent-related settlement, and Intel took the opportunity to replace their ailing i860 and i960 designs with the StrongARM. Today these are known by the name XScale.

ARM Thumb *N.* A 16-bit variant of the 32-bit ARM instruction set. ARM processors that support the Thumb instruction set can be switched in and out of "Thumb mode" via a bit in a register. Once in the Thumb mode, the CPU fetches special 16-bit instructions from memory. The advantage of these instructions is that they can be fetched more quickly across a narrower data bus and consume less memory. Not all of the ARM's capabilities are supported in Thumb mode, however.

ARP (rhymes with harp) *abbr.* A mechanism for mapping a destination IP address to its corresponding MAC address so that an IP packet can be routed over a specific physical network such as Ethernet. Short for Address Resolution Protocol. RFC 826.

Each node on a network has both a logical (IP) address and a physical (MAC) address. When sending a packet to a specific node, the application software provides only the IP address. The protocol stack, via ARP, must determine the specific MAC address for that IP address before it can finalize and send the network frame that will contain the IP packet.

In practice, it is inefficient to make ARP requests and receive replies before each packet is sent, so a table is kept (typically at the network driver) of all the known IP–MAC address pairs. Only if the MAC address of a particular destination IP address cannot be found in that table is the ARP protocol invoked. The results are added to the table then so they can be used later. *See also* RARP.

FURTHER READING: http://www.netrino.com/Connecting/2000-07/

array   *n.* A set of variables of common type arranged adjacently in physical memory.

array bounds overflow   *n.* A run-time situation in which memory outside an array is accessed accidentally or illegally through the array and its index.

   EXAMPLE: If the array `foo` is declared as `int foo[4];`, it has four elements (`foo[0]`, `foo[1]`, `foo[2]`, and `foo[3]`). For a variety of reasons, any C/C++ compiler will allow the programmer to directly or indirectly access `foo[5]`, `foo[-1]`, or any other nonexistent array element, which could result in corruption of other variables. In some languages, like Java, an attempt to read or write memory before or after an array will result in an exception.

arrival time   *n.* The time at which some signal or event occurs. In the case of an interrupt, the arrival time is the time at which the signal is asserted. Some delay, called latency, can occur before the arrival of this signal or event is noted by the software.

Art of Computer Programming   *N.* A three-volume book that illustrates numerous important algorithms used by programmers. (Knuth, Donald. *The Art of Computer Programming, 2nd Edition.* Addison-Wesley, 1998.) A bit dated—he used an artificial assembly-like language called MIX—this work includes many of the basic algorithms we use. Written with style, elegance, and wit, it presents the math behind each algorithm, with cookbook implementations.

Art of Electronics   *N.* The standard reference to practical electronic circuit design (Horowitz, Paul and Winfield Hill. *The Art of Electronics, 2nd Edition.* New York: Cambridge University Press, 1989.) The most comprehensive and lucid book on electronics ever written, it should be on the desk of everyone working in embedded systems. The authors completely cover the basics of electronics, analog design, and much of digital engineering. It is a little dated, but that is exhibited mostly by reference to older components.

artificial intelligence   *n.* The application of reasoning in machines, perhaps ultimately leading to human-like consciousness. Abbreviated AI.

No one knows how to define AI properly or even knows what intelligence is, but like pornography, we feel we'll know it when we see it. Some researchers think AI will self-organize and create awareness when the complexity of computers reaches levels similar to the human brain (1 trillion-plus connections); others suspect there's an as yet unknown spark required to initiate such intelligence.

Regardless, everyone agrees that the government will tax it when it arrives. *See also* Turing test.

AS   (as letters) *abbr. See* address strobe.

as   *See* binutils.

ASCII   (as-key) *abbr.* A popular mapping of the American character set to a 7-bit binary value. Short for American Standard Code for Information Interchange. See table on page 289. *See also* extended ASCII, Unicode.

ASIC (ay sick) *abbr. See* application-specific integrated circuit.

aspect ratio 1. *n.* A ratio of width to height.

USAGE: Aspect ratio is used in many fields. Regular televisions, for instance, have a 4:3 aspect ratio, so they are wider than they are high. Common monitor resolutions, like 640 × 480, 800 × 600, and 1024 × 768 share TV's 4:3 aspect ratio. High-definition TV changes the ratio to the movie-like 16:9 and thus eliminates the need for letterbox-presentation formats.

2. *n.* Outside of electronics, a ratio of height to width. Sails, for example, have a high aspect ratio if they are very tall and narrow.

assembler *n.* A software development tool that translates human-readable assembly language programs into machine-readable code that the target processor can understand and execute.

USAGE: Assembler also can mean assembly language, as in, "I wrote that part of the code in assembler."

assembly *See* assembly language.

assembly language *n.* A human-writable form of a processor's native instruction set. In its typical form, each line of assembly code represents a single CPU instruction. The human-readable representation of each opcode is called a mnemonic.

assert 1. *v.* To change the voltage on an electrical signal, such as an interrupt. In the case of an active high signal, to assert the signal is to set it to a positive voltage, such as 5 V. In the case of an active low signal, it is set to 0 V.

2. *See* ASSERT().

ASSERT() *n.* A widely used C preprocessor macro for checking an assumption at run time. If an assumption, such as ASSERT(param > 10);, is ever found to be false, the filename and line number of the failed assertion are generally printed or logged, and the program is often halted. It's a very useful feature during debug and a great tool for handling unanticipated situations gracefully in the field.

asserted *n.* To be in a logic 1 state, as a signal. *See also* assert.

assembly language An example of an assembly language subroutine for the PIC16F877 microcontroller. The code reads two ASCII bytes from the serial port, interprets them as hex digits (0 ... F), and combines them to form a byte of binary data.

```
GetHexByte: call    SerialReceive   ;get new byte from serial port
            addlw   0xBF            ;add -'A' to Ascii high byte
            btfss   STATUS.C        ;check if positive
            addlw   0x07            ;if not, add 17 ('0' to '9')
            addlw   0x0A            ;else add 10 ('A' to 'F')
            movwf   HexByte         ;save nibble
            swapf   HexByte.F       ;move nibble to high position

            call    SerialReceive   ;get new byte from serial port
            addlw   0xBF            ;add -'A' to Ascii low byte
            btfss   STATUS.C        ;check if positive
            addlw   0x07            ;if not, add 17 ('0' to '9')
            addlw   0x0A            ;else add 10 ('A' to 'F')
            iorwf   HexByte.F       ;add low nibble to high nibble
            movf    HexByte.W       ;put result in W reg
            return
```

assertion *n.* An assumption check, typically implemented in software via an ASSERT( ) macro.

astable *adj.* The state of a circuit that is likely to flip states without any further input. The circuit is "hanging fire," ready to change, rather like a ball atop a perfectly smooth hill.

EXAMPLE: An astable multivibrator is a circuit that uses a pair of gates in a feedback loop. Only one or the other can be at 1; however, the circuit is not stable, so it oscillates.

astable multivibrator *n.* A circuit with no stable state. The output oscillates between 0 and 1. Although it's pretty easy to build an astable multivibrator using a pair of transistors with plenty of resistors and capacitors, the classic design uses a pair of inverters tied in a loop. Today, most people would use the venerable 555 timer instead, since it can be configured to oscillate with reasonable accuracy at a wide range of frequencies. *Contrast with* monostable multivibrator.

asymptotic *adj.* A mathematical function that will approach, but never quite reach, a limiting value.

EXAMPLE: The function $1/x$ is asymptotic to 0; as x goes to infinity, the function gets smaller and smaller—practically to zero, but never quite there.

async (eh sink) *abbr. See* asynchronous.

asynchronous *adj.* A signal that is not related in the time domain to another signal is asynchronous. Abbreviated async. Each signal or event occurs at its own rate. Designers who try to synchronize two async signals will very often find this creates a metastability, which is a probabilistic situation where the two deterministic events can yield a random output.

EXAMPLE: Two microprocessors, each using their own clock, are asynchronous. Even if the clocks have exactly the same frequency, they are unrelated in time. Thermal changes and component differences ensure that the clocks will drift slightly, so even if the two could be synchronized, they'd quickly drift out of sync.

asynchronous bus *n.* A bus that does not use a clock to coordinate data transfers. Asynchronous buses generally use data strobes (like read and write) to indicate that data is available. Systems with asynchronous buses don't have to use a common clock, so processors running at different frequencies and with different clock phases can safely transfer data. *Contrast with* synchronous bus.

EXAMPLE: The VME bus is asynchronous.

asynchronous communications *n.* A communications scheme that transmits data over a single wire, sending bits one at a time in sequence. The timing of each bit is known by both transmitter and receiver. Each transmitted data byte begins with a start bit that starts the receiver's timing circuitry. Critical to the success of asynchronous communications is that the data bits have well-defined widths. *See also* start bit. *Contrast with* synchronous communication.

EXAMPLE: The best known asynchronous communications scheme is RS-232.

asynchronous logic *n.* An unclocked digital circuit or part of a circuit. Asynchronous logic changes state when any input changes. This can lead to race conditions and transient errors. *Contrast with* synchronous logic.

EXAMPLE: An address decoder is asynchronous. Its outputs will go to insane values as the input address changes, but this isn't a problem because a control line (read or write) is also applied to the memory circuits, in effect synchronizing the system.

ATE (as letters) *abbr. See* automatic test equipment.

atom *n.* The smallest building block of chemical reactions. All atoms are composed of protons and electrons and, with the exception of the most common form of hydrogen, neutrons. Taxonomy is driven by the number of protons, which determines the element. A varying number of neutrons creates different isotopes of an atom or element.

atomic 1. *adj.* An operation that cannot be interrupted is considered atomic. Atomic operations are inherently reentrant; they complete without fear of preemption or corruption by other tasks. A single opcode that does a read-modify-write, for instance, modifies a shared variable without the risk of an intervening interrupt causing the variable to be used in a half-changed state. Software developers can turn nonatomic operations into atomic ones by disabling interrupts. *See also* swap, test-and-set.

2. *adj.* Used to indicate measurement scales. Atomic scales are on the order of angstroms.

EXAMPLE: Semiconductor manufacturing is done on atomic scales. A 100-nm geometry, for example, results in lines 1,000 angstroms wide.

attenuation *n.* The reduction of a signal by some amount. Attenuation is the opposite of amplification. Analog signals are often too strong, so a circuit reduces their amplitude.

EXAMPLE: Any decent short-wave radio has a manual control to adjust attenuation, reducing the incoming signals by 10 dB or more. This adjustment is useful to avoid overloading the radio's front end when working with a nearby strong transmitter, but it is used more often when picking up weaker signals. The attenuator reduces broadband noise, essentially raising the weak, narrowband signal from the noise floor.

ATVEF (at vef) *abbr.* A standard for creating enhanced, interactive television content and for delivering that content to a range of television, set-top, and PC-based receivers. Short for Advanced TeleVision Enhancement Forum (http://www.atvef.com/). ATVEF defines the standards used to create enhanced content that can be delivered over a variety of media, including analog (NTSC) and digital (ATSC) television broadcasts, and a variety

of networks, including terrestrial broadcast, cable, and satellite. It is based on HTML.

FURTHER READING: http://www.netrino.com/Articles/ATVEF/

`auto` *res.* A little-used storage class specifier in C and C++. By default, variables declared at the heads of functions or code blocks within functions have local extent. The `auto` keyword can be used to force that extent upon such a variable but is rarely if ever used by programmers since that is the default behavior.

auto-zero *adj.* Describes a type of circuit that automatically compensates for drifting offsets. Autozero circuits go "offline" periodically, turning the input off and using feedback to figure out the current DC offset level. These levels change because of thermal drift and component aging. The new offset is then applied as a correction to the circuit's transfer function.

autoindexing *adj.* An addressing mode that extracts the destination address from a register and increments the register's contents after the data is transferred.

HISTORY: First used on the DEC PDP-11 series of minicomputers, the autoindexing addressing mode allowed any register to be a stack pointer and greatly simplified processing lists of data. The 68000, which has an instruction set that was patterned after the PDP-11, was the first microprocessor to employ autoindexing.

EXAMPLE: On the 68k series of processors, the instruction `MOVE.W (A0)+,D0` transfers data from memory at the address in A0 to register D0, and then adds 2 (one word) to A0.

automatic *See* automatic variable.

automatic test equipment *n.* A device that tests a complete PCB assembly without human intervention. Abbreviated ATE. ATE systems are typically big and complex, sporting hundreds of points that sense nodes on the PCB. These arrays, coupled with custom programming in the ATE device developed for each kind of PCB tested, can identify bad parts, practically eliminating skilled component-level technicians. *See also* bed of nails, JTAG.

automatic variable *n.* A variable that is defined within a function and, therefore, located on the stack. However, local variables declared static in C/C++ are not included in this classification.

autovector *adj.* A way of managing interrupts without supplying an external vector. An autovector cycle uses the interrupt's priority level as the vector instead of expecting an external controller to supply it. Invented by Motorola for the 68000 when hardware was relatively expensive, autovectored interrupts let designers eliminate hardware in systems with few interrupt sources.

average *n.* The sum of a series of values divided by the number of values in the series. Also called the mean.

$$average = \frac{A_1 + A_2 + ... + A_n}{n}$$

Averages are often used in digital filtering, to smooth noisy analog data.

average-case execution time *n.* The average amount of time to execute a section of code. It may be helpful to define the jitter and standard deviation along with such averages. Although the average-case execution time might be interesting in some applications, the worst-case execution time is typically of far more interest, particularly in real-time systems.

awk *n.* A pattern-matching and -processing language. An awk tool searches one or more specified files, checking for records that match a prespecified pattern. If awk finds a match, it performs the action specified for that pattern.

Awk is a flexible utility that programmers often use to automate complicated text-processing work. The syntax can be cryptic, but most awk scripts are only a few lines of code and can be simple throwaway items written as a quick solution to a temporary problem.

B

backdoor *n.* A way of circumventing a system's security, usually known only to the software developer(s). In less of a security context, backdoors called "cheat codes" are often included in video games. Once known to the user, these can be used to access secret play levels or obtain superpowers.

background debug mode *n.* A resource contained in many modern processors that can be used to help

isolate defects in a program. Abbreviated BDM. Many CPUs include quite a bit of extra logic just to give developers a debugging interface. A few pins are either multiplexed with other functionality or dedicated to debugging.

BDM resources include a high-speed synchronous communications link to a connected development computer, which issues commands to the BDM logic in the CPU. This interface lets the programmer see and alter all registers, memory, and I/O, as well as set breakpoints, run, stop, and single step. A few processors dedicate more pins to debugging and can echo limited real-time trace data out of the pins on command.

HISTORY: For many years, the in-circuit emulator was the most common debugging tool used in embedded systems development. With the advent of very-high-speed CPUs, however, creating a reliable electrical connection between the ICE and the target CPU became difficult and expensive. Caches and address-translation mechanisms (e.g., pipelines and MMUs) removed any correlation between the signals at the processor's pins and the program flow, further rendering ICEs problematic. Finally, very fine pitch surface mount and BGA packages created mechanical-connection difficulties that were never solved satisfactorily. A BDM bypasses all of these problems by giving direct access to the processor's core at a point before the cache or MMU, at reasonable speeds, and using just a few pins to simplify the tool connection.

background task *n.* A portion of a program that runs on its own as time permits, but which is currently suspended or currently has fewer CPU resources allocated to it than the foreground task.

HISTORY: "Background task" is a term now mostly obsolete. In the olden days (e.g., Data General's Nova systems), multitasking was the sharing of a single processor between exactly two tasks: one running in the foreground and the other in the background. Today's systems more likely consist of a large jumble of tasks executing at varying rates with a range of priorities. Although only one task has control of the processor at a given time, each is equally important, so none deserve the diminutive label "background."

backlight *n.* A local light source often used to make an LCD more readable in low- or no-light situations.

backplane *n.* A physical and electrical common bus that connects multiple printed circuit boards. The backplane is primarily a wiring and mounting framework but also can include electronics to match the impedance of the signals propagated through it.

EXAMPLE: A VME backplane is a large PCB containing connectors for each inserted PCB.

bad block *n.* A block on a disk that is no longer usable.

bad code *n.* An ugly program. Pretty much every program ever written is bad code. Most developers figure that if architects made buildings the way programmers write code, the first woodpecker that came along would destroy civilization.

USAGE: Typically, any program not written by oneself will be referred to as "bad code."

ball grid array *n.* A type of package for ICs. Abbreviated BGA. BGA packages have no pins per se; instead, all connections go to half-round balls on the bottom of the package. Hot air solders these balls to the circuit board. The advantage of BGA packaging is very short wire lengths, giving much better high-speed response. The BGA package

The underside of a BGA part packing 357 connections into a square inch of surface area.

also makes it possible to bring many hundreds of pins to the circuit board in a small-form factor.

bandpass filter *n.* A circuit that blocks all frequencies except those in a specified range. Bandpass filters can be made of capacitors and inductors, as active filters using op-amps, or implemented on a DSP. Examples include lowpass filters, which block all frequencies above a certain value, and highpass filters, which do the opposite.

bandstop filter *n.* A filter that blocks one specific frequency range. Often used when heavy narrowband interference exists, such as in a plasma heater. A bandstop filter eliminates this energy, letting other signals of interest pass. *Contrast with* bandpass filter.

bandwidth 1. *n.* The frequency range of a signal or circuit. A signal's bandwidth is the difference between its lowest and highest frequency components.

EXAMPLE: The bandwidth consumed by a particular signal might not be intuitively obvious. For example, an AM signal might require only 5 kHz to express the data's frequency range, but when transmitted, it often consumes several times that bandwidth in the radio spectrum for the two sidebands and carrier.

bang-bang control *See* on–off control.

bank *See* memory bank.

banked *adj.* Said of memory that is broken into two or more banks.

barrel shifter *n.* A circuit that moves bits in a register left or right quickly. All processors have the ability to right- or left-shift registers, usually implemented in a serial fashion. Thus, a 10-bit shift requires at least 10 clock cycles. Barrel shifters are gigantic arrays of logic that shift any number of bits in a single clock cycle. This faster shifting capability comes at the cost of much more electronics, but in an IC, transistors are cheap.

base *n.* The terminal of a bipolar transistor that functions to control the flow of current between emitter and collector.

base-n *n.* A generic notation for representing numbers. No matter how you choose to represent numbers, if you have a herd of 25 sheep, the herd will always have the same number of members. Because people have 10 fingers and 10 toes, numbers are represented in base-10, so sheep are counted $1, 2, \ldots, 9, 10, 10 + 1, 10 + 2, \ldots, 10 +$

$9, 2 \times 10, 2 \times 10 + 1, \ldots, 2 \times 10 + 5$ for a total of 25_{10} (i.e., base-10). If people had eight fingers, sheep would probably be counted $1, 2, \ldots, 7, 8, 8 + 1, 8 + 2, \ldots, 8 + 7, 2 \times 8, 2 \times 8 + 1, \ldots, 3 \times 8 + 1$ for a total of 31_8 (i.e., base-8).

Using base-10 (a.k.a., decimal), a third digit is needed at $10 \times 10 = 100$ and a fourth at $10 \times 100 = 1000$. In base-8 (octal), that third digit is needed earlier, at $8 \times 8 = 64$; the fourth at 512.

Computers generally use base-2, which is called binary. They count sheep $1, 2, 2 + 1, 4, 4 + 1, 4 + 2, 4 + 2 + 1, \ldots, 16 + 8 + 1$ for a total of 110012_2. People tend to find binary dreadfully slow to decode. Unfortunately, it's not easy to lump bits together into base 10, so memory dumps are assembled into groups of 4 bits, called nibbles, and 8 bits, called bytes. Each nibble can represent a number 0 through 15, which leads naturally to base-16 (hexadecimal) notation; the values 10 through 15 are represented by the characters A through F. In hexadecimal, the total number of sheep is $16 + 8 + 1 = 19_{16}$.

Although binary, octal, decimal, and hexadecimal are the most commonly used notations, any base, n, can be used. The formula for converting the value to decimal is always $a \times n^m + b \times n^{m-1} + \ldots + d \times n + e$, where coefficients a, b, etc. are in the range 0 to n-1. If n is greater than 36 (the ten digits 0 to 9 plus the twenty six letters A through Z), however, you'll have to come up with a new system for representing digits.

base-plus-offset addressing *n.* One of many ways an instruction can fetch data from memory. This mode forms an address by adding a number, encoded in the instruction, to the contents of a register.

EXAMPLE: On an ARM processor, the instruction

```
LDR r0,[r1,#16]
```

loads from location $r1 + 16$, where the content of register $r1$ is the base and literal 16 is the offset.

bash *cmd.* A Linux shell compatible with the Unix Borne shell. An acronym for "Borne again shell."

BASIC (basic) *abbr.* An early, usually interpreted, high-level language that's easy to learn. Short for Beginners All-purpose Symbolic Instruction Code. Some wags claim that programmers who learn their craft in BASIC can never create good code because the early forms of this language encouraged the most unstructured practices. It's virtually never used in embedded systems, with the possible exception of those poor unfortunates writing Visual Basic code on embedded PCs.

HISTORY: John G. Kemeny and Thomas E. Kurtz invented BASIC in 1964 for use at Dartmouth College and then made it freely available to the rest of the computer community.

basic input/output system *n.* In a PC, the low-level drivers that handle I/O, usually stored in ROM. Abbreviated BIOS. The BIOS is essentially the firmware component of a general-purpose computer. The folks who develop PC BIOS are, therefore, embedded software developers.

HISTORY: In the early days of CP/M and DOS, the BIOS lived in PROM or EPROM and was unchangeable. Today's PC BIOSes usually reside in flash, making them as upgradable as Internet Explorer—and sometimes as buggy.

BASIC Stamp *N.* A tiny single-board computer manufactured by Parallax based on an 8051, PIC, or other microcontroller. The BASIC Stamp is about the size of a postage stamp (hence the name) and executes a variant of BASIC called PBASIC. Inexpensive, self-contained, and easy to program, they're used in education and simple embedded systems that require little horsepower but rapid delivery.

A BASIC Stamp collection.

battery *n.* A device that uses chemical reactions to produce or store power. Batteries come in many flavors (lithium ion, nickel cadmium, lead acid, etc.), each targeted to different applications. Some manufacture power; others store it when charged.

battery-backed *adj.* A circuit kept alive by power provided by a battery. Most battery-backed systems keep SRAM data alive when power fails. SRAM is volatile, losing data when there's no power. However, a small Ni-Cad or lithium ion battery can provide just enough juice to retain that data for years.

HISTORY: Battery backup circuits are notoriously badly designed, leading to the pandemic of embedded systems that mysteriously lose setup data. Building electronics that keep RAM supplied with power is but part of the problem; other issues include ensuring the CPU doesn't do anything crazy as it loses power and forcing the software to a safe state.

battery backup *n.* A battery that's only used when another power source is lost.

baud 1. *n.* A unit of signaling speed equal to the number of discrete events per second.

2. *n.* Incorrectly, but most commonly, used to indicate the bit rate of a serial transmission. This casual usage generally assumes that a 9600-baud signal, for example, transmits 9600/8, 8-bit characters per second. However, each character is in fact prefixed with a start bit and suffixed with one or more stop bits and perhaps a parity bit as well. Actual transmission rates vary, depending on the protocol and hardware used.

HISTORY: Named for the French engineer Emile Baudot (1845–1903).

baud rate *n.* The number of discrete events transmitted per second over a serial link. A rate of 1200 baud means the signal can change its value 1200 times per second. If 1 bit is one change, then the bit and baud rates are the same. This is true for most digital systems, which generally use just two voltages: one each to represent a 0 and a 1. However if, for instance, eight different voltage levels were used, then each level of the voltage represents 3 bits, so the bit rate is three times the baud rate. *See also* baud.

BCD (as letters) *abbr. See* binary-coded decimal.

BDM (as letters) *abbr. See* background debug mode.

bed of nails *adj.* An apparatus to check the operation of assembled printed circuit boards. Bed of nails testers are used on the production floor of high-volume manufacturing operations to both check for and diagnose PCB problems. Physically resembling the name, they are dense matrices of spring-loaded pins that connect to many nodes on the board. A very large and expensive machine measures the signals at each point, comparing them to the expected values. Programmers can spend months to years writing test code specific to the testing of an individual board to isolate failures.

HISTORY: Although bed of nails testers are still common, the JTAG interface is, in many cases, replacing these devices. JTAG uses a boundary scan methodology to look for unconnected nodes.

behavioral inheritance *n.* The relationship between a substate and its (direct or transitive) superstate in a hierarchical state machine. A substate (nested state) in a hierarchical state machine need only define the differences from the superstates (surrounding states). A substate can easily share (reuse) the behavior from its superstate(s) by simply ignoring commonly handled events, which are then automatically handled by higher-level states. This semantics of state nesting allows a substate to inherit all aspects of behavior from its ancestors (superstates); therefore, it's called behavioral inheritance.

Behavioral inheritance in Quantum Programming, just as class inheritance in object-oriented programming, combines abstraction and hierarchy and allows building whole taxonomies of states. As with class inheritance, behavioral inheritance is subject to the same fundamental law of generalization (the Liskov Substitution Principle extended to nested states), and, as with any other kind of inheritance, behavioral inheritance supports reuse through programming by difference.

bel *See* decibel.

benchmark 1. *n.* A specific standard for comparing the performance of processors or systems, such as Dhrystone MIPS. *See also* synthetic benchmark.
2. *n.* A numerical value that results from benchmarking a processor or system and that represents its performance relative to some standard.

benchmarking *n.* The act of measuring the performance of a processor or system against an objective standard.

BeOS *n.* An operating system designed for use in multimedia applications and Internet appliances. In late 2001, Be Inc. decided to close its doors and sold the code for BeOS and related intellectual property to Palm Inc. Although widely hailed for its unique journaling filesystem and innovative user interface, BeOS was a flop in the commercial marketplace. Perhaps it was just before its time. The expected growth of embedded systems of the Internet-appliance type failed to materialize once the dot com and telecommunication bubbles burst.

BER (as letters) *abbr. See* bit error rate.

best-case execution time *n.* The least amount of time required to run a particular piece of code. Compare to worst-case execution time.

BGA (as letters) *abbr. See* ball grid array.

bias 1. *n.* An offset either in a system or applied to one. 2. *v.* To apply an offset to a system or circuit.

USAGE: A bias is often a constant voltage applied to a transistor or IC to change the device's transfer function. For example, transistors are not linear at low base voltage levels. By adding a small bias, it's possible to linearize the device's response by keeping base voltages high.

bidirectional *adj.* Describes a type of device or bus that supports two-way data transfers. To reduce wiring, connectors, and pin counts, it's common to share data on one bus. Data can move from device A to B or from B to A, though not at the same time. *Contrast with* unidirectional.

EXAMPLE: A bidirectional data bus is present on pretty much every microprocessor. A single bus transfers data to and from memory and I/O. Control signals police the transfers, ensuring that there are no attempts to transfer data in both directions at the same time.

bidirectional buffer *n.* An integrated circuit that both drives signals down a bus and receives data on the same bus from other drivers.

EXAMPLE: The 74LS245 is a single IC containing eight bidirectional bus drivers. Control signals select which direction the data goes through the IC.

bidirectional bus *n.* A group of wires over which data is transferred in any direction.

EXAMPLE: Data buses are almost always bidirectional, since data can be both read from and written to memory and I/O over the same group of wires.

bidirectional port *n.* A parallel I/O device that can either send data out of the processor/system or accept data in. As transistor prices on ICs plummet, more vendors provide smarter on-board I/O ports. Many parallel ports are bidirectional. Control ports internal to the CPU select the function of each bit: input, output, high impedance, bus drive characteristics, and so on. This flexibility lets

the developer configure the generalized port into exactly the configuration needed by a system.

big iron *n.* A slang expression meaning a mainframe computer, often referring to one from IBM.

big-endian *adj.* A data representation for a multibyte value that has the most significant byte stored at the lowest memory address. Note that only the bytes are reordered, never the nibbles or bits that comprise them. Every processor stores its data in either big-endian or little-endian format. Sun's SPARC, Motorola's 68k, and the PowerPC families are all big-endian. The Java virtual machine is big-endian as well. Similarly, every communications protocol must define the byte order of its multibyte values. TCP/IP uses big-endian representation.

EXAMPLE: If the 32-bit value 0x12345678 is located at address 1000d in memory, its most significant byte, 0x12, would be found at location 1000d. Location 1001d would contain the next most significant byte, 0x34; location 1002d would contain 0x56; and location 1003d would contain the least significant byte, 0x78.

bill of materials *n.* A comprehensive list of every part needed to build a particular system or subsystem. Abbreviated BOM. Young engineers dream of a job of endless creativity. However, the true nature of engineering is a bit of inspiration followed by a lot of mind-numbing paperwork. A working design is useless if it cannot be manufactured. The BOM is a tedious, carefully cross-checked list of parts correlated to an assembly drawing that shows where each part goes. Modern tools greatly speed the creation of these lists but require carefully defined databases to track all the ever-changing details necessary to place orders for the parts.

bin2hex (bin to hex) *n.* A development tool that converts a binary file containing an executable into an Intel Hex format file. Such a tool is often needed so that the executable can be downloaded to the target over a serial port.

binary 1. *n.* A number system that uses only the two symbols, 0 and 1. Binary makes sense for digital systems because the 0 and 1 states can be represented by a voltage being above or below some level. Analog drift and noise do not corrupt the data.

2. *n.* Describes an operator that takes two inputs. In high-level languages, operators transform one or more input arguments. A binary operator requires exactly two inputs. For example, + is a binary operator taking two inputs and returning their sum.

binary encoder *n.* A rotary encoder that translates shaft angle into an n-bit binary count, where 2^n is the resolution of the device. Used to provide feedback to embedded systems that control or sense real-world motion (e.g., in the joint of a robotic arm). *Contrast with* Gray code encoder, quadrature encoder.

binary point *n.* A convention used when representing integers and fractions in one word that sets where the integer ends and the fractional part begins. Often used in fixed-point math. The binary point doesn't really exist; it's merely a reference so the software knows how to process the word. For example, a fixed-point number might be represented by 16 bits, the upper 4 bits of which are the integer portion and the rest the fraction. The binary point is then between bit positions 2^{12} and 2^{11}.

binary portability *n.* The ability to execute the same program on multiple platforms without recompiling.

binary prefixes *n.* The International Electrotechnical Commission has defined precise names for the binary multipliers used so casually by computer folk. *Very few people use these terms correctly.*

- 2^{10} is called a kibi and abbreviated Ki
- 2^{20} is called a mebi and abbreviated Mi
- 2^{30} is called a gibi and abbreviated Gi

Generally, the prefix refers to bits or bytes, as in kibibytes. Bytes are abbreviated B, and bits are bit. Typical forms are

- KiB and Kibit,
- MiB and Mibit, and
- GiB and Gibit.

These prefixes for binary multiples were developed by IEC Technical Committee 25, Quantities and Units. The complete citation for this revised standard is IEC 60027-2, 2nd edition, 2000-11. See table on page 290. *See also* decimal prefixes.

EXAMPLE:
- 1 kibibit: 1 Kibit = 1,024 bits
- 1 kibibyte: 1 KiB = 1,024 bytes
- 1 mebibit: 1 Mibit = 1,048,576 bits
- 1 mebibyte: 1 MiB = 1,048,576 bytes
- 1 gibibit: 1 Gibit = 1,073,741,824 bits
- 1 gibibyte: 1 GiB = 1,073,741,824 bytes

HISTORY: Confusing? You bet. But consider the normal definition of "K"—a binary thousand—which isn't a decimal thousand or even really a binary thousand. (A binary thousand would be 1000b, right? That's 8 decimal.) Rather, K is the binary number (1024) closest to a decimal thousand. This has proven so completely confusing that it has become a standard.

FURTHER READING: http://physics.nist.gov/cuu/ Units/binary.html

binary semaphore *n.* A type of semaphore with just two states. Often used to guarantee mutual exclusion. *Compare to* mutex.

binary-coded decimal *n.* A way of representing base 10 numbers in base 2. Abbreviated BCD. Assigns four binary bits per decimal digit, encoding each digit in conventional binary. Thus, 4 bits express the numbers 0 to 9, with the other values unused. This representation is inefficient and cumbersome to work with.

HISTORY: IBM's 1602 processor, dating from the late 1950s, pioneered the use of a computer that performed all computations, internally and externally, in BCD. Although this simplified I/O, since punched cards naturally adapt to BCD encoding, programming and hardware complications led to the demise of BCD machines. Still used as a transitional coding scheme when dealing with I/O.

binutils (bin you tills) *n.* A collection of binary utilities associated with gcc. The most notable utilities are the GNU linker (ld) and assembler (as). Other tools in the set perform profiling (gprof), archiving (ar), and help programmers analyze the contents of object files (nm, objdump, strings, and readelf).

BIOS (buy oase) *abbr. See* basic input/output system.

bipolar transistor *n.* A three-terminal transistor in which current flows between the emitter and collector and which is controlled by small signals into the base.

bison *n.* The GNU version of yacc. Cleverly named as a play on the pronunciation of yacc. *See also* flex.

BIST (rhymes with mist) *abbr. See* built-in self-test.

bistable *adj.* A device that can be in either of two states.

EXAMPLE: A bistable multivibrator is the fancy name for a flip-flop. Its output is a 1 or 0, depending on the inputs. Once in either state, it will stay there until the inputs change in a manner proscribed by the type of flip-flop.

bistable multivibrator *See* flip-flop.

bit *n.* A binary digit. Each bit holds either 1 or 0 and, as such, represents the smallest unit of information a computer can process.

bit bang *v.* To transfer data serially under software control. *See* bit banger.

bit banger *n.* A piece of software that exchanges data serially with another processor or a device like an EEPROM by manually reading or writing one or more GPIO pins. When transmitting, a bit banger generates a serial data stream by shifting data onto an ouput pin one bit at a time. If there is no inherent clock or baud rate, the transmitter may also be responsible for generating a clock signal on a second output pin. When receiving, a bit banger reads an input pin, converting the sequence of bits found there into a byte (or bytes) of data. The code will append or strip start and stop bits as needed.

In the case of RS-232, the bit banger code is critically dependent on matching the baud rate. Such delicate code is very difficult to tune and tends to break when ISRs run or when CPU cycles are in short supply.

bit banging *n.* The process of transferring serial data under software control. *See* bit banger.

bit error rate 1. *n.* How often a serial data stream loses or mangles transmitted bits. Abbreviated BER. Digital engineers define the bit error rate as the number of incorrect bits divided by the total number of bits transmitted. The result is a percentage.

2. *n.* RF engineers define BER, in decibels, in terms of noise as

$$BER = \frac{E_b}{N_0} = C - N_0 - 10\log(f_b)$$

where

- f_b = transmission bit rate (Hz)
- N_0 = noise spectral density (dB-m/Hz)
- E_b = energy per bit (dB-m/Hz)
- C = carrier power (dB-m)

bit rate *n.* The number of bits transmitted over a channel per unit time. *See also* bps, baud rate.

bit stuffing *n.* The process of inserting nondata binary digits into a stream of binary data. Bit stuffing is necessary only when the electrical rules used to indicate 1s and 0s on the channel require voltage-level changes every so often.

EXAMPLE: If only four consecutive 1 bits can be received properly, a single nondata 0 bit must be stuffed into the channel after the fourth 1 to ensure proper receipt. In this situation, the receiver will always ignore the first 0 following any string of four 1s.

bitfield *n.* A field of 1 or more bits within a larger integer value. C/C++ compilers support the declaration of bitfields in `struct` definitions. To create a 1-bit bitfield, simply append `:1` to the end of that field's definition. That field's name then refers only to that one bit, which is useful when interacting with peripheral registers through memory-mapped I/O. However, be aware that the ANSI C standard is silent on the subject of bit ordering; programs that use bitfields might not be portable across compilers.

bitmap 1. *n.* A graphics file format. Windows' bitmap-format files have extension .BMP.

2. *n.* A data structure that compactly represents the status of a large number of items. Each item of interest is assigned a single bit in the bitmap.

EXAMPLE: The status of a large number of blocks in a memory pool can be kept in a bitmap. If the corresponding bit is set, that block might be considered in use.

bitmask *n.* A constant value used to mask off the unimportant bits of a larger field.

In this code fragment, the constant DATA_READY_FLAG is a bitmask.

```
#define DATA_READY_FLAG   0x10

if (status & DATA_READY_FLAG)
{
    // receive data here
}
```

USAGE: The term "bitmask" also is used sometimes to describe a similar constant value used to set or clear a particular bit.

bitstream *n.* Any continuous flow of binary data in a channel.

bitwise *adj.* Said of a logical operator that directly manipulates individual bits within a larger field. For example, a bitwise-OR (like C's | operator) performs a logical-OR of each bit.

black box *n.* Any software or hardware component or system, the internals of which are not visible to the user or tester. At its most fundamental level, anything can be a black box. An adder is simply a black box with two inputs and one output that performs a particular function on the inputs. A filter is a black box with one input stream and a corresponding output stream. The effect of the filter as a black box is called its transfer function.

Each black box is defined by the number and type of its inputs and outputs and by the effect that it produces. The concept is often used for system decomposition and during the testing of subsystems. But, of course, reverse engineering is the process of determining the implementation underlying a specific black box.

black box testing *See* functional testing.

bleeder resistor *n.* An electrical part or circuit that quickly drains a power supply's latent charged current to ground. A bleeder resistor is more often than not one large power resistor connected across the terminals of a power supply. Not much of a concern in low-voltage logic, bleeders become critical with high-voltage power. It's not much fun to carefully turn power off on a system, unplug it for safety's sake, and then get zapped because a capacitor maintains several hundred volts, sometimes for many minutes!

block 1. *n.* A sector of a disk drive or flash memory.

2. *v.* To wait for an event to occur via a system call. *See also* blocked.

blocked *n.* A task state indicating that the task is waiting for some event external to itself, such as completion of an I/O request, to occur. While a task is blocked, it uses no CPU cycles and is not available to be selected by the scheduler to run. Many tasks can be in the blocked state, though they are usually tracked separately based on the events for which they are waiting.

blue noise *n.* A type of noise in which power density increases 3 dB per octave with increasing frequency (density proportional to f) over a finite frequency range. *See also* pink noise, white noise.

BNF (as letters) *abbr.* A formal way to describe a language. Short for Backus–Naur Form. BNF is used to define the grammar of the language. BNF is so unambiguous that one can actually construct a parser for the language automatically. Programs that do this are commonly called compiler compilers. The most famous of these is yacc, but there are many more.

HISTORY: Developed by John Backus and Peter Naur to describe the syntax of the Algol 60 programming language.

BNF productions *n.* The rules associated with a grammar defined by BNF. The following line is a typical production:

symbol := option a | option b | option c

A production rule simply states that the symbol on the left-hand side of the := must be replaced by one of the options on the right-hand side, each of which are separated by the vertical bar. Options usually consist of both symbols and terminals. Terminals are pieces of the final string that are not symbols. They are called terminals because there are no production rules for them: they terminate the production process.

board support package *n.* Part of a software package that is processor or platform dependent. Abbreviated BSP. Typically, sample source code for the BSP is provided by the package developer. To port the larger package, only the code in the board support package must be modified. Most commercial real-time operating systems have a BSP to make porting easy.

Bode plot *n.* A graph of log(amplitude) vs. log(frequency). The Bode plot describes the output response of a frequency-dependent system. Bode plots show the transfer function of a system. They make multiplication of amplitudes a simple matter of adding distances on the graph, since log(ab) = log(a) + log(b).

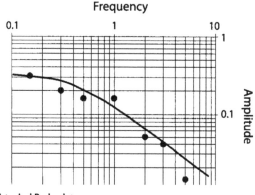

A typical Bode plot.

BOM (as letters) *abbr. See* bill of materials.

bond-out processor *n.* A special version of a processor that has some of the internal signals brought out to external pins. Bond-out processors are designed to be used within an in-circuit emulator and are not typically used in any other kind of system.

bondout *See* bond-out processor.

bool *res.* A 1-byte type defined in header file `std-bool.h` with values restricted to 1 (true) or 0 (false). *See also* _Bool.

_Bool *res.* In C99, a 1-byte primitive data type used specifically to represent Boolean values. Redefined as `bool` in header file `stdbool.h`.

Boolean *adj.* Describes a binary true/false variable or result. *See also* Boolean algebra.

Boolean algebra *n.* A combinatorial system that combines propositions with logical operators like AND, OR, and NOT. Boolean algebra provides rules to operate on two binary values. It includes the following laws, as well as others.

- A commutative law:
  a AND b = b AND a

- An associative law:
  (a OR b) OR c = a OR (b OR c)

- A distributive law:
  a OR (b AND c) = (a OR b) AND (a OR c)

Boolean algebra forms the basis of all computer logic.

HISTORY: Invented by George Boole (1815–1864).

Boolean logic *n.* An implementation of a Boolean truth table using electronic components. *See also* Boolean algebra.

boost *v.* To step up, as in a voltage multiplier or charge pump.

boot *v.* To start a system.

boot ROM *n.* A ROM that stores the code that executes each time a system boots.

boot-block flash *n.* A flash memory device that has at least one sector (or block) that can be hardware locked to ensure it is never reprogrammed. The bootloader, if present, would normally be kept in the boot block.

bootable *adj.* Describes an executable that can start a system.

bootloader *n.* A small program stored in ROM and responsible for initializing the hardware to a known initial state and making it possible to download application software to the system to be run. These capabilities are often built into a debug monitor.

BOOTP (boot pee) *abbr.* A communications protocol for establishing a system's boot parameters, including its IP address, from a server on the same IP network. Short for Bootstrap Protocol. RFC 951.

bootstrap loader *See* bootloader.

boss *n.* A four-letter word referring to the creature, sometimes of the species *Homo sapiens*, responsible for capricious schedules, inadequate resources, and rapidly changing specifications. Responds well to groveling, a torrent of acronyms, and promises of a bonus. "Big bosses" are often found nesting with accountants and lawyers or in front of Congressional committees.

bounce *n.* The erratic oscillation of a mechanical contact when it closes or opens. Switches and other mechanical devices used as inputs are springy. When closed or opened, they bang back and forth for a handful of milliseconds. To a computer, this looks like multiple opens and closes. If connected to an interrupt input, the CPU might see hundreds of interrupts, even though the switch closed just once. All wise developers include either debouncing hardware that removes the bounces totally or smart software that lets the contacts settle before returning an open/close value.

boundary condition *n.* An input with a value that is at the extreme edge of an algorithm's design. Boundary conditions are responsible for a huge number of bugs. Developers are notoriously sloppy about testing their routines at these edges.

EXAMPLE: Every square root algorithm has an implicit boundary condition at zero; an input smaller than zero should create an error. Another example is the thermostat designed to keep a building habitable: what happens if, for some reason, the input temperature soars to an unexpected value like 110 degrees?

boxcar integrator *n.* An algorithm that smooths data by averaging the most recent values.

$$boxcar_i = \frac{(D_{i-n+1} + D_{i-n+2} + D_{i-n+3} + \dots + D_i)}{n}$$

where D_i is the current input datapoint and n is the number of readings to average.

Boxcar integrators, because they average only the most recent data, are fast to respond to changing inputs. They are typically used to remove analog noise from input data.

bps (as letters) *abbr.* A common unit for expressing bit rates. Short for Bits Per Second. *Contrast with* cps. *See also* baud rate.

branch instruction *n.* A machine or assembly language instruction that causes the computer to transfer to a different address. On many computers, branch instructions are distinct from jumps: a branch is a short transfer of control, whereas a jump is used to go to addresses further away from the current location. Branches can be unconditional (always taken) or conditional; in the latter, the transfer may or may not occur, depending on the result of a previous instruction.

branch table *n.* A software decision matrix embodied in a table of destination addresses. When a complex decision can result in a program vectoring off to one of many possible addresses, programmers often create a branch table of these addresses, with code that indexes into the table to find the correct destination.

Compilers often create branch tables to implement large switch statements.

breadboard *n.* A hardware prototype. Breadboards are never (in healthy organizations) shipped as final products. They're used by engineers to perfect the design. Sometimes a breadboard is wire-wrapped, a PCB, or even a "3D" circuit (parts soldered together, suspended by their leads).

break 1. *v.* To stop a running program manually, such as by pressing Ctrl-C in a debugger or shell. 2. *See* breakpoint.

breakpoint *n.* A location in a program at which execution is to be stopped and control of the processor switched to the debugger. Mechanisms for creating and removing breakpoints are provided by most debugging tools. *See also* tracepoint, hardware breakpoint.

breakpoint counter *n.* A debugger resource that lets the program run through a test condition a specified number of times before stopping execution. Breakpoint counters exist on software-only debug monitors and BDMs (in which case they do not run in real time) or on in-circuit emulators (in which they are hardware resources and so do not affect program execution).

EXAMPLE: When debugging a looping program, the developer might want to see what happens just before the loop exits by setting the breakpoint counter to a value just less than the number of loop iterations left and letting the program run. It'll then stop, as desired, shortly before exiting.

brick wall filter *n.* A lowpass filter with a very steep cutoff (20 dB per octave or more) so that virtually nothing that's out of band passes through.

bridge chip *n.* A chip that bridges two buses.

bridge rectifier *n.* A circuit of four diodes that cuts off the negative part of a sine wave, doubling the frequency of the positive part. Bridge rectifiers offer high-efficiency rectification. They also are used sometimes on devices that take DC

A bridge rectifier.

power in to make the input independent of polarity. Even if power is reversed, the circuit gets proper DC polarity.

broadcast *v.* To send a message or network packet to all possible receivers.

brownout *n.* The condition when power supplied to a system drops below specifications but does not go completely away. In the U.S., household power is about 120 VAC. During the summer months, it's not unusual for air conditioning demands to create short drops of 70 or 80 V. This is sure to drive the system's power supply out of regulation. If power just went away, things wouldn't be so bad, since restoration of power would result in a complete system reset. A brownout, though, might leave just enough voltage on the system's circuits to bias the reset logic to a confused state, so the device would never come back to life properly. Poorly designed reset circuits are endemic in this industry.

brownout detector *n.* A circuit that senses partial losses of power and then cleanly resets the processor. A brownout occurs when the AC mains dip below the allowed levels but do not entirely go away. In the U.S., for instance, a 100-VAC supply is below standards and will likely cause most DC power supplies to go out of regulation. If power dropped to zero, any reasonable reset circuit would first safe a microprocessor and then cleanly reset it after power was restored. During a brownout, though, the DC supply might go to some intermediate value that confuses a poorly designed reset circuit. Brownout detectors clamp the processor's reset line just before the DC levels fall out of the processor's legal range.

browser *n.* A content viewer for HTML, XML, or WML.

brush motor *n.* A motor that applies power to a rotating armature via contacts that rub on the armature. Brush motors are typically DC motors, which use carbon brushes to supply power to the motor's armature. The brushes rub on an alternating sequence of copper contacts called the commutator. Each pair of commutator contacts applies power to the armature's coils in alternating directions, creating the push–pull forces that spin the armature.

brushless motor *n.* A motor that uses a passive armature and no brushes. Brushless motors have permanent magnets on the armature. The stationary windings that surround the armature apply the push–pull torque needed to rotate the armature. Commutation occurs by smart electronics that alternate power to the stationary windings. Brushless motors offer certain advantages over their brush motor cousins; notably, lower power requirements and higher efficiencies because of the lack of drag from the brushes.

BSP (as letters) *abbr. See* board support package.

BSS segment (bee ess ess segment) *abbr.* A segment in an object file that contains uninitialized data. An acronym for Bulk Storage Segment. The startup code may or may not initialize the uninitialized data memory area before starting the program. *See also* data segment.

buck *v.* To step down, as in a voltage regulator.

buffer 1. *n.* An array of data memory. Buffers can be implemented in hardware (aka FIFOs) or software but generally exist to smooth out short-term variations in the arrival rate of data. Sizing buffers to prevent overflow and wasted memory is the subject of queueing theory. *See also* message queue.

2. *n.* A hardware device that isolates two circuits (e.g., two computer buses) and that increases the drive capability of the circuit. Buffers are used in many applications, such as driving DRAM, which is highly capacitive. Most DRAM arrays require far more drive than a CPU can generate.

bug *n.* A flaw in a piece of hardware or software. Also called a defect.

HISTORY: U.S. Navy Admiral Grace Hopper coined the term after finding an actual moth in one of the early computers she worked on. The moth was found inside an electrical switch, where the short it created caused her program to malfunction.

bug-tracking software *n.* A project-management database that follows the progress of software or hardware defects from first detection, through assignment to an individual engineer, and eventually to elimination. Also called defect-tracking software.

build 1. *v.* To (re)generate an executable from its source code.

2. *v.* The specifics of this process for a particular project. As in, "the build failed."

3. *v.* To assemble components into a circuit.

4. *n.* A compiled and linked program, created by a make operation.

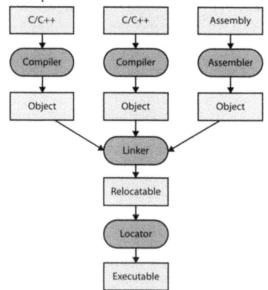

This executable must be rebuilt from three source files, one of which is in assembly language.

built-in self-test *n.* Hardware or software that checks functionality of a system. Abbreviated BIST. High-reliability systems often employ BIST to ensure correct system operation. Some run the self-test continuously in the background.

HISTORY: The PC's original 1981-era BIOS included an exhaustive, even obsessive, self-test, including a test of every 8088 instruction.

burst *n.* Any short but dense blast of data.

DMA can occur in bursts, where the transfer requires much CPU overhead for a short period of time. Datacomm often occurs in packetized bursts. Even analog data acquisition can come in bursts, especially when vast numbers of A/D conversions are needed over a short time to overcome the Nyquist limits on a short bit of signal.

burst transfer *n.* A fast but short transfer of a multiword block of data. Usually refers to DMA transfers.

bus 1. *n.* A set of electrical signals with a group function. For example, the data bus is a set of *n* pins used by a processor to read and write *n*-bit data values or opcodes from a memory device. *See also* address bus, data bus.

USAGE: Pluralization of this term is difficult. The options are buses and busses, both of which are acceptable by the standards of the English language. However, buses is preferable to us and already more popular within the computer community.

2. *n.* A vehicle you don't want the lone guru to get hit by.

bus analyzer *n.* A device used to monitor and track operation of a specific bus. A typical bus analyzer is a hardware device similar to a logic analyzer, though with additional intelligence to understand the protocols and timing of the specific bus (say, VME) being monitored. Bus analyzers are used to diagnose tough real-time hardware design issues.

bus arbitration *n.* The process of deciding which of two or more computers or systems gets access to a shared bus. Bus arbitration occurs whenever one bus (perhaps controlling a shared memory bank) can be controlled by more than one device. Any of a number of algorithms can be used by the hardware to restrict access to a single controller at a time. The other is held off until the first completes its transaction.

bus bridge *See* bridge chip.

bus contention *n.* A condition where more than one device attempts to place data on a bus at the same time. In this case, the logic signals go to indeterminate states. Bus contention results from timing or logic design errors and is usually mitigated by proper bus arbitration logic.

bus cycle *n.* One or more clock intervals in which a complete bus transfer occurs. All synchronous digital computers work in intervals of clocks. A bus cycle, which is the smallest unit of data transfer, comprises one or more clock periods. A typical bus cycle will include production of an address and subsequent transfer of the data at that address.

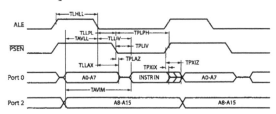

An 8051 memory bus cycle for external memory reads.

bus driver 1. *n.* An integrated circuit that places data on a shared bus. Bus drivers generally exhibit enhanced electrical parameters, notably the ability to drive more power than a conventional logic device, and more highly capacitive loads. A bus might have many connected devices or might go through a long bit of wiring through the backplane, requiring the extra horsepower.

2. *n.* Career path for engineers who don't read *Embedded Systems Programming*.

bus grant *n.* A condition where the current bus master signals bus availability to another device. On multimaster buses, a device requiring access to the bus issues a bus request signal to the master. When ready to release the bus from its own use (so the requester can use the bus), the master issues a bus grant signal.

bus master *n.* A computer, system, or controller (e.g., a DMA controller) that may have exclusive access to a bus and which arbitrates multiple requests for that bus. *See also* bus slave.

bus request *n.* A signal issued by a device wanting exclusive access to a bus. In multimaster bus systems, a device requiring access to the bus issues a bus request signal to the master. When ready to release the bus from its own use (so the requester can use the bus), the master issues a bus grant signal.

bus slave *n.* A computer, system, or controller that may access a bus when given permission by a dominant controller (the bus master). *See also* bus master.

bus width *n.* The number of electrical signals that compose a bus. For example, an 8-bit data bus is a set of eight wires running from the processor to its memory and peripheral devices.

buses *n.* The plural of bus.

Busicom *N.* A Japanese company that, in 1971, used Intel's new single-chip 4004 processor to create what were arguably the world's first embedded systems: a family of 12 business calculators.

HISTORY: Prior to the 4004 microprocessor, which then–memory maker Intel had just conceived, software was only used in stand-alone and mainframe computers. Devices like Busicom's previous business calculators were designed entirely with custom hardware. For its new line of 12 calculators, which differed only in feature sets, though, Intel engineer Ted Hoff proposed that using the same hardware in each device, coupled with device-specific software (stored in an Intel memory chip, of course) would reduce development costs. The calculators were a bust but the 4004 a big hit. Processors soon found their way into traffic signal controllers, telecom network components, ICBMs, and, eventually, virtually every electronic device.

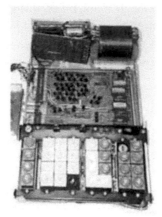
One of the Busicom calculators that spawned a revolution.

busy wait *v.* To waste precious CPU cycles polling.

Butterworth filter *N.* A type of filter with a very flat passband.

The response of a Butterworth filter is

$$output = \frac{1}{\sqrt{1 + input^{2n}}}$$

where *n* is the filter's order.

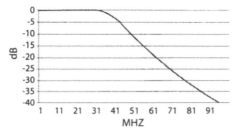

The response of a 5th order low-pass Butterworth filter.

button *n.* A press-to-operate momentary switch.

buy versus build *n.* The process of deciding whether 'tis nobler to invent in-house or purchase a solution from an outside vendor. Purchased solutions can be off-the-shelf products or contracted development from an outside source. *See also* commercial off-the-shelf.

bypass capacitor *n.* A device that removes much of the noise on power and ground signals. The average digital circuit board is peppered with bypass capacitors. As digital signals switch, they induce high-frequency noise on the power lines—a very bad thing that can lead to improper switching and even device failure. A board typically has a few bulk (large-value, on the order of 10μF) bypass devices that provide stored energy for a few nanoseconds of switching. Additional smaller capacitors (0.001 to 0.1μF) are connected very close to the power and ground leads of nearly every IC to remove the high-frequency noise.

byte *n.* An 8-bit value.

byte order *See* endianness.

byte-wide pinout *n.* A way of bringing signals to pins on an IC in a single group of eight. Byte-wide pinouts were a great innovation when they appeared. Perhaps the most famous SSI part was the 74245, a byte-wide bidirectional bus driver. Memory chips quickly assumed this layout (though bit-wide pinouts were not uncommon in the early LSI days). Today, byte-wide pinouts are the norm on 8-bit devices; larger memories offer 16, 32, or more bits, often in configurations best suited to PCs.

bytecode *n.* One of the opcodes of the Java virtual machine. Java's opcodes are called bytecodes because they are only 1 byte wide.

EXAMPLE: Bytecode jsr has numeric value 0xA8. It is a call (JSR is short for Jump to SubRoutine)

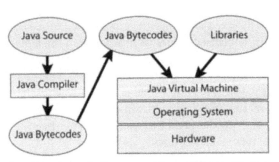

A set of Java bytecodes forms a portable executable module that can be run on any JVM or Java processor.

instruction that makes a branch based on the 16-bit parameter that follows.

FURTHER READING: Tim Lindholm and Frank Yellin. *The Java Virtual Machine Specification.* Addison-Wesley, 1997.

C

C *N.* A hugely popular procedural programming language. C has some similarities to assembly language in terms of compactness and direct hardware access. C cross-compilers are widely available, as are skilled C programmers. *See also* K&R C, ISO C.

HISTORY: Developed by Dennis Ritchie at Bell Labs in 1969–1973. The typeless BCPL and B languages, which derived from Algol, preceded it and gave it some of its features.

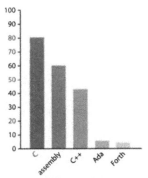

[Note: Multiple choices were possible.]

C is the lingua franca of embedded systems programming, as can be seen in these results from an October 2000 survey of *Embedded Systems Programming* subscribers.

FURTHER READING: A wonderful history of the language, written by its creator, is available at http://cm.bell-labs.com/cm/cs/who/dmr/chist.html.

c *n.* The speed of light in a vacuum: 299,792,458 meters/second. It's important to note that the length of the meter is now precisely defined by international convention as the distance light travels in $1/c$ seconds.

C run time *n.* Various pieces of ancillary code required to run a C program. The C run time typically consists of startup code and standard libraries.

C threads *n.* A library-level threading package developed for use with Mach OS. A new C thread is created by calling cthread_fork(). Once spawned, this thread has access to the global variables of its parent and siblings. Cooperative multithreading is accomplished via calls to cthread_yield(). *See also* green threads.

C# (C sharp) *N.* A programming language similar to Java but invented by Microsoft. Like Java, C# is object-oriented and has an associated virtual machine.

C++ (C plus plus) *N.* An object-oriented programming language that is based on and backward-compatible with C. Many say that C++ is partly crippled by an overly complex syntax, further weakened by the insistence on backward compatibility, and hurt by the many variants that appeared in the marketplace while the details of the ANSI standard were fought over a decade too long. The result is a language that often seems designed for memory leaks but also does have some useful features (notably classes and exceptions). The Embedded C++ subset tries to find a happy medium.

HISTORY: Developed by Bjarne Stroustrup at Bell Labs, who added Simula-like encapsulation, inheritance, and polymorphism to C.

C/SLIP (see slip) *abbr.* A variant of SLIP that uses compressed IP and TCP headers to increase throughput once a connection has been established. Short for Compressed SLIP. RFC 1144. *See also* PPP.

C99 *N.* A 1999 update to the international standard for the C programming language. The updated standard is formally known as *ISO/IEC 9899: Programming Languages—C*. From an embedded systems programming perspective, one of C99's most exciting enhancements is built-in definition of signed and unsigned integer data types of 8, 16, and 32 bits. (They are typedef'd as `uint8_t`, `int8_t`, `uint16_t`, etc. in the platform-specific library header file `stdint.h`.) The C99 standard also recognizes C++-style comments (`//`) and makes several other long-overdue language improvements.

USAGE: In standard C, the size of primitive types `short`, `int`, and `long` are only loosely defined. On one platform, an `int` can be 16 bits; on another, 32 bits. For many years, embedded sys-

tems programmers have defined their own typedefs for fixed-sized signed and unsigned integers. Finally, standard names were assigned in the C99 updated language standard. If you don't have a C99-compliant compiler and library at your disposal, you can `typedef` these constants yourself. Now that C99 has standardized their names, we strongly recommend that you make your fixed-size type names comply.

cache *See* cache memory.

cache coherency *n.* The process of ensuring that the content of cache is the same as that of main memory. On processors with data caches, there's little incentive to echo writes that occur to cache all the way to main memory. After all, accesses to this big data store are slow.

Various schemes can be employed to ensure that cache values changed by writes are updated to RAM before the cache is reloaded. However, in a multiprocessor system, it's important to guarantee that main memory is always correct: that cache coherency is maintained. The simplest method is to use a write-through cache, where all writes immediately update RAM. More sophisticated methods use less bus bandwidth at the cost of more complexity. *See also* cache, write-through.

cache hit *n.* A memory access that finds the needed code or data already in the cache. The total memory-access time for a cache hit is the time to check the cache for the needed code or data plus the access time for the cache.

cache hit ratio *n.* The percentage of time that a cache hit occurs relative to the total number of memory accesses made while a program runs. The higher the hit ratio, the fewer cache misses there will be and the lower the overall memory access time.

cache memory *n.* Very-high-speed memory that supplies the most recently used instructions and/or data to the CPU with few if any wait states. The bottleneck on computers today is memory and bus speeds. Processors are much faster than either. One solution is to insert a small amount of very fast memory—the cache—between the system RAM/ROM and the CPU. The cache generally runs at zero wait states, so it keeps up with the processor's needs. Sometimes two or more levels of cache are used: one level is zero wait states; the next level, which is larger, uses a few waits.

EXAMPLE: Consider the state of desktop processors today. At 1 GHz, not particularly fast by modern standards, the CPU executes one machine cycle per nanosecond. To avoid wait states, a RAM with 1-ns access time is needed. That sort of memory is staggeringly expensive and difficult to build in large quantities, so the fast cache supplies instructions to the processor. The system's normal RAM might have a 50-ns access time. Every cache miss results in the system undergoing 50 wait states while data is moved from system memory.

cache miss *n.* A memory access that does not find the needed code or data in the cache. The total memory access time for a cache miss is the time to check the cache for the needed code or data plus the access time for the memory.

cache miss penalty *n.* The cost, in time, of a cache miss relative to a cache hit.

cache, data *n.* A cache for program data memory.

cache, instruction *n.* A cache for program instruction memory.

cache, write-through *n.* A type of cache memory in which every write to a cache location is immediately echoed to the main system memory. Write-through cache ensures that the content of main memory is always accurate. A write-through cache is one solution to the coherency problem in multiprocessor systems that share the same bus. *See also* cache coherency.

CAD (rhymes with had) *abbr. See* computer-aided design.

CAE (as letters) *abbr.* Equivalent to computer-aided design. Short for Computer-Aided Engineering. *See* computer-aided design.

Calculus, the *N.* A branch of mathematics that uses infinitesimals to describe the infinite. The Calculus primarily deals with change: slopes, motion, rotating vectors, and so on. Most engineers are familiar with its integrals and derivatives.

HISTORY: Newton and Leibniz get most of the credit for independently inventing modern calculus.

calibration *n.* The process of correlating an embedded system to real-world parameters. Embedded systems live in a digital world isolated from the realities of physical phenomena. When an instrument reads 11011b from an A/D converter, it must somehow transform that binary number to temperature, velocity, or some other physical parameter. Often the data comes in skewed, offset, or multiplied by unavoidable small errors in the system's electronics. When the device is calibrated, these errors are removed.

Other systems require calibration to determine the transfer function between the input and the output data. It's not unusual to read an item and feed it through a polynomial with coefficients that are determined when the instrument is calibrated. This usually occurs when there's no clear and fixed algorithm relating input and output.

CAM (rhymes with ham) 1. *abbr.* Short for Computer-Aided Manufacturing.

2. *abbr. See* content-addressable memory.

CAN (as in tin can alley) *abbr. See* controller area network.

Canadian cross *N.* The process of building a cross-compiler on a platform other than the host that it will ultimately run on. This concept is most commonly encountered with the highly portable GNU tools. For example, it is often far easier to build the GNU compiler variant you require on Unix, even though it will be used on a Win32 system to build for a MIPS target.

candela *n.* A standard unit of luminous intensity. Abbreviated cd.

CANopen *n.* An networking technology implementing a higher-layer protocol for the CAN physical layer. Relevant standards are maintained and updated by the CAN in Automation (CiA) group. CANopen is a European standard (EN50325-4).

cap (rhymes with tap) *abbr. See* capacitor.

Capability Maturity Model *N.* Probably the most well-known of the heavyweight software processes. Abbreviated CMM. The CMM rates organizations into one of five maturity levels, determined by the practices used to produce software. The levels are:

1. *Initial.* The software process is characterized as ad hoc, and occasionally even as chaotic. Few processes are defined, and project success depends on individual effort and heroics.
2. *Repeatable.* Basic project-management processes are established to track cost, to establish a schedule, and to define functionality. The necessary process discipline is in place to repeat earlier successes on projects with similar applications.
3. *Defined.* The software process for both management and engineering activities is documented, standardized, and integrated into a standard software process for the organization. All projects use an approved, tailored version of the organization's standard software process for developing and maintaining software.
4. *Managed.* Detailed measures of the software process and product quality are collected. Both the software process and the products are quantitatively understood and controlled.

5. *Optimizing.* Continuous process improvement is enabled by quantitative feedback from the process and from piloting innovative ideas and technologies.

Very few organizations have achieved CMM Level 5.

capacitance *n.* The ability of a part or circuit to store electrical energy in an electrostatic field. Measured in farads (F).

capacitive coupling *n.* The transfer of energy between two unconnected signals via a changing electrostatic field. Run two signal wires in close proximity and some energy will be coupled between them as their signals vary—usually producing an undesired effect. In a sense, the entire universe is capacitively coupled, in that a changing field anywhere has some effect on all metallic objects. However the effect declines with $1/distance^2$, so for practical purposes, most of this is seen within a circuit board.

capacitive load *n.* A driven node with impedance that is purely capacitive. A perfect capacitor is the quintessential capacitive load. Any electrical circuit, cable, component, or system may appear highly capacitive to its driver. A capacitor—and hence a capacitive load—requires $I = dV/dt$ amps from its driver, so any fast logic transition consumes (for a brief time) a large amount of current. Capacitive loads are notoriously difficult to drive.

In the real world, most components, even a wire, exhibit both resistive and reactive characteristics. The input of a CMOS gate might exhibit almost an infinite resistive load but look rather capacitive at 10 pF or so. This load limits the number of devices that a gate can drive. *See also* fan-out.

EXAMPLE: Large DRAM arrays can be highly capacitive, so standard design practice includes placing series resistors inline with the drivers. This slows access somewhat but increases the system's time constant, reducing current.

capacitive reactance *n.* The resistance of a capacitive circuit to the flow of AC current.

$$X_c = \frac{1}{(2\pi f C)}$$

where *f* is frequency in hertz and *C* is capacitance in farads. Thus, as the frequency increases, capacitive reactance decreases; ditto for the value of the capacitor.

capacitor *n.* A device that stores energy in an electrostatic field. Abbreviated cap. Capacitors are one of the fundamental building blocks of circuits. A capacitor is essentially two metal plates separated by an insulator. The plates do not touch; as a result, a perfect capacitor has infinite resistance to DC current. However, AC induces a changing field from one plate onto another, so AC signals can and do pass through such parts. As frequencies increase, capacitors exhibit less resistance (reactance) to the signal. *See also* bypass capacitor, filter capacitor.

The schematic symbol of a capacitor.

EXAMPLE: Capacitors are used in embedded systems in analog front ends to manage AC data, in power supplies to smooth rectified AC, and all over PC boards as decoupling devices to eliminate high-frequency AC on the power lines.

capital equipment *n.* Literally, equipment that can be written off over a period of years under IRS rules. More commonly, any gear not used in a product that has long-term value. Includes even development tools used only for one short-term project.

card *n.* A printed circuit board.

card cage *n.* A mechanical and electrical enclosure that holds multiple interconnected printed circuit boards. Popular in VME systems.

care and feeding *n.* The part of a hardware design that provides the power and reset circuitry for a processor.

carriage return *n.* An ASCII character that denotes the end of a line. Abbreviated CR. ASCII 0x0D. Called "Enter" on PC keyboards.

HISTORY: Before the invention of monitors, Teletypes were the standard computer interface for real-time computing. These bulky and noisy machines were marvels of mechanical engineering, with many hundreds of parts moving in an intricate dance. The print head moved across the page; the carriage return key brought it back to the left side of the paper.

carry 1. *n.* An overflow from a shift or add operation.

EXAMPLE: If an 8-bit adder sums the (unsigned) values 1011 0011b and 1001 0010b, the result is too large to fit in 8 bits. Every computer has an extra bit of logic that captures this overflow carry bit so that it can be applied to a subsequent operation.

2. *n.* The processor flag that indicates whether the previous instruction resulted in a carry.

Cartesian coordinate *N.* A two- or higher dimensional coordinate system in which the distance to a point is its distances from the perpendicular axes. Any point's location can be expressed as an ordered pair, triple, etc., such as (2, 4).

HISTORY: Named for the French mathematician Rene Descartes (1596–1650).

CAS (rhymes with raz) *abbr. See* column address select.

CASE tool *n.* Tools to assist in the design or implementation of a product. Short for Computer-Aided Software Engineering. Typical CASE tools include complexity analyzers, code generators, UML tools, and state machine builders.

cast *v.* To change the type of a piece of data, say, by promoting it from a character to an integer. *See also* explicit cast, implicit cast.

cathode *n.* The element of a semiconductor device that donates electrons. In a diode, for example, current passes from the anode to the cathode. On a diode, the cathode is the terminal marked by a band.

cc (as letters) *abbr.* The C compiler that comes standard with many Unix workstations. Short for C Compiler. Unfortunately, cc is not available in cross-compiler versions. For that, most Unix-based developers install the GNU C compiler (gcc).

CCD (as letters) *abbr. See* charge-coupled device.

CCITT (as letters) *abbr.* An international telecommunications standards body that became the telecom sector of the ITU (ITU-T) in 1993. Short for International Telegraph and Telephone Consultative Committee.

CDC (as letters) *abbr.* A J2ME configuration describing a minimal set of JVM features and class libraries for devices that have a few megabytes of ROM and RAM, plug into an electrical outlet, and have an always-on network connection. Short for Connected Device Configuration. In practice, although the CDC libraries are much smaller than J2SE libraries, the embedded systems that implement CDC are very-high-end devices (like set-top boxes) that have almost as many resources as general-purpose computers. *Contrast with* CLDC.

CE (as letters) *abbr.* The mark needed on most products sold to EU countries. Short for the French version of European Conformity. The CE certification procedure mainly has been set up to harmonize the varying national regulations for consumer and industrial products in European member states to encourage a single market, to increase cost savings for producers, to enhance the safety of products, and to supply public bodies with a uniform procedure that can be checked against a common standard.

The CE mark.

ceiling *n.* A mathematical function that returns the smallest whole number larger than a given real number. *See also* floor.

EXAMPLE: The ceiling of 13.91 (often expressed $\lceil 13.91 \rceil$) is 14.

center frequency *n.* The midpoint of a signal or filter band. Not surprisingly, engineers work with frequencies in the frequency domain: they plot amplitude on a vertical axis and frequency on the horizontal. This approach makes it easy to see passbands, center frequency, sidebands, and so on.

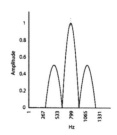

The vertical line shows the center frequency of this signal, which has two sidebands.

central processing unit *n.* The part of a processor that executes instructions.

certification 1. *n.* The process of confirming that a product meets standards set by some outside body. Examples include the European CE mark, Underwriter's Labs UL certification, or the FCC's EMI emission standards. Typically costly and fraught with peril (your gadget might fail the test), yet required for many products. 2. *n.* A process that might ensure that firmware developers have certain minimal skills. Feared by all developers, the idea of certification rears its ugly head from time to time. No one can agree on what certification should entail, what it means, and who is qualified to either be certified or administer such a test. Some U.S. states offer a P.E. designation for software engineers who've passed a standardized exam, though the value of such a test alone is questionable at best.

Chai (rhymes with high) *n.* Hewlett Packard's Java virtual machine.

chaotic system *n.* A system in which the response appears random but in fact is drastically dependent on the initial conditions. Chaotic systems seem to give random outputs, but in fact, they respond quite repeatedly if you can set up their initial conditions exactly; problem is, it can't be done. An error below noise levels will skew the output dramatically. But there are patterns within the seeming noise: outputs cluster around "attractors" and phase plots show ranges of outputs that seem drawn to a value. Chaotic systems are all nonlinear; their behavior is described by an equation with a polynomial of order two or more. It turns out that many of these yield unpredictable results when iterated.

EXAMPLE: The classic example of a chaotic system is the weather. A butterfly flapping its wings in Brazil is theorized to affect local weather, which will affect regional weather, which will eventually change conditions in Boise. No one is smart enough, no computer vast enough, to cope with these tiny variations in input that so dramatically affect the results.

char (like the start of carrot) *res.* A primitive data type in C and several related languages that declares a character variable. In C and C++, the size of a char is always an 8-bit ASCII-encoded value. In Java, a char is always a 16-bit Unicode value. In both languages, strings are zero-terminated arrays of char values.

character generator *n.* A device that converts an ASCII character to pixels for display on a CRT or LCD. The input to the character generator is an ASCII character extracted from memory by scanning logic, which reads memory in sync with the display rate of the screen. The character generator outputs one line of pixels. It's trivial to build one from a ROM that maps characters and line scan information to pixels.

HISTORY: In today's highly integrated age, character generators seem an anachronism, but every fancy display controller includes one, buried in gates and transistors.

character literal *n.* A single ASCII character, such as an "a," passed as a parameter to a function or assigned to a variable.

characteristic 1. *n.* The exponent part of a floating-point number. *See also* IEEE 754.

2. *n.* A typical parameter of an electrical component.

EXAMPLE: The characteristic impedance of the universe is 377 ohms.

charge pump *n.* A circuit that transforms a DC input voltage to a different DC voltage. In a charge pump, the incoming DC powers an oscillator with an output that is voltage multiplied using diodes or that goes into a switching power supply circuit. Few charge-pump circuits provide more than a few tens of milliamps of output current.

EXAMPLE: An early and still-popular IC using a charge pump is the MAX-232A, which is a driver and receiver for RS-232. The MAX-232A uses only a single 5-V supply, yet produces the +/- 10-V swings needed to drive RS-232. It requires external capacitors, which are difficult to fabricate on silicon, to support the internal charge pump and voltage-doubler circuit. The MAX-233 requires no external caps.

charge-coupled device *n.* A semiconductor device that is sensitive to light and that is organized in massive matrices to detect many individual pixels of light. Abbreviated CCD. CCDs sense light intensity then shift their data out to analog electronics for further processing. Widely used in digital cameras.

chassis ground *n.* The point at which the system's common signal point (ground) connects to the enclosure or main metal structure. Sometimes called frame ground. Grounds abound in an embedded system. The word chassis is rarely heard anymore; once all enclosures were steel or aluminum and clearly required a ground for safety's sake. Today the chassis ground is often the ground return to the AC outlet.

check in *v.* To save the current version of a file in a version-control system.

check out *v.* To make a writable copy of a previously saved version of a file in a version-control system. First, the file is checked out; then changes are made and tested; then it is checked in.

checkerboard *n.* A pattern of data corresponding to alternating 0x55 and 0xAA bytes. In binary, this looks like the black and red squares of a checkerboard.

```
01010101
10101010
01010101
10101010
```

checkerboard test *n.* A memory test that writes a checkerboard pattern to the device and reads it back to verify that the data pins are properly wired. *See also* walking 0s test.

checkpoint *n.* The saved state of a program or its data. *See also* roll back.

checksum *n.* A numerical check value calculated from a larger set of data. A checksum is most often used when sending a packet of data over a network or other communications channel. One checksum formula is a simple addition, with overflow ignored, wherein the bytes of the packet are added together into a variable of a fixed size/width (say, 16 bits) as they are sent. The checksum is typically sent at the end of the packet and used at the receiving end to confirm the integrity of the preceding data. *See also* Internet checksum.

child state *See* simple state.

chip *n.* An informal but very common name for an integrated circuit. A packaged IC might look

awfully complex, but the bare die resembles a small part of a potato chip.

chip puller *See* IC extractor.

chip select *n.* A signal that enables a memory chip or I/O device. Abbreviated CS. Chip selects go to each memory chip and peripheral in the system; only when its individual CS is enabled will that particular device turn on (all others being off).

HISTORY: Once upon a time, chip selects came from a decoder chip, were it a 74LS138, PAL, or FPGA. Today, many embedded processors provide an abundance of programmable CS outputs. The hardware initialization code configures each CS via various control registers that define each select's address range, wait states, and other properties.

choice pseudostate *n.* A notational shorthand in UML statecharts for dynamic conditional branches. Represented by a diamond (or an empty circle). A choice pseudostate is most often used to split a transition based on the results of prior transition actions. *Compare to* fork pseudostate, junction pseudostate.

choke *See* inductor.

chop 1. *v.* A technique used in an oscilloscope to display two signals on one screen. Prior to the complete digitization of scopes, they all worked by sweeping the beam from the left to the right side of the screen. When displaying two or more channels of information, the user had a choice of selecting "alternate" (display each signal on alternate sweeps) or "chop." The chop mode mixed both signals with a square wave: one channel effectively modulated the top of the wave; the other channel modulated the bottom. Because the chop frequency was unlikely to be related to either of the channel inputs, the screen appeared to show two distinct signals, although setting the trigger and sweep controls pathologically could make the chopping square wave appear.

2. *v.* A method to provide faster current rise in an inductive load such as a relay or motor coil.

CiMM (as letters) *abbr.* Defined by an Air Force major as a supplement to the CMM. Short for Capability iMmaturity Model. CiMM defines the negative levels of software maturity typical of most development organizations.

0.   *Negligent.* Indifference.
-1.   *Obstructive.* Counterproductive.
-2.   *Contemptuous.* Arrogance.
-3.   *Undermining.* Sabotage.

circuit *n.* A group of electronic components that implements a particular function. All circuits are closed systems; current flows through the circuit and back to the source.

circuit board *See* printed circuit board.

circuit breaker *n.* A hardware device that prevents overloads by removing the current source when loads get too high. Most circuit breakers resemble switches, but when current flow gets too high, an overheat sensor shuts the circuit down. Users often confuse breakers with switches, but a lot of these have limited cycles. Big circuit breakers, such as those powering buildings, will tolerate only two or three overcurrent conditions before failing. And, oh, what a failure! When a 50,000-A circuit goes, you're looking at a Fourth of July fireworks display.

Circuit Cellar *N.* A monthly magazine specializing in coverage of practical techniques for circuit and software design. The magazine is popular with electronics hobbyists and home enthusiasts. Subscriptions are not free. *See also Embedded Systems Programming.*

FURTHER READING: http://www.circuitcellar.com

circular buffer *n.* A data structure that's implemented as an array but automatically wraps from the end back to the beginning. Circular buffers are implemented by incrementing the array-indices mod-

ulo n, where n is the total number of elements. See code listing for an example.

circular wait *n.* One of four conditions necessary for deadlock. When one thread holds a resource that another needs and the pattern of resource holds and needs is circular, a deadlock is said to exist. But if one of the other three conditions are not met in the system, it's possible for the operating system to break the impasse.

EXAMPLE: Thread t1 acquires mutex m1, then tries to acquire mutex m2. But m2 is already held by thread t2, which is blocked waiting for m1, which will never become available to t2 because t1 will block waiting for m2, which will not be released by t2 because it is already blocked waiting for m1. A circular wait prevents either thread from proceeding.

CISC (rhymes with risk) *abbr. See* complex instruction set computer.

class *n.* The design-time specification for a set of similar instances. A class consists of data and functions that operate on that data. Functions defined within a class are called methods; data elements are members. Each instance of a class is an object. *See also* object-oriented programming.

class A amplifier *n.* An amplifier with output that faithfully reproduces the input. A sine wave applied to a class A amplifier will experience no clipping.

Class A amplifiers give the maximum linearity but at the expense of low efficiency, typically in the 25 to 30% range.

class B amplifier *n.* An amplifier that faithfully passes the positive part of its input signal but clips the negative cycles. Class B amplifiers are reasonably linear in their conduction region and offer efficiencies approaching 65%.

class C amplifier *n.* An amplifier that clips all negative excursion of the input signal and has an output

circular butter An implementation of a circular buffer in C.

```c
typedef struct
{
    int   size;       // Number of items in array.
    item array[];     // Dynamically allocated storage.
    int   count;      // Initially zero.
    int   read;       // Read index (0 to size-1)
    int   write;      // Write index (0 to size-1)

} CircBuf;

int
insert(CircBuf * pBuf, item data)
{
    /*
     * Ensure the buffer is not full.
     */
    if (pBuf->count == pBuf->size) return (false);

    /*
     * Add new data to the array.
     */
    pBuf->array[pBuf->write] = data;
    pBuf->count++;

    /*
     * Update the write index circularly.
     */
    pBuf->write = (pBuf->write + 1) % pBuf->size;

    return (true);

}   /* insert() */

int
remove(CircBuf * pBuf, item * pData)
{
    /*
     * Ensure the buffer is not empty.
     */
    if (pBuf->count == 0) return (false);

    /*
     * Extract next item from the array.
     */
    pData = pBuf->array[pBuf->read];
    pBuf->count--;

    /*
     * Update the read index circularly.
     */
    pBuf->read = (pBuf->read + 1) % pBuf->size;

    return (true);

}   /* remove() */
```

stage that is off when the input is zero. A class C amplifier is very efficient (80%) and has awful linearity. The output resembles a stream of digital pulses.

class D amplifier *n.* A type of amplifier that is very efficient but that, in its analog form, massively distorts the signal. Class D amplifiers essentially turn the input wave into on–off output excursions. Because their distortion makes them almost useless in the analog era, they now are the future of amplifiers in power-limited devices like cell phones. A processor drives a class D amp using PWM; filters on the amp's output recreate the analog waveform.

Class D amplifiers are typically 80 to 90% efficient.

class diagram *n.* A static view of a (sub)system's design that shows the object classes and their relationships. At run time, the dynamic state of the system will take one of many possible forms based on the class diagram. UML is one popular notation for drawing class diagrams.

class library *n.* A set of classes packaged together for use by one or more programs. *See also* library.

CLB (as letters) *abbr. See* configurable logic block.

CLDC (as letters) *abbr.* A J2ME configuration describing a minimal set of JVM features and class libraries for devices that have only kilobytes of ROM and RAM, are battery powered or handheld, and have an intermittent network connection. Short for Connected Limited Device Configuration. In practice, it is possible to implement a CLDC runtime environment on a 16-bit processor with 128 KB of ROM and 32 KB of RAM (for the heap), although you might want additional memory for one or more J2ME profiles and your application code. *Compare to* CDC.

clear to send *n.* A flow-control signal, popular in serial communications, asserted by a receiving device when it sees RTS asserted and is ready to receive more data. Abbreviated CTS. *See also* request to send, hardware flow control.

ClearCase *N.* A popular version-control system from Rational.

Clementine *N.* A NASA mission that suffered serious software problems. Clementine was a lunar explorer. A software glitch caused nearly all of its fuel to vent. Although the spacecraft was recovered, its mission was severely degraded.

The proximate cause of the failure remains unknown. Logs show that just before the fuel dump, the software experienced a floating-point exception. However, over 3000 such exceptions had happened previously and were safely handled. (Which begs the question: Why so many errors?) Apparently, immediately after this last exception, the software locked up for some unknown reason and fired thrusters.

Fuel is precious on these missions, so a timeout had been established to shut thrusters down after too much firing. That was in software; the code was hung, and the timeout did not occur.

Ultimately, ground control sent a hard reset to the spacecraft that brought the errant code under control, though with nearly dry tanks.

After the mission, developers wished they had implemented a watchdog timer. The hardware was there ... but no one had written the code. Odds are that adding this trivial bit of code would have saved the mission. *See also* Mars Pathfinder, Ariane 5, Therac-25.

CLI (as letters) 1. *abbr. See* command-line interface.

2. *res.* The 80x86 instruction for disabling interrupts. Short for CLear Interrupt flag.

clipping *n.* A condition created by a nonlinear circuit that cuts off all signals above or below a certain level.

An input wave to a class B amplifier (the sine wave) and its (slightly delayed) clipped output.

clock *n.* A (generally) square wave that sequences all operations of a digital computer. Sometimes called the processor clock. A wag once said that the purpose of time is "to keep everything from happening all at once." That's a pretty good description of the function of a clock in a computer.

Clocks give the digital logic ICs time to complete their functions. In a single clock cycle, the system does one thing. If the processor issues an address to RAM, by the next clock cycle, the memory has had time to decode the address and access the data; now the processor reads this stable information. *Compare to* system clock, real-time clock.

clock frequency *n.* The rate at which the CPU clock runs. Measured in hertz (usually MHz or GHz, though some systems do run in the kHz range to save power).

USAGE: Clock frequency usually refers to the processor's effective clock rate—the speed at which it runs. Some CPUs have clock multipliers that convert a low-frequency crystal input (e.g., 32 kHz) to a much higher rate (say, 16 MHz). Clock frequency refers to that higher rate.

clock skew *n.* An undesirable effect of propagating high-frequency signals around a board, resulting in clock timing errors. At high clock rates, the speed of light and propagation delays inside components create slight timing changes in all signals. The clock is one signal that typically runs all over a board. Buffers ensure that it does not become corrupt, but these buffers (plus the track lengths) induce timing errors, referred to as clock skew.

clock tick *See* timer tick.

close() *n.* A system-call complement to open() that closes files that were previously opened or created new. A part of the standard Unix API for files and I/O devices, once a file has been close()'d successfully, it can no longer be read or written. *Contrast with* open().

closed loop *adj.* Describes a type of system that uses feedback to control a device. Sensors measure important parameters of the system and feed that data back to the firmware, which then corrects the output to control the process.

EXAMPLE: An example closed-loop controller is a system that dyes fabric. A colorimeter senses the resulting color; the computer constantly reads the colorimeter's output and adjusts the dye or process as needed to maintain the desired color.

Another example is a boat's autopilot, which reads a flux-gate compass and adjusts the boat's heading to conform to the user's desired course.

closed-loop control *n.* The use of feedback in a control system. Many real-time embedded systems make control decisions. These decisions are usually made by software and are based on feedback from the hardware under control (termed the plant). Such feedback commonly takes the form of an analog sensor that can be read via an A/D converter. A sample from the sensor might represent position, voltage, temperature, or any other system parameter of interest. Each sample provides the software with additional information on which to base its control decisions. *See also* on–off control. *Contrast with* open-loop control.

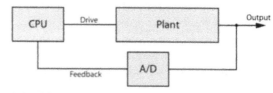

A closed-loop control system.

closed-loop gain *n.* The constant multiplier applied to a feedback signal.

CMM (as letters) *abbr. See* Capability Maturity Model.

CMOS (see moss) 1. *abbr.* The flash or battery-backed SRAM that holds the configuration parameters used by the BIOS.

HISTORY: Oddly, the PC's battery-backed RAM has acquired the common name CMOS because that is the technology used to build the memory (CMOS devices require virtually no power and so are ideal for backups). It's rather like calling a Corvette a "Fiberglass," but the inaccurate moniker has stuck.

2. *abbr. See* complementary metal-oxide silicon.

CMOS latchup *See* SCR latchup.

coaxial cable *n.* A type of wire consisting of an inner signal strand, a layer of insulation, an outer braid that cylindrically encloses the inner strand, and a final layer of insulation. Often called coax for short. The outer braid is generally connected to ground, so it forms a Faraday shield around the inner signal strand. Coax cable is thus ideal for propagating low-level analog signals because it protects them from interference from outside sources. Conversely, it's also used to transmit signals, particularly high-powered signals (as from a radio transmitter).

There are many types and configurations of coax, each having its own impedance. Engineers match the impedance of the coax to the transmitter, thus enabling the low-loss transmission of the signal long distances to an antenna.

COCOMO (cocoa-mo) *abbr. See* constructive cost model.

code 1. *n.* An element of an encoding scheme. The code 0x41, for example, is the code for the ASCII character that represents the letter "A."

2. *n.* The software part of a project. The code includes the language statements that implement the project.

3. *v.* The act of writing software. Coding does not include high-level functions like specification and documentation. It refers specifically to generating the statements in C, assembly, or another language.

code compression *n.* Any of several techniques that reduce the amount of ROM required to store an executable program. In most instances, the code is expanded and copied into RAM before it is run.

code coverage *n.* A quality-assurance strategy that ensures all of the software has executed at least once. Code coverage is almost always coupled with a tool that monitors code execution via software that instruments the code being tested or hardware that watches the bus. The tool tells the development team which statements have and have not executed; the team then devises tests to exercise the remainder of the code. Code coverage is not a panacea, because there could be many ways in which a particular function or statement can run, but because some observations suggest that as much as 50% of the software in an embedded system is never tested, its use at least leads to much better testing.

code inspection *n.* A formal process where multiple people review software before it's tested. Various studies show that inspection is 20 times cheaper at finding bugs than traditional testing. The typical inspection uses a team of four or five people, including the code's author, who individually examine the software for errors. Then, at an inspection meeting, the team goes over the entire function line-by-line, looking for and noting possible errors, without attempting to find fixes. Note that the inspection should take place after a clean compile but before the code is tested.

HISTORY: Invented by Michael Fagan at IBM in 1976 and further developed by Tom Gilb and others.

code memory *n.* The computer memory that holds executable instructions. Embedded systems generally keep code in nonvolatile spaces like ROM and flash.

code review *See* code inspection.

code segment *n.* On an 80x86 processor, the region of memory selected by the CS register. *See also* text segment.

code size *n.* The amount of memory space consumed by a program's code and constant data. The greater the code size of a compiled program, the larger the ROM needs to be. Many compilers can optimize the compiled code to minimize code size at the expense of efficiency.

codec *n.* Hardware or software that converts analog sound, speech, or video to digital and back. Short for COder–DECoder. Codecs reproduce and compress/decompress the signal. Widely used in virtually all communications and multimedia applications.

coding standard *n.* A document that describes the way in which an organization writes software, including style, naming conventions, commenting requirements, and more. Coding standards are a key tool to producing software that can be inspected; without the standard, inspection meetings would collapse in a flurry of arguments over stylistic issues. Standards also ensure that developers avoid dangerous or hard-to-debug constructs (like nesting if statements 10 deep), leading to better code.

coefficient *n.* A constant term that multiplies a variable in a polynomial.

EXAMPLE: In the polynomial $3x^2 + 4$, the number 3 is a coefficient.

COFF (as in coffee) *abbr.* A widely used object file format. Short for Common Object File Format. *See also* ELF, a.out.

COGS (rhymes with hogs) *abbr. See* cost of goods sold.

coherency *See* cache coherency.

coil 1. *n.* A type of inductor formed by winding wires in a loop.

2. *See* inductor.

cold boot *n.* Complete system startup by applying power with no assumed initial conditions. A cold boot starts the system off from scratch. It is possible to maintain previous state information in nonvolatile memory, though such data must be checksummed or otherwise validated to ensure that it's not random uninitialized memory. *See also* boot.

cold solder joint *n.* A soldered connection that was not properly heated or that moved while the solder cooled. Cold solder joints are the bane of electrical circuits because they often work just fine—until the ambient temperature changes, humidity increases, or the PCB flexes just a little.

collector *n.* One of the three terminals of a bipolar transistor; current flows between the collector and emitter, controlled by small inputs to the base. *See also* emitter, base.

column address select *n.* A signal from a DRAM controller telling DRAM that the current address information is the column address. Abbreviated CAS. DRAMs don't take a normal binary address; the DRAM controller breaks addresses into rows and columns, dumping first one then the other into the chip. *See also* refresh, DRAM refresh.

combinatorial logic *n.* A digital circuit with no state information. The output of a combinatorial circuit always reflects its inputs; there is no history. That essentially means no flip-flops or other memory devices are included. *Contrast with* sequential logic.

EXAMPLE: A binary adder is combinatorial: the output is given by a simple truth table and is nothing more than the sum of the two inputs plus a carry. Change any input, and the output will go to a new value.

comm port *n.* A communications channel. One usually thinks of the PC COM1 and COM2 ports, but in embedded systems, an Ethernet link is a comm port, as are RS-422, USB, and many other types of connections.

command line *n.* The generally 80-column-wide place where skilled operators enter Unix, DOS, or proprietary commands. *See also* command-line interface.

command-line interface *n.* An alternative to GUIs, where the user enters program and script names in a nonintuitive text form. Abbreviated CLI. Command-line interfaces are simple and very powerful. Even the most complex of GUIs often have command-line interfaces for automating complex tasks and as a backdoor for sophisticated users of the system. Windows' DOS-like command prompt and the many Unix shells are representative of command-line interfaces in general.

comment drift *n.* A highly undesirable yet all too common condition where programmers change code without updating the comments embedded within it. Comment drift converts even the best documentation into garbage. Worse, experienced developers expect such drift to be the norm, so they never trust any comment.

comments *n.* The nonexecutable part of computer code that describes the author's intentions. Despite the widespread belief that well-written code is self-documenting, years of experience have shown either that there's no such thing as well-written code or that the theory is wrong.

Comments help the author and other programmers understand what the code does and how. Comments are in plain language, use regular sentence structure and punctuation, and are descriptive. Poor comments lead to unmaintainable code.

HISTORY: It has been shown that the first Hippocratic Oath of Software Engineering ("Never include a comment to help people understand your code. If they understand it, they don't need you.") is incorrect.

commercial off-the-shelf *adj.* A subsystem that's purchased rather than developed. Abbreviated COTS. The term is widely used in the DoD community to describe standard commercially-available (nonmilitary) hardware components.

common subexpression elimination *n.* A compiler optimization that removes redundant operations. Sometimes abbreviated CSE.

EXAMPLE: In the expression $2*a + 2*a + 3$, the second $2*a$ subexpression is redundant and can be eliminated and the result of the first calculation used in its place.

common-mode *adj.* An undesired signal that appears on both the signal wire and its return. Every wire is an antenna that picks up interference from all sorts of sources, such as the (in the U.S.) 60-Hz power lines, lightning, etc. A system working with low-level analog inputs is very susceptible to such signals. When sending an analog level over a distance, it's often prudent to send both a ground and signal; at the receiving end, these are applied to a differential amplifier. Common-mode signals will be on both wires; the amp will thus subtract these, producing a clean output.

Communications *n.* The name of the primary monthly magazine of the ACM. Formally, *Communications of the ACM.* All active ACM members receive a subscription to this magazine. Other journal subscriptions are optional and cost extra.

comp.arch.embedded *n.* A USENET newsgroup that serves the embedded hardware and software design communities.

FURTHER READING: news:comp.arch.embedded

comp.realtime *n.* A USENET newsgroup that serves the real-time hardware and software design communities.

FURTHER READING: news:comp.realtime

comparator 1. *n.* An analog op-amp circuit with output that swings to one rail if the + input exceeds the − input and to the other rail in the opposite case. In effect, the comparator produces a digital output based on the relative magnitudes of the two inputs.

2. *n.* A digital combinatorial circuit that subtracts two inputs, producing a <, >, or = result, but that does not output the difference between the inputs.

compensation, scope *n.* The process of adjusting an oscilloscope probe so its response is the same regardless of input frequency. A scope probe is more than a wire; its length alone, given that it samples high-frequency signals, means it exhibits enough capacitance and inductance to corrupt the signals being measured. All decent scope probes have a compensation adjustment, generally a little screw that turns a variable capacitor. Before taking any important AC measurements, the scope user connects the probe to a square wave source (typically provided on the scope's front panel just for this purpose) and turns the screw until the displayed waveform is perfectly square.

compilation *n.* The process of converting a program or module written in a high-level language (like C or C++) into machine instructions the processor can execute. Compilers are the software tools that do the translation.

compiler *n.* A software-development tool that translates high-level language programs into the

machine-language instructions that a particular processor can understand and execute. However, the object code that results is not yet ready to be run; at least a linker or link-step must follow.

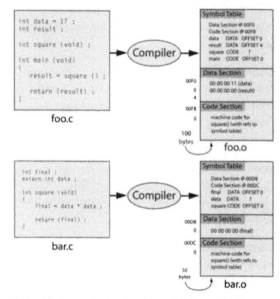

A simplified example, showing the results of compiling the contents of two source modules into corresponding object files.

complementary metal-oxide silicon *n.* A type of logic that uses metal-oxide silicon transistors, where the gate is physically insulated from the source and drain by a thin layer of oxide. Abbreviated CMOS. In logic ICs (including memory and processors), CMOS transistors are always configured in pairs, so when one is on, the other is off. In a static state—since one transistor is always off—no power flows from V_{cc} to ground, making CMOS ideal for low-power applications.

HISTORY: CMOS was originally very slow; therefore, it targeted only a very small range of applications. The N-channel metal-oxide semiconductor (NMOS) dominated all IC products until the late 1970s, when ICs started using so many transistors that the power consumed was more than the die could handle; that is, ICs were creating more heat than designers could get rid of. CMOS processes were improved, so speeds skyrocketed. Today, most high-density parts use CMOS technology.

complex breakpoint *n.* A debugging resource that stops program execution when an event more complex than encountering an address occurs. Complex breakpoints are simulated on software-only and BDM debuggers, so the target program runs at a crawl. An ICE includes hardware resources that execute at full speed while monitoring the bus for the breakpoint condition(s).

EXAMPLE: Every debugger has its own feature set and capabilities, but a complex breakpoint command might look as follows:

```
break when 0x1234 read from variable foo
```

complex conjugate *n.* A complementary version of a complex number that differs from its brother only in the sign of the imaginary term. *See also* complex number.

EXAMPLE: The complex numbers $(3 + 4i)$ and $(3 - 4i)$ are complex conjugates.

complex instruction set computer *n.* Describes the architecture of a processor family. Abbreviated CISC. So-called CISC processors generally feature variable-length instructions and multiple addressing formats and have a small number of general-purpose registers. Intel's 80x86 family is the quintessential example of CISC. *Contrast with* reduced instruction set computer.

complex number *n.* A number that has the square root of -1 as a component. The square root of -1 is represented by i by mathematicians and j by electrical engineers. Complex numbers have both a real and an imaginary part: an example is $(3 + 4i)$, in which 3 is real and $4i$ is imaginary. Complex numbers are often treated as orthogonal components on a Cartesian plane.

complex programmable logic device

n. A larger, more capable PLD. Abbreviated CPLD. Each CPLD typically consists of several programmable logic blocks plus a matrix of programmable interconnecting paths. CPLDs can be used to create larger and more advanced logic circuits than PLDs but are generally smaller and less flexible than FPGAs.

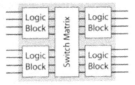

A CPLD is typically a single-chip collection of PLDs plus a switch matrix.

component 1. *n.* A physical electronic device that is a part of a circuit, such as an IC, coil, or resistor.

2. *n.* A subunit of a program that is a functional entity within itself. Analogous to electronic components, though the art of software components is still in its infancy. Practitioners have long dreamed of "software ICs" that would function as off-the-shelf solutions to common problems.

composite state *n.* A state that contains one or more other states. Also called a parent state. *See also* simple state.

computer *n.* Any electronic device that reads instructions from memory, using data stored from the same or different memory, and carries out those instructions. Essentially, all computers are synchronous digital devices, though analog versions were once common, and asynchronous digital versions seem likely to appear.

HISTORY: Before the digital revolution, vast computational activities were quite important. Ballistic tables were used to aim naval guns. Math tables contained massive amounts of trig, log, and other data. Ephemeris tables showed the positions of the planets and stars for astronomers and navigators. These were created by "computers"—typically armies of women who worked in big rooms carrying out calculations by hand and orchestrated by a (male) boss.

computer operating properly *n.* Motorola's name for its watchdog timer system, which is included in some of its microcontrollers. Abbreviated COP.

computer-aided design *n.* The use of a computer to create electronic or mechanical drawings and documentation. Abbreviated CAD. CAD is a broad term that encompasses many facets of design work, from schematic capture to PCB routing to generation of BOMs and all aspects of mechanical design and packaging. CAD has replaced the drawing board.

condition code *n.* A value stored in a special latch inside of a processor that maintains the status of an operation. Condition codes vary from processor to processor but typically include zero, carry, parity, etc. When a math instruction (say, an add) finishes, the condition codes are set appropriately. The next instruction can then test these codes to make decisions. Be warned that different processors use condition codes in wildly different ways. For example, the move instruction on most CPUs does not change the saved codes, but on the 68k, most move instructions will alter the codes.

EXAMPLE: On an x86 processor, a loop might look as follows.

```
loop:
  ; do something
  dec ax
  jne loop
```

Register ax is the loop counter; decrementing it affects the condition codes. When ax reaches zero, condition code zero is asserted, so the jne instruction falls through.

condition variable *n.* A synchronization primitive used for signaling between threads within the same monitor. Condition variables are somewhat like counting semaphores, except that either a blocked thread wakes immediately after another thread signals a condition variable (in a Hoare monitor), or the signaling thread must completely exit the monitor before the blocked thread becomes ready to run.

The biggest difference, however, is that condition variables don't have an integer value that is tracked, incremented, and decremented, so a call to signal a condition variable can be lost if there are no threads already waiting on it.

conditional instruction *n.* The machine code or mnemonic form of an instruction that makes a decision. Most conditional instructions will result in a call or jump to a new location if the condition is met. *See also* branch instruction.

EXAMPLE: The Z80 instruction JR Z,dest will jump to dest if the previous instruction results in a 0; otherwise, execution continues with the next instruction.

conductance *n.* The measure of a material's ability to transmit a current. The inverse of resistance. Denoted by the symbol G.

$$G = \frac{1}{R}$$

The unit of conductance is the siemens.

conduction *n.* The process of carrying an electrical current. Conduction is inhibited by resistance, which is measured in ohms. *See also* conductor, ohm.

conductor *n.* Any material that carries an electrical current. Conductors can be perfect (a superconductor has 0 ohms), pretty darn good (copper), or rather nebulous depending on how they're used (semiconductor). *Contrast with* insulator.

configurable computing *n.* The use of FPGAs in a system so that the hardware design can be changed simply by uploading a new logic design and reprogramming the FPGA(s). Unlike its cousin reconfigurable computing, FPGAs need not be dynamically reprogrammable to achieve configurable computing. The FPGA(s) can simply be reprogrammed at each system startup. Configurable computing is already in use in many systems. *Contrast with* reconfigurable computing.

configurable logic block *n.* A collection of gates that can be assigned a behavior in a programmable logic device. Abbreviated CLB. Most programmable logic chips consist of a set of CLBs and routing resources that can be used to connnect their inputs and outputs. *See also* LUT.

configuration management *See* version control system.

connectivity *n.* A very qualitative measure of how well a system connects. Connectivity is often used in a binary sense, as to whether a system is or is not connected to the Internet.

connector *n.* An electronic component that ties two subsystems together in a nonpermanent fashion. Connectors come in thousands of varieties and are used in virtually all electronic systems. *See also* D-type connector.

console *n.* An increasingly obsolete term designating the control head of a system. Most often, it refers to a terminal-like interface that includes a keyboard and CRT.

const *res.* A qualifier keyword used when declaring a constant variable in C and various related languages. A statically checked type qualifier that declares that the associated object will not change during its lifetime.

USAGE: There is no specific required location for the const qualifier in a declaration. However, we recommend

```
float const a = 3.1e-8;
float const * p = &a;
```

which can be read (top to bottom) as "constant floating-point value" and "pointer to a constant floating-point value," respectively.

To declare a pointer with a value that cannot change, use

```
float const * const p = &a;
```

which declares p a constant pointer to a constant floating-point value. (Hopefully, the proper placement of const for a constant pointer to a nonconstant value object is now also clear.)

constant *n.* A value that never changes. A variable that is constant can be declared using the C const keyword, which allows it to be stored in ROM. A constant value, such as π, alternatively can be included in a program via a #define.

constraint *n.* A requirement expressed as a range.

EXAMPLE: If the total RAM available is limited to 128 KB, the range of this constraint is 0 to 128 KB.

constructive cost model *n.* A scheduling technique for estimating development time described in Barry Boehm's book *Software Engineering Economics* (Prentice-Hall, 1981). Abbreviated COCOMO. Development time is

$$time = constant(KLOCs)^{exponent}$$

where constant and exponent are functions of other project parameters.

constructor *n.* A function that is called when each new instance of a data type is created. In C++, the constructor for a class Foo is named Foo:: Foo(). That method of the class is called automatically whenever a new Foo is created.

consultant *n.* An individual who first appears when the project is in distress, tells management exactly what engineering has been saying for months (which is immediately adopted), gets paid three times the highest engineer's hourly rate, and leaves before testing any solution.

content-addressable memory *n.* An almost mythical memory device that accepts data and returns the address at which that data is stored. Abbreviated CAM. CAMs are enormously complex parts, so they exist only in very small configurations. They are used for extremely fast look-up table storage because, in one cycle, they return the result of a search.

context *n.* The current state of the processor's registers and flags. The context must be saved when an interrupt occurs or when an operating system selects a new task to run and preempts the previously running task.

context switch *n.* The process of switching from one task to another in a multitasking operating system. A context switch involves saving the context of the running task and restoring the previously saved context of the other. The piece of code that does this is necessarily processor specific.

contiguous *adj.* The relationship of two or more adjacent areas that share a boundary. The term contiguous is often used when discussing memory areas; two are contiguous if one immediately follows the other without a break.

continuity *n.* The condition where current flows through a loop.

USAGE: "There's continuity" is often heard when an engineer measures a circuit or, more often, wires leading somewhere, with an ohmmeter. This means the circuit is not open, and the resistance is low.

control bus *n.* The group of signals from a microprocessor that has timing and control information for the rest of the system. The control bus includes signals like R/~W and HLDA. When data and address appear on their respective buses, it's the control bus signals that cause memory to perform a read or write operation or to exchange data with a peripheral.

control plane *n.* The path of network packets that change the characteristics of the network connection. Most network processors recognize two different paths through a piece of network equipment such as a router: the control plane and

the data plane. Packets containing data to be routed to an endpoint pass through the optimized data plane. Those packets containing configuration instructions destined for or of interest to the local node are deemed part of the control plane. Most common data plane packet processing can be accomplished in hardware. The control plane packets must be processed by software as well.

control system *n.* An embedded system that manipulates a physical device. Common examples of control systems are thermostats, elevators, and cruise control. *See also* closed-loop control, open-loop control.

control, proportional–integral–differential *See* PID.

Ctrl-Q handshake *n.* A way of mediating serial communications to avoid overflowing the receiver. When transferring ASCII data, the device receiving data may halt the transmitter by sending a Ctrl-Q character (also known as XOFF and represented by 0x11). Ctrl-S (XON, 0x13) tells the transmitter to resume sending.

controller area network *n.* A serial bus system well suited to the task of interconnecting real-time systems. Abbreviated CAN. Multimaster capabilities and broadcast messaging are key features. Although originally developed for intra-automotive controller networks, CAN is common in industrial automation as well.

convection *n.* The transfer of heat in a gas or liquid by the circulation of currents in that medium. Convection is one of the three forms of heat transfer, the others being radiation and conduction.

cooperative multitasking *n.* A scheduling algorithm alternative in which there is no preemption, but tasks periodically yield, offering the operating system a chance to select another task to run. The problem with cooperative multitasking is that the system is only as strong as its weakest task. If a task doesn't cooperate, either by design or as the result of a bug, the whole system will lock up. This is exactly what used to happen in the Microsoft operating systems, like Windows 3.11, that were based on DOS.

COP (rhymes with mop) *abbr. See* computer operating properly.

COP8 (cop eight) *N.* A family of microcontrollers from National Semiconductor.

coprocessor *n.* A separate IC that provides extra functionality to a microprocessor system by monitoring the bus in parallel with the CPU and executing special instructions targeted at this extra IC. A coprocessor is essentially a special-function processor that executes its own instruction set. What makes it distinct from other computer systems is that it and the main CPU share the same address and data buses. The coprocessor is idle until it sees an instruction it understands. Most coprocessors employ a busy flag so the main CPU can continue to fetch and execute instructions while the coprocessor is executing one of its own, perhaps very slow, instructions.

EXAMPLE: Intel's 8087 was the first true coprocessor. It added floating-point math to the x86 processor line. An 80387 came out to do the same for the 80386 processor. When Intel introduced the 80486, the coprocessor instruction set was included on-chip.

copyleft *n.* A method for making software free by requiring all derived versions of the program to be made available free. Whereas a copyright is attached to something to keep it under proprietary control, a copyleft is attached to set it free and prevent future enhancements from becoming proprietary.

core 1. *See* core memory.

2. *See* hard core, soft core.

core dump *n.* A record of the contents of memory after a system crash. Core dumps show every location in memory so that a programmer can supposedly track down the root cause of a system crash.

HISTORY: Core dumps come from the days of mainframe computers, when debugging tools were minimal. When the mainframe crashed, most operating systems automatically printed the entire contents of memory (back then, 256 KB of memory was a lot, so the printouts weren't too huge). System programmers combed the dump to find out why the OS crashed. Although it sounds impossible, some programmers got quite good at this.

Those were the days of core memory, hence the name. Today, core dumps are almost unknown, as better development tools somewhat ease the pain of tracking the cause of crashes.

core memory *n.* An obsolete memory device that stored data in ferrite toroids. Core memory used one toroid per bit of storage. The earliest devices were almost the size of Cheerios; later versions were barely visible to the naked eye.

Four wires typically ran through each toroid. Organized and addressed in an x–y matrix, one x and one y wire each received one-half the current needed to flip the magnetic state of a stored bit. Where the x–y addresses came together, the toroid had enough current to flip, creating a magnetic pulse detected by a third wire common to all cores in a plane. The fourth wire biased the array to reduce drive requirements. All reads were destructive, changing the stored data, so every read was followed by a write to restore the data.

Core memory was very reliable and resilient to radioactive fields, so it and a derivative (plated wire) were used into the 1980s on spacecraft. However, the technology more or less died in the 1970s for commercial applications because of the much lower cost per bit and the reduced size of semiconductor memories.

correlation *n.* The amount of correspondence between two sets of data. If two signals are exactly the same in all respects, they will have a correlation of 1.0 and they are said to be fully correlated. If two signals have no similarity whatsoever, they will have a correlation of 0.0, and they are uncorrelated.

cosine *n.* A trigonometric function that is the ratio of the side of a triangle adjacent the angle of interest to the hypotenuse. Abbreviated cos.

$$\cos(\alpha) = \frac{adjacent}{hypotenuse}$$

cost of goods sold *n.* The cost to manufacture a product in production. Abbreviated COGS. A product's cost of goods sold includes components and labor, but excludes sales, G&A, and other costs. It's usually compared to nonrecurring engineering (NRE) costs. Depending on volumes, it may or may not make sense to heavily invest in extra NRE to reduce COGS. *See also* nonrecurring engineering cost.

cost per seat *n.* The per-workstation cost of a development tool. Most EDA tools and some compilers and debuggers are licensed for use only on one workstation (or by one developer) at a time. The cost of these tools is generally linear with the number of development seats your company will require.

COTS (rhymes with pots) *abbr. See* commercial off-the-shelf.

coulomb *n.* A standard unit of electric charge. Abbreviated C. One coulomb is 6.25×10^{18} electrons.

counter 1. *n.* A piece of test equipment that counts an input.

2. *n.* A peripheral that counts external events. In practice, counters are almost always capable of timing (counting processor cycles) as well as counting external events. *Compare to* timer. *See also* counter/timer.

counter/timer *n.* A common peripheral that counts either external events (counter mode) or processor cycles (timer mode). Virtually every microcontroller has one or more on-board counter/timers. Most operate in a vast number of modes; some have dozens of control registers (Motorola's TPU has more than 50).

Counter/timer hardware has more uses than can be imagined, including as input devices to count events, as outputs to drive pulse-width modulation devices, and as internal units to create regular interrupts for RTOS context switching.

counting semaphore *n.* A type of semaphore with more than two states. A counting semaphore is typically used to track multiple resources of the same type. An attempt to take a counting semaphore is blocked only if all of the available resources are in use. *See also* semaphore.

coupling *n.* A (generally undesirable) link between two source modules. If a change in module A causes code in module B to fail, then the two modules are said to be coupled. Proper use of encapsulation will separate the interface from the implementation of each module. Once that's done, changes to either module's implementation should not affect the other module, which helps aid reuse and lower maintenance costs.

coverage *See* code coverage.

cowboy *adj.* Used to describe someone who will obey no rules, has no concept of software process, and typically generates a spaghetti mess of code no one can possibly maintain.

USAGE: Almost always used as an adjective before the word programmer or coder.

CPLD (as letters) *abbr. See* complex programmable logic device.

cpp (as letters) *abbr.* The most common name for the C preprocessor when it is a distinct tool. Short for C PreProcessor.

cps (as letters) *abbr.* A common unit of bit rate. Short for Characters Per Second. Because of overhead like start, stop, and parity bits, the cps of a transmission is not generally just the raw bps/8. *See also* baud rate.

CPU (as letters) *abbr. See* central processing unit.

CPU utilization *n.* The amount of time required by a program versus time available, measured as a percentage. Usually measured as the opposite of idle time. If the processor is idle 6% of the time, its CPU utilization is 94%.

CPU-bound *adj.* Describes a thread that needs lots of processor cycles to complete its work. It's best if CPU-bound threads take advantage of spare cycles while the I/O-bound threads are waiting for an I/O operation to complete. In other words, these are generally background threads with lower priority.

CPU32 *n.* The CPU architecture of a number of Motorola microcontrollers. Although CPU32 processors share the same instruction set (similar to and based on the 68k ISA), each has a different mix of peripherals and different packaging options. Examples include the 68332, 68340, etc.

CR/LF (see-are ell-eff) *abbr.* A pair of ASCII characters often used to terminate each line of a file. Short for Carriage Return/Line Feed.

crash 1. *n.* The state of a system in which a program or OS has wandered from a normal execution stream. Crashes have many different symptoms, but in general the computer continues to run … something. The crash might be intercepted by an exception handler, but more often, one finds the system completely unusable until rebooted.

2. *n.* To discontinue operating as expected.

CRC (as letters) *abbr. See* cyclic redundancy code.

CRC-16 (as letters and number) *N.* A specific 16-bit cyclic redundancy code. The following parameters apply to this CRC.

- generator polynomial = $x^{16} + x^{15} + x^2 + 1$ (0x18005)
- initial remainder = 0x0000
- final XOR value = 0x0000
- data bits reflected
- remainder bits reflected

If you implement a CRC-16, be sure to test the result on the string "123456789"; the result should be 0xBB3D.

CRC-32 (as letters and number) *N.* A specific 32-bit cyclic redundancy code. The following parameters apply to this CRC.

- generator polynomial = 0x104C11DB7
- initial remainder = 0xFFFFFFFF
- final XOR value = 0xFFFFFFFF
- data bits reflected
- remainder bits reflected

If you implement a CRC-32, be sure to test the result on the string "123456789"; the result should be 0xCBF43926.

CRC-CCITT (as letters) *abbr.* A specific 16-bit cyclic redundancy code specified by the CCITT. The following parameters apply to this CRC.

- generator polynomial = $x^{16} + x^{12} + x^5 + 1$ (0x11021)
- initial remainder = 0xFFFF
- final XOR value = 0x0000
- data bits not reflected
- remainder bits not reflected

If you implement a CRC-CCITT, be sure to test the result on the string "123456789"; the result should be 0x29B1.

critical path *n.* The part of a project that is most directly delaying completion. Unfortunately, many managers don't seem able to anticipate what other parts of the project might be in the critical path once the current problem is overcome. As a result, such managers cause the next set of critical-path problems to occur simply by focusing all available developers on the current critical-path component.

critical section *n.* A sequence of instructions that must be executed in sequence and without interruption to guarantee correct operation of the software. If the instructions are interrupted, a race condition might occur.

criticality 1 failure node *n.* A NASA term indicating a failure that will result in the loss of a manned spacecraft. Criticality 1 failure nodes have no backups. An external tank rupture is an example.

cross-assembler *n.* A software tool that converts assembly mnemonics to machine instructions, yet runs on a development system that might have a different instruction set.

EXAMPLE: A developer might use a cross-assembler that assembles 68332 code on a PC; the output, once linked and located, will be downloaded through a debugger for execution on the target 68332 platform.

cross-compiler *n.* A compiler that runs on a different platform from the one for which it produces object code. Often even the processor architecture/family of the host and target platforms differ.

FURTHER READING: http://www.netrino.com/Articles/CrossCompilers/

cross-platform development *n.* The process of creating software for a target microprocessor using a host computer with a different CPU. Cross-platform development is the essence of embedded systems work; most developers work with a Unix or PC host yet generate code for target processors ranging from PICs to DSPs.

crosstalk *n.* The undesirable coupling of signals between two conductors. Every wire is an antenna that both radiates and receives energy.

When signal wires or tracks run close together, especially if one of them has a very high impedance, it's possible and common for signals from one wire to appear on the other.

crowbar *n.* A circuit that places a low-resistance load on the output of a power supply to quickly bring its output to zero. Linear power supplies typically have huge filter capacitors (thousands of microfarads) that can retain energy for minutes after the system is turned off. That's dangerous for repair technicians if the voltages are high. It will also make the system less tolerant of brownouts, since the stored energy will usually immediately droop to some extent, crashing the processor, yet maintain enough voltage to cause erratic operation of the reset circuit.

HISTORY: Named after the old safety practice of discharging filter capacitors by dropping a wrench, crowbar, or other massive metal object across the cap's terminals.

CRT (as letters) 1. *abbr.* A vacuum tube with a phosphorescent screen used for displaying data and other information. Abbreviation for Cathode Ray Tube.

2. *n.* Colloquially used to mean a computer monitor that uses a cathode ray tube. All PCs and workstations employ some sort of monitor to display information to the user. Until the late 1990s, this was invariably a CRT, though LCD screens are common now as well.

crystal *n.* A two-terminal electronic device that sets an oscillator's frequency. Crystals are nothing more than carefully shaped pieces of quartz sandwiched between a pair of metal plates attached to wires. A small applied current causes the quartz to oscillate at a very precise frequency determined by the quartz's shape and size; this vibration sets up an electric field. Important characteristics include: *frequency*, the speed of oscillation; *cut*, which determines the axis in which the quartz vibrates; *mode*, the preferred harmonic (some crystals oscillate at a harmonic of the quartz's natural resonant frequency); *stability*, drift versus temperature. Decent crystals that operate above 20 MHz or so are hard to make, so most high-frequency parts operate at the third or fifth harmonic.

crystal, CPU *n.* The device that sets a processor's clock frequency. Processor crystals range from 32-kHz devices designed for wrist watches to many-megahertz parts. Often the crystal is packaged inside a more sophisticated part that converts a crystal's natural sine wave output to digital. *See also* crystal.

crystal, real-time clock *n.* The device that sets the time base for a time-of-day oscillator. The vast majority of real-time clocks use a 32,768-Hz crystal. Because these are in all wrist watches, they are cheap and small. *See also* crystal.

CS (as letters) 1. *abbr. See* chip select.

2. *n.* A computer scientist or their university degree.

CSE (as letters) *abbr. See* common subexpression elimination.

CTS (as letters) *abbr. See* clear to send.

cubicle *n.* A tiny box, much like an abandoned refrigerator carton, housing one to twelve programmers. Developers serve out their sentences for up to 12 hours a day in this cramped cell while the warden (boss) patrols the compound making sure each prisoner stays occupied producing code.

cubicle farm *n.* A refugee camp for programmers that features high density, overpopulation, and poor living conditions. Designed to maximize noise and interruptions and (most importantly) minimize productivity, cube farms demonstrate management's commitment to using developers as interchangeable components in a vast software factory. An underground movement spearheaded by DeMarco and Lister's *Peopleware* (New York:

Dorset House Publishing, 1987) aims to eliminate this form of slavery. The revolution is now!

current *n.* The flow of electrons in a closed circuit. Measured in amperes. *See also* amperage.

current loop 1. *n.* A way to transmit analog data in noisy industrial conditions with two wires. It's common to send analog data throughout a factory via the two-wire current loop. The input must be scaled to a range of 4 to 20 mA.

2. *n.* An obsolete method of sending serial data between two devices. Teletypes, most famously the ASR-33, transmitted and received ASCII characters via a 20-mA current loop. Twenty milliamps of flowing current (i.e., the circuit was closed) designated a "marking" condition. A "space" was specified by no current flow (an open circuit), as all old developers found by the horrible buzzing noise the Teletype let out whenever its signal cable became unconnected.

current sink *n.* A component or circuit that draws a constant current from a source. Although a resistor is indeed a current sink, the current it draws varies with the applied voltage. Packaged current sinks, though, offer constant draw regardless of voltage. Often used to drive LEDs and laser diodes when a precise level of current is needed.

EXAMPLE: Sharp's IR2C53 is a constant current sink for driving visible and IR LEDs.

current source *n.* A component or circuit that provides an accurate current level at a very low noise. Widely used in D/A converters, which typically source current into a resistor array.

EXAMPLE: Analog Device's ADN8810 is a current source providing a programmable current level.

cursor *n.* On a GUI, a visible indication of the user's current location in a text-entry field. *See also* mouse pointer.

curve *n.* The output of a function exercised over all possible inputs. A function, and therefore the curve it produces, is differentiable; thus, it has no discontinuities and can never result in more than one unique value for any particular input.

curve fitting *n.* The process of determining the coefficients of a polynomial to approximate a function. Three kinds of curve fits are used in embedded systems development. The first is to approximate complex functions that have no easily computed results, such as trigonometric functions (cosine, sine, tangent, etc.), roots (square roots and others), and more exotic functions like Bessel functions.

The second is to approximate aspects of reality that have no known transfer function. For example, it's possible to measure the percentage of protein in grains by measuring reflected light at hundreds of wavelengths from a sample and then combining these readings in a polynomial. No one knows how to compute the coefficients, so the instrument must be calibrated: hundreds of samples with known concentrations of protein are run through the machine, and then a curve-fitting program determines those coefficients.

Finally, curve fitting is occasionally used to reduce noise in a sequence of analog input data. If there's some *a priori* knowledge about the expected shape of the data, it's possible to do a least-squares fit. The resulting curve is a more accurate, smoothed representation of the data. Least-squares curve fitting can also almost automatically generate the first and second derivative of the data.

CVS (as letters) *abbr.* A popular open source version control system. Short for Concurrent Versions System.

FURTHER READING: http://www.cvshome.org

cycle time, memory *n.* The total time a memory array or device needs to start and complete an access and then be ready for the next access. Cycle and access times are equivalent on most of today's memory devices; a recovery period is no longer needed between accesses. This was not true 20

years ago; an access could complete, but a small settling time was needed before the memory could successfully start another access.

cycle-level simulator *n.* A simulation engine that is faithful to the real system's behavior down to the cycle level. Simulation is inherently slow and difficult. It's nice to make certain assumptions about a system's behavior to speed simulation execution, which is quite common on instruction-level simulators. A cycle-level simulator, though, must be precise down to the timing of the target system.

cyclic executive *n.* A simplistic "operating system" that calls each of several functions in a cyclic fashion. Each function is allocated a specific time slot in the larger cycle, much as each transmitter has a prespecified time slot in a TDM system. Some "tasks" might use their slot each time it comes; others might spread their work across multiple slots. A set of tasks with harmonic periods generally works best.

In certain types of systems, cyclic executives are far more useful than preemptive, real-time operating systems. However, there are no notable commercial players, since a decent cyclic executive is also easily and inexpensively developed in-house.

The determinism and timing accuracy of a cyclic software architecture are valuable in real-time systems, particularly when the periods of the various jobs to be done coincide precisely or harmonically.

cyclic redundancy code *n.* A powerful and useful checksum based on modulo-2 binary division. Abbreviated CRC.

When computing a CRC of width c bits on a message of length m bits:

- the message bits are appended with c zeroes; this augmented message is the dividend
- a predetermined (c + 1)-bit binary sequence, called the generator polynomial, is the divisor
- the checksum is the c-bit remainder that results from the division operation

In other words, you divide the augmented message by the generator polynomial, discard the quotient, and use the c-bit remainder as your checksum.

The mathematically appealing aspect of division is that remainders fluctuate rapidly as small numbers of bits within the message are changed. Sums, products, and quotients do not share this property, so remainders make the best checksums.

As is the case with other types of checksums, the width of the CRC plays an important role in the error detection capabilities of the algorithm. Ignoring special types of errors that are always detected by a particular checksum algorithm, the percentage of detectable errors is limited strictly by the width of a checksum. A checksum of c bits can only take one of 2^c unique values. Because the number of possible messages is significantly larger than that, the potential exists for two or more messages to have an identical checksum. If one of those messages is somehow transformed into one of the others during transmission, the checksum will appear correct and the receiver will unknowingly accept a bad message. The chance of this happening is directly related to the width of the checksum. Specifically, the chance of such an error is $1/2^c$. Therefore, the probability of any random error being detected is $1 - 1/2^c$.

To repeat, the probability of detecting any random error increases as the width of the checksum increases. Specifically, a 16-bit checksum will detect 99.9985% of all errors. This is far better than the 99.6094% detection rate of an 8-bit checksum, but not nearly as good as the 99.9999% detection rate of a 32-bit checksum. All of this applies to both CRCs and addition-based checksums. What really sets CRCs apart, however, is the number of special cases that can be detected 100% of the time. For example, two opposite bit inversions (one bit becoming 0, the other becoming 1) in the same column of an addition would cause the errors to be undetected. But that's not the case with a CRC.

By using one of the mathematically well-understood generator polynomials to calculate a checksum, it's possible to state that the following types of errors will be detected without fail.

- A message with any one bit in error
- A message with any two bits in error (no matter how far apart, which column, etc.)
- A message with any odd number of bits in error (no matter where they are)
- A message with an error burst as wide as the checksum itself

The first class of detectable error is also detected by an addition-based checksum, or even a simple parity bit. However, the middle two classes of errors represent much stronger detection capabilities than those other types of checksum. The fourth class of detectable error sounds at first to be similar to a class of errors detected by addition-based checksums, but in the case of CRCs, any odd number of bit errors will be detected. So the set of error bursts too wide to detect is now limited to those with an even number of bit errors. All other types of errors fall into the relatively high $1 - 1/2^c$ probability of detection.

For most people, the overwhelmingly confusing thing about CRCs is the implementation. Knowing that all CRC algorithms are simply long division algorithms in disguise doesn't help. Modulo-2 binary division doesn't map well to the instruction sets of general-purpose processors. So, whereas the implementation of a checksum algorithm based on addition is straightforward, the implementation of a binary division algorithm with an $(m + c)$-bit numerator and a $(c + 1)$-bit denominator is nowhere close. For one thing, there aren't generally any $(m + c)$- or $(c + 1)$-bit registers in which to store the operands.

FURTHER READING: Complete C and C++ implementations of a CRC algorithm flexible enough to be used for CRC-16, CRC-32, CRC-CCITT, or any other standard cyclic redundancy code are in the public domain. These can be found at http://www.netrino.com/Connecting/2000-01/crc.zip and http://www.boost.org/libs/crc/, respectively.

Cygwin (sig win) *N.* A package of software from the company formerly called Cygnus (now owned by RedHat) that makes running the GNU tools on Windows platforms reasonable. Hence, Cyg-Win. (Note the GNU in Cygnus as well.) At its core, the product is basically just a Unix-like command shell for Windows. Many embedded systems programmers use Cygwin along with the GNU tools to develop and test their firmware from a PC host.

FURTHER READING: http://www.cygwin.com

cylinder *n.* On a disk drive, a collection of tracks equidistant from the center but on distinct platters. A large part of the delay in transferring data to or from a disk is the seek time, which involves moving the head out to the appropriate track and then waiting for the requested sector to come into view. By organizing tracks into cylinders and recording adjacent blocks of a file entirely on tracks of the same cylinder, movement of the heads (which are all always the same distance from the center) is kept to a minimum.

D

D-cache (dee cache) *abbr. See* cache, data.

D-type connector *n.* A connector often found in embedded and desktop systems. When viewed from the pins, the connector looks much like the letter 'D'. The most common D-type connectors are

- 9-pin serial cables for RS-232 communications,
- 15-pin video cables for monitors and LCD projectors, and
- 25-pin parallel cables for printer connections or, in very old systems, RS-232.

D/A (D-to-A) *abbr. See* D/A converter.

D/A converter *n.* A hardware device that takes a set of bits, typically from a processor, as input and produces an analog signal proportional to the digital input as output. Short for digital-to-analog converter. D/A converters might be as simple as an array of resistors configured in the typical "R-2R"

fashion or a hybrid module that generates very precise results with many bits of resolution. A simple use is to vary the intensity of a lamp (another approach that avoids the messy analog world is a pulse-width modulator that uses different switching rates and pulse lengths to control intensity).

D/A converter, multiplying *n.* A peripheral device that converts a digital word to an analog voltage using a reference voltage to scale the result. Many D/A converters use a precisely regulated reference voltage as the basis for the analog out. In some, the reference is required to be more or less a certain value. Others take virtually any value, which results in a transfer function like

$$output = input \times reference$$

hence, "multiplying."

DAC (dack) *abbr. See* D/A converter.

daisy chain 1. *n.* A digital circuit that propagates a signal into and out of a series of components. Because a daisy-chained signal passes through each connected component, any of them can block the signal from passing further down the chain. Daisy chains are slow but simple.

EXAMPLE: The Z80 used a daisy-chained interrupt structure: the interrupt request line passed from the lowest priority peripheral toward the CPU through every other peripheral. The last one in line, which tied directly to the Z80's interrupt input, had the highest priority. When a peripheral requested an interrupt, the request passed along the chain. Any device closer to the processor could block the request and pass its own request on, thus implementing a crude priority scheme.

2. *v.* To connect a series of devices in a daisy chain.

dangling input *See* floating input.

dangling pointer *n.* A pointer to an object that no longer exists. Although the pointer variable still contains a valid memory address, the data at that address is no longer in active use, usually because it was previously `free()`d. In fact, the same memory location might have since been reallocated for another purpose. The risk inherent in the existence of the dangling pointer is that the new data at that location can be corrupted by the owner of the old pointer.

dangling reference *n.* A pointer to an object that no longer exists in memory. Although the object might have been `deleted` properly, another copy of the reference was still around. If that other reference is ever used to access the object, it is possible that some other object created in the space freed by the original will be corrupted.

das blinkenlights *n.* ACHTUNG! Das machine is nicht für gerfingerpoken und mittengraben. Ist easy schnappen der springenwerk, blowenfusen und corkenpoppen mit spitzensparken. Ist nicht für gewerken by das dummkopfen. Das rubber-necken sightseeren keepen hands in das pockets. Relaxen und vatch das blinkenlights!

data *n.* Information used by a program but that is not part of the executable code. Data includes variables, items declared as `const`, and information read from or written to peripherals.

data acquisition *n.* The process of sucking in analog data and converting it to digital for further processing. A common part of many embedded systems, such as a digital scope, which might acquire a billion analog samples per second.

data acquisition system *n.* Any of a wide class of systems that convert analog inputs into digital signals for further processing. Data acquisition is often the front end of an embedded system.

There are quite a few vendors for preconfigured modular data acquisition (sub)systems that can be plugged together using a common bus structure.

data bits *n.* The string of binary data being sent in a network frame or asynchronous serial character. The data bits are generally surrounded by framing bits at the start and end of the transmission. *See also* 8N1.

data bus *n.* A set of electrical signals connected to the processor and all of the memory and peripheral devices with which it communicates for the purpose of transferring data between them. When the processor wants to read (write) the contents of a memory location or register within a particular peripheral, it sets the address bus pins appropriately and receives (transmits) the contents on the data bus. One unit of data is transferred in each memory cycle.

data collection *n.* The sampling and recording of data for later processing. Data-collection systems can take in either digital or analog data. For example, scientific instruments that measure ocean temperature over the course of months or years later report that data back to researchers when the instrument is retrieved.

data direction register *n.* One of several registers used to control parallel ports that can be used as either inputs or outputs. Often abbreviated DDR. Most bidirectional ports can be programmed bit by bit as inputs or outputs. The DDR holds these selections and sets the hardware up appropriately. *See also* bidirectional port, general-purpose I/O.

data link layer *n.* The protocol layer responsible for sending and receiving data over a physical communications medium. Layer 2 of the OSI reference model. In the TCP/IP protocol suite, the data link layer lies partly in hardware (the network interface controller) and partly in software (the driver for that card, ARP, and RARP). *See also* physical layer, network layer.

data memory *n.* A storage area that holds values, such as variables and constants, referenced by the program code. Data memory is in RAM or, in some cases, flash or EEPROM. Most often, data memory contains the program variables, but in some very rare cases, a bit of self-modifying code might live in a small section of this memory.

USAGE: It's tempting to call RAM data memory, but this is not always accurate. Fast RAM chips are much cheaper than most fast nonvolatile devices (e.g., EPROM). Some embedded systems, therefore, copy the program from EPROM to RAM at startup, then execute from RAM at higher speeds (fewer wait states).

data plane *n.* The optimized path of data packets routed through a network processor. Packets handled in the data plane are not individually opened and are typically handled entirely at the network layer. A router is a network node that specializes in shuttling such packets on toward their destinations very efficiently. *See also* control plane.

data segment 1. *n.* A segment in an object file that contains initialized data. The data segment is

located in RAM, though the initial values for those variables must be copied from an equal-sized segment in ROM.

2. *n.* On an 80x86 processor, the region of memory selected by the DS register.

data selector *See* digital multiplexer.

data sheet *n.* The complete specification of a particular hardware component, such as an IC. Data sheets contain all of a part's electrical, timing, and interface parameters. The data sheet for a resistor might be a single paragraph; that for a complex IC might rival *War and Peace* in length. Developers ignore even the most obscure footnote at their peril. Refer to "How to Get the Right Information from a Data Sheet," Appendix F of Bob Pease's book *Troubleshooting Analog Circuits* (Butterworth-Heinemann, 1991).

data terminal ready *n.* An RS-232C signal that informs the DCE that the DTE is alive and well. Abbreviated DTR. DTR is normally set to the ON state (logic 0) by the DTE at power-up and left there. Note that a typical DCE must have an incoming DTR before it will function normally.

databook *n.* A bound volume describing the use and specifications of one or more components. *See also* data sheet.

datacom *adj.* Of or relating to the transfer of nontelephony data over a communications network. *Compare to* telecom.

datagram *n.* A UDP packet. Unlike TCP, UDP is connectionless. Each datagram is considered a distinct communication between the sender and receiver. If more than one datagram is sent along that path, they could arrive out of order, or some might not arrive at all.

datalogger *n.* A device (typically an embedded system) that continuously collects and records data of some sort.

EXAMPLE: A water flow datalogger might record the water level every minute in a particular section of sewer. The system's memory can later be uploaded to a central database or used for analysis of the sewer's performance during a storm.

date code *n.* A marking on many components, especially ICs, that indicates when the device was manufactured. The date code lets vendors track problems with manufacturing defects, since slight variations in process technology, humidity, vibration, and sometimes seemingly even the phase of the moon can affect a part's performance. Date codes vary in format but often look like "9843," which means the part was made in the 43rd week of 1998.

daughterboard *n.* A circuit board that attaches to a larger circuit board, often via a header. *See also* motherboard.

daughtercard *See* daughterboard.

dB (dee-bee) *abbr. See* decibel.

dB-m *n.* A unit of power measured in decibels, referenced to one milliwatt. Also called dBm. The dB-m of a signal = 10 log((signal in watts)/(0.001 watt)). Engineers use the decibel to compare the magnitudes of two signals; they are not absolute measures in any sense. dB-m, though, is an absolute measure.

dBm0 *n.* A measure of power, in decibels relative to a zero signal at 1 mW. *See also* dB-m.

DC (as letters) *abbr. See* direct current.

DC bias *n.* A constant voltage applied to an analog circuit, usually by a constant-voltage source or resistor. Circuits get a DC bias for many reasons, often to keep an inherently nonlinear system operating in a linear subset of its range.

DC motor *n.* A motor powered by a source of DC current. Motors, by their nature, are AC devices,

since a stationary winding or magnet must alternately attract and repel the moving armature. A process of commutation converts the DC input to an alternating magnetic field. On brush motors, commutation takes place by the brushes engaging alternating windings on the armatures. Brushless motors employ fancy electronics that reverse the EMF field, in effect turning the DC into AC before applying it to the motor. *See also* brush motor, brushless motor.

DC–DC converter (DC-to-DC converter) *n.* A type of voltage regulator. Transforms a DC voltage to another voltage, passing through an AC stage on the way.

DCE (as letters) *abbr.* One of the endpoints of an RS-232 serial communications channel. Short for Data Communications Equipment. *See also* DTE.
EXAMPLE: A modem.

DDS (as letters) *abbr. See* direct digital synthesis.

dead code elimination *n.* A compiler optimization that removes instructions that have no effect.
EXAMPLE: With dead code elimination enabled and variable x not read until after the following code snippet, the entire sequence

```
x = 1;
...
x = 2;
if (x == 2)
{
    x = 3;
}
```

could be replaced by

```
...
x = 3;
```

deadline *n.* In a real-time system, the time at which a particular set of computations or data transfers must be completed. There are typically consequences associated with missing a deadline. If the deadline absolutely, positively must be met every time or else, it is called a hard deadline. Hard deadlines have dire consequences when missed. Other deadlines are said to be soft deadlines.

deadline-monotonic algorithm *n.* A priority-assignment algorithm for use with a real-time operating system that uses fixed-priority preemptive scheduling. Abbreviated DMA. Like rate-monotonic algorithm, DMA is a technique for setting the priorities of each thread relative to the others. The difference is that DMA considers the deadlines of each thread rather than their periods. The deadlines of the threads are assumed to be known *a priori*; the shorter the deadline of a particular thread, the higher its assigned priority (hence, "deadline"-monotonic). DMA is equivalent to RMA in the special case that all tasks have deadlines equal to their periods. *Compare to* earliest-deadline-first.

deadline-monotonic analysis *n.* The process of analyzing a real-time system to assign individual thread priorities according to the deadline-monotonic algorithm.

deadlock *n.* An unwanted software situation in which an entire set of tasks is blocked, waiting for an event that only a task within the same set can cause. If a deadlock occurs, the only solution is to reset the involved set of tasks or the entire system. However, it is usually possible to prevent deadlocks altogether by following certain software-design practices. Consult an operating systems textbook for details.

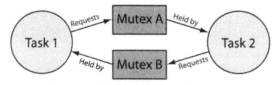

A key condition for deadlock is a circular wait, such as that shown here.

deadly embrace *See* deadlock.

deadman switch *n.* A safety-control device that prevents a system from operating except when an

operator is present. Some systems are so potentially dangerous that the designer wants to ensure that they do not continue to operate if the user is no longer at the controls or has lost consciousness; for example, weight detectors on the seat of a speedboat to disable the engine if the driver is missing.

deadtime *n.* An interval of time after which a control decision is made and the drive signal is adjusted before the plant responds. Deadtime makes closed-loop control difficult. Unless you can compensate for the plant's delayed reaction to new drive signals, it's probably a bad idea to make any further changes until after the deadtime has elapsed. In that sense, deadtime introduces an upper bound on how frequently the control system can make adjustments.

debounce *v.* The process of eliminating uncertainty from a mechanical input, such as a switch. Any contact "bounces" when actuated. Computers are so fast, they can see a rapid succession of opens and closes; it's hard to know which state is correct. Debounce algorithms make that determination.

One simple approach is to read the input a few times with a short wait between each (several milliseconds). See code listing for an example. Repeat until all readings are the same. Hardware approaches use flip-flops and double-throw switches. *See also* bounce.

debug agent *See* debug monitor.

USAGE: This variant of the terminology seems to be most common in the GNU community, where a gdb stub is the embedded agent. We do like that this form emphasizes the active side of working in target on behalf of the remote debugger but still suggest "debug monitor" as the better choice in most contexts.

debug monitor *n.* A piece of embedded software that has been designed specifically for use as a debugging tool. It usually resides in ROM and communicates with a debugger via a serial port or network connection. The debug monitor provides a set of primitive commands to view and modify memory locations and registers, create and remove breakpoints, and execute your program. A remote debugger with knowledge of the command format communicates with the debug monitor and combines these primitives to fulfill higher-level requests like program download and single-step.

debugger *n.* A tool used to test and debug software. A typical remote debugger runs on a host computer and connects to the target through a serial port or over a network. Using the debugger, you can download software to the target for immediate execution. You can also set breakpoints in the code and examine the contents of specific memory locations and registers.

debugger, source-level *n.* A software program that runs on a host (desktop) computer used to find bugs, but that correlates all low-level target machine instructions and hex addresses to the user's high-level language source files. Working with hex addresses and data isn't too terrible when programming in assembly language, because there's a one-to-one mapping between all of these values. In C or other HLLs, it's very difficult. For example, a source-level debugger can see that a program stops at address 0x123A, but it will call up the user's source file and highlight the C statement represented by that address.

Such debuggers therefore need a tremendous amount of information about a program, from where the source files can be found and their names to complete linkage information, as well as knowledge of how the compiler translates HLL statements to machine instructions. There is no

debounce A function like this will debounce up to eight input pins. Simply call it each time the raw state is reread and use the returned value for the debounced signals. To require three or more consecutive readings be the same, simply replace `previous` with two or more prior states.

```
uint8_t
debounce(uint8_t current)
{
    static uint8_t  asserted = 0x00;
    static uint8_t  previous = 0x00;

    /*
     * Compare the current and previous states of each input.
     */
    asserted |= (previous & current);   // Assert newly "on" inputs.
    asserted &= (previous | current);   // Clear newly "off" inputs.

    /*
     * Update the history.
     */
    previous = current;

    /*
     * Return the debounced inputs to the caller.
     */
    return (asserted);

}   /* debounce() */
```

generic source-level debugger; each is either sold with a specific compiler or comes with translation programs specific to compilers. The compiler usually must be set to generate "debug info" (in files) for the source-level debugger to use.

debugging *n.* The process of removing defects from a program. Bugs range from errors in specifications to mistakes made while generating code. Regardless, debugging is the act of fixing these problems after writing and starting to test the system. Debugging is often the most expensive part of system development, and it is one that often gets shortchanged, which explains why so many electronic products run so poorly.

Although debugging will probably always be a part of programming, wise developers minimize such effort using proven software-development processes that reduce bugs, such as code inspections.

decade *adj.* A factor of ten. *Compare to* octave.

USAGE: Often used to describe the characteristics of some system. For example, a resistor decade box is a piece of test equipment that lets the user select almost any resistor value in increments of 10, 100, 1000 ohms, and so on.

deceleration *n.* Acceleration that is negative, meaning that velocity is decreasing.

decibel *n.* One tenth of a bel (no kidding!). Abbreviated dB (since a bel is abbreviated B). A bel is the log of the power ratio

$$bel = 100\log(P_1/P_2)$$

so a decibel is

$$dB = 10\log(P_1/P_2)$$

HISTORY: The bel was named for Alexander Graham Bell.

decimal *n.* A number in base-10 notation. Reputedly common because we have 10 fingers and learned to count on those digits. Base-10 is singu-

larly useless in computer applications (except when interacting with humans) because it packs so poorly into binary words. *See also* binary-coded decimal.

HISTORY: There were computers in the 1950s and 1960s that used decimal, expressed in BCD, as their native way of computing. IBM's 1620 was tremendously popular in its day. But binary is much more efficient, so decimal machines eventually went the way of the dinosaurs.

decimal point *n.* The symbol that expresses the change from integers to fractions of an integer when working with base 10 numbers. Decimal points are usually expressed via the period symbol.

EXAMPLE: In the number 12.34, the decimal point indicated by the period separates the whole from the fractional part of the number.

decimal prefixes *n.* The standard prefixes specified by the SI system to express multiples of 10.

- 10^3 is called a kilo and abbreviated k
- 10^6 is called a mega and abbreviated M
- 10^9 is called a giga and abbreviated G

See table on page 290. *See also* binary prefixes.

EXAMPLE:

- 1 kilobit: 1 kbit = 1,000 bits
- 1 kilobyte: 1 kB = 1,000 bytes
- 1 megabit: 1 Mbit = 1,000,000 bits
- 1 megabyte: 1 MB = 1,000,000 bytes
- 1 gigabit: 1 Gbit = 1,000,000,000 bits
- 1 gigabyte: 1 GB = 1,000,000,000 bytes

decision point *n.* A step in an algorithm at which point the step that follows varies based on some computable result. Each decision point must lead to one of two or more possible algorithmic paths being chosen. In a C program, for example,

```
if (x == 0)
{ ... }
else
{ ... }
```

represents a decision point with two possible paths. Adding additional `else if` statements increases the number of possible paths..

decoder *n.* A circuit that selects one of a number of possibilities. Decoders take many inputs and have many outputs; however, only one output will be active at a time, depending on the inputs. Generally the inputs are binary numbers.

EXAMPLE: The 74LS138 chip takes a 3-bit binary number as input and asserts one of eight outputs. Its most common application is to select one of many memory or I/O chips. Some number of address bits are decoded to enable just one device.

decompression *n.* The process of extracting the information hidden inside a compressed image. Compression is frequently used to reduce the amount of data transferred over modems and networks. Decompression must therefore be done by hardware or software on the receiving end.

deconstructor *See* destructor.

decoupling capacitor *n.* A device that removes much of the noise on power and ground signals. The average digital circuit board is peppered with decoupling capacitors. As digital signals switch, they induce high-frequency noise on the power lines, which is a very bad thing that can lead to improper switching and even device failure. A board typically has a few bulk (large-value, on the order of 10μF) decoupling devices that provide stored energy for a few nanoseconds of switching. Additional smaller capacitors (0.001 to 0.1μF) are connected very close to the power and ground leads of nearly every IC to remove the high-frequency noise.

decrement (deck reh ment) *v.* To decrease by one. *See also* −−.

decryption *n.* The process of unscrambling an encrypted message to recover the information it contains. The decryption algorithm and any related keys are necessarily dictated by the encryption process used to scramble the data.

deep-history pseudostate *n.* A visual shorthand for the complicated idea of having a parent state remember which child state was last active. Similar to the shallow-history pseudostate, but with a depth of memory that its return to history lacks. Shown as a circled "H★" in UML. A transition to a composite state's deep-history pseudostate reverts that state to its complete saved extended state—not just into a particular substate. To implement this, additional memorization of state information is required when leaving the composite state.

defect *n.* A flaw or error in the requirements, specification, or implementation of a system or subsystem that manifests itself in dangerous or incorrect system behavior. Also called a bug.

defect-tracking software *See* bug-tracking software.

deferred event *n.* Any event that is not handled immediately, as it occurs. For example, if an interrupt occurs and the ISR simply notes its occurrence but doesn't take any action in response, and the action is taken later in the mainline code, then that interrupt is a deferred event.

deferred procedure call *n.* A function that is called in response to an interrupt but does not necessarily execute immediately. Abbreviated DPC. Interrupts occur asynchronously to other parts of the program. Although the interrupt controller or generating peripheral might need to be serviced promptly, some actions can be deferred. In fact, good software engineering practice dictates that ISRs be made as short as possible. The ISR could, however, register a DPC to be scheduled later by the operating system.

degrees of freedom *n.* A property of a movable object that specifies the number of directions in which it can be moved. Abbreviated DOF. *See also* 6DOF.

EXAMPLE: A washer on a screw is limited to movement in two directions, so it has 2 DOF, maximum. At either end of the screw, however, it has just 1 DOF; when the nut is tightened, the washer is no longer able to move at all, so it has 0 DOF.

delay *n.* A period of time a program or task pauses. Often, when a program needs to wait for a while, it executes a delay function. An example is a debounce routine, where the code reads a switch and waits a few milliseconds before rereading it.

A simple delay is an empty `for()` loop, but this is a computationally expensive way to do nothing. It's more efficient to set a timer (software or hardware) to interrupt program execution once the desired time has elapsed, leaving the CPU available for other uses in the meantime.

delayed branch *n.* An opcode that indicates a new instruction-pointer value but defers that jump until after the instructions that immediately follow in the program. Delayed branch instructions are associated with pipelined CPUs, which use them to avoid fetching instructions that won't be executed as a result of a pending jump. Problem is, many compilers don't use these instructions properly, resulting in a lost opportunity to increase processor bandwidth.

delayed sweep *n.* A feature on many oscilloscopes that lets the user zoom in on an event that takes place long after the trigger event. Delayed sweep requires two time bases and two trigger mechanisms. One time base is triggered by an initial event. The sweep starts at this time base's rate. A delay feature holds off on triggering the second time base until a specified period elapses; then, the second triggering circuit is armed. Any event that then satisfies the second trigger condition engages the second time base, so the sweep speeds up to the base rate.

HISTORY: The best analog scopes all sported delayed sweep. Digital scopes may or may not include this feature, since some acquire so much data with each sweep that the same information is available simply by expanding a segment of the screen.

delete *res.* An operator used to free heap objects in C++ programs. Objects are allocated dynamically on the heap via the `new` operator, then used by the program. When or if the program no longer needs the storage, it must be freed manually, via `delete`.

In Java, which also has a `new` operator, there is no matching `delete`. Instead, a garbage collector thread automatically frees heap objects that are no longer in use.

deliverable *n.* A work product, often associated with a project milestone, that is in a finished form. Deliverables for embedded systems typically include the project requirements, a design specification defining the planned system and its subsystems, and the actual hardware, firmware, and final product implementations.

delta *n.* Any small difference or change.

demodulation *n.* The process of extracting information from a signal. Also called "detection." Analog data rarely exists in isolation. When transmitted, it's usually combined with a carrier of some sort. In a process called modulation, the transmitter modulates, or modifies, the carrier to add the signal. Demodulation is the opposite and happens in the receiver, where the signal is extracted.

EXAMPLE: In AM, the information is multiplied by a fixed carrier frequency, varying the carrier's amplitude in sync with changes in the signal. An AM demodulator is nothing more than a diode, which rectifies the signal (removing the excursions below zero), and a small capacitor, which filters out the high-frequency carrier.

Other demodulators are much more complicated. Single sideband, for instance, requires precision filters and other electronics.

DeMorgan's theorem *n.* An utterly indispensable mathematical way to simplify combinatorial circuits. DeMorgan's theorem has two equivalent expressions.

$$/(A \text{ AND } B) = /A \text{ OR } /B$$

$$/(A \text{ OR } B) = /A \text{ AND } /B$$

The theorem provides a way to change ANDs into ORs and back again.

demultiplexer *n.* An electronic component that connects an input to one of a number of outputs. Sometimes called a "demux." A binary input selects to which of the outputs the digital signal goes.

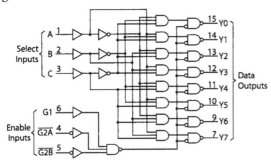

TI's classic 74LS138 demultiplexer, which sends an input to one of eight outputs.

demultiplexing *n.* The process of sending a digital signal to one of a number of outputs. *See also* demultiplexer.

demux (de-mucks) *abbr. See* demultiplexer.

Department of Defense *n.* The U.S. military establishment and a huge consumer of embedded systems of all stripes. Abbreviated DoD.

deprecated *v.* No longer supported, as in: Method A() of class Foo is no longer supported and will eventually be removed. Although not a new concept, this term gained popularity with Java—perhaps because there were so many changes to the standard Java class libraries in its early years.

dereference *v.* To access data through a pointer or reference.

derivative *n.* A mathematical operation that yields the rate of change of a function. The derivative of $f(x)$ is denoted by $f'(x)$.

$$f'(x) = \frac{f(x + h) - f(x)}{h}$$

as h approaches zero.

EXAMPLE: The derivative of position is speed; that of speed is acceleration. Thus, the second derivative of position is acceleration.

derivative control *n.* A form of closed-loop control in which each adjustment made to the drive signal is a function of the rate of change of the plant's state. Derivative control is rarely used by itself. More typically, it is combined with proportional control.

The biggest problem with proportional control alone is that you want to reach new desired outputs quickly, avoid overshoot, and minimize ripple once you get there. Responding quickly suggests a high proportional gain; minimizing overshoot and oscillation suggests a small proportional gain. Achieving both at the same time might not be possible in all systems.

Fortunately, information about the rate of change of the plant's state is generally available (or can be derived). If the state is changing rapidly, overshoot or undershoot could lie ahead. In that case, a derivative-control component can reduce the size of the change suggested by the proportional controller.

The rate of change of a signal is also known as its derivative. In a sampled system, the derivative at the current time is simply the change in value from the previous to the current sample. This implies that one should subtract a change of:

$$change = D \times (current - previous)$$

where D is a constant gain. The only other thing needed is to save the previous sample in memory.

In practice, proportional derivative (PD) controllers work well. The net effect is a slower response time with far less overshoot and ripple than with a proportional controller alone. *See also* PID.

desktop *See* desktop computer.

desktop computer *n.* A reasonably priced general-purpose computer that runs thousands of applications. Sometimes used as a host for embedded systems software development—when no one is around to play Quake. The x86 architecture and its derivatives dominate the desktop computer market, a battle formerly waged between the PC, Apple, and various Unix machines. Most run a flavor of Windows. And even the Unix boxes have mostly migrated to the x86, with x86-based Linux now stealing market share from both Windows and the more traditional Unix variants.

destructor *n.* In C++, a method of a class that is called automatically when any instance of that class is destroyed. The destructor for `class MyClass` is always named `MyClass::~MyClass()`. The automatic call of the destructor offers the programmer an opportunity to free other memory no longer in use. For example, if an object created on the heap with `new` contains an array of characters that was dynamically allocated in the constructor, the destructor should free the array. If no destructor is defined in the class definition, then a default destructor may be run by the C++ run-time environment.

determinism *n.* The Cartesian dream of knowing precisely what will happen and precisely when. Destroyed at the atomic level by quantum mechanics in the early 1900s, its macroscopic reign, too, is less viable because of chaotic uncertainties in nonlinear systems.

In the embedded systems realm, the term suggests that a real-time multitasking system will always perform as advertised. This, sadly, is all too often more hope than fact, as complex timing from interacting tasks renders most forms of analysis

helpless. RMA, when applied correctly, can at least ensure determinism in task execution.

developer license *n.* The rarely read fine print attached to software tools. Developer licenses usually limit the use of a purchased tool to single instances, though site licenses are more forgiving—and expensive. Developer licenses are often on a "per seat" basis, where a company pays a generally not-insignificant fee for each development station that uses a tool.

The license is enforced by methods ranging from trust to hardware interlocks to legions of lawyers. It's always worth studying, sometimes surprising, and at times so repressive as to make a particular tool choice unwise.

HISTORY: Repressive licenses and fees created a movement toward free software, embodied by GNU and Linux. Business models surrounding free software abound, and the jury is still out on their viability in a market economy. At the least, they offer an interesting alternative to traditional software pricing and sales strategies.

development seat *n.* One workstation containing the tools used to create an embedded system. Generally used only when talking to tool vendors, who often charge on a per-seat basis. *See also* developer license.

development system *n.* A workstation that includes all of the software and some of the hardware tools used by a firmware engineer. Compilers, linkers, debuggers, and editors are all part of a development system.

USAGE: Although this term includes hardware devices like ICEs and BDMs, it usually excludes hardware tools designed for hardware engineers, like oscilloscopes and logic analyzers.

development tools *n.* The complete set of compilers, assemblers, linkers, locators, remote debuggers, and other tools used by an engineer to implement, debug, and test a new system. In most embedded systems work, the development tools run on a host PC or Unix workstation, rather than on the target processor.

device driver *n.* A software module that hides the details of a particular peripheral and provides a high-level programming interface to it. Each device driver is typically a piece of operating system–specific software that makes it possible for application software to attach to, read and write data from, and change the behavior of the peripheral device. The more complex the operating system environment, the more likely it is that the device driver code will have to conform to a certain high-level API. For example, Windows and Unix both require every network device driver to conform to a common API.

device programmer *n.* A tool for programming EPROMs, PLDs, nonvolatile memories, and other electrically programmable devices. Typically, the programmable device is inserted into a socket on the device programmer, and the contents of a memory buffer are then transferred into it. So-called gang programmers create several devices from the same image simultaneously.

DFM (as letters) *abbr.* A design-time emphasis on the manufacturability of a final hardware product. Short for Design For Manufacturability. Manufacturability concerns include parts, tooling, factory labor costs, expected failure rates, and inventory management.

DFT (as letters) *abbr.* A design-time emphasis on the testability of a system. Short for Design For Testability. As systems become ever more complex, it's more difficult to create comprehensive manufacturing test procedures. DFT addresses testing from the outset of the system's design, rather than as an afterthought.

DHCP (as letters) *abbr.* A follow-on to BOOTP that is more dynamic in its allocation of IP addresses.

Short for Dynamic Host Configuration Protocol. RFC 2131.

Whereas a BOOTP server maintains a static list of recognized MAC addresses along with their specific IP address and other configuration parameters, a DHCP server simply maintains a list of available IP addresses (typically in some configurable range) and parcels one out to each new requester.

Dhrystone (dry stone) *n.* One of the most commonly used processor benchmarks. Dhrystone is a synthetic integer-only benchmark that, despite its popularity, is not very useful for comparing processors, because it doesn't test them in a way they are actually used by application programs. It's also very easy to exploit the tests to achieve better results, which is often done, since benchmarks are used primarily for marketing purposes.

One aspect of the Dhrystone program that receives much attention is the relatively high dependency on string functions for the overall performance. Between 10 and 20% of the benchmark execution times are typically taken by the `strcpy()` and `strcmp()` library routines.

HISTORY: Created by Dr. Reinhold P. Weicker, then of Siemens, to measure the performance of computer systems (not embedded processors).

diagnostic *n.* A function or program that either tests a system or isolates the causes of the system's problems. *See also* built-in self-test.

die *n.* The silicon part of an IC. Most ICs consist of a die plus packaging, but in some high-volume applications, the die is bonded directly to the PCB. Vendors often will sell bare die for later custom packaging by their customers.

die size *n.* The dimensions of the silicon portion of an IC. Die size is measured in millimeters or square millimeters (mm, mm^2) and expressed as the area of the chip or by its rectangular measurements. Die sizes range from a few to several hundred square millimeters.

dielectric *n.* The insulating layer in capacitors and other electronic components. Dielectric materials are rated by their breakdown voltage—the voltage that arcs through the material—and their dielectric constant, K, defined as the ratio of capacitance of a capacitor made from the dielectric material to the capacitance of a capacitor using a vacuum as the dielectric. By definition, $K = 1$ for a vacuum. Tantalum pentoxide $K = 28$, which is why tantalum capacitors offer so much capacitance in such small packages.

differentiator *n.* A circuit that computes a derivative. The cheapest differentiator is just a capacitor connected to a logic gate. As the gate changes state, it induces a pulse into the cap; the response is a decaying negative or positive spike, since the transfer function of a cap is related to dV/dT. Differentiators often are used to isolate the leading or trailing edge of a pulse.

digital 1. *adj.* Describes a signal or data that is expressed by a finite number of states. The digital world is quantized: everything exists as combinations of discrete states with no in-between states. This is the opposite of analog, where the magnitude of the signal is its size.

In the embedded world, despite some flirtation with trinary (three states) in the 1970s, all digital systems are binary and use only two states (1s and 0s).

2. *adj.* Describes a device or system that uses discrete states. A whole generation of consumers now uses digital to refer to types of devices and information: digital TV, digital cell phones, digital music, etc. *Contrast with* analog.

digital filter *n.* A filter that's implemented digitally. A digital filter accepts digital inputs (typically samples read from an A/D converter) and produces

digital outputs. The data is processed in firmware running on a DSP.

digital multiplexer *n.* A device that selects one input from a number of digital inputs based on a binary value. Also sometimes called a data selector. Digital multiplexers typically have from 3 to 16 digital inputs. A binary input code selects one of these, funneling the selected one to the output. *Contrast with* demultiplexer.

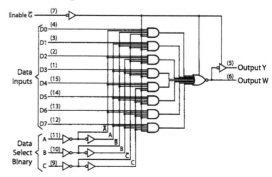

TI's 74LS251 selects one output from eight inputs.

digital signal processing *n.* The process of extracting information from an analog signal using a DSP and signal-processing algorithms such as filters and Fourier transforms. *See* digital signal processor.

digital signal processor *n.* A device that is similar to a microprocessor, except that the internal CPU has been optimized for use in applications involving discrete–time signal processing. Abbreviated DSP. In addition to standard microprocessor instructions, DSPs usually support a set of specialized instructions, like multiply-and-accumulate, to perform common signal-processing computations quickly. A Harvard architecture, featuring separate code and data memory spaces, is commonly used to speed data throughput. Common DSP families include Texas Instruments' 320Cxx and Motorola's 5600x series.

digital storage oscilloscope *n.* An oscilloscope that records data digitally. Abbreviated DSO. All oscilloscopes are tools that display analog or digital signals in circuits; digital scopes acquire the data and convert it to digital form; a computer then processes and displays the signals.

Unlike most analog scopes (except analog storage scopes, which are now obsolete), digital scopes store acquired data. Thus, an event that occurs just once and lasts but a microsecond will be captured and displayed. This is critical for debugging digital circuits. Digital scopes also offer various signal-analysis features, such as smoothing and measurements (voltage, time, delta time, etc.).

Unlike analog scopes, which use a single moving dot to display the data, a digital scope's display is really a computer monitor. It's trivial to show alphanumeric characters describing the instrument's settings and information about the displayed signals. *See also* oscilloscope.

digital voltmeter *n.* A piece of test equipment that reads voltage, displaying it with digits instead of a needle pointing to a scale. Abbreviated DVM. Most DVMs also measure resistance and current; some include frequency, capacitance, and other nifty features.

digital-to-analog converter *See* D/A converter.

digitizing oscilloscope *See* digital storage oscilloscope.

Dijkstra, Edsger *N.* (1930–) Inventor of the semaphore and the related primitives P( ) and V( ).

DIMM (dim) *abbr.* A form factor for RAM banks that's widely used in PCs. Short for Dual Inline Memory Module.

diode *n.* A two-terminal semiconductor device that passes current in one direction only. Used for many purposes, most commonly for rectifying AC in power supplies. Also often used across inductive loads, like relays, to remove the spike that occurs when the load is switched on or off. *See also* rectifier.

diode–transistor logic *n.* A very old and totally obsolete way of building logic devices. Abbreviated DTL.

HISTORY: DTL was the first of the 5-V logic families. It used diodes on the inputs in a diode-NAND configuration, with a couple of output transistors in a push–pull configuration to amplify the signal. DTL was supplanted by the faster and more versatile TTL logic.

DIP (dip) 1. *abbr. See* dual inline plastic.

2. *abbr. See* dip switch.

dip switch *n.* A group of switches, usually SPST, in a dual inline package. DIP switches, available in through-hole and SMT configurations, offer lots of switches in a very small and very cheap package. They're not meant for applications requiring lots of switching; most often, they are used to set up an instrument's operating parameters.

Dirac impulse function *n.* A mythical signal with zero width and infinite height. In other words, it is infinitely powerful for an infinitely short period of time. Such a function is interesting because, in signal processing, it provides a way of setting a system ringing at its natural frequency, without itself becoming involved in the effect.

direct current *n.* A constant, or very slowly changing, voltage. Abbreviated DC. DC is the kind of power from a battery. Power supplies often convert AC to the DC needed by digital and analog circuits.

direct digital synthesis *n.* A technique for computing the analog values of an output, such as sound, that does not depend on computing sine or cosine terms at run time. Abbreviated DDS. For example, DDS can be used to generate the PWM duty cycles (or analog voltage levels, via D/A) necessary to achieve the combination of two sine waves used in DTMF. The technique works by adding samples of the two sine waves at some sampling rate. The samples can come from a sine lookup table.

direct memory access *n.* A technique for transferring data directly between two peripherals (usually memory and an I/O device) with only minimal intervention by the processor. Abbreviated DMA. DMA transfers are managed by a third device called a DMA controller, which shares the memory bus with the processor. Unused memory cycles are stolen by the DMA controller. The processor is only involved, via an interrupt, once the entire block of data has been transferred. In that way, the processor is freed to do other things and overall throughput is increased.

directory *n.* In a filesystem, a special kind of file-like object that holds other files. A directory is basically a binary file containing a special data structure. There is generally one entry in this data structure for each file or subdirectory.

disable *v.* To turn something off, usually temporarily. In embedded systems, often refers to interrupts: instructions disable and enable interrupt sources.

disable interrupt 1. *v.* To temporarily turn one or more interrupts off. In most systems, it's possible to globally disable interrupts (turn them all off) as well as disable individual interrupts. The hardware automatically disables at least the interrupting source when the interrupt occurs (some CPUs shut all of them down). It's up to the software to reenable them when all of the nonreentrant processing is done. *See also* interrupt enable.

2. *n.* The opcode that turns off all interrupts. *See also* global interrupt enable.

disassembler *n.* A software tool that converts machine code back to assembly mnemonics. Disassemblers are specific to a particular processor because they must understand that CPU's opcodes. Some are table based; by changing tables and rules, they will work with a variety of processor families. Most will generate label names to help understand calls and branches. The best disassemblers try to differentiate between data and

code (since, in a Von Neumann machine, there is no implicit difference between the two).

disassembly *n.* The process of converting machine instructions back to crude assembler mnemonics. Often done when trying to reverse-engineer a product for which there is no documentation. Of course, this helps little when the original source was in an HLL, but with astronomical amounts of expensive engineering time, it's possible to make some sense of the code. There's probably no more expensive way to patch-in a feature.

discipline *n.* In software engineering, the much ignored and oft-maligned idea that creating programs is more science than art. Disciplined development means always following a procedure of some sort. That might mean using the CMM, the PSP, XP, or even an *ad hoc* combination of techniques. The goal is to reduce bugs and build firmware faster. It's well known that the opposite of disciplined development (cowboy coding) yields buggy projects, late, along with more inconsistent results across projects.

HISTORY: The firmware field was started by EEs who both designed hardware and wrote programs, generally using no more discipline than heroics. This worked well when address spaces were small and programs rarely exceeded 16 KB. As the 1990s spawned new classes of utterly huge firmware projects comprising hundreds of thousands or millions of lines of code, it became obvious that heroics were simply not enough to ensure timely delivery of decent code. But by and large, most firmware organizations have been unable or unwilling to adopt more disciplined methods.

discontinuity *n.* A break in a graph or a function. Discontinuities are abrupt changes in a function's behavior. An embedded system sam-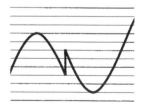

A function with a discontinuity.

pling a continuous function might see sudden discontinuities that arise from corrupt data, noise sources, or failed sensors.

Discontinuous functions are not differentiable, though it's common to break the function's transfer function into multiple subsets, each of which is continuous and therefore differentiable.

discrete *adj.* Said of a function or data that is quantized into a finite number of levels. The entire digital world is discrete, all processing and data handling is done in a discrete manner, and nondiscrete data is sampled into discrete levels before being processed. Even normal continuous mathematical functions are implemented by discrete alternatives. *Contrast with* analog.

discrete logic *n.* A digital circuit implemented using small-scale integration parts. Discrete logic is the converse of highly integrated logic, such as that found in an ASIC or FPGA.

disk drive *n.* Any secondary storage device utilizing rotating magnetic or optical material. Examples of disk drives include floppy drives, hard drives, and CD-ROM drives. *See also* flash filesystem.

display 1. *n.* An LED-, LCD-, or CRT-based output device used to communicate information to a system's human operator(s). Oscilloscopes, logical analyzers, PDAs, cell phones, car stereos, and many other everyday embedded systems include displays.

2. *v.* To present information to the user.

distortion *n.* Any unwanted corruption of a signal. Usually measured as a percentage.

distributed system *n.* A system in which the topology is spread among numerous computers. Distributed systems use multiple computers to implement a function. Advantages over big iron include higher redundancy, the ability to survive partial failures, and localization of computation (the work gets done near where it's needed).

EXAMPLE: The Internet is perhaps the best example of a distributed system; in fact, it's so distributed, no one really knows much about most of the connected computers. The Internet can continue to function despite significant outages, such as attacks on multiple root servers (9 of 13 were brought to their knees by a distributed denial of service attack as this was written, yet few users noticed).

distributor *n.* A critical type of company in the electronic-component supply chain that buys parts in bulk from vendors and then resells to customers. Distributors insulate big vendors from customers who purchase in small-to-medium quantities. No manufacturer wants to sell three $2 ICs to an OEM, yet those customers must be served. OEMs often buy huge volumes from distributors but can sometimes negotiate a better deal with the manufacturer themselves. *See also* original equipment manufacturer.

disturbance 1. *n.* An effect on The Force that can be sensed by any Jedi Knight. Often presages Luke Skywalker or Darth Vader's leitmotiv and a scene change.

2. *n.* A similar change that causes a control system to readjust. For a brief period, the system's behavior becomes less stable as a result of the disturbance; however, if the system is properly damped, oscillations will die out quickly as the system finds a new stable point.

dither *n.* A slight change around a nominal value. Dither can be an undesired aspect of the signal—say, if it should be a constant amplitude but in fact varies just a bit around the expected value. It's also employed to help tune circuits: an oscillator designed to work at some precise frequency might have an adjustment that lets the operator move the frequency a few hertz either side of center. On single-sideband radios, there's often a dither knob, called receive independent tuning, that lets one move the receive frequency a few hundred hertz away from the transmitter, in case the other station being worked is a bit off-frequency.

divide-by-zero *n.* When the denominator of a division is zero. Basic math tells you that you cannot divide anything by zero, because the result is indeterminate. It's worse on a computer, since, as the denominator approaches zero, the result of the division quickly overflows the result register. Most processors include a trap that catches such errors; wise developers install a trap handler to detect and/or recover from such a problem, which usually results from a flaw in the logic.

DLL (as letters) *abbr. See* dynamically linked library.

DMA (as letters) 1. *abbr. See* direct memory access.

2. *abbr. See* deadline-monotonic analysis.

DMA acknowledge *n.* A signal from the processor to a DMA controller indicating that the processor grants control of its memory bus. Depending on the hardware configuration, the DMA controller can use either the memory bus to complete one transfer or an entire series of them. In the latter case, the processor might be forced to stop executing for a long period of time, possibly increasing interrupt latency or causing a missed deadline. *See also* hold acknowledge.

DMA controller *n.* Hardware that manages DMA transfers. DMA operations take place independently of the processor, though they do share the same bus. The DMA controller arbitrates control of the bus between the CPU and DMA and runs the DMA cycles. Many microcontrollers include a DMA controller on-chip, though plenty of DMA controllers are also available in IC form.

DMA interrupt *n.* The interrupt that signals completion of a set of DMA transfers. The DMA controller starts and manages DMA cycles, sharing the bus with the CPU as needed. A typical DMA transfer moves many bytes between sections of

memory or between memory and a peripheral. When the entire transfer completes, the controller issues an interrupt to the CPU (if so configured).

DMA request *n.* A signal from a DMA controller to a processor indicating that the DMA controller would like to use the memory bus. Once the request is acknowledged, the DMA controller can take control of the bus to complete its transfer.

DNS (as letters) *abbr.* A protocol for converting domain names to IP addresses. Short for Domain Name System. When you direct your browser to embedded.com, that name must first be sent to a DNS server to be turned into the appropriate IP address. That address is then used to send requests to the HTTP server on the appropriate network node.

DO-178B (dee oh one seventy eight) *N.* A standard for the production of high-reliability software that complies with the safety requirements for airborne systems. Known as ED-12B in Europe.

Created and maintained by RTCA (Radio Technical Commission for Aeronautics) and accepted by the FAA, the goal of DO-178B was to develop objectives for the life-cycle processes, to provide a description of the activities and design considerations for achieving those objectives, and to provide a description of the evidence indicating the objectives have been satisfied.

There are five levels of DO-178B certification:

- Level A: Failures are catastrophic
- Level B: Failures are hazardous to life
- Level C: Failures have major cost effects
- Level D: Failures result in minor cost effects
- Level E: Failures have little consequence

FURTHER READING: http://www.rtca.org

documentation 1. *n.* Generally external materials used to explain the function of a program. Documentation comprises specifications, design notes, user manuals, and much more. *See also* internal documentation, external documentation.

2. *n.* The most precious stuff in the universe. Or seemingly so, since there's never enough of it around when you need it.

DoD (as letters) *abbr. See* Department of Defense.

don't care *n.* A truth table or logic equation entry where the state of a bit does not matter. One thinks of bits as being in either a 1 or 0 state only, but in fact, engineers use two other states as well. A don't care bit, represented by "X" in a truth table, indicates that either a 1 or a 0 is permissible. For example, the data input to a D–flip-flop can be either a 1 or 0 if clock isn't asserted—it has no effect on the output. Instead of making two entries in the flop's truth table (1 in yields stored state out, 0 in yields stored state out), using the don't care condition shortens the table and makes it easier to create a simpler circuit. Note that there is no physical representation of don't care; it's an aid to designers only.

In addition to 1, 0, and don't care, digital circuits also often put bits into a tristate, which is a high-impedance state: neither 1 nor 0. Tristates let other drivers get access to a shared bus. This should not be confused with a don't care.

dongle *n.* A hardware-based copy-protection mechanism sometimes used to enforce the per-seat licenses for expensive software or hardware-development tools. A typical dongle looks like a gender changer and connects to the parallel port of the host workstation. The physical presence of the dongle is confirmed each time the licensed program is run.

doorstop *n.* What most embedded systems are useful for once they fail.

DOS (like moss) *abbr.* Any of several nonpreemptive, non–real-time operating systems originally used in personal computers. Short for Disk Operating System. *See also* ROM-DOS.

double *res.* A double-precision floating-point data type. Though the standard is flexible, C's double primitive type generally conforms to the IEEE 754 standard for representation of double-precision floating-point data. C++ and Java have an equivalent data type of the same name. In memory, an1 IEEE 754 double consumes 8 bytes. *Compare to* float. *See also* long double.

double buffer *n.* A software technique that uses two buffers for transmitting or receiving data, so software delays in processing the data do not affect the transmission/reception. In a double-buffered receive scheme, there are two identical memory buffers: A and B. When buffer A is full, its data is made available to the system, and the receive routine starts filling buffer B. The program's actions in processing the data in A have no effect on the incoming data that's now being funneled into B.

double sideband *See* double-sideband modulation.

double-precision *adj.* Generally refers to a floating-point number with twice the number of bits as a single-precision number. Most embedded systems use 32-bit single-precision floating point, making double-precision numbers 64 bits (though more might be used in the computation inside the floating-point unit). *See also* IEEE 754. *Contrast with* single-precision.

double-sideband modulation *n.* A form of modulation that suppresses the carrier but transmits the information in two identical lobes: one on either side of the carrier's frequency. Abbreviated DSB. Never used anymore, DSB was a temporary solution to the problem of wasted energy in AM transmissions.

Virtually all of the energy in AM is in the carrier. When viewed in the frequency domain (amplitude vs. frequency, say, on a spectrum analyzer), an AM signal has a very strong carrier with two sidebands (two lobes), one on each side of the carrier. The sidebands have much lower energy than the carrier yet carry all of the information. Double-sideband modulation removes the carrier and transmits just the sidebands. However, each sideband has identical information, so DSB isn't nearly as efficient as single-sideband modulation, which eliminated both the carrier and the redundancy and displaced DSB as a technology.

double-sided PCB *n.* A printed circuit board that uses exactly two layers of tracks. Double-sided PCBs are most often made of a fiberglass board with layers of copper glued to each side. An etching process uses acid to eat away unneeded copper, leaving just the tracks. Vias drilled through the board and then plated connect signals between the top and bottom layers.

down counter *n.* A counter that counts down, from its maximum value toward zero. *Contrast with* up counter.

download *v.* To move data or code into a target's memory over a communications channel such as a serial port.

downtime *n.* The duration for which a system cannot be used normally. If a product fails in the field and a technician has to go to the customer's site to fix it, that entire period is downtime. The customer cannot use the product until it has been fixed. *See also* five nines, high-availability.

DPC (as letters) *abbr. See* deferred procedure call.

DPDT (as letters) *abbr.* A type of switch that has two independent sets of contacts (poles). Each pole connects a common pin to one of two contacts (throws). Short for Double Pole, Double Throw. Note in the figure that both totally separate sets of contacts are actuated by one handle. *Contrast with* DPST.

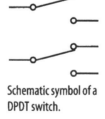
Schematic symbol of a DPDT switch.

dpi (as letters) *abbr.* A unit of resolution. Short for Dots Per Inch.

DPST (as letters) *abbr.* A type of switch that has two independent sets of contacts (poles). Each pole makes a connection to a contact (throw). Short for Double Pole, Single Throw.

Schematic symbol of a DPST switch.

The picture is a schematic symbol for a DPST switch. Note the two totally separate sets of contacts, both actuated by one handle. *Contrast with* DPDT.

drain *n.* The terminal on an FET to which current flows.

DRAM (dee ram) *abbr.* A type of RAM that maintains its content only as long as the data stored in the device is refreshed at regular intervals. Short for Dynamic Random Access Memory. The repetitive row by column refresh access cycles are usually performed by a peripheral called a DRAM controller. If this isn't done every few milliseconds, some or all of the data stored in the memory can be lost. DRAM is much cheaper per byte than SRAM because it requires just one transistor per bit rather than four to six; however, it has longer access times. DRAM's lower cost per byte makes it attractive whenever large amounts of RAM are required. Many systems include both types: a small block of SRAM (a few kilobytes) along a critical data path and a much larger block of DRAM (megabytes perhaps) for everything else.

DRAM controller *n.* A device that generates the special refresh cycles needed by DRAM devices to keep those memories from developing amnesia. DRAMs use a single transistor to store each bit. A charge in the transistor's gate is stored by the capacitor formed by the insulating layer between the gate and channel. This capacitance is on the order of a few picofarads, so the stored voltage representing the bit discharges rapidly, on the order of milliseconds.

The DRAM controller steals bus cycles from the processor to recharge the capacitors. DRAM controllers can be external ICs or a peripheral included within a microcontroller. *See also* DRAM refresh.

DRAM refresh *n.* The process by which a DRAM controller recharges the capacitors in dynamic memories. DRAM memory cells retain the stored data in very leaky capacitors: the junction between the transistor's gate and channel. Periodic refresh cycles recharge these cells. Most DRAM devices require a complete refresh every 2 to 4 ms.

DRAM devices are organized as *x*–*y* matrices, with each memory cell at the intersection of a row and column. To access any cell, the processor sends a row address with the RAS (Row Address Strobe) signal asserted, and then the column address with CAS (Column Address Strobe) asserted.

Refresh cycles are basically simplified reads. Two basic refresh methods exist. The first is RAS refresh, which is accomplished by sequentially addressing the row addresses and asserting RAS. This causes every memory cell in the row to refresh. The second method is CAS-before-RAS refresh; the CAS signal is asserted before the RAS signal, and the memory chip uses an internal counter to form a row address. This can be intermeshed with a normal memory access so that less bus bandwidth is consumed for refreshing.

Note that refresh is basically the methodical reading of row addresses. A demonic programmer could build refresh code by writing a background task that simply issues a read to an incrementing row address.

drive-by-wire *adj.* Describes a ground-based system in which the human operator controls a computer, which in turn actuates mechanical effectors. The human has no direct control over the mechanism. Drive-by-wire systems offer many advantages over conventional mechanical linkages. Weight is saved since the signals propagate via copper or fiber. Smart firmware can do a better job than a distracted or frightened driver.

This assumes, of course, that the software is correct—a very difficult thing to ensure. *See also* fly-by-wire.

driver 1. *n.* A collection of software functions and optional ISR(s) that encapsulates access to a peripheral. Short for device driver. Good firmware limits access to hardware devices; only one routine (the driver) should ever issue I/O instructions for each connected device. If many parts of the code talk to a device, debugging becomes difficult, reentrancy issues abound, and updating code to deal with hardware changes becomes expensive.

2. *n.* A hardware device or circuit that amplifies logic levels. Bus drivers (like the classic 74LS244) increase the fanout of logic signals to drive highly capacitive buses on a single PCB. Many peripherals (e.g., lamps and motors) require much more current than a digital chip can supply; driver circuits convert the logic level to much higher currents.

Communications links often use special driver chips to create the appropriate signal levels; the MAX232, for instance, adapts TTL signals to RS-232 levels.

droop rate *n.* The rate at which an analog signal leaks off toward zero. Droop rates are important in sample-and-hold circuits, which, at heart, are capacitors that store signals for a period of time. If the droop rate exceeds the system's resolution, errors will occur.

DSL (as letters) *abbr.* A type of broadband network connection. Short for Digital Subscriber Line. DSL is generally used over standard telephone cables and in the last mile.

DSO (as letters) *abbr. See* digital storage oscilloscope.

DSP (as letters) *abbr. See* digital signal processor.

DTE (as letters) *abbr.* One of the endpoints of an RS-232 serial communications channel. Short for

Data Terminal Equipment. Any PC or workstation is a DTE device. A DTE's serial port can be connected to a DCE's serial port via a standard RS-232 cable. To connect two DTE serial ports, you need a null modem cable, which has some of the signal wires crossed. *See also* DCE.

DTL (as letters) *abbr. See* diode–transistor logic.

DTMF (as letters) *abbr. See* dual-tone multiple frequency.

DTR (as letters) *abbr. See* data terminal ready.

dual inline plastic *n.* A type of IC package in which the pins run down two sides of the device. Abbreviated DIP. DIP packages are through-hole mounted; their pins are inserted into holes in the PCB and then soldered. Plastic packaging is used, which makes the devices very cheap but limits the temperature range (typically 0 to 70°C).

USAGE: Some surface-mounted parts are plastic and have pins on two sides but are not through-hole mounted; they are, therefore, not DIPs.

dual-port RAM *n.* A memory device with two buses that lets two different systems access memory concurrently. Dual-port RAMs include their own arbitration logic to avoid conflicts. They're useful for sharing data in multiprocessor systems.

dual-tone multiple frequency *n.* The pairs of pure frequency tones added together to convey one of a standard 12 touch tones. Abbreviated DTMF. Because these tones are sent through the telephone channel, DTMF is an example of in-band signaling.

DTMF frequency pairs.

	1209 Hz	1336 Hz	1477 Hz
697 Hz	1	2	3
770 Hz	4	5	6
852 Hz	7	8	9
941 Hz	*	0	#

DUART (dew-art) *abbr.* An IC that contains a pair of UARTs. Short for Dual Universal Asynchronous Receiver–Transmitter. Philips, Motorola, Exar, and others make DUARTs that contain a pair of common UARTs. For instance, the 68681 implements two 6850 devices.

dumb terminal *n.* A monitor and keyboard that communicate with a host computer, generally over an RS-232 link. Dumb terminals can include a processor (embedded!), but the CPU does nothing other than control the terminal. There's no user-accessible local intelligence.

HISTORY: DEC introduced one of the first dumb terminals, called the VT05, in 1970. In 1975, Lear Siegler came out with the ADM-3A, an inexpensive and wildly successful unit found on many early microprocessor systems. The character set of DEC's 1978 VT100 became an industry standard that is still emulated today.

duplex (dew plex) *adj.* Bidirectional. *See* half-duplex, full-duplex. *Contrast with* simplex.

duty cycle *n.* How often a signal is asserted, expressed as a percentage. Duty cycle is a crucial parameter in many applications, such as power calculations. A ¼-W resistor cannot take 1 W of power forever (100% duty cycle), but it can survive the same 1 W if the total average power is less than ¼ W—a 25% duty cycle. *See also* pulse width modulation.

DVM (as letters) *abbr. See* digital voltmeter.

dword (dee-word) *n.* A unit of data that is two words wide. Short for Double Word. Often 32 bits, though almost exclusively processor specific.

dynamic memory allocation *n.* Use of the heap to create instances of classes and other data objects at run time. *See also* malloc( ), fragmentation, memory leak, garbage collector.

dynamic priority *n.* A priority that can be changed at run time. *Contrast with* static priority.

dynamic RAM *See* DRAM.

dynamic variable *n.* A variable for which storage is created only at run time, typically on the heap. Calls to `malloc()` in C and `new` in C++ and Java create dynamic variables. Calls to `free()` in C and `delete` in C++ cause that storage to be returned to the heap for possible reuse.

Automatic variables, which are created at run time but are stored on the stack instead of the heap, are not considered dynamic.

dynamically linked library *n.* A library that isn't linked into the application code that uses it until the code is loaded into memory or the first call to a function in the library is made. Abbreviated DLL. Rarely used in embedded systems (which are statically linked), DLLs are widely used on Windows and Unix workstations.

E

e *n.* A mathematical constant representing the base of the natural log (ln). About 2.71828. *See also* `exp()`.

E²ROM *See* EEPROM.

earliest-deadline-first *adj.* Describes a preemptive scheduling algorithm in which thread priorities are changed on the fly so that the thread with the shortest time remaining before its next deadline is selected to run. Abbreviated EDF. The ready thread with the most imminent deadline is guaranteed to be running every time. EDF scheduling can achieve higher processor utilization than RMA or any static priority scheme but requires the operating system to support dynamic priorities.

Unfortunately, EDF scheduling degrades poorly. If the system experiences a transient overload, it is impossible to predict which threads will miss their deadlines. For that reason, RMA is more commonly used in hard real-time systems, with the trade-off that more processing power must be

applied to the problem to offset RMA's lower utilization.

Note that the deadline monotonic algorithm is different from EDF. DMA assigns static priorities based on deadlines so that each thread always has the same priority each time it runs. With EDF scheduling, a thread's priority can increase as its very next deadline draws near.

easter egg *n.* A hidden credits screen or other fun stuff that can be made visible only through a semisecret sequence of user inputs. Although fun for developers and some users, these are often removed from the final versions of products once management learns of their existence.

EXAMPLE: If you have a Tektronix 1240 Logic Analyzer, try this sequence: cursor up-arrow, enter DAD. Depending on the version of the firmware, you might be rewarded by meeting the development team.

EBCDIC (ebb suh Dick) *abbr.* A character set used by IBM's mainframe computers. Short for Extended

Binary-Coded Decimal Interchange Code. Although rarely seen outside IBM anymore, the EBCDIC set is perhaps the second-best-known character set. It was originally developed for storage of data on punched cards. *See also* ASCII.

EC++ (as letters) *abbr. See* embedded C++.

ECL (as letters) *abbr. See* emitter-coupled logic.

ECO (as letters) *abbr. See* engineering change order.

eCos (ee-cos) *abbr.* An open source embedded operating system. Short for Embedded Configurable Operating System. Created by Cygnus; acquired with Cygnus by Red Hat. Sold under the Red Hat eCos Public License until August 2002; it's now available under the less-restrictive GPL.

EDA *n.* Tools and processes for hardware design, layout, and synthesis. Short for Electronic Design Automation.

EDF (as letters) *abbr. See* earliest-deadline-first.

edge connector *n.* A connector formed by cutting the edge of a PCB into a rectangular shape, etching copper connection tabs on the rectangle, and plating these with gold to increase corrosion immunity and reduce resistance. Edge connectors are used in many systems with a backplane. Each PCB plugs into connectors on the backplane using their edge connectors (VME is a notable exception: high-density right-angle connectors are used instead of edge connectors to achieve a higher pin count).

edge-sensitive input *n.* A processor input that responds only to signal transitions. Edge-sensitive inputs do nothing when subjected to a prolonged 1 or 0. They watch for the signal to change from 0 to 1 or vice versa. *Contrast with* level-sensitive input.

edge-triggered latch *n.* A flip-flop or group of flip-flops that transfers data from the inputs to the out-

put only when the clock transitions from 0 to 1 (or 1 to 0).

EXAMPLE: The 74LS161/163 4-bit latches are classic edge-triggered latches.

edit–compile–test *n.* A commonly repeated cycle of software-development steps. Changes are made to the source code in an editor, and then the new code is compiled; finally, the executable is downloaded and run. If the software doesn't work or does not yet support all of the required features, the cycle repeats. A typical day for most software developers includes numerous edit–compile–test cycles.

editor *n.* A program for editing text files. Editors provide basic file-entry and modification facilities, as well as more sophisticated functions like (depending on the editor) binary editing, macros, and the ability to emulate other editors. Some are highly integrated into the IDEs of complete toolchains.

Editors rouse more love and hate than any other software-development tool. One person's pet editor is another's bane.

EXAMPLE: Popular editors include Ultraedit, Emacs, vi, CodeWright, and (gag) Windows Notepad.

EE (double-ee) *abbr.* An electrical engineer or their university degree.

EE Times *n.* A popular free weekly trade magazine that covers business and new technology issues. Short for *Electronic Engineering Times. EE Times* is a must-read publication for hardware designers, but it comes too frequently for most to really study.

FURTHER READING: http://www.eetimes.com

EEMBC (embassy) *abbr.* A nonprofit organization founded in 1997 that develops and certifies benchmarks and benchmark scores to help designers select the right embedded processors for their systems. Short for Embedded Microprocessor

Benchmarking Consortium. These benchmarks are application specific and intended to help provide customers with an objective means of evaluating processors and controllers. The organization provides scores for a number of processors free online.

FURTHER READING: http://www.eembc.org

EEPLD (as letters) *abbr.* A programmable logic device that is in-circuit reprogrammable. Short for Electrically Erasable Programmable Logic Device.

EEPROM (double-ee prom) 1. *abbr.* A type of ROM that can be erased electronically and reprogrammed in-circuit (or with a device programmer). Short for Electrically Erasable Programmable Read Only Memory. From the programmer's perspective, EEPROM is very similar to flash memory. The biggest difference is that the bytes (words) of an EEPROM can be erased individually.

2. *n.* A nerd dominated high-school dance.

effective address *n.* The final address generated by a machine code instruction before being applied to an MMU or similar hardware. The effective address contains the result of all address math done in the instruction, including adding index and base registers, displacements, and offsets. *See also* addressing mode.

EIA (as letters) *abbr.* A trade organization representing a large number of U.S. manufacturers, particularly in the electronics industry. Short for Electronic Industries Alliance. The EIA is a lobbying and standards-making body. Affiliated organizations include the CEA (Consumer Electronics Association), the TIA (Telecommunications Industry Association), JEDEC, (Joint Electron Device Engineering Council), and others.

FURTHER READING: The standards defined by EIA are available from http://www.global.ihs.com.

elapsed time *n.* The interval between a start and end event. Often used in profiling the efficiency of communications channels.

electricity *n.* The flow of electrons in a conductor.

electrolytic capacitor *n.* A type of capacitor that uses aluminum foil plates separated by a conducting chemical. The dielectric is formed when a field is applied to the device through electrochemical actions. Electrolytic capacitors offer very high capacitances in a small area and are the standard filtering component in power supplies.

electromagnetic interference *n.* Unwanted distortion inductively coupled onto a signal. Abbreviated EMI. Generally used to refer to a transmitter's output that interferes with other radio services. For instance, a ham radio operator's transmitter might cause electromagnetic interference on his neighbor's TV.

electromagnetic spectrum *n.* The entire range of possible frequencies, from DC to gamma rays and beyond. The spectrum is measured in terms of wavelength or frequency, where wavelength in meters = 3×10^8/frequency in hertz. AM radio is at the low end of the spectrum, from 500 kHz to 1.6 MHz; FM radio is around 100 MHz, cell phones at 800 MHz, radar from 2 to 14 GHz, and visible light around 10^6 GHz.

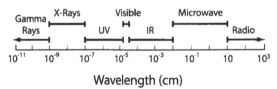

The electromagnetic spectrum.

electromagnetics *n.* The study of the electric and magnetic fields. Maxwell's equations are expressed in terms of four vectors: electric field (**E**), electric flux (**D**), magnetic field (**H**), and magnetic flux (**B**). The equations are interlinked because each vector force is described in terms of another. The equations state that when an electric field moves, it creates a magnetic vortex—a kind of swirl or wake in space–time. Likewise, when a magnetic field moves, it creates an electric vortex. Light, x-rays, radio waves, and the like are merely ripples in our space–time continuum, where the electric and magnetic aspects of the force travel together as electromagnetic waves, which propagate at the speed of light.

HISTORY: James Clerk Maxwell (1831–1879) showed quantitatively how electrical and magnetic fields interact via a set of four equations that have tormented aspiring EEs for a century. Maxwell realized that magnetism, electricity, and light were different aspects of the same force described by his vector equations.

electromotive force *n.* The attraction between charged particles. Abbreviated EMF. EMF is measured in volts, where 1 V is the electrical force between two points for which 1 amp of current will do 1 joule of work.

electron *n.* An elementary particle that orbits an atom's nucleus in a probabilistic cloud. Electrons are negatively charged and, although only $1/1800$th the mass of a proton, are the basic unit of electric current flow. Trading of electrons is the basis for most chemical bonds.

electron gun *n.* A device that emits and aims electrons, shooting them through a vacuum at a distant target. Electron guns are the basis for all CRT displays. They're composed of an electron emitter, which is a heated filament; an accelerator, a highly charged (20,000 V!) plate that attracts electrons and zooms them away from the emitter; and aiming mechanisms. In a TV or computer monitor, which always sweeps the electron beam in exactly the same pattern, the aiming is performed by electromagnets positioned around the CRT. An analog oscilloscope, which positions the beam anywhere on the screen at any time, uses charged plates that steer the beam electrostatically.

electrostatic discharge *n.* The flow of electrons through an arc. Abbreviated ESD. Increasingly, ESD is a problem for embedded systems that must meet regulatory requirements. In Europe, most electrical devices must meet the CE requirements, one of which specifies an immunity to ESD. The voltages in any ESD spark are enormous, though usually the current is very low.

ELF (like a Tolkien immortal) *abbr.* A common object file format. Short for Extensible Linker Format. *See also* a.out, COFF.

embedded C++ *n.* A subset of the C++ programming language that is optimized for embedded systems use and supported by some compiler vendors. Abbreviated EC++.

FURTHER READING: http://www.caravan.net/ec2plus/

embedded database *n.* A database engine to be run out of ROM. Both flat and relational database products are available for sale in the embedded systems marketplace. They are generally designed to operate out of a small ROM or RAM.

embedded Linux *n.* Any Linux distribution that is targeted at resource-constrained hardware, such as that found in embedded systems. *See also* uClinux.

embedded PC *n.* A PC-compatible motherboard or complete system, typically running a DOS or Windows OS, that serves as the processing engine for an embedded system.

embedded processor *n.* Any processor in an embedded system.

USAGE: Be aware that many use this term when they really mean microcontroller.

embedded programming *v.* Writing firmware for embedded systems. A popular career.

embedded software *See* firmware.

embedded system *n.* A combination of computer hardware and software, and perhaps additional mechanical or other parts, designed to perform a dedicated function. In some cases, embedded systems are part of a larger system or product, as in the case of an antilock braking system in a car. *Contrast with* general-purpose computer. *See also* Busicom.

EXAMPLE: Microwave ovens, cell phones, calculators, digital watches, VCRs, cruise missiles, GPS receivers, heart monitors, laser printers, radar guns, engine controllers, digital cameras, traffic lights, remote controls, bread machines, fax machines, pagers, cash registers, treadmills, gas pumps, credit/debit card readers, thermostats, pacemakers, blood gas monitors, grain analyzers, and a gazillion others.

Embedded Systems Conference *N.* The largest convention dedicated to embedded systems development. Abbreviated ESC. At the time of this printing, the ESC was held annually in San Francisco, Boston, and Chicago. Several hundred classes are offered at each, along with a large vendor display of tools and resources.

FURTHER READING: http://www.esconline.com

Embedded Systems Programming *N.* A free monthly trade magazine that has been serving the embedded design community since 1988. As of this printing, it had more than 60,000 subscribers, all of them embedded systems hardware and software developers. To subscribe, visit their website at http://www.embedded.com.

Embedded.com *N.* An online community for embedded systems developers run by the publishers of *Embedded Systems Programming* and promoters of the Embedded Systems Conference.

EMI (as letters) *abbr. See* electromagnetic interference.

emitter *n.* The terminal of a bipolar transistor from which current flows. In a bipolar transistor (not an FET), current flows between the emitter and collector, controlled by small signals into the base. *See also* collector, base.

emitter-coupled logic *n.* A type of logic device designed for high speeds. Abbreviated ECL. ECL came out in the 1960s as a fast alternative to the slow 74-series (TTL) logic then available. Very power hungry, speeds to 500 MHz were available, though only in small-scale integration. ECL used a negative power supply and closely spaced logic levels.

empirical value *n.* A number determined by experiment.

emulation RAM *n.* Memory physically located inside of a debugging tool that can be logically mapped into the target processor's address space. Sometimes called overlay RAM. Primarily found in ICEs and ROM emulators, emulation RAM lets the developer download and test code in target memory address ranges that might not normally support downloads. Sometimes engineers use this feature to start debugging code even before the target hardware exists: the emulation RAM, plus the ICE's access to the internal peripherals of the CPU, gives a partial target environment useful for testing a good deal of an application.

emulator 1. *See* in-circuit emulator.

2. *n.* Any debugging tool that pretends to be a system resource and adds additional functionality or remote visibility. *See also* ROM emulator.

enable *v.* To turn something on, usually temporarily. Often refers to interrupts in embedded systems: instructions disable and enable interrupt sources.

enable interrupt 1. *v.* To temporarily turn one or more interrupts on. In most systems, it's possible to both globally enable interrupts (turn them all on) and individually enable interrupts. *See also* interrupt enable.

2. *n.* The opcode that turns on all interrupts. *See also* global interrupt enable.

encapsulation *n.* An approach to software design that involves hiding implementation details to eliminate coupling between modules. The key to encapsulation is to keep the interface separate from the implementation. The upside is that the implementation details can be changed without affecting any of the users of the interface.

Along with inheritance and polymorphism, encapsulation is one of the three pillars of object-oriented programming. Of the three, it is easiest to achieve encapsulation without an OO language.

In C++ and Java, encapsulation is achieved by defining a class and allowing users of the class to interact only through its public methods. In C, you can accomplish much the same by creating a header file that defines only the API; keep the implementation data and code inside the source module and declare it `static`.

enclosure *n.* The mechanical package that houses an embedded system's electrical guts. Enclosures can be made of metal, plastic, or more bizarre materials (e.g., the paper of an electronic greeting card or a Barbie doll's head).

encoder 1. *n.* A device that translates one set of bits into another. For instance, a priority encoder takes multiple input sources and outputs a single code, which is the highest priority asserted interrupt.

2. *See* rotary encoder.

encryption *n.* The process of hiding information by scrambling data. There are a number of popular encryption algorithms, including PGP (Pretty Good Privacy) and DES (Data Encryption Standard). *See also* decryption.

endian *See* endianness.

endianness *n.* The attribute of a hardware or software architecture that indicates how multibyte values are represented and stored. The two possibilities are called big-endian and little-endian.

HISTORY: The origin of the odd terms big-endian and little-endian can be traced to the 1726 book *Gulliver's Travels*, by Jonathan Swift. In one part of the story, resistance to an imperial edict to break soft-boiled eggs on the little end escalates to civil war. (The plot is a satire of England's King Henry VIII's break with the Catholic Church.) A few hundred years later, in 1981, Danny Cohen applied the terms and the satire to our current situation in *IEEE Computer* (vol. 14, no. 10).

FURTHER READING: http://www.netrino.com/Publications/Glossary/Endianness.html

energy 1. *n.* In an electrical system, the amount of work performed measured in watts times time. A familiar energy measure is the household electric bill, which is commonly computed in units of kilowatt-hours.

2. *n.* Amount of work performed. Work is force times a distance and is measured in joules (J).

engineer 1. *n.* A person who uses technology and analysis to solve problems. The public often confuses engineers and scientists, which work in orthogonal fields. Scientists discover basic principles of nature; engineers use those principles to build things.

2. *v.* To create a product.

engineering change order *n.* A formal change to a circuit design. Abbreviated ECO.

entry action *n.* An action that executes as a state is entered. *See also* exit action.

entry point 1. *n.* The starting address of a function or subroutine. Fifty years of software engineering have taught us to build functions with single entry and exit points. Unhappily, developers seem to thwart even the rigors of languages that attempt to enforce this rule.

2. *n.* The starting address for an entire program. The developer typically needs to provide this information to the locator so that a jump to the

entry point can be inserted at the processor's reset vector.

enum (ee noom) *res.* In C and various related languages, a keyword for declaring a new enumeration type.

Declaration of an enumeration type in C.

```
enum month
{
    January = 1, February, March, April, May,
    June, July, August, September, October,
    November, December
};
```

enumeration *n.* A custom integer data type that can only be defined a value from a predefined set. *See also* enum.

eof (as letters) *abbr.* Short for End Of File.

EOF (as letters) 1. *abbr.* An end-of-file character. Short for End Of File.

2. *n.* The end of an open file, as indicated by an unsuccessful read() call. *See also* append.

EOT (as letters) *abbr.* The ASCII character meaning End Of Tape. Assigned the ASCII code 0x04.

EPLD (as letters) *abbr.* A programmable logic device that can be erased, typically via exposure to ultraviolet light, and reprogrammed in a device programmer. Short for Erasable Programmable Logic Device.

EPROM (ee-prom) *abbr.* A type of ROM that can be erased by exposing it to ultraviolet light. Once erased, an EPROM can be reprogrammed with a device programmer. Short for Erasable Programmable Read Only Memory. A window in the device allows ultraviolet radiation to enter the device and reset the ROM circuitry to its initial state.

erasable *adj.* Capable of having its contents reset to their factory state. Said of memory devices.

errata *n.* An addendum to a datasheet or databook that identifies known bugs in the part or its original documentation.

errno (err-no) *n.* A popular name for a global variable that indicates the cause of the last failed library call. The convention for doing this comes from POSIX. Generally speaking, a library routine that sets errno will return an error code, such as −1, indicating to the caller that some sort of an error has occurred.

EXAMPLE: On success, fork() returns the child's PID to the parent and 0 to the child. If the call was unsuccessful, no child process is created and −1 is returned to the caller. The would-be parent can then check the value of errno to see what went wrong.

USAGE: If you decide to implement an errno variable in a multitasking environment, be sure that you actually write and read only the errno of the running task. Each task must have its own errno (typically in its TCB) to prevent the library from being nonreentrant.

error, single-bit *n.* A garbling of a stream of binary data that results in a single bit flip. Single-bit errors are easily detected even by the simplest additive checksum algorithms, that is, assuming that the checksum is itself transmitted without error.

ESD (as letters) *abbr. See* electrostatic discharge.

Esterel *N.* A system-design language that can generate complex state machines automatically.

estimation *n.* A promise made to management about delivery or performance of a system. Estimations can be made by careful analysis of a problem, with detailed design showing the exact scope of the solution, or by a wild, off-the-cuff guess made in a desperate attempt to deliver what the boss expects. The latter approach is more common, unfortunately.

Even the most disciplined development teams often fail spectacularly at estimations if requirements change constantly. Virtually all new software development methodologies recognize change and try to avoid serious up-front delivery date promises with a more realistic approach to estimation that favors evolving dates over the course of the project. However, most bosses still demand a cast-in-stone end date—even when everyone knows it's meaningless.

Ethernet *N.* The ubiquitous LAN standard defined by IEEE 802.3. Ethernet is the most common networking standard for short-range applications. Originally limited to 10 Mbps, most implementations now run at 100 Mbps.

Ethernet is the physical link as well as the data link protocol, acting as the two lowest levels of the OSI reference model.

Ethernet connects multiple computers using the carrier sense multiple access with collision detection (CSMA/CD) schema.

HISTORY: Invented by Robert Metcalfe in 1973 at the Xerox Palo Alto Research Center. Metcalfe went on to found networking giant 3Com.

Ethernet address *See* MAC address.

ethics *n.* The standards with which one makes important decisions. Engineers are usually hired as technical experts to build products. Few bosses expect the engineering team to question the nature of the good or evil engendered by their creations; yet, engineers build everything from irrigation systems for poor countries to nuclear weapons.

Smaller decisions that never make the headlines are often more ethical than technical: Do you ship with bugs? Can this technology be diverted in bad ways? Must you admit that there are still flaws in this product, even when such an admission might ruin your career?

William LeMessurier was a structural engineer profiled in the May 29, 1995, issue of the *New Yorker* for revealing that the Citicorp building in New York, which was his design, had serious structural flaws resulting from decisions made by the contractors. Despite knowing he'd be sued (he was) and that his career might end (it didn't), he went to the customer and convinced them to spend millions to fix the defects.

Roger Boisjoly is another engineer who famously put his career on the line to object to the launch of the space shuttle Challenger. His data showed clearly that the low temperatures at the pad that awful day could cause serious erosion of the O-rings. Overruled at the time, he was later proven correct.

Euler's formula *n.* An important mathematical equation that links imaginary numbers to trigonometry.

$$e^{ix} = \cos(x) + i\sin(x)$$

evaluation board *n.* A complete working embedded computer implemented on a single-board computer. Sometimes abbreviated EVB. Every reputable microprocessor vendor offers an EVB for each type of CPU they offer. The board lets designers experiment with the processor, learn its characteristics, and test the tools before selecting the chip.

EVBs can be astonishingly effective at shortening the development cycle: you can start testing firmware early using the evaluation board, instead of waiting for your proprietary hardware (which will always be late).

even parity *n.* A type of parity in which a bit is appended to the data to make an even number of 1s. Used by the receiver to ensure correct data transmission. *Contrast with* odd parity. *See also* parity.

EXAMPLE: ASCII character "A" (0x41), if transmitted with even parity, would be sent as 010000010b. The LSb is the parity bit and is not set, since the character already has an even number of 1s. ASCII "a" (0x61) would be sent as 011000011b, which has the parity bit set to 1.

event *n.* An occurrence in time and space that has significance. UML clearly distinguishes between an event (type of occurrence) and an event instance (concrete instance of that occurrence). For example, Keystroke is an event for the keyboard; however, each press of a key is not an event but a concrete instance of the Keystroke event. Also of interest for the keyboard might be the Power-on event, but turning the power on tomorrow at 10:05:36 will be just an instance of the Power-on event.

An event can have associated parameters, allowing the event instance to convey not only the occurrence of some interesting incident, but also quantitative information regarding that occurrence. For example, the Keystroke event generated by pressing a key on a computer keyboard has associated parameters that convey the character scan code, as well as the status of the Shift, Ctrl, and Alt keys.

An event instance outlives the instantaneous occurrence that generates it and might convey this occurrence to one or more state machines. Once generated, the event instance goes through a processing life cycle that can consist of up to three stages. First, the event instance is received when it is accepted and awaits processing (e.g., it is placed on the event queue). Later, the event instance is dispatched to the state machine, at which point it becomes the current event. Finally, it is consumed when the state machine finishes processing the event instance. A consumed event instance is no longer available for processing.

event counter *n.* A variable that tracks the number of occurrences of a given event.

event-driven *See* reactive system.

exa- *pre.* The prefix meaning 10^{18}. Abbreviated E.

exception *n.* A detected error condition. Exceptions typically cause the equivalent of a software interrupt. Note that exceptions are a special class of errors that are always detected, either by the hardware or a software run time. Ordinary error conditions can occur but be ignored (e.g., malloc() returning an error that no one looks at), so C++, Java, and Ada include exception support that can force errors to be handled.

Hardware exceptions are generally termed traps.

USAGE: It's common to use the phrase "throwing an exception" when such errors occur.

exception handler *n.* A software routine that is invoked when an error is detected. Exception handlers are often software interrupt handlers. They take some reasonable action when something goes wrong. An example is divide-by-zero, which throws an exception on many processors, or a nuclear power plant overheat condition, which hopefully also is treated promptly and correctly.

Exception handling is one of the more difficult problems in firmware development. If a divide-by-zero handler is invoked for any one of hundreds of possible divides sprinkled throughout the code, what action should that handler take? Or if there's a memory-allocation error, should the system reboot? Worse, it is notoriously hard to test for exceptions, so most exception handlers go untried, ready to create their own set of bugs when the worst happens at the customer's site.

Excess-3 *N.* An ancient coding scheme used with BCD math that simplified dealing with multidigit arithmetic. BCD math is somewhat difficult because of carries. Adding two BCD digits can yield a 5-bit result, with the carry embedded in the result (not as a separate bit). To tell whether there's a carry, you must compare the result to 10 (01010b), which is expensive to do using old-fashioned transistor or vacuum-tube logic.

Excess-3 BCD overcomes the carry problem as follows. The digits 0 through 9 are encoded as 0011 ... 1100 (add three to the normal BCD representation). When adding two digits: if there is no decimal carry, then there is no binary carry; if there is a decimal carry, then there is a binary carry, too. Because each operand is encoded as true-value + 3, the sum will be encoded as true-value + 6. If the sum is ≤9, its encoding will be ≤15; if it is ≥10, its encoding will be ≥16 (which involves a carry out of a 4-bit encoding).

If there is no carry, the sum must be corrected by subtracting three. If there is a carry, correct the sum by adding three.

Complicated? Yes, but it reduced parts counts. When each bit needed its own transistor or tube, any simplification was important. Today, transistors cost nothing, so such complex shortcuts are no longer used.

EXAMPLE: 3 + 6 = 0110b + 1001b = 1111b. Removing the excess 3: 1111b − 0011b = 1100b, which is the Excess-3 code for 9.

3 + 7 = 0110b + 1010b = 0000b with a carry. Adding the Excess-3 code yields a carry and 0011b, or zero and overflow.

HISTORY: The UNIVAC 1, completed in 1951, represented numbers in Excess-3 notation, which had also been used in the Bell Telephone Laboratories Model I Relay Calculator built in 1940.

exclusive-OR *See* XOR.

executable *n.* A file containing object code that is ready for execution on the target. All that remains is to place the object code into a ROM or download it via a debugging tool.

execute-in-place *adj.* Said of a program that runs from its storage medium. Abbreviated XIP. ROMed programs, for instance, are sometimes copied to a much faster RAM before being executed; these are not execute-in-place programs.

execution speed *See* processor speed.

execution time *n.* The amount of time required to run a function, periodic thread, or other piece of software.

executive *See* cyclic executive.

exit action *n.* An action that executes as a state is exited. *See also* entry action.

exp( ) (exponential) *fn.* A library routine for raising *e* to some power.

explicit cast *n.* A type conversion that is coded explicitly by the programmer. Information could be lost in such a conversion (e.g., if a 32-bit integer is cast to a 16-bit integer), but the compiler will not prevent this. *Contrast with* implicit cast.

EXAMPLE:

```
uint8_t    small;
uint16_t   large;

...

large = (uint16_t) small;
```

exponential growth *n.* A mathematical way to compute the increase of a population.

$$\frac{dN}{dt} = rN$$

N is the growing population size, and r is the constant rate of growth.

Often expressed in the integrated form.

$$N_t = N_0 e^{rt}$$

See also geometric growth.

exponential notation *n.* A technique used to express numbers that cover a wide range. Exponential notation is a formal mathematical way to express numbers as a combination of a mantissa and a characteristic. The general form of the expression is

$$number = mantissa \times 10^{characteristic}$$

although often written 4×10^{-7}, 4e-7, or 4E-7.

Computer systems use registers with limited numbers of bits to express various quantities. A 32-bit variable can handle a range of only billion (or about nine decimal digits) unless an alternative approach is used. Exponential notation is that alternative. *See also* floating-point, IEEE 754.

extended ASCII *n.* One of several proprietary encoding schemes that use the eighth bit in a computer's byte to double the size of the 7-bit ASCII character set.

extended state machine *n.* A state machine with memory. The basic function of the system is a function of the state, which describes how it behaves qualitatively. Within that state, however, one or more extended state variables may describe quantitative aspects of the system.

EXAMPLE: Consider a device for performing laser eye surgery. To ensure proper behavior during each surgery, the designers might want to limit the number of operations that can be performed between calibrations. If that number is, say, 100, a state machine without extended state variables would need to implement 100 copies of the "operating" state, differing only in the state to which they transition to when the surgery is complete. An extended state machine implementation would simply track with a variable the number of operations since the last calibration and transition from "operating" to the "needs calibration" state when that variable reaches 100.

extended state variable *n.* A variable associated with an extended state.

extent *n.* The lifetime of a variable or storage area. The extent of a global variable is the lifetime of the program, meaning the location in data memory reserved for it is created as the program is loaded and freed only when the program exits. By comparison, a local, or automatic, variable has only the lifetime of the function in which it is declared.

extern *res.* In C and various related languages, a keyword indicating that a variable or function is declared in another module at global scope. If you're doing things properly, you should never need to use the extern keyword outside of a header file that's included by all of the involved source modules.

extern "C" *res.* In C++, a way of declaring that a particular external function is implemented in C and compiled via the C compiler. Its use instructs the C++ compiler not to "mangle" the name of the prototype.

This step is completely unnecessary if all of the code will be compiled as C++ by a C++ compiler. Note, though, that even many C++ compilers will default to C's behaviors when compiling source files ending with a .c extension. *See also* mangled name.

How a C++ module might provide for proper linkage to C code.

```
extern "C"
{
    #include <cmodule.h>
}
extern "C" int anotherCfunc(void);
```

external 1. *adj.* On the outside.

2. *n.* A variable with storage information that is declared in a different module. The compiler cannot determine where externals are stored. The linker resolves all externals, plugging the appropriate addresses into the compiled code. *See also* public.

external documentation *n.* Documentation, like a user's manual or specification, that is separate from a work product. *See also* internal documentation.

external fragmentation *n.* A specific type of fragmentation, in which the fragments lie outside the dynamically allocated areas. The C standard library's malloc() function and the C++ new operator suffer from external fragmentation, since a large amount of available heap storage can ultimately wind up split into lots of small free chunks.

When each free chunk is physically separated from its neighbors by a fully used allocated chunk like this, the fragmentation is said to be external. Therefore, external fragmentation occurs whenever allocated blocks vary in size according to the size of the request. *Contrast with* internal fragmentation.

external reference *n.* A mention in one source file of a variable of a function that is declared in another source file. It is the linker's job to match the unresolved symbol in the first file to the resolved symbol in the second. Both the name and the type (or prototype, in the case of a function) must typically match to avoid a link error. In C and C++, global variables that are to be referenced this way must be declared `extern` within the file that references them.

extrapolation *n.* The process of estimating a result by inferring the result from known data. If one knows the general response of a system, it's easy to extrapolate data a little beyond the known data; extrapolations fail when they reach much beyond empirical results. The classic extrapolation mistake is drawing a curve from a single point of data.

eXtreme Programming *n.* One of the more popular of the agile-development methods that stresses code over design. Abbreviated XP. Extreme programming has a dozen practices.

1. *The planning game.* With regard to business and technical decisions, a foggy view of the future is okay.
2. *Small releases.* Get versions out often.
3. *Metaphor.* Create a high-level description of the system.
4. *Simple design.* Limit anticipated needs.
5. *Testing.* The test code is as important as the real code.
6. *Refactoring.* Never fear tossing out code if there's a better approach.
7. *Pair programming.* Use a two-person development team.
8. *Collective ownership.* Anyone can make changes anytime.
9. *Continuous integration.* Allow all-up testing all the time.
10. *40-hour week.* Never work overtime 2 weeks in a row.
11. *On-site customer.* As a part of team, answers questions, evaluates releases, and refines requirements.
12. *Coding standards.* All code conforms to a standard.

F

f/w (firmware) *abbr. See* firmware.

FAA (as letters) *abbr.* Federal Aviation Administration.

factorial *n.* The product of all positive integers from 1 to a given number. Expressed as $n!$.

EXAMPLE: $5! = 5 \times 4 \times 3 \times 2 \times 1 = 120$.

fail-safe *adj.* Said of a strategy that handles errors in a way that ensures the system will go into a nondangerous mode if the software or hardware crashes. It is often thought that fail safe means the system cannot fail. That's impossible because everything physical can break. Instead, a fail-safe system dies in a safe mode: the nuclear power plant that shuts down instead of melting down, the ABS brakes that turn control over to a backup mechanical hydraulic system, and so on.

Fail Safe *N.* A fascinating 1964 movie about what happens when a system fails in an unexpected mode. Starring Dan O'Herlihy, Walter Matthau, Frank Overton, Henry Fonda, and Larry Hagman. Directed by Sidney Lumet.

failover EXAMPLE: In the case of the space shuttle, a watchdog checks that one of the computers has generated engine power calculations every 18 ms. If it fails to produce the calculations in that time, then it will failover to a hot backup, which already should have performed those calculations.

failure *n.* An unwanted operation of a system. Failures might be relatively benign or even unnoticed, as when a watchdog resets the system without notifying the user. Others can result in death and destruction. *See* Clementine, Mars Pathfinder, Therac-25.

failure mode *n.* The way in which a system breaks or stops functioning properly. Failure modes range from catastrophic (the Takoma Narrows bridge fell down) to safe (the X-ray machine that fails with the X-ray source turned off). In-between modes might include the World Trade Centers, which stood long enough to allow some 15,000 people to escape from the lower floors.

fall time *n.* The length of time for a logic signal to transition from a 1 to a 0. Perfect digital signals would need no time to fall, but in the real (capacitive) world, these times can run to the tens of nanoseconds. Fast logic (e.g., 74F) minimizes both rise and fall times at the expense of decreased signal integrity because of electromagnetic effects.

falling edge *n.* The portion of a logic signal that transitions from a 1 to a 0.

false *res.* An operator used for comparison and asserting Boolean falsehood in C++, Java, and several other languages.

C99 adds `false` to C's lexicon, in header file stdbool.h. *See also* `true`. *Contrast with* `FALSE`.

FALSE *lit.* A popular, but nonstandard, `#define` indicating a Boolean falsehood in C programs. *See also* `TRUE`. *Contrast with* `false`.

fan *n.* A mechanical device that circulates air to cool components. The annoying and inescapable Second Law of Thermodynamics implies that action releases heat. This applies to electronics, of course, so ICs get warm or even dangerously hot as they function. Some parts (notably some of Intel's Itanium family) can dissipate well over 100 W, enough to destroy any IC unless the heat is removed. Fans, peltier plates, and even liquid cooling systems all serve this purpose. *See also* heat sink, smoke.

fan-in *n.* The number of inputs a gate has.

EXAMPLE: A four-input NAND gate has a fan-in of 4.

fan-out *n.* The power output of a logic gate, rated in the number of other gates it can drive. Fan-out refers specifically to the current drive and sink capabilities of the driving gate. A 74LS device, for instance, might be able to drive 10 other 74LS devices; however, excessive capacitance in the system reduces this drive.

far *adj.* In real-mode x86 code, a function or data that is not in the current (code or data) segment. Far pointers must be dereferenced through the combination of a segment and an offset register. *Contrast with* near.

far *res.* A special non-stanard reserved word recognized by some x86-specific C compilers. Used to declare functions or data as far.

farad *n.* A standard unit of capacitance. Abbreviated F.

$$C = \frac{V}{Q}$$

C is the capacitance in farads, V is the potential in volts, and Q is the charge in coulombs.

One farad is a huge value, not often encountered in real circuits (with the exception of the Supercaps made by Panasonic and others, which offer values into the tens of farads). More often, caps are in the microfarad and picofarad ranges.

HISTORY: Named for Michael Faraday (1791–1867).

fast *adj.* A term indicating relative speed. Fast means little without a common frame of reference. A 1-GHz PC is no longer fast, yet a 250-MHz embedded system is (today) pretty darn speedy. Yesterday's fast is today's painfully slow: the 12-MHz 286 screamed compared to its 8086 predecessor, yet today it couldn't run any common application.

FAT (as letters) *abbr. See* file allocation table.

fatal error *n.* A failure mode that results in system shutdown. Some applications might come back to life via a watchdog after a fatal error; others stay crashed until an operator intervenes. Fatal errors do not necessarily result in fatalities.

fault *n.* A system error to be handled in software, such as a page fault or segmentation fault. *See also* exception, bug.

USAGE: Often misused broadly to mean any software crash or error in a program.

FCC (as letters) *abbr.* The U.S. agency that regulates various wireless frequency spectrums and licenses transmitters. Short for Federal Communications Commission.

FDA (as letters) *abbr.* The U.S. agency that regulates medical device manufacturers, among others. Short for Food and Drug Administration.

FDMA (as letters) *abbr.* A technique for dividing a communications channel into several narrower bandwidth subchannels and granting exclusive use of each to a specific transmitter. Short for Frequency Division Multiple Access. *Compare to* TDMA.

feature creep *n.* The common condition wherein a specification grows in complexity over time. Specifications are very fluid and never satisfy everyone. Feature creep results when engineering caves to these demands for extra functionality. Sometimes it's a good thing, when customers suggest a feature that will truly make a unit more usable.

EXAMPLE: The sales team often uses feature creep to make up for their inability to sell: "I can't sell that blasted thing without these extra features!" The extra engineering time buys them another 6 months of poor sales without too much pressure from management.

features *n.* The set of behaviors an embedded system exhibits to customers. Customers see features, not design. Code quality, structure, and language are invisible except in how they affect a particular feature's operation. *See also* feature creep.

feed-forward *adj.* Said of a technique that uses intermediate results to speed up a circuit. See figure.

EXAMPLE: An example is an adder. The output of each stage requires the carry input from the previous stage, making the circuit intrinsically slow. It's possible to break a 16-bit adder, for example, into four 4-bit adders and add extra logic that quickly computes the carry result from each 4-bit adder. This is fed forward to the successive stages, greatly speeding the calculation.

feedback 1. *n.* A portion of a circuit's output that is coupled into the same circuit's input. Negative

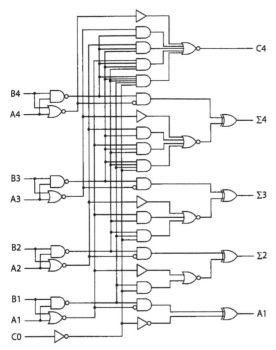

feed-forward A 4-bit adder. Note that the carry output is computed in parallel with the summation. A feed-forward technique then applies it to successive stages.

feedback stabilizes systems and reduces oscillations. Positive feedback creates an unstable, oscillating, system. *See also* negative feedback, positive feedback, closed-loop control.

2. *n.* A way of improving behavior (of people, software-development processes, etc.) by studying a result and then changing the actions that gave that result.

EXAMPLE: The husband who listens and then never again forgets his wedding anniversary uses feedback to improve his marriage. The teacher who corrects homework but adds suggestions for improvement provides feedback.

feedback loop *n.* The path through which a signal travels on its way from a system's output back to the input.

feedthrough 1. *See* via.

2. *n.* A component that passes an electrical signal through a shielded box. High-frequency or especially sensitive analog electronics is often encased in a Faraday shield—a metal box that blocks radiated electromagnetic fields. Feedthroughs soldered onto the box transmit signals, but not RF energy, in and out of the box.

female *n.* The end of a connector or cable into which the male end's protuberance can be plugged. In order for cables to be connected together and properly wired through, there are distinct male and female ends. In many cases, it is easy to tell which is which.

femto- *pre.* The prefix representing a numerical multiplier of 10^{-15}. Abbreviated f.

femtoamp (fem-toe-amp) *n.* 10^{-15} amperes. A very small amount of current.

ferrite bead (fair-ite) *n.* A type of inductor, shaped like a cylinder, through which passes a wire. The inductor reduces transmission of high-speed signals, which, if the ferrite is employed, are presumably not wanted.

Ferrite beads are a class of toroidal inductors, but in embedded systems, they are almost universally strung on a wire with none of the conventional transformerlike turns commonly used with other toroids in RF work. One application is to put the bead over a DC or slow analog signal to remove some of the noise coupled in from the logic circuits.

FET (like bet or as letters) *abbr. See* field effect transistor.

fetch–execute cycle *n.* The entire process of running a single machine instruction on a processor. Each such cycle begins by reading the instruction from memory (the fetch). The CPU then executes that instruction.

Most 16- and 32-bit processors do not have identifiable fetch–execute cycles. Prefetchers and pipelines separate these two operations into very different time segments, as the processor fetches whenever it can, executing when it must.

FFS (as letters) *abbr. See* flash filesystem.

fiber optic cable *n.* A cable made of plastic or glass strands that is flexible and efficiently propagates light. Sometimes called simply fiber (U.S.) or fibre (U.K.). Fiber optic cable transmits light efficiently because each internal reflection is at a very low angle of incidence, resulting in little loss of energy. Used to transmit data of all sorts by modulating the light source, the light acts as a carrier signal; its frequency is so high that vast amounts of information can be modulated onto it.

Fibonacci sequence *n.* A sequence of integers formed by adding the previous two numbers.

$$f_n = f_{n-1} + f_{n-2}$$

Strangely, Fibonacci sequences are found in many natural phenomena. The study of recursion is often centered on a function that computes the digits of this sequence.

EXAMPLE: 1, 1, 2, 3, 5, 8, 13, 21, 34, 55, 89, …

fidelity *n.* The degree to which an electronic system accurately reproduces the sound or image of its input signal.

EXAMPLE: Before stereos, the word hi-fi (high-fidelity) was used to mean a sound system, to distinguish those (at the time) high-tech, high-performance devices from earlier mechanical sound systems.

field effect transistor *n.* A type of transistor in which the major current flow is through an N- or P-type channel. An FET has three terminals: the source and drain, which are the two endpoints of the channel, and the gate. Current flows through the device from the source to the drain. An electric field applied to the gate modulates the current flow. In the absence of a gate voltage, the FET's

drain-source resistance is very low, generally from 1 to 100 ohms

FETs are almost always constructed of silicon, but some GaAs devices exist and yield fantastic frequency responses. Ironically, because FETs are voltage devices, their operation more closely resembles that of a vacuum tube than of a transistor. *See also* MOSFET.

field trial *n.* A real-world test of a system installed at a customer's site. Unhappily, field trials all too often reveal all of a system's flaws.

field, in the *n.* The physical location where the model of reality developed in the lab ceases to work as expected. It's often where the rubber meets the road … and fails. Software that worked perfectly at the factory might not even boot in the field; hardware fries and smokes, and the algorithms developed by a brigade of theorists are shown to be fatally flawed.

field-programmable gate array *n.* A logic chip that has thousands of internal gates and can be programmed. Abbreviated FPGA. FPGAs are especially popular for prototyping integrated circuit designs. However, once the design is finalized, hard-wired chips called ASICs are often used instead for their faster performance and lower cost.

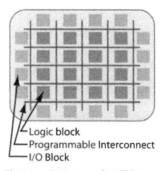

The internal structure of an FPGA.

FIFO (fie-foe) 1. *abbr.* A type of queue that is sorted so that the earliest addition will be the next item removed. Short for First In, First Out. *Contrast with* LIFO.

2. *n.* An IC that implements a FIFO function. Often used to buffer data between two systems, since hardware FIFOs can be both read and written at the same time. As long as the designer can guarantee the FIFO will never overflow, the two systems can be asynchronous.

filament (fill-uh-mint) *n.* The part of a vacuum tube or incandescent lamp which, when heated by current flow, emits light or electrons. Before transistors, vacuum tubes were the basic element of electronic circuits. A filament (generally powered by 6.3 or 12.6 VAC) emitted a stream of electrons aimed at a plate and modulated by the grid. With the exception of CRTs, tubes are rare today.

file *n.* A named sequence of binary or character data bytes. Files are stored on a disk or in a flash filesystem.

file allocation table *n.* A data structure that contains a description of the files in a directory (name, location, permissions, etc.), such as that used in Microsoft's FAT16 and FAT32 filesystems.

file descriptor *n.* A handle for an open file.

filesystem *n.* A directory structure that allows files to be stored on a disk and retrieved by name. The most popular standard filesystem format used in embedded systems is FAT16, often implemented on a flash memory instead of a rotating disk. Other popular filesystems include Windows' FAT32 and NTFS and Linux's ext2fs.

filter 1. *n.* A signal conditioner. All filters function by accepting an input signal, blocking prespecified frequency components, and passing the original signal minus those components to the output.

EXAMPLE: A typical POTS phone line acts as a filter that limits frequencies to a range considerably smaller than the range of frequencies human beings can hear. That's why listening to CD-qual-

ity music over the phone is not as pleasing to the ear as listening to it directly.

2. *v.* To remove unwanted frequency components from an input signal. *See* digital signal processing.

filter capacitor *n.* A device that converts rectified AC to smooth DC. Linear power supplies are simple devices that take AC in and pass it through a rectifier (diode or group of diodes), clipping all excursions below 0 V. This gives an AC signal that's entirely positive but still changing rapidly. A filter capacitor is a huge device (thousands of microfarads) that converts the rectified signal to pure DC.

filter length *n.* The number of taps in a digital filter. *See* filter taps.

filter taps *n.* The number of past inputs weighted to produce the output of a digital filter. *See* finite impulse response.

finite impulse response *adj.* Describes a type of digital filter that is implemented as a weighted moving average. Abbreviated FIR. The output is a function of the last n inputs, where n is the number of taps or the filter length. The name is derived from its behavior when an impulse function is provided as input at any specific time; the function will cease to affect the filter's output after some finite amount of time has elapsed. *Contrast with* infinite impulse response.

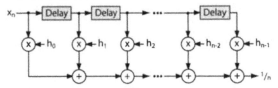

The logical structure of an FIR filter.

A simple implementation of an *N*-tap FIR filter in C.

```
/*
 * Sample the input signal (perhaps via A/D).
 */
sample = input();

/*
```

A simple implementation of an *N*-tap FIR filter in C. (Continued)

```
 * Insert the newest sample into an N-sample
 * circular buffer. The oldest sample in the
 * circular buffer is overwritten.
 */
x[oldest] = sample;

/*
 * Multiply the last N inputs by the
 * appropriate coefficients. Their sum is
 * the current output.
 */
y = 0;
for (k = 0; k < N; k++)
{
    y += h[k] * x[(oldest + k) % N];
}
oldest = (oldest + 1) % N;

/*
 * Output the result.
 */
output(y);
```

finite state automaton *See* finite state machine.

finite state machine *n.* An abstract machine that defines a finite set of conditions of existence (called states), a set of behaviors or actions performed in each of those states, and a set of events that cause changes in states according to a finite and well-defined rule set. Abbreviated FSM. FSMs are an efficient way to specify constraints on the overall behavior of a system. Being in a state means that the system responds only to a subset of all allowed inputs, produces only a subset of possible responses, and changes state directly to only a subset of all possible states. *See also* Moore automaton, Mealy automaton.

FIR (as letters or fir) *abbr. See* finite impulse response.

firewall *n.* A hardware device or software package that shields a network from (hopefully) all of the forces of evil on the Internet. Firewalls typically hide the LAN from the Internet by assigning false IPs, while also disabling access to vulnerable ports.

Firewalls are ironically designed by the same sorts of fallible humanoid creatures who built the extremely buggy set of software that leads to security vulnerabilities. That means the firewalls themselves are often defective. Happily, installing one leads to a false sense of security that eases workplace stress while letting the evil ones slip into the LAN undetected.

firmware *n.* Executable software that is stored within a ROM.

USAGE: This term is interchangeable with embedded software and sometimes is used even when the executable is not stored in ROM.

firmware standards *n.* A set of rules defining how code will be written. Firmware standards abound, but few developers employ any standard other than "make it work." The result: millions of lines of poor, undocumented, and unmaintainable code. A good standard is concise and employed religiously.

EXAMPLE: See http://www.ganssle.com/misc/fsm.doc for one standard.

first-come first-served *n.* A nonpreemptive scheduling algorithm that runs threads in the order that they are spawned or become ready to run. Abbreviated FCFS. Sometimes even a preemptive operating system will use FCFS scheduling to resolve conflicts within a particular priority level. That is, if two threads are both ready and have equal priority, an RTOS might choose to run the one that became ready first.

five nines *n.* A measure of system reliability corresponding to 99.999% uptime. To achieve this target, a system must be down no more than about 5 minutes per year!

fixed priority *See* static priority.

fixed-point 1. *adj.* A way of representing numbers with a large range that allows relatively fast computations. Fixed-point math assigns a binary point at some location in an otherwise integer word or words. Fairly simple algorithms can perform the normal four arithmetic functions on these values. Typical representations use words of 16 bits, of which 4 are a biased exponent, 1 is a sign bit, and the rest are fractional values.

2. *adj.* Said of a microprocessor, DSP, or software package that doesn't support floating-point math. *Contrast with* floating-point.

EXAMPLE: Many applications can get by with a much cheaper fixed-point DSP and some carefully honed firmware.

FURTHER READING: Labrosse, Jean. *Embedded Systems Building Blocks.* R&D Books, 2000.

flag *n.* Any Boolean variable or bit in a register that indicates the state of something. For example, each bit in an interrupt status register is a flag representing the state of one of eight interrupt sources. If a bit is set, the related interrupt is asserted. *See also* mutex.

flag register *n.* A processor register, such as the x86's FLAGS, that contains the zero, carry, and other result flags. *See also* condition code.

flash 1. *v.* To download new firmware into a flash memory. A bootloader typically facilitates this process by communicating with a program on the host, erasing the flash memory, and writing the new code. The sector of the flash memory that contains the bootloader's code must not be overwritten in the process.

USAGE: For example, "Let's flash the board and try it."

2. *See* flash memory.

flash filesystem *n.* A directory structure that allows files to be stored in a flash memory device and retrieved by name. Sometimes abbreviated FFS. Most flash filesystems are nonhierarchical and have limited filename lengths. They are not typically designed to have their contents changed frequently and lack security.

flash memory *n.* A RAM–ROM hybrid that can be erased and rewritten under software control. Flash is an in-circuit programmable nonvolatile memory segmented into blocks called sectors. Each sector can be individually erased, then the data within it rewritten. Flash memory is common in systems that require nonvolatile data storage at very low cost. In some cases, a large flash device can be used instead of a disk drive. Although there is a theoretical limit to the number of times a flash memory can be erased and rewritten successfully, this limit is seldom reached in practice.

USAGE: To capitalize or not to capitalize? That is indeed the question. Although it makes little sense to capitalize, the practice is quite widespread. We recommend against it.

flat real mode *n.* An unsupported trick mode, wherein Intel's 80386 processor can access more than a megabyte of memory without going into protected mode. The trick involves switching into protected mode, configuring the ES (extended segment) register to access memory beyond the 1-MB real-mode boundary, returning to real mode, then accessing the extra region of memory via ES.

flat ribbon cable *n.* A group of wires bound into a single flat cable by an outer plastic coating. Computer systems require vast numbers of wires to send data between boards and peripherals. Flat ribbon cable combines many conductors (typically 10 to 60) into a single cable that can be mass-terminated (i.e., a single compression operation with a special tool connects all of the wires to a connector).

An example of flat ribbon cable.

Many variations exist. One popular approach is called twist and flat, which combines many pairs of wires in a single cable. Each pair is twisted together to offer reasonable impedance control and low susceptibility to induced fields.

flat-panel display *n.* An LCD-based, rather than a CRT-based, display, such as those used in laptop computers.

flex *n.* The GNU version of lex. *See also* bison.

flip-flop *n.* A logic element that maintains state information. Sometimes called simply a flop. Flip-flops remember previous inputs. A D-flop locks in the input data when a clock is asserted, remembering that input until the clock changes again, for example. Every register and latch is comprised of at least one flip-flop per bit.

flip-flop, D *n.* A logic device that saves state information. D flip-flops have two inputs—clock (CLK) and data (D)—and two

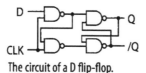

The circuit of a D flip-flop.

outputs (Q and its inversion, /Q). Optional preset and reset inputs can exist as well. The Q output follows the D input when clock goes high. When clock falls, whatever was on the D input is then latched until clock again goes high. *Contrast with* flip-flop, JK.

flip-flop, JK *n.* A logic device that saves state information. The JK flip-flop has three inputs (J, K, and clock) and two outputs (Q and its inversion, /Q). Optional preset and reset inputs can exist as well.

JK flip-flops are edge-triggered; that is, their outputs will change only on the falling edge of clock. If both J and K are 0, then the flop's output will not change. If both are logic 1, then the flop toggles (changes state) every time clock falls. If J is 1 and K is 0, Q will go to 1 when clock falls. The reverse is true if K is 1 and J is 0. *Contrast with* flip-flop, D.

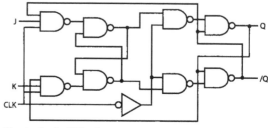

The circuit of a JK flip-flop.

HISTORY: The inputs are named for the inventor, John Kardash.

float *res.* A single-precision floating-point data type. Though the standard is flexible, C's float primitive type generally conforms to the IEEE 754 standard for representation of double-precision floating-point data. C++ and Java share this data type and its meaning. In memory, an IEEE 754 float consumes 4 bytes. *Compare to* double.

floating input *n.* An input to any logic device that is not connected to anything. Sometimes called a dangling input. Floating inputs were once thought to be safe. In the days of bipolar logic (e.g., 74LS), these inputs had weak internal pullups. Today, this is much less common. CMOS logic in general does not have these pullups (though some microprocessors do on some inputs).

Leaving a CMOS input unconnected will almost certainly—at a point usually after the customer takes delivery of your system—result in the device self-destructing from SCR latchup. *See also* SCR latchup.

floating-point 1. *adj.* A way of representing numbers that require huge dynamic ranges with fractional values. Generally supported by the run-time library supplied with a compiler or via a dedicated floating-point unit.

2. *adj.* Said of a microprocessor, DSP, or software package that has floating-point math built in. *Contrast with* fixed-point. *See also* IEEE 754.

EXAMPLE: Prior to Intel's launch of the Pentium, floating-point coprocessors were a popular add-on to fixed-point 386- and 486SX-based PCs. These chips were known as the 80387 and 80487, respectively. Only the 486DX processor supported floating-point math directly.

floating-point coprocessor *n.* A coprocessor IC that provides floating-point arithmetic operations. Generally used alongside a fixed-point processor. *See also* coprocessor.

floating-point processor *n.* A processor with an integrated floating-point unit. Floating-point units generally drive up chip prices, so they are little used in embedded systems. Software developers who use integer-only processors must either avoid the use of floating-point math in their programs, manipulate floating-point values in integers, or rely on a slow and bulky floating-point emulation library.

floating-point unit *n.* A hardware device that performs floating-point math. Abbreviated FPU. Most floating-point units are very fast. Some are coprocessors.

HISTORY: One of the first floating-point units was AMD's 9511, widely used on early 8-bit systems. Later, Intel introduced the 8087, a coprocessor for the 8086/88. Often sold as options on PCs until Intel introduced the 486, which included an on-chip FPU (though the 486SX variant of the chip was sold without the FPU).

floor *n.* A mathematical operation that returns the largest whole number smaller than a given real number. *See also* ceiling.

EXAMPLE: The floor of 13.91 (often expressed ⌊13.91⌋) is 13.

flop *See* flip-flop.

floppy disk *n.* An inexpensive removable storage media comprising a rotating mylar disk enclosed in a plastic protective shield. Floppy disks range in storage capacity up to a few megabytes. They're rarely used in embedded systems.

flow control *n.* The capability to start and stop communications. When two devices communicate over a serial port or other channel, there might be times when one of the devices is no longer able to buffer or process incoming data. When that happens, the receiver needs a way to tell the sender there's no more room. By asserting a flow control "pause," it's possible for the sender to be made aware of the receiver's condition. *See also* software flow control, hardware flow control.

flush 1. *v.* Any process of deleting unneeded data. Common uses include cache flushes (clearing the cache memory) and pipeline flushes (clearing a CPU's pipeline when an interrupt, jump, or call occurs).

2. *v.* To force data from a buffer to an output device, such as a display, before returning to the caller.

EXAMPLE: `fflush()` can be called after `fprintf()` to force the string to be written to the file. If the string ends with a '\n', the flush is implied.

flux 1. *n.* A chemical contained in the hollow tube of solder that cleans the metal as the connection is made. Solder joints made to dirty wires and leads will never be reliable. Flux is a tan-colored chemical that cleans the contacts. Acid flux is especially effective, but will attack components, so it should never be used in electronic circuits. Rosin is the preferred material.

2. *n.* A state of chaos. Any project described as being "in flux" surely hides a lurking disaster of unknown magnitude.

fly-by-wire *adj.* Describes an aircraft system in which the human operator controls a computer, which in turn actuates mechanical effectors. The human has no direct control over the mechanism. Fly-by-wire systems are common in aircraft today. They offer many advantages over conventional mechanical linkages. Some fighter aircraft, for instance, are so unstable they cannot be controlled by even the most testosterone-laden fighter jock. Fly-by-wire systems naturally integrate into autopilots, save weight, and can adapt to changing aircraft flight envelopes automatically.

flyby transfer *n.* A DMA transfer that performs both the data read and write operations in a single memory cycle. Flyby transfers are supported by the ISA bus and its embedded cousin PC/104 but are rarely used in other systems with DMA.

FM (as letters) *abbr. See* frequency modulation.

FMEA (as letters) *abbr.* A systems safety engineering technique that attempts to discover all the problems that could occur in the use of a device. Short for Failure Mode and Effects Analysis. The probability of an occurrence and the seriousness of the risk involved are assigned to each possible failure. Then a solution—such as improved design, testing, labeling, or training—is proposed to mitigate the problem.

FMECA (as letters) *abbr.* Short for Failure Mode Effects and Criticality Analysis. *See* FMEA.

`foo` *lit.* A common name for a variable or function in a quick (back-of-napkin) piece of disposable code. Other common names include `bar` and `baz`. Good programming practice dictates that such meaningless names be avoided in production code.

footprint 1. *n.* The amount of memory required by a program.

2. *n.* The physical dimensions of an IC.

foreground task *n.* A portion of a program that runs whenever it needs to. The background task, if there is one, is suspended while the foreground task runs. *See also* background task.

foreground/background system *n.* A design pattern for embedded software consisting of an infinite loop in `main()` and one or more ISRs.

USAGE: Sometimes used to denote a simple system with exactly two tasks.

`fork()` *fn.* The POSIX system call to spawn a child process. The call to `fork()` creates an identical copy of the parent process and assigns it a unique process ID (PID). When the `fork()` call returns to the parent process, the child's PID is returned. The child process, which is running the identical code, sees `fork()` return 0 instead, so it can execute different code in the parent to load a different program. See listing.

fork *v.* To create a new thread of execution by first making a copy of the current thread. *See* `fork()`.

fork pseudostate *n.* A notational shorthand used in UML statecharts to split an incoming state transition into two or more transitions. Shown as a vertical bar with one transition going into it and two or more coming out. Because a system can only be in one state within a given orthogonal region at any point in time, the transitions coming out of the fork pseudostate must each end in distinct orthogonal regions. *Compare to* join pseudostate.

form factor *n.* The shape or size of a circuit board or product.

form feed *n.* The ASCII character represented by `0x0C`. Abbreviated FF. The same as Ctrl-L. In olden days, the form feed character was used to advance a printer to a new sheet of paper.

Forth *N.* A niche programming language originally designed for real-time control of telescopes. An ANSI standard since 1994 (X3.215). Forth has a simple syntax and many keywords, unlike C/C++ and similar languages, which are the opposite. Forth programs are made up of many small procedures, and math is via RPN. These procedures are compiled, though Forth has no compiler in the traditional sense. Forth is essentially just a collection of procedures, called words, and an interpreter.

Nowadays, Forth is used primarily to test and debug hardware and bring up systems. Only about 2% of the subscribers of *Embedded Systems Programming* reported using Forth regularly in a 2001 survey.

Interestingly, some Unix workstations boot a small Forth interpreter before the rest of the operating system. One such environment is Sun's Open Boot, which provides Forth programming capabilities right out of ROM and a small bootloader

fork() Pseudocode for spawning a child process.

```
#include <sys/types.h>

main()
{
    /*
     * Try to spawn a child process.
     */
    pid_t pid = fork();

    if (pid == 0)
    {
        /*
         * This is the child process' copy.
         * Load and execute another program.
         */
        exec(...);

        /*
         * The child will never get here.
         */
    }
    else if (pid < 0)
    {
        /*
         * Something went wrong, check errno.
         */
    }

    /*
     * The new parent continues.
     * It can use wait() to sync with the
     * child later.
     */
}
```

that enables the operating system to be manually or automatically loaded and run from a disk drive or over a network. IEEE 1275 defines a standard based on Open Boot.

EXAMPLE: When interpreted in Forth, the simple program

```
: BIGGEST OVER OVER < IF SWAP THEN DROP ;
5 9 BIGGEST .
```

first compiles the new word BIGGEST, which compares the two numbers at the top of the parameter stack and leaves only the larger behind, then pushes the numbers 5 and 9 onto the stack and compares them in this way. The period (.) at the end of the program prints the result.

FURTHER READING: The Forth Interest Group maintains a website at http://www.forth.org with links to books and other resources.

Fortran *N.* The first common high-level language. Short for FORmula TRANslation. Fortran was originally targeted at scientific applications. It, and eventually Cobol, dominated information processing throughout the 1960s and early 1970s. The standard for Fortran 95 is ISO/IEC 1539-1997. Amazingly, a standards body continues work on upgrading the language, with the current tentative standard named Fortran 200x.

Fortran is essentially unused in embedded systems.

HISTORY: The first commercial Fortran ran on an IBM 704. It was written in 1954–1957 by an IBM team lead by John W. Backus, of BNF fame.

Fourier series *n.* A series expansion that can express any periodic signal as the sum of sine/cosine waves, each of which is a harmonic of the fundamental frequency.

$$x(t) = a_0 + a_1 \cos(\omega_0 t + \Theta_0)$$
$$+ a_2 \cos(2\omega_0 t + \Theta_1) + \dots$$
$$+ a_n \cos(n\omega_0 t + \Theta_{n-1})$$

where the coefficients an are non-negative, ω_0 is the fundamental frequency, and Θn are phase shifts.

HISTORY: Named for Jean Baptiste Joseph Fourier (1768–1830).

FPGA (as letters) *abbr. See* field–programmable gate array.

FPU (as letters) *abbr. See* floating-point unit.

fragment *n.* One part of a network packet that is too large to be sent as a whole. *See also* fragmentation and reassembly.

fragmentation *n.* The tendency of dynamically allocated memory regions to become cluttered with noncontiguous chunks of free space. In the aggregate, there might be sufficient free space on the heap to make an allocation possible, but if there are no contiguous chunks of at least the requested size, a `malloc()` or `new` will fail.

Fragmentation also affects disk blocks and other dynamically allocated resources. *See also* internal fragmentation, external fragmentation.

fragmentation and reassembly *n.* A feature of the IP layer in a TCP/IP protocol suite that provides for the capability to send and receive upper-layer packets of a size larger than the maximum frame size supported by the physical layer. Large data packets are divided up into smaller fragments and sent with a special fragment number in their header. The IP layer on the receiving end is responsible for reassembling these fragments back into a whole before passing them on to the layers above.

Fragmentation and reassembly is one of the most complex jobs assigned to the IP layer. It is far simpler to implement a subset of IP functionality that does not include this one feature and restrict TCP and UDP packet sizes to the MTU of the underlying network.

FURTHER READING: Jeremy Bentham's book *TCP/IP Lean: Web Servers for Embedded Systems* (CMP Books, 2002) includes a very nice discussion of the tradeoffs involved in the decision to support packets larger than the MTU.

FRAM (eff ram) *abbr.* A type of RAM that retains the data it stores even when no power is applied. Short for Ferro-electric RAM. FRAM offers the best of RAM and ROM; write times are fast and the memory can be used as nonvolatile storage. It has a mixture of existing memory features: the one-transistor cell of DRAM, the price of SRAM, and some of the persistence of flash. It seems a perfect combination, but it isn't. Because of the physical nature of the FRAM cell, there is a limit to the number of accesses it will tolerate before it loses its nonvolatility.

FRAM takes its name from the ferro-electric crystal at the heart of the memory. This material might not be what you think it is. The "ferro" could lead you to believe that the material has something to do with magnetism—it doesn't. The "electric" suggests the memory is a storage of charge—it isn't.

Ferro-electric materials store state based on the position of free atoms within the crystal. There are only two stable positions for the free atoms. One of those stable positions is used to hold logic 1, the other logic 0. The nice thing about the crystal's behavior is that it requires no power to preserve state. That is how FRAM achieves nonvolatility. Turn off the power, and your data will still be there for you a decade later.

Despite these advantages, FRAM is not a popular choice for memory technology.

frame ground *n.* The ground connection to the system's chassis. Also called chassis ground. *See also* safety ground.

`free()` *fn.* A function in the C standard library that is the counterpart to `malloc()`. Once a heap object has been created via a call to `malloc()`, it must be released via a corresponding call to `free()`. This function takes a pointer to the heap object as its only argument. *Compare to* `delete`.

free 1. *adj.* Available for use, as in a block of heap memory or a data structure. *See also* free list.

2. *v.* To release memory that was previously allocated dynamically. *See also* `free()`, `delete`.

free list *n.* A data structure that indicates which blocks of memory or disk are currently unallocated. The free list need not be maintained in linked list form.

free software *n.* Software that comes with source code, so that users are able to run, copy, distribute, study, change, and improve it.

Free software is all about access to source code. The free software movement is as much a political organization as anything else. Under the free software licensing model, it is your right to use the software, modify it, and redistribute it in any way you like. It's even okay for you to charge for your distribution. However, these broad rights are conditioned upon your commitment to provide similar access to your modifications and to never narrow the licensing rights as a condition of distribution.

Proponents of free software generally believe that all information, especially source code, has a right to be free. Therefore, they mean free software in the "free speech" sense, not as in "free lunch." They advocate attachment of a copyleft, which says that "anyone who redistributes the software, with or without changes, must pass along the freedom to further copy and change it." *Contrast with* proprietary software, open source, public domain.

FURTHER READING: http://www.fsf.org

frequency *n.* The rate, in hertz, at which something periodic occurs. *See also* wavelength.

frequency components *n.* The individual frequencies that compose a periodic but nonsinusoidal waveform. Any periodic waveform can be decomposed as the sum of sine waves of different amplitudes and frequencies; each of these is a frequency component of the original signal. *See also* Fourier series.

frequency counter *n.* A tool that measures an input signal's rate of oscillation. The measured signal need not be periodic or digital. Many multimeters include a frequency counter.

frequency domain *n.* A view of a signal in terms of signal strength versus frequency. Most developers think of signals as they'd be displayed on an oscilloscope: amplitude on the vertical axis versus time on the horizontal. That's a measure of how the signal changes over time and

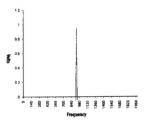

A 1000Hz sine wave viewed in the frequency domain. Compare this to the same sine wave in the time domain (see sinusoid).

is called the time domain. But it's often valuable to think (and measure) in the frequency domain, which is what a spectrum analyzer displays. For instance in the frequency domain, an AM signal looks like a carrier at the nominal frequency surrounded by a pair of sidebands.

frequency generator *n.* Traditionally, a piece of test equipment that generates a sine wave at a frequency selected by the user. Today, these are largely replaced by arbitrary waveform generators, which can create sine, triangle, step, and just about any other sort of waveform.

frequency hopping *n.* A technique used in spread-spectrum communications.

frequency modulation *n.* A way of sending information over a communications link by dithering a carrier frequency by an amount proportional to the input signal. Abbreviated FM. The carrier frequency (the nominal frequency of the signal) is shifted by the modulating input. FM tends to be less susceptible to noise than AM.

frequency response *n.* The effect in the frequency domain of an amplifier, filter, or black box on an input signal. A stereo's frequency response would ideally be flat over the audible frequency range; that is, it would show exactly the same gain at all of those frequencies. A filter's response is quite different, accentuating or attenuating signals in the passband as required by the design. Frequency response plots are made in the frequency domain, plotted as amplitude versus frequency. *See also* transfer function.

front panel   *n.* The part of a system containing the user interface.

EXAMPLE: The front panel of a typical oscilloscope features an LCD or CRT display, one or more connectors for probes, and a variety of knobs and buttons.

FSM   (as letters) *abbr. See* finite state machine.

FTP   (as letters) *abbr.* A client–server TCP/IP protocol for moving files from one node to another. Short for File Transfer Protocol. RFC 959. An FTP server application listens on well-known TCP port 21, waiting for client connections. Once a control connection is established on port 21, one or more data connections between the pair can be established for the transfer of each requested file.

fudge factor   1. *n.* The key to developing accurate schedules. One rule of thumb is to carefully decompose a problem into its component parts, schedule each one, develop a total system schedule, and then multiply by a number between two and three (the fudge factor). Pessimists increase the fudge factor by any amount needed to seemingly guarantee on-time delivery, but it's generally still going to be delivered late.

2. *n.* Any estimated multiplier grabbed out of thin air.

full-duplex   *adj.* Said of a communications link over which data can be sent in both directions at the same time. *Contrast with* half-duplex.

full-scale   *adj.* Applied to an analog input that's equal to the maximum value the system can read.

function   *n.* Formally, a subroutine that takes arguments, performs work based on those arguments, and returns a result. Informally, any subroutine. *See also* procedure.

function overloading   *n.* Including two or more functions or methods of the same name in a single program. This is not supported by C and is only possible in C++ or Java when each of the functions has a different number or type of parameters or return type. *See also* mangled name.

function pointer   *n.* The address of a function. In C and C++, the name of every function can (with the parentheses removed) be assigned to a pointer. Then the pointer can be dereferenced (with the parentheses back in place) to call the function. This is most useful when implementing jump tables.

functional testing   *n.* A test or test procedure that exercises the firmware's features. Functional tests are created from the system's spec, not from the structure of the code. Although seemingly an ideal approach—because the system is tested the way the customer uses it—the tests tend to miss more complicated issues. IF statements nested five deep create permutations usually missed by functional tests. Decisions made by programmers, like exception handling, are also missed.

Some development methodologies, like eXtreme Programming, stress generating tests in parallel with code development. Just as functional tests miss low-level design decisions, these parallel tests often miss global structural design decisions. The best approach is probably a combination of detailed unit testing, advocated by XP and other methods, coupled with carefully designed functional tests. *See also* unit test, eXtreme Programming.

fuse 1. *n.* A sacrificial component designed to fail open when excessive current passes through it, protecting the circuit from damage. A fuse is most often a strip of metal contained in a package made of metal and glass. Every fuse has an amperage rating; exceed that rating by some amount, for at least some specified time, and the resulting thermal stresses will cause the strip of metal to melt, breaking the circuit.

2. *n.* The basic component of some kinds of semiconductor memory, such as fusible link ROMs. The fuse is usually a polysilicon layer that is destroyed or left intact when the device is programmed, permanently recording a 0 or 1 in that location. *See also* anti-fuse.

fuzzy control *n.* Any control system technique using fuzzy logic.

fuzzy logic 1. *n.* A methodology that makes it possible to make decisions based only on ambiguous or imprecise input data. Fuzzy logic can be implemented in software or hardware. As a first step, the possible inputs are grouped into sets. Decisions are then made based on the partial membership of inputs in these sets (according to fuzzy set theory), rather than the specific values of the input signals. The overlap of these partial set memberships results is a specific decision.

2. *n.* A multivalued set theory. *Contrast with* Boolean logic.

FURTHER READING: The FAQ for newsgroup comp.ai.fuzzy is a good place to start. Find it at http://www.faqs.org/faqs/by-newsgroup/comp/comp.ai.fuzzy.html

G

G (jigga) *abbr. See* giga-.

GaAs (gallium arsenide) *abbr. See* gallium arsenide.

gain *n.* The scaling factor of an amplifier or other circuit or software that transforms a signal. *See also* offset.

EXAMPLE: Consider a simple op-amp used as a linear amplifier. Its transfer function will be

$$output = X \times input + offset$$

where X is the gain.

GAL (rhymes with pal) *abbr. See* generic array logic.

gallium arsenide *n.* A material used instead of silicon for manufacturing some specialized ICs. Abbrevi-

ated GaAs. Gallium arsenide is a mixture of two elements, gallium (Ga) and arsenic (As). Gallium is a by-product of the smelting of other metals, notably aluminum and zinc, and it is rarer than gold. Arsenic is not rare, but it is very poisonous.

GaAs ICs offer low noise and good gain even at very high frequencies (tens of GHz). Unfortunately, they're expensive and have only a third of the thermal conductivity of silicon. Chips made from GaAs run hot.

garbage collector *n.* Part of a run-time environment that automatically reclaims areas of dynamically allocated memory (on the heap) that are no longer being used by the application. All Java run-time environments include a garbage collector. In

C++, which does not have a garbage collector by default, it is possible to add one with a third-party package. If you don't have a garbage collector, though, you need to manually reclaim memory that is no longer being used with the `delete` keyword.

The big advantage of a garbage collector is that it can prevent memory leaks, which result from a programmer's failure to delete heap variables that are no longer in use. It will also prevent dangling pointers, which occur when variables that are still being used are inadvertently deleted.

The trade-off is that the garbage collector generally consumes some processor cycles and is not as efficient in reclaiming memory as a perfect programmer would be.

gate 1. *n.* The basic component of combinatorial circuits. Short for logic gate. Gates include ANDs, ORs, XORs, and NOTs, plus a number of variants. With enough gates, it's possible to build any logic device—from a flip-flop to a computer.

2. *n.* One of a field effect transistor's three terminals. The electric field on the gate modulates the current flow from source to drain.

gate array *n.* An IC consisting of tens or hundreds of thousands of uncommitted logic gates that can be fairly easily customized to a particular application. Many ASICs are customized gate arrays. The gate array has lots of logic gates, all unconnected. Customers design a digital circuit, which is implemented by a single extra manufacturing step of adding a metallized layer that connects the gates as needed. This is faster and cheaper than designing an IC from scratch.

gateway *n.* A network node responsible for bridging networks that speak different protocols.

GB (jigga-byte) *abbr. See* gigabyte.

Gbit (jigga-bit) *abbr. See* gigabit.

gcc (as letters) *abbr.* A popular open source C cross-compiler used by many embedded systems programmers. Short for GNU C Compiler and sometimes capitalized. A large number of host–target combinations is possible; most 32-bit CPUs and some others are supported as targets.

gcj (as letters) *abbr.* An open source cross-compiler for Java. Short for GNU Compiler for Java and sometimes capitalized. *See also* ahead-of-time compiler.

gdb (as letters) *abbr.* A remote debugger that's part of the GNU tools. Short for GNU DeBugger and sometimes capitalized.

gdb stub *n.* A debug monitor compatible with the GNU debugger, gdb.

gender changer *n.* A special adapter that converts a male cable end to a female, or vice versa.

generic array logic *n.* A variant of the PAL, introduced by Lattice, Inc., which is electrically reprogrammable and which has configurable output macrocells. Abbreviated GAL. PALs are fixed in function. A 20R8, for instance, has 20 inputs and eight registered outputs. If you need a different configuration, you buy a different part. Because GALs are configurable at programming time, a single part implements most PAL chips.

general-purpose computer *n.* A combination of computer hardware and software that serves as a general-purpose computing platform. PCs, Macs, and Unix workstations are the most popular modern examples. *Contrast with* embedded system. *See also* basic input/output system.

EXAMPLE: Any mainframe, Unix workstation, PC, MAC, laptop, or other computer that looks and acts like a computer.

general-purpose I/O *n.* Customizable input/output pins on a microcontroller. Abbreviated GPIO. By wiring the hardware appropriately and configuring the GPIO port in software, one pin can be used as input to read a switch, another as an output to control a status LED, and a pair to serve as clock and data for a serial EEPROM.

generator polynomial *n.* A polynomial that provides the binary coefficients for the divisor of a particular CRC algorithm. An n-bit CRC algorithm will always have a generator polynomial that begins with x^n and ends with 1.

EXAMPLE: The generator polynomial for CRC-16 is

$$x^{16} + x^{15} + x^2 + 1$$

Extracting just the binary coefficients of these terms results in the 17-bit value 1 1000 0000 0000 0101. The uppermost bit is always a 1 and is dropped at times; the divisor for CRC-16 is, therefore, officially 0x8005.

geometric growth *n.* A mathematical way to compute the rate at which a population increases.

$$N_t = G^t \times N_0$$

where N_0 is the initial population size, G is the growth rate over t generations, and N_t is the current population after t generations.

Geometric growth is often confused with exponential growth.

EXAMPLE: If a population of 100 very friendly programmers has a 5% growth rate per generation, then after three generations, there would be

$$N_1 = 1.05 \times 100$$

$$N_2 = 1.05 \times 1.05 \times 100$$

$$N_3 = 1.05 \times 1.05 \times 1.05 \times 100$$

equals 116 developers.

GHz (jigga-hurts) *abbr. See* gigahertz.

Gi (gib-bee) *abbr. See* gibi-.

GiB (gib-bee-byte) *abbr. See* gibibyte.

gibi- (gib-bee, hard g as in gig) *pre.* The prefix designating 2^{30}. Abbreviated Gi. 1 gibibit:
- 1 Gibit = 1,073,741,824 bits
- 1 gibibyte: 1 GiB = 1,073,741,824 bytes

See also binary prefixes.

gibibit *n.* 1,073,741,824 bits. Abbreviated Gibit. *See also* binary prefixes.

gibibyte *n.* 1,073,741,824 bytes. Abbreviated GiB. *See also* binary prefixes.

Gibit (gib-bee-bit) *abbr. See* gibibit.

giga- (jigga) *pre.* The prefix meaning 10^9. Abbreviated G.
- 1 gigabit: 1 Gbit = 1,000,000,000 bits
- 1 gigabyte: 1 GB = 1,000,000,000 bytes

See also decimal prefixes.

gigabit *n.* 1,000,000,000 bits. Abbreviated Gbit.

gigabyte *n.* 1,000,000,000 bytes. Abbreviated GB. *See also* decimal prefixes.

gigahertz *n.* One billion cycles per second. Abbreviated GHz.

GIGO (guy-go) *abbr.* Short for Garbage-In, Garbage-Out. A reminder that seemingly bad results are sometimes more an indication of invalid input data. For example, if your system or algorithm isn't designed to handle input values above some level, its improper behavior could be more a result of bad assumptions than bad code. Perhaps you need to filter out that garbage data or rethink what is and isn't valid input.

glitch *n.* An unwanted, spurious logic pulse of very short duration. Any unwanted, erratic, and generally nonreproducible behavior of a system is termed a glitch. Most result from poor timing or bad combinatorial design.

A glitch is also the standard excuse for a single irreproducible failure. Experienced developers know that the phrase, "It must've just been a glitch," really means, "I have no idea what just happened, but maybe if I ignore it, the problem will go away." Unfortunately, it seldom does.

glitch trigger *n.* A feature of logic analyzers that captures very short transient events. Useful for finding the causes of glitches; trigger on the event and capture enough other state information to identify the design error.

global *See* global variable.

global interrupt enable *n.* The processor flag that enables interrupts. Often abbreviated GIE, though each processor family gives it a unique name. There are typically several levels of interrupt enables in a system. In addition to setting the GIE flag, the programmer typically also needs to enable the interrupt at the source, and perhaps at an intermediate interrupt controller as well.

Global Positioning System *N.* A satellite-based radion-avigation system developed by the DoD that became available for commercial use in 1995. Abbreviated GPS. The constellation comprises 24 operational satellites. GPS provides two levels of service: Standard Positioning Service (SPS) and Precise Positioning Service (PPS).

SPS is a positioning and timing service available to all GPS users on a continuous, worldwide basis with no direct charge. It provides a predictable positioning accuracy of 100 meters (95%) horizontally and 156 meters (95%) vertically and time transfer accuracy to UTC within 340 nanoseconds (95%).

PPS is a highly accurate military positioning, velocity, and timing service available to users authorized by the U.S. government. In 2000, President Clinton authorized general availability of PPS, which provides a predictable positioning accuracy of at least 22 meters (95%) horizontally and 27.7 meters vertically and time transfer accuracy to UTC within 200 nanoseconds (95%).

In times of war, unfortunately, PPS (or even SPS) might be unavailable to the general public; yet, that hasn't stopped the burgeoning industry for GPS receivers and dependent navigational devices.

GPS signals are transmitted on 1575.42 and 1227.6 MHz.

global variable *n.* Any variable with a scope that makes it available to the entire program. As a group, sometimes called globals for short. Globals are dangerous, since any part of a program might alter them, making debugging very difficult. Worse, when changed in a nonatomic manner, nightmarish race conditions can occur. Yet a global is the fastest way to pass data around, so they cannot always be avoided entirely. Good design minimizes globals, excluding them for all but essential purposes, and ensures atomic updates. *Contrast with* local variable.

glue logic *n.* The address decoding and other messy circuitry (or programmable logic) that ties together a system. It's called glue logic because it's what holds the entire system together.

glueless interface *n.* A connection between components that does not require any additional logic. One reason microprocessor vendors offer complete families of components (e.g., a processor and related peripherals) is that all parts connect together with a minimum of glue logic. So Intel's 8259 interrupt controller seamlessly connects to an 8086, yet would be a nightmare to hook to a 68000. *See also* glue logic.

GMT (as letters) *abbr.* The time in Greenwich, England, as defined by the Royal Observatory, Greenwich. Short for Greenwich Mean Time. From 1884 to 1986, the time in each of the world's 25 time zones [GMT − 12 ... GMT ... GMT + 12] was calculated as an offset from the current time at the Royal Observatory.

In 1986, calculations of time based on the Earth's rotation were replaced by atomic measurements. The current standard for world time is now called Coordinated Universal Time (UTC). Greenwich, England, is still the base for calculating time zone offsets.

HISTORY: The establishment of Greenwich, England, as the center of timekeeping was the result of an international conference hosted by the U.S. in 1884 in Washington, DC. The goal of the conference was to standardize the length of the day and other timekeeping measures across countries for purposes of international commerce.

GNAT (like the insect) *abbr.* An Ada 95 front end for the GNU compiler. Short for GNU Ada Technology. Although GNAT is free software, a commercial "Pro" version and paid support are available from Ada Core Technologies.

FURTHER READING: http://www.gnat.com

GND *See* ground.

GNU (like the animal) *abbr.* A collaborative project launched in 1984 to create a free and complete Unix-like operating system. Short for Gnu's Not Unix.

FURTHER READING: http://www.gnu.org

GNU compiler *See* gcc.

GNU compiler for Java *See* gcj.

GNU debugger *See* gdb.

GNU Lesser General Public License *N.* An alternative to GPL for open source libraries that can be legally linked (statically or dynamically) with proprietary software. Abbreviated LGPL.

The LGPL is used to license free software so that it can be incorporated into both free software and proprietary software. In other words, it is a less protective sibling of GPL. The rules are basically the same, with one major exception: the requirement that you open up the source code to your

own extensions to the software is removed. So although LGPL components remain free software, they can be included within a larger proprietary software package.

The real downside of the GPL, particularly for embedded systems developers, is that it's designed to discourage the creation of proprietary software and to encourage free software. If you wanted to build your firmware around a GPL package or library, you could be forced (legally) to give away the source code to your firmware unless you follow certain rules. But this is not a problem with an LGPL package like the GNU C library, which can be legally included as part of any proprietary software.

FURTHER READING: http://www.fsf.org/licenses/licenses.html#LGPL

GNU Public License *n.* A licensing scheme associated with open source software. Abbreviated GPL.

Since 1984, the goal of the GNU project has been to develop a complete Unix environment that is licensed as free software. Although some of the code involved is public domain, the vast majority is licensed under GPL.

GPL is a specific implementation of copyleft. This is analogous to copyright law, in which there is a general legal right that is implemented in various specific ways in different contracts and print and electronic publications. GPL prohibits proprietary patents related to modifications of the software, prohibits royalties, and requires that the same terms be attached when redistributing the software or a derivative of it. Of course, anyone can create software and then license it under these same terms. Use of the GPL language is not restricted to GNU-related projects. (Their copyleft is not copyrighted.)

The popular GNU compiler and associated tools are licensed under GPL, as is Linux. This means that anyone making a new and improved GNU compiler or Linux variant must give their new source code back to the community. However, it is important to note that this does not mean that software built with the compiler or run on the operating system must also become free. It is legal to use a free software tool to produce proprietary software. *Compare to* GNU Lesser General Public License.

FURTHER READING: http://www.fsf.org/licenses/licenses.html#GPL

GNU tools *n.* A broad generic name for the popular GNU compiler (gcc), debugger (gdb), binutils, and related software development tools.

Goertzel algorithm *N.* An alternative to the FFT that is much faster to compute. The Goertzel algorithm can be used when tones of just a few frequencies need to be detected. For example, it finds application in touch tone (DTMF) and call progress tone detection.

`goto` (go to) *res.* The C equivalent of an unconditional branch instruction. The subject of much controversy, the actual use of `goto` is rare for good reason. However, there might be occasions in which its use is helpful; for example, `goto` offers a nice way to exit a function from multiple points in the code, all via the same block of cleanup code.

GPIB bus *See* HP-IB bus.

GPIO (as letters) *abbr. See* general-purpose I/O.

GPL (as letters) *abbr. See* GNU Public License.

gprof *See* binutils.

GPS (as letters) *abbr. See* Global Positioning System.

grammar *See* BNF.

graphical user interface *n.* A visual display, such as a CRT or LCD, and its content. Abbreviated GUI. The term is generally reserved only for use with complex two-dimensional displays like those on PCs, ATM machines, Palm PDAs, and cell phones. Simple LCD text displays and banks of LEDs don't rate.

graphics coprocessor *n.* A processor or ASIC dedicated to manipulating and/or displaying GUI data. The use of a graphics coprocessor generally speeds up display capabilities while also freeing up the main processor to deal with other issues.

Gray code *N.* Any of several possible mappings of the integers from 0 to $2^n - 1$ to a set of n-bit binary values such that only 1 bit differs between each successive binary value. The mapping that's typically used is formally known as binary reflected Gray code. Generating a set of that form involves starting with 0...000b and always flipping the rightmost bit that will give a new value.

Applications abound. Consider a shaft encoder with a 4-bit parallel output. Encoders use brushes or optical techniques to report position; these are mechanical and, therefore, imperfect implementations. An encoder that outputs normal binary, if positioned between 3 (0011b) and 4 (0100b), might dither with 3 bits changing. The processor might read (serially) 0011b (3), 0100b (4), or 0111b (7)—the latter a hugely incorrect value. If a Gray code is used, the data will dither between 0010b (3) and 0110b (4); the only possible values seen by the computer are those two, both of which are off by one from each other, and either of which is a reasonable approximation of the position.

EXAMPLE: n = 3: { 000b, 001b, 011b, 010b, 110b, 111b, 101b, 100b }

HISTORY: Named for Bell Labs engineer Frank Gray, who developed a binary reflected code for use in communication and later patented their use for shaft encoders in 1953, though such codes were known to others in the late 1800s.

Gray code encoder *N.* A rotary encoder that translates a shaft's angle into an n-bit Gray code, where 2^n is the resolution of the device. The use of Gray code reduces errors from reading the encoder as the shaft rotates. *Contrast with* binary encoder, quadrature encoder.

green threads *n*. User-level threads that share the context of a single kernel-level thread. Green threads are cooperative and can be implemented without assistance from the operating system. In fact, the operating system is not even aware that the one thread it knows of is actually sharings its use of the processor. (Think of a landlord who is unaware that a tenant is subletting a part of her house to other tenants.)

To make them easier to implement, most user-level threads are spawned using a thread library. Thread libraries make the creation of user-level threads easy and define the mechanisms through which they can communicate and synchronize their behavior.

The big problem with user-level threads is that, because the OS doesn't know they exist, if any one user-level thread blocks by making a system call, that whole group will be unable to use the CPU until the awaited event occurs. Also, green threads cannot be run in parallel, even if multiple processors are available.

Some Java virtual machine implementations use green threads, since that makes the whole JVM more portable. However, there is grave risk in doing this. It is far better to map each Java thread to a native OS thread instead. *See also* pthreads, C threads.

green wires *n*. The physical manifestation of a hardware bug fix. EEs fix design errors by cutting PCB tracks and reconnecting the tracks to other signal nodes with green or blue wire-wrap wire. It's possible to gauge a designer's prowess by examining a working prototype PCB. More green wires suggests a sloppier designer. *See also* re-spin.

ground *n*. The negative reference point for all signals in a system. Often shortened to GND, especially on schematics. It's tempting to think of signals as existing in isolation—you see 1s and 0s, 5 and 3.3

V propagating all over a system. Yet every electrical signal exists as part of a pair; every voltage is referenced to some point. That reference point is called ground. Even radio waves, which exist as electromagnetic waves in the air, are referenced to the earth. Hence the name. *See also* chassis ground, signal ground, safety ground.

ground bounce *n*. A condition where an IC's ground pin momentarily goes to a voltage level above or below ground. Ground bounce is a serious problem in digital systems. Although lasting for sometimes less than a nanosecond, if it occurs on a latch or flip-flop, there's a very good chance the device will change state, probably crashing the system.

Found in high-speed systems and caused by poor PCB design practices. Avoided by dedicating an entire PCB plane to nothing but ground. *See also* ground plane.

ground loop *n*. A condition in a system that has multiple ground points, in which some of these grounds are at different voltage levels. In low-level analog design, ground loops couple noise into the connected components. Analog designers know to float their scope ground (disconnect the ground pin in the power cord) to avoid creating a ground loop between the scope and system being probed.

Sometimes ground loops can be dangerous; incorrectly grounded outlets can lead to large voltage differences between plugged-in devices and can shock or kill users.

ground noise *n*. Any unwanted signal on the ground line. Often caused by ground loops.

ground plane *n*. A layer in a multilayer PCB that provides an electrical ground for connections from other layers. Especially in high-speed systems, the ground plane must have low inductances and resistances to avoid voltage drops. This requirement mandates a solid layer of copper.

FCC and CE rules require low emitted RF radiation. Many designers achieve this by putting ground and/or power planes on the outside layers of their circuit boards. These layers act as a poor man's Faraday shield.

grounding mat *n.* A flat piece of conductive plastic used by people assembling and working on electronic circuits to prevent static electricity from destroying or injuring components. The person is connected to the ground mat via a conductive strap. Static is therefore coupled around the PCB being worked on. *See also* static electricity, grounding strap.

grounding strap *n.* The connection between a person who is working on a circuit board and a ground point, usually a ground mat. The ground strap and mat work together to divert static electricity from the person around the PCB, protecting delicate components. *See also* static electricity, grounding mat.

guard *See* guard condition.

guard condition *n.* Boolean conditions of extended state variables that affect the behavior of a state machine by enabling or disabling certain operations (e.g., change of state). Often shortened to guard. Extended state machines often react to stimuli based not only on the qualitative state (extended state) but also on the value of the extended state variables associated with that state. For instance in the keyboard example (see expla-

nation to extended state machine), when the keystroke counter exceeds a certain value, the state machine alters its behavior by changing state. In fact, the logical condition (comparing the keystroke counter with the threshold) is tested by every keystroke, but the change of state occurs only when the condition evaluates to TRUE. This example illustrates the general mechanism by which extended state variables influence behavior. Guard conditions (or simply guards) are evaluated dynamically based on the value of extended state variables and affect the behavior of a state machine by enabling or disabling certain operations (e.g., change of state).

The need for guards is the immediate consequence of adding memory (extended state variables) to the state machine formalism. Used sparingly, guards and extended state variables form an incredibly powerful mechanism that can immensely simplify designs. Used too liberally, however, guards can easily defeat the purpose of using state machines in the first place. The misuse or overuse of guards is a common way to make state machine implementations overly difficult to comprehend.

guesstimate 1. *v.* The process of estimating through educated guesswork.

2. *n.* The result of such a process.

GUI (as letters) *abbr. See* graphical user interface.

guru *See* lone guru.

H

H-infinity filter *n.* A Kalman-like filter that is more robust in the face of modeling errors and noise uncertainty. The goal is to find a state estimate, J < $1/\gamma$, where γ is an arbitrary value chosen to increase the accuracy of the estimate. The estimate can be calculated by the following equations.

$$L_k = (I - \gamma Q P_k + C^T V^{-1} C P_k)^{-1}$$

$$K_k = A P_k L_k C^T V^{-1}$$

$$\hat{x}_{k+1} = A\hat{x}_k + Bu_k + K_k(y_k - C\hat{x}_k)$$

$$P_{k+1} = A P_k L_k A^T + W$$

where I is the identity matrix, K_k is the filter gain matrix, initial state estimate $\hat{x}_0$ is a best guess, and P_0 is set to give acceptable filter performance. The ratio of the estimation error to noise will always be less than $1/\gamma$, regardless of the amount and type of noise in the actual environment!

The Kalman filter was very successfully applied to aerospace control problems in the 1960s. However, when it was later applied to problems in industrial control, it was found to be problematic. Accurate system models are not as readily available for industrial problems. In addition, engineers rarely understand the statistical nature of the noise processes that impinge on such systems. The H-infinity filter is more robust in the face of such uncertainties.

h/w (hardware) *abbr. See* hardware.

HA (as letters) *abbr. See* high-availability.

hack 1. *v.* To write software, typically in an unprofessional manner.

2. *v.* To attempt access to or control of a computer system in an unauthorized manner.

3. *n.* A clever programming trick or workaround.

half-duplex *adj.* Said of a communications link over which data can be sent in one direction at a time. A half-duplex link can operate over a single pair of wires (e.g., as the old-style Teletype did); in this case, the two devices communicating take turns transmitting. *Contrast with* full-duplex.

half-power point *See* 3-dB.

Hall effect *N.* The production of a voltage in a current-carrying semiconductor in the presence of a magnetic field.

Hall effect sensor *N.* An electronic component that detects and measures a magnetic field. Hall effect sensors generate either a linear voltage (on the order of 1 to 2 mV per gauss of applied field) or a discrete 1 or 0, indicating the presence of a field of a given strength. The latter are extensively used in switches.

Hall effect switch *N.* A device that uses the Hall effect to sense contact closures. Closing a Hall effect switch moves a magnet near a semiconductor sensor, which returns a switch-closed indication to the computer. *See also* Hall effect sensor.

halt *n.* An opcode that turns the processor's execution unit off. Once it has executed the halt instruction, the CPU will cease fetching instructions and can only be awoken again by an interrupt.

Typically, the only time a programmer will ever code a program that includes the halt instruction is in the startup code that handles the case that the call to main() returns, which should never happen. Generally speaking, processors that have low power modes won't call the instruction that enters that mode by this name. Not all processors include a halt instruction.

ham radio *n.* A radio service licensed by the FCC and authorities in most other countries to provide noncommercial hobby and emergency access to the radio waves. Known officially as amateur radio. Ham radio gives hobbyists access to a vast range of frequencies, from under 1 MHz to the hundreds of gigahertz. Using the correct bands, hams (as the operators are called) can communicate over tens of thousands of miles. Bands are set aside by international convention for their use.

In emergencies that knock out normal telephone service, hams have many times provided communications for locals.

Many embedded systems engineers got their start in ham radio in their youth. One of the authors of this books has ham call sign N3ALO.

Hamming distance *n.* The number of bit positions in which any two equal-length binary strings differ. The Hamming distance represents the number of bit errors that must occur if one of those strings is to be incorrectly received as the other.

EXAMPLE: The two binary strings 1001001b and 1011010b are separated by a Hamming distance of 3. To see which bits must be changed, simply XOR the two strings together and note the bit positions that are set. In our example, the XOR result is 0010011b, which has 3 bits set.

HISTORY: Named for Dr. R.W. Hamming (1915–1998), who developed the theory of error-correcting codes at Bell Labs in the 1940s and 1950s.

handheld PC *n.* A PDA-like gadget that runs Windows CE and is used as a compact mobile sidekick to a PC. The question of whether or not PDAs and handheld PCs are embedded systems is a challenging one. Although they are similar in design to embedded systems, the capabilities of these products are more in line with those of general-purpose computers.

handle *n.* Any value or variable that serves to select a particular item from a set, typically for use with an API.

EXAMPLE: A file descriptor is a handle for one of the files in the filesystem. This handle is returned by the filesystem's open() call and subsequently supplied as a parameter to each read(), write(), or close() operation that follows.

handshake *n.* An arbitrated exchange of signals that initiates and/or concludes some function. Handshakes ensure that both participants agree to the course of action that will be taken.

EXAMPLE: DMA transfers use a handshake so the DMA controller can gain access to the bus. A DMA request signal from the controller asks the processor for exclusive bus access. When the CPU is ready to release the bus, it informs the controller of the fact via a DMA acknowledge signal.

hard core *n.* A processor that's included in silicon embedded in an array of programmable logic. *See* platform FPGA.

hard deadline *n.* A deadline that must be met, or else. If a hard deadline is not met, the consequences are dire. The loss of human life is certainly the gravest of such consequences, though others are possible. *See also* soft deadline, hard real time.

hard real time 1. *adj.* Pertains to a system with deadlines that absolutely, positively must be met every time … or else. *Contrast with* soft real time.

2. *n.* A deadline that absolutely, positively must be met.

USAGE: As in, "This operation must be performed in hard real time."

hardware 1. *n.* The part of the system you can kick. 2. *n.* The physical manifestation of a system. The boundary between hardware and software is blurring. Once upon a time, the code was that which was stored in memory; everything else was hardware. Today, lots of "hardware" exists inside FPGAs, PLDs, and PALs and is created via a process nearly identical to programming. In some cases, the hardware equations are downloaded to the … er … hardware at system boot time.

Unfortunately, as hardware design more and more resembles software development, the hardware inherits all of software's evils: late delivery, bugs, and misinterpreted specs.

hardware address *See* MAC address.

hardware breakpoint *n.* A hardware debugging resource that stops a program's execution when a condition specified by the developer occurs. Hardware breakpoints, unlike their software counterparts, don't change memory locations. Thus, they are useful for debugging code that's in ROM and for working on pathological code that modifies or reads the program space (like a ROM checksum). They also run at full speed; there's no need to slow the system down. A software complex breakpoint, for instance, essentially emulates the program as it tediously checks each executed statement against the break condition. Several types of these breakpoints exist. *address breakpoints*: The program stops when a particular address occurs. The developer might specify a break condition, like "stop on first line of function `foo()`." Address breakpoints are usually implemented with a 1-bit RAM memory equal in size to the CPU's address space (sometimes tricks are used to make the RAM look like it's that large). Thus, there's no real limit to the number of address breakpoints the user can set. *complex breakpoints*: These match data patterns. A user might specify, "stop when `read_data=0x11a`." Because they require lots of logic, few debuggers offer more than a handful of these. *nested breakpoints*: The combinations of com-

plex and address breakpoints into a sequence so that users can command, "break when `read_data=0x11a` only after `rd_isr()` returns." Hardware breakpoints are primarily found in in-circuit emulators and on some on-chip debuggers. In most cases, single stepping in an emulator uses hardware breakpoints. *See also* software breakpoint, in-circuit emulator, breakpoint.

hardware flow control *n.* A flow control technique that uses dedicated hardware signals to pause and resume communications. *See also* request to send, clear to send. *Contrast with* software flow control.

hardware object *n.* A functional or logical hardware component that contains its own configuration and state information. Used in (re)configurable computing, each hardware object is a piece of logic that can be executed in an FPGA. Hardware objects should be independent of position, or relocatable, to allow them to be executed from any convenient and available location within the configurable logic array.

hardware prototype *n.* The first physical manifestation of a new chip or board design. Fortunately, hardware prototypes are generally better documented and planned than software prototypes, though they aren't always without bugs.

hardware-in-the-loop simulation *n.* Any simulation environment in which part of the target hardware is available and interfaced with other simulated components. Abbreviated HILS. Many complex systems, such as those used in dangerous or remote locations, can never be fully tested without some aspect of its behavior being simulated. These require hybrid test environments involving some real and some simulated hardware.

Harel statechart *N.* A visual formalism for describing states and transitions in a modular fashion. Invented by David Harel in the early 1980s, such diagrams show state nesting and concurrency. Among other things, Harel statecharts add AND-states and OR-states to conventional state diagrams. The two essential ideas enabling this extension are the provision of hierarchical states and the notion of orthogonality. In a nutshell, one can say:

statechart = state diagrams + state hierarchy + broadcast communication

See also UML statechart.

FURTHER READING: David Harel, "Statecharts: A Visual Formalism for Complex Systems", *Science of Computer Programming*, 8, 1987, pp. 231-274.

Harvard architecture *N.* A processor architecture that separates data and instructions into different memory spaces. The Harvard architecture is most popular on DSPs, where the benefit of simultaneous instruction and data fetches can significantly increase signal processing throughput.

hash function *n.* Any algorithm that takes a set of data as input and outputs a key based on that data. Very desirable properties of hash functions include speed and a resulting normal distribution of keys across the full set of likely or possible input data. *See also* hash table.

EXAMPLE: The simplest of all possible hash functions takes an ASCII string as input and outputs just the first letter or two of the string as the key. Such a hash can be used to sort a large set of strings into a set of more quickly searched buckets.

hash table *n.* A dynamic data structure that is an alternative to a sorted linked list, with faster insertions, removals, and lookups. For each item of data stored, a hash value is computed. These values are used to sort the items as they are stored in the data structure. To perform a lookup (e.g., to determine whether a particular item of data is already in the data structure), the value is hashed and the resulting hash is used to quickly determine whether the value is in the data structure.

An example of a simple hash algorithm is one that takes a search string and returns the first letter. In this way, a collection of names can be sorted by

the first letter for quick retrieval. However, if a lot of names are stored, numerous entries will reside within each letter's "bucket," and some buckets, like M and S, typically will have more entries than the others.

For optimal results, therefore, the algorithm to compute the hash should be designed to produce (approximately) unique, randomly distributed values. In that way, the best- and average-case lookups will require only the length of time to compute the hash and check one bucket.

HAVi (ha-vee) *abbr.* A networking protocol for consumer electronics devices that was designed to run over IEEE 1394. Short for Home Audio/Video Interoperability. Sponsored by Grundig, Hitachi, Philips, Sony, and others, HAVi defines a set of protocols and APIs to support audio/video device abstraction and control, an addressing scheme and lookup service, plug-and-play capability, and management of isochronous data streams. *See also* UPnP, Jini.

FURTHER READING: http://www.havi.org

HDL (as letters) *abbr.* A programming language used to design hardware. Short for Hardware Description Language. Verilog and VHDL are both popular HDLs.

header 1. *n.* A connector for multiple pins. Headers are generally specified by the number of pins, such as in "connect the logic analyzer to the 32-pin header next to the CPU."

2. *n.* Bytes containing metainformation about a data packet to be sent over a network. Short for packet header.

3. *See* header file.

header file *n.* A file of general information—not code—that will be included by reference into source files. Header files usually contain macro definitions, function prototypes, external reference links, and definitions of symbolic equivalents used throughout the program. *See also* #include, extern.

heap *n.* An area of memory used for dynamic memory allocation. Calls to malloc() and free() and the C++ operators new and delete result in runtime manipulation of the heap. In Java, there is a heap and a new keyword, but no way to manually free the space. A garbage collector does that automatically.

heap fragmentation *See* fragmentation.

heap segment *n.* A region of memory reserved for the heap. The startup code may or may not initialize the heap memory area to zero before starting the program.

heartbeat *n.* An LED flashing at a steady rate, indicating that the system is functioning normally.

heat sink *n.* A device that passively extracts heat from (usually) a semiconductor. The miracle of Moore's Law has changed the world by packing astonishing numbers of transistors on a single die. But there's no getting around the Second Law of Thermodynamics, which tells us each transistor generates waste heat. Removing that heat, especially as transistor counts soar, is a great challenge. Intel's Itanium 2 can dissipate more than 100 W—enough to destroy the chip if not properly managed.

A typical heat sink.

Heat sinks, thermally bonded to the semiconductor, draw the heat out, dumping it in the air or, in more exotic applications, to a cooling fluid.

hello world *n.* The smallest program that does anything visible. Compiling a trivial program, like "hello world," is always a good first exercise when learning any new language or new development environment. The "hello world" program is small enough that one can reasonably expect to type it correctly or to be able to spot any errors by

inspection. Thus, it makes an excellent first test of whether the programmer understands the fundamental steps in using the development environment.

The classic "hello world" program (in C).

```
#include <stdio.h>

main()
{
    printf("hello, world\n");
}
```

First published by Kernighan and Ritchie in *The C Programming Language*

Unfortunately, getting "hello world" to run on an embedded system is much more challenging than on a desktop computer. This typically depends on complex devices like UARTs and writing driver code to initialize and use them. It's far easier to write an LED blinker, which is the embedded equivalent.

henry *n.* The unit of inductance. Abbreviated H.

$$L = V / (dI/dt)$$

where L is inductance (henries), V is voltage (volts), I is current (amperes), and t is time (seconds).

A changing magnetic field induces an electric current in a loop of wire located in the field. Although the induced voltage depends only on the rate at which the magnetic flux changes (measured in webers per second), the amount of the current depends also on the physical properties of the coil. A coil with an inductance of 1 henry requires a flux of 1 weber for each ampere of induced current. If, on the other hand, it is the current that changes, then the induced field will generate a potential difference within the coil: if the inductance is 1 henry, a current change of 1 A/s generates a potential difference of 1 V.

The henry is a large unit; inductances in practical circuits are measured in millihenrys (mH) or microhenrys (μH). *See also* inductance.

USAGE: The plural is sometimes spelled henrys, but in English it is correct to spell it henries.

HISTORY: The unit is named for the American physicist Joseph Henry (1797–1878).

hertz *n.* A standard unit of frequency. Abbreviated Hz. One hertz is equal to 1 cycle per second.

HISTORY: Named for Heinrich Rudolph Hertz (1857–1894).

hex (hecks) *abbr. See* hexadecimal.

hex file *n.* A file in the Intel Hex format.

hexadecimal *n.* The representation of a number in base-16 notation. Because only 10 numerals are available but 16 values are used, the letters A, B, C, D, E, and F are appropriated to represent digits weighted 10 through 15, respectively. In C and various related languages, an integer constant that begins with either 0x or 0X is interpreted in hexadecimal notation. Outside of C, appending a lowercase h to the number is a common alternative representation.

EXAMPLE: Hexadecimal 0xA2 (sometimes A2h) converted to decimal is

$$(10 \times 16^1) + (2 \times 16^0) = 162$$

hierarchical state machine *n.* An extended state machine that supports hierarchical decomposition of states by allowing the nesting of states within states. Abbreviated HSM. An HSM has characteristics of both a Mealy automaton and a Moore automaton, in that actions generally depend on both the state of the system and the triggering event, as in a Mealy automaton. Additionally, an HSM provides optional entry and exit actions, which are associated with states rather than transitions, as in a Moore automaton.

HSMs allow the nesting of states within states with the following semantics. If a system is in the nested state "s11" (called substate), it also (implicitly) is in the surrounding state "s1" (the super-

state). This HSM will attempt to handle any event in the context of state s11 (which is in the lower level of the hierarchy). However, if state s11 does not prescribe how to handle the event, the event is not quietly discarded (as in a classical finite state machine); rather, it is automatically handled in the higher level context of state s1. This is what is meant by the system being in state s1 as well as s11. Of course, state nesting is not limited to one level only, and the simple rule of event processing applies recursively to any level of nesting.

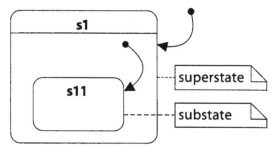

A simple HSM with state s11 nested inside state s1.

States that contain other states are called composite states; conversely, states without internal structure are called simple states. A nested state is called a direct substate when it is not contained by any other state; otherwise, it is referred to as a transitively nested substate.

The semantics of hierarchical state decomposition are designed to allow sharing (reuse) of behavior. The substates (nested states) need only define their differences from the superstates (surrounding states). A substate can easily reuse the common behavior from its superstate(s) by simply ignoring commonly handled events, which are then automatically handled by higher level states. In this manner, the substates can share all aspects of behavior with their superstates. For example, in a state model of a simple toaster oven, states toasting and baking share a common transition to state doorOpen, defined in their common superstate, heating.

Hierarchical state decomposition can be viewed as the classical exclusive-OR applied to states. For example, if a system is in state heating, it means that it's either in state toasting OR baking. That is why state hierarchy is alternatively called OR-decomposition and the nested states are called OR-states.

high *n.* The voltage, typically positive, associated with a logic-1. As in, "That input is pulled high." A signal is typically pulled high via connection to V_{cc} through a pullup resistor. *Contrast with* low.

high impedance *n.* A qualitative expression indicating that the AC resistance of a node is significantly greater than that of another, connected, node.

EXAMPLE: The output impedance of a tube amplifier is high (thousands of ohms) compared to that of a speaker (4 to 8 Ω), so a matching transformer must be used. By contrast, a transistor amplifier's output impedance closely matches that of the speaker.

See also impedance.

high-availability *adj.* Needing to be up 99.999% (or more) of the time. Abbreviated HA. *See* five nines.

high-level language *n.* A language, such as C, C++, Ada, or Java, that is processor independent. Abbreviated HLL. When programming in a high-level language, it is possible to concentrate on algorithms and applications without worrying about the details of a particular processor.

HISTORY: The first high-level language (Fortran), when invented in the 1950s, was criticized as generating slow and bloated machine code. Despite a half century of progress in language and compiler design since then, many still wage code bloat versus programmer efficiency flame wars.

high-order 1. *adj.* Said of a filter with many terms. High-order filters have tens to even hundreds of terms; as such, they offer very sharp cutoffs but are expensive to implement in hardware.

EXAMPLE: The high-order byte of a word is the most significant byte; the high-order bit is the most significant bit.

2. *adj.* Said of a filter with many terms. High-order filters have tens to even hundreds of terms; as such, they offer very sharp cutoffs but are expensive to implement in hardware.

higher-layer protocol *n.* Any application layer software that runs over a particular "lower-layer" physical interface. The standards for many communications interfaces used in embedded systems, such as SPI, I^2C, and CAN, only define the physical connection. A higher-layer protocol can be added to enhance communication capabilities over such a link. *See also* CANopen.

highest locker *n.* The highest priority thread that accesses a particular shared resource. The priority ceiling for that resource is typically set either to the priority of the highest locker or incrementally higher. *See also* priority ceiling emulation.

highest locker protocol *See* priority ceiling emulation.

highpass filter *n.* A digital or analog filter that allows only high-frequency components of the input signal to pass to the output. In theory, a highpass filter removes frequency components below some threshold frequency completely and allows the components above that threshold to pass through unchanged. In practice, however, the low-frequency components are merely highly attenuated, the high-frequency components might have their magnitude or phase slightly changed, and the cutoff occurs more gradually over a range of threshold frequencies. *Compare to* lowpass filter, bandpass filter.

EXAMPLE: A highpass filter is often used to remove the 60-Hz signal that is endemic in the U.S. because of its use in AC power circuits (50 Hz in some other parts of the world).

HILS (hills) *abbr. See* hardware-in-the-loop simulation.

history pseudostate *See* shallow-history pseudostate. *See also* deep-history pseudostate.

hit rate *n.* In a system with a cache, the percentage of time that a cache hit occurs out of the total number of cache lookups. The higher the hit rate, the greater the speedup resulting from the addition of the cache. If there are separate L1 and L2 caches or data and instruction caches, there will be distinct hit rates associated with each cache. Hit rates vary based on the characteristics of the executed programs and the size and properties of the cache itself. *Contrast with* miss rate.

HLDA (hold ack) *abbr. See* hold acknowledge.

HLL (as letters) *abbr. See* high-level language.

hold acknowledge *n.* A signal on Intel processors that indicates the CPU has granted bus control to another master. Abbreviated HLDA. HLDA comes in response to a hold request; thus, it is half of the DMA bus request/grant signal pair.

hold time *n.* The length of time a flip-flop's input data must remain stable after each clock transition. Violating the hold time parameter will create a metastable state. *See also* setup time, metastability.

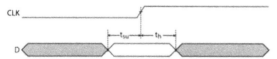

Clock is the top graph; the flip-flop's input data is the bottom graph. Hold time (t_h) is the time the input data must be stable after clock transitions.

hook *n.* An easy way to attach a function call. For example, some RTOSes will include hooks for calling a user-specified function on every context switch. You could hook a function to toggle task-specific I/O pins to collect run-time timing data

for each of the tasks in the system on a logic analyzer.

host *n.* A general-purpose computer that communicates with the target via a serial port or network connection.

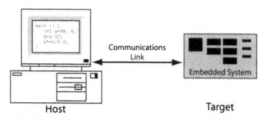

The host is used to develop and debug firmware for the target.

USAGE: This term usually distinguishes the computer on which the compiler and debugger are being run from the embedded system for which software is being developed.

host byte order *n.* The native endianness of a computing platform. The host byte order for an 80x86-powered system is little-endian.

USAGE: Use of this term is largely restricted to comparisons of the native endianness to the endianness of the network protocol the system uses to communicate with other systems.

hot swap *v.* To remove and insert a board on a bus or backplane while power is still applied to the bus.

HP-IB bus (as letters) *n.* A bus for connection and control of any kind of programmable lab instrument (e.g., scopes, logic analyzers, power supplies, counters, etc.) that provides a standard interface for communication between instruments from different sources. Also called GPIB. IEEE Std 488.2-1987.

Three types of devices can be connected to the HP-IB bus: listeners, talkers, and controllers. Some devices include more than one of these functions. The standard allows a maximum of 15 devices to be connected on the same bus. A minimum system consists of one controller and one talker or listener.

HISTORY: Hewlett Packard originally developed the interfacing technique and called it HP-IB (for Hewlett Packard Interface Bus). However, the interface quickly gained popularity in the entire industry. Because the interface was so versatile, the IEEE committee renamed it GPIB (General Purpose Interface Bus).

HSM (as letters) *abbr. See* hierarchical state machine.

HTML (as letters) *abbr.* A text-based data format that presents information in a platform-independent manner. Short for HyperText Markup Language. If you're reading this dictionary electronically via a Web browser, it's probably in HTML format. *See also* XML.

`htonl()` (host-to-network long) *fn.* A function or macro for converting a 32-bit value from host to network byte order. *See* code listing.

`htons()` (host-to-network short) *fn.* A function or macro for converting a 16-bit value from host to network byte order. *See* code listing.

HTTP (as letters) *abbr.* A communications protocol used to remotely access files on a Web server. Short for HyperText Transport Protocol. RFC 1945. The files retrieved could be in HTML, text, or any other format.

hub *n.* A local area networking device that connects two or more computers. A hub operates only at the physical layer, so it does not restrict the flow of packets as a switch would. Any network frame sent to the hub by one node will be echoed out to all of the nodes attached to it. Hubs are distinguished by the types of physical networks they support, such as 10 Mbps Ethernet, 100 Mbps Ethernet, etc.

human–machine interface *n.* The part of the system where flesh and eyeballs meet metal and silicon. Encompassing more than just the display or look and feel of a GUI, the human–machine interface is the sum total of the user's physical experience of using a device. It includes elements as diverse as weight and physical dimensions, ease of use, the physical location of knobs and buttons, and the readability of displays.

Hungarian notation *n.* A variable naming convention that encodes a variable's type as a prefix to its name. A variable naming convention that encodes a variable's type as a prefix to its name. For example, an integer might be named `iVariableName`,

`htonl()` If the network protocol is TCP/IP, which uses a big endian representation, this C macro will perform the byte reordering.

```
#if defined(BIG_ENDIAN)
#define htonl(A)  (A)
#elif defined(LITTLE_ENDIAN)
#define htonl(A)  (((((uint32_t) (A) & 0xff000000) >> 24) | \
                    (((uint32_t) (A) & 0x00ff0000) >> 8)  | \
                    (((uint32_t) (A) & 0x0000ff00) << 8)  | \
                    (((uint32_t) (A) & 0x000000ff) << 24))
#endif
```

`htons()` If the network protocol is TCP/IP, which uses a big endian representation, this C macro will perform the byte reordering.

```
#if defined(BIG_ENDIAN)
#define htons(A)  (A)
#elif defined(LITTLE_ENDIAN)
#define htons(A)  (((((uint16_t) (A) & 0xff00) >> 8) | \
                    (((uint16_t) (A) & 0x00ff) << 8))
#endif
```

with the leading i denoting the variable's type. Hungarian notation is promoted as a readability aid, which helps the programmer avoid the headache of digging through typedefs and include files to determine a variable's type.

Hungarian notation is essentially a commenting technique. Comments often lie, though, when they become outdated—a huge source of problems with the notation. Change the type of a variable (say, when porting the code from a 16- to a 32-bit processor), and you have to search out and change the name of every use of that variable. That rarely happens, of course, as in wParam in Microsoft's Win32 APIs: the type changed from a 16-bit value (w stands for word) to a 32-bit value (which should have been dwParam).

In practice, the prefix idea is extremely valuable for marking two common variable types in C programs: pointers and binary flags. These two types are also unlikely to change as the program evolves.

By preceding a pointer variable with p, dereferencing the right number of times becomes easy. Whereas pFoo refers to the pointer, *pFoo and pFoo-> refer to the actual object. Likewise, if you have a pointer to a pointer, label it with a pp.

Binary variables labeled with a preceding b are easy to spot in a code listing and make their use in tests easy to get right. You would never write x = bReady + 1;, for example. Although if (!bReady) { ... } makes perfect sense.

HISTORY: Invented by Charles Simonyi of Microsoft. The programmers there looked at the convoluted, vowel-less variable names produced by his scheme and, like everyone else who has come into contact with them since, must have said something like "This might as well be in Greek—or even Hungarian!". They almost certainly had in mind, as well, another kind of mathematical system called Polish notation. They put the two together and made up the name "Hungarian notation."

FURTHER READING: See http://www.gregleg.com/oldHome/hungarian.html for a list of common prefixes.

HW (hardware) *abbr. See* hardware.

hybrid module *n.* A circuit implemented in an IC-like module, though made by assembling many discrete components and semiconductors. Sometimes called hybrids for short. Hybrids incorporate components that cannot be put easily onto an IC, like inductors and capacitors. Typical applications include RF transmitters/receivers, and modulators for Ethernet and telephony.

hypertext *n.* ASCII text with embedded links, a la HTML. When users view the document in a browser and select one of the words or phrases with a link, the linked document is retrieved and displayed.

hysteresis 1. *n.* A lag in the response of a system to a change in its input.

2. *n.* The failure of a system to come back to its original state. Systems that exhibit hysteresis are those that maintain some memory of their previous states. Pull on a spring and then release it: if it doesn't quite return to its previous length, the spring exhibits hysteresis.

EXAMPLE: Ferromagnetic components can be flipped to a different state by applying a magnetic field; when the field is removed, the part stays in its new state, an attribute exploited by disk drives and core memory.

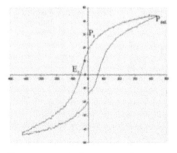

The response of a ferromagnetic part to a field. The vertical axis indicates the magnetic field strength, the horizontal axis the electric field strength.

Hz (hurts) *abbr. See* hertz.

I

I-cache (eye cache) *abbr. See* cache, instruction.

I/O (as letters) 1. *abbr.* Short for input/output.

2. *n.* The interface between a processor and the world around it. The simplest examples are switches (inputs) and LEDs (outputs).

I/O device *n.* A piece of hardware that interfaces between the processor and the outside world. Common examples are switches, LEDs, serial ports, and network controllers.

USAGE: This term is generally interchangeable with peripheral.

I/O map *n.* A table or diagram containing the name and address range of each I/O device addressable by the processor within the I/O space.

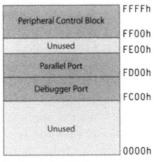

An I/O map for a 186 microcontroller with its peripheral control block left in the I/O space.

I/O pin *n.* An individual input or output pin. *See also* general-purpose I/O.

I/O port *n.* A particular address in a processor's I/O space.

I/O register *n.* A control or status register in a peripheral. *See also* memory-mapped I/O.

I/O space *n.* A special memory region provided by some processors and generally reserved for the attachment of I/O devices. Memory locations and registers within a processor's I/O space can only be accessed via special opcodes. For example, processors in the 80x86 family have special I/O space instructions called `in` and `out`. *Contrast with* memory space.

I/O-bound *adj.* Pertains to a thread that needs lots of I/O operations to complete its assigned work. It's generally best if I/O-bound threads can get quick access to the CPU (i.e., they have high priority) when they need a few processor cycles to set up the next I/O operation. *Contrast with* CPU-bound.

I²C (eye squared see) *abbr.* An inexpensive chip interconnection popular on circuit boards. Short for Inter-Integrated Circuit bus. Featuring a two-wire synchronous (data and clock) connection, I²C can run at speeds up to 100 kHz ("standard") or 400 kHz ("high speed") and is multidrop. *See also* SPI.

FURTHER READING: Kalinsky, David and Roee Kalinsky. "Introduction to I²C," *Embedded Systems Programming,* August 2001.

IC (as letters) *abbr. See* integrated circuit.

IC extractor *n.* A tool for removing a chip from a socket.

ICE (like frozen water) *abbr. See* in-circuit emulator.

ICMP (as letters) *abbr.* A network layer protocol (IP peer) used to ping remote hosts to see if they are alive and able to successfully receive and send packets over the data link and physical layer. Short for Internet Control Message Protocol. RFC 792.

The use of this protocol also tests any nodes and networks between the pair that are involved in routing the test and its response.

icon *n.* A small graphic, typically on a GUI.

IDE (as letters) *abbr. See* integrated development environment.

idle loop *n.* A simple block of code within an operating system that contains an infinite loop for the processor to execute when none of the tasks are ready to run.

```
idle:
 jmp idle
```

idle task *n.* A task that runs when none of the others is ready to run. In most operating systems, there is really no actual idle task; rather, a part of the scheduler executes an idle loop whenever there's no task to run. If there are hooks in the OS, it might be possible to specify a function to run instead of the idle loop, which could be useful for calculating the CPU's idle time.

idle time *n.* The percentage of a processor's time that is spent in the idle loop.

IEEE (eye-triple-ee) *abbr.* A nonprofit professional association serving the electrical engineering community. Short for Institute of Electrical and Electronics Engineers. The IEEE's hundreds of thousands of members in over 150 countries specialize in everything from computer engineering to biomedical technology to electric power generation and distribution. In addition to publishing almost a third of the world's journals relating to these and other fields, the IEEE is also an accredited standards body.

FURTHER READING: http://www.ieee.org

IEEE 1003.1 *See* POSIX.

IEEE 1003.1b *N.* A set of process-level real-time extensions to the POSIX standard. IEEE Std 1003.1b-1993.

IEEE 1003.1c *See* pthreads.

IEEE 1149 *See* JTAG.

IEEE 488 *See* HP-IB bus.

IEEE 754 *N.* The standard way to express floating-point numbers on most modern processors.

Under IEEE 754 rules, single-precision numbers are constructed using a 32-bit binary value in which the MSb is the sign bit, S; the next 8 bits are the exponent bits, E; and the final 23 bits are the fraction, F. (The fraction is also called the mantissa and the exponent the characteristic.)

To determine the value V represented as a single-precision number:

- if E = 255 and F is nonzero, then V = NaN (not a number)
- if E = 255 and F is zero and S = 1, then V = $-\infty$
- if E = 255 and F is zero and S = 0, then V = ∞
- if 0 < E < 255, then V = $(-1)^S \times 2^{(E-127)} \times$ (1.F), where 1.F represents the binary number created by prefixing F with an implicit leading 1 and a binary point
- if E = 0 and F is nonzero, then V = $(-1)^S \times 2^{(-126)} \times$ (0.F), which is called an unnormalized value
- if E = 0 and F is zero and S = 1, then V = -0
- if E = 0 and F is zero and S = 0, then V = 0

IEEE 754 also supports 64-bit double-precision words in which the MSb is again the sign bit, the next 11 bits are the exponent bits, and the final 52 bits are the fraction.

To compute the value of a double-precision number:

- if E = 2047 and F is nonzero, then V = NaN
- if E = 2047 and F is 0 and S = 1, then V = $-\infty$
- if E = 2047 and F is zero and S = 0, then V = ∞

- if $0 < E < 2047$, then $V = (-1)^S \times 2^{(E-1023)} \times (1.F)$
- if $E = 0$ and F is nonzero, then $V = (-1)^S \times 2^{(-1022)} \times (0.F)$
- if $E = 0$ and F is zero and $S = 1$, then $V = -0$
- if $E = 0$ and F is zero and $S = 0$, then $V = 0$

IEEE-ISTO 5001 *See* Nexus.

IEEE-IX *N.* A name briefly used (in 1986 or so) for the standard that would eventually be called POSIX. Short for IEEE's version of Unix.

IETF (as letters) *abbr.* In its own words, the IETF is an "open international community of network designers, operators, vendors, and researchers concerned with the evolution of the Internet architecture and the smooth operation of the Internet." Short for Internet Engineering Task Force. It is the IETF that defines and refines protocols in the TCP/IP protocol suite, through working groups focused on routing, security, and other aspects of the network.

FURTHER READING: http://www.ietf.org

IGMP (as letters) *abbr.* A protocol used between IP hosts and gateways to establish multicast groups. Short for Internet Group Management Protocol. RFC 1122.

IIR (as letters) *abbr. See* infinite impulse response.

image 1. *See* memory image.

2. *n.* A graphic, such as an icon or bitmap.

imaginary number *n.* A number based on the square root of a negative number. Imaginary numbers have a real part (an ordinary number) and an imaginary part (that based on the square root of a negative number) expressed as

$$R + I\sqrt{-1}$$

where R is the real part and $I\sqrt{-1}$ the imaginary part. In math $\sqrt{-1}$ is called *i*; EEs call it *j*.

Although imaginary numbers might seem bizarre and pointless, in fact, they're used throughout math and engineering. *See also* Euler's formula.

immediate addressing mode *n.* An addressing mode in which the address is encoded as part of the instruction.

EXAMPLE: The x86 instruction

```
MOV AX, (0x1234)
```

reads data from an address (0x1234) that's part of the instruction.

immediate operand *n.* A parameter used by an opcode that is included as part of the instruction. Instructions might require data from registers, memory, I/O, or other sources. Immediate arguments are encoded directly into the instruction.

EXAMPLE: In the Z80 instruction

```
LD BC, 0x1234
```

the 16-bit value 0x1234 is encoded into the instruction. An assembler would generate a 3-byte opcode: 01 34 12 (shown in hex).

impedance (impede-ance) *n.* The sum of resistance (R) and reactance (X) expressed in ohms. Can be thought of as AC resistance at a particular frequency. Represented by the symbol Z.

In a series circuit,

$$Z = \sqrt{R^2 + X^2}$$

In a parallel circuit,

$$Z = \frac{RX}{R^2 + X^2}$$

At high speeds, it's critical to match the impedance of a driving gate and its receiver, especially as wire or track lengths get long (more than a few inches). Mismatches create ringing, in which the signal bounces back and forth between the two nodes. Large amounts of ringing can confuse 1s and 0s; larger amounts can destroy CMOS parts.

impedance matching *n.* The process of designing circuits that makes a driver's impedance match the receiver's. When a driver and receiver have mismatched impedances, incorrect data can be transferred or the parts destroyed by SCR latchup. Engineers match impedances by using networks of resistors, resistors and capacitors, or, in extreme cases, active components.

implicit cast *n.* A type conversion that is not coded explicitly by the programmer. *Compare to* explicit cast.

impulse function *See* Dirac impulse function.

impulse response *n.* The reaction, in terms of output, of a filter to an impulse function at its input.

in-circuit emulator *n.* A debugging tool that takes the place of (emulates) the processor on the target board. Abbreviated ICE and often called an emulator for short. The ICE is a bridge between the target system and a software debugger running on the host. It provides the resources needed to access the target microprocessor. An emulator connects to or completely replaces the target CPU via a large cable, which routes all signals to the ICE unit. In-circuit emulators frequently incorporate a special bond-out version of the target processor that brings normally buried signals out of the chip to the ICE's logic circuits.

An emulator from Applied Microsystems.

HISTORY: Intel invented the emulator in the mid-1970s with the first of their famous "blue boxes" for the 8080 microprocessor. Emulators and microprocessors evolved concurrently for many years, CPU manufacturers often paying ICE vendors' NRE costs to build units for each new processor. But bond-out parts are very expensive and ship in miniscule volumes, so semiconductor vendors became more reluctant to produce them. As more components migrated onto the chip (prefetchers, cache, pipelines, etc.) bond-outs became ever more necessary. Furthermore, higher speeds and difficult packages made ICEs more and more problematic. For these reasons, the emulator's past dominance is diminishing in favor of JTAG and BDM debuggers.

in-circuit programmable *adj.* Said of an electrically erasable and programmable device such as an EEPROM or EEPLD. The contents of such devices can be (re)written while on the circuit board and do not require a device programmer.

in-system programming *n.* The act of programming a memory chip (like an EPROM) without removing it from the embedded device. Abbreviated ISP. In-system programming uses extra circuits on the target board to program the device. The advantage is that parts can be soldered to the board yet still be (re)programmed. Flash memories are inherently in-system programmable (typically requiring no extra circuits) and are almost always programmed that way.

incomplete decoding *n.* A circuit that selects memory or I/O devices based on a partial match of address lines. Incomplete decoding saves logic devices, and thus reduces costs. In a very simple 16-bit system with 64 KB (2^{16} bytes) of address space, the designer might use this strategy by enabling RAM if A15=1, and ROM if A15=0, even if each of the attached memory devices are in fact much smaller than the implied 32 KB.

increment *v.* To increase by one. *See also* ++.

incremental release *n.* A development strategy that produces deliverables frequently, allowing customers and users to conduct tests and see how well the partial product meets their needs. A policy of incremental releases is the opposite of building the entire product and, only then, letting users and QA start their tests. It's part of every modern agile method.

Older up-front design and build approaches pretend that requirements are static; history, though, has shown that they change often. Incremental releases *provoke* requirements change, as users see very early how the product actually fits their needs. Although such change is scary, it's better to find out what's wrong with a product 6 months before final delivery, than 2 weeks after.

index 1. *n.* A value added to an address to form a pointer to memory. Indexes can be part of an addressing mode or something constructed by a programmer to access a data structure. It's not unusual to load a register with the base of a table of data (say, for interpolation) and then add another register (the index) to get to a particular value. *See also* indexed address.

2. *n.* Any integer offset into a table.

3. *v.* To add one, as in "the program indexes the stepper motor to the next position."

index register *n.* A high-speed memory location inside a CPU, the contents of which are added to something else to form the complete address of a variable or function.

EXAMPLE: The Z80 instruction

```
ld   D, (IX+12)
```

forms the address of the argument by adding 12 to the value stored in index register IX.

indexed address *n.* An address formed by adding the contents of an index register to other parameters (e.g., a displacement or the contents of another memory location).

inductance *n.* The ability to store electrical energy in a magnetic field. *See also* inductor, henry.

induction motor *n.* An AC motor in which the field windings are powered by energy coupled from the stator. Induction motors have a fixed stator with windings much like those of a synchronous motor. The rotor (also called an armature) also has

windings; however, these are each closed loops of wire. The changing magnetic field of the stator induces current in the rotor, leading to a repulsive and attractive effect with the stator's windings.

inductive load *n.* A device driven by a circuit that exhibits a primarily inductive reactance. Inductive loads require heavy starting currents since, at low frequencies, they appear to be almost a short circuit. Examples include motors and relays. *See also* inductance.

inductive reactance *n.* The resistance of an inductive circuit to the flow of AC current.
$$X_L = 2\pi f L$$
where f is frequency in hertz and L is inductance in henries. Thus, as the frequency increases, inductive reactance also increases. This is intuitively obvious, since an inductor is a coil of wire that offers little resistance to DC signals.

inductor *n.* A device formed by wrapping turns of wire around a core. Also called a coil or choke. Inductors can have air cores; larger units use iron or ferrites to increase the device's inductance. *See also* inductance.

Schematic symbol for an inductor.

Industrial, Scientific, and Medical band *N.* A region of the frequency spectrum made available for unlicensed—but lightly regulated—transmitters. Abbreviated ISM. In the U.S., the 900-MHz and 2.4-GHz bands are currently licensed this way, though there are others. These ISM bands are shared by a variety of devices, including consumer cordless telephones, garage door openers, and wireless LANs.

inertia *n.* The tendency of a body to resist changes in its motion. Also used in electronics to describe any resistance to change. For instance, thermal inertia is the lag in temperature change in something being heated.

infinite impulse response *n.* A type of digital filter that uses feedback. Abbreviated IIR. The output is a function of the last *n* inputs and outputs, where *n* is the number of taps or the filter length. The name is derived from the fact that an impulse function provided as input to such a filter at any specific time will never cease to affect its output. *Contrast with* finite impulse response.

infinite loop *n.* A chunk of code that repeats forever. Usually avoided except in the case of the system's main loop that runs forever, or in individual tasks that have no need to exit (they might run all the time or wait on availability of some resource).

information hiding *n.* An important aspect of abstraction. Details of the implementation of a function or data type are best hidden from other software modules. In C++, the implementation of public methods and everything about private methods and data members is hidden.

The big advantage of information hiding is that it creates a separation that makes it possible to change the implementation of one module without affecting other modules. In effect, it reduces coupling between modules.

infrared *adj.* Light at wavelengths longer than that of red. Typically in the 700- to 1000-nanometer range. Often used as the carrier frequency for very short range communication, such as in TV remote controls and PDAs.

inherent address *n.* An addressing mode in which all parameters needed to form the address are known a priori by the CPU.

EXAMPLE: The 68HC11 processor's aba instruction adds what is in accumulators A and B, and stores the result in accumulator A.

inheritance *n.* An approach to software design that involves the sharing of behaviors between similar classes. Using inheritance, a class can be defined in terms of one or more parent classes; this "subclass" derives its interface and implementation details

from the base class. Of course, inheritance is only useful if the subclass differs in some way from the parent(s). Some methods of the subclass will be overridden and/or others may be added.

Inheritance is one of the three pillars of object-oriented programming and is supported by C++ and Java directly. The general rule of thumb is that every derived class "is a" specialization of the more general base class. For example, every square "is a" rectangle.

initial conditions *n.* A system's starting parameters.

EXAMPLE: Science's success at explaining the nature of the universe leads some religious people to speculate that perhaps God doesn't exert control over the universe but at least specified the initial conditions. Everything else followed deterministically from there. Ironically, chaos theory suggests in nonlinear systems that it's impossible to specify initial conditions accurately enough for a system to be deterministic.

initial pseudostate *n.* A source for the default transition in a state diagram. Shown as a black dot in UML. There can be no more than one initial pseudostate within each composite state.

initialized data *n.* Static variables that have an initial value when the program starts. In an embedded system, these initial values are typically stored in the ROM image alongside the code and copied to RAM by the startup code. *Contrast with* uninitialized data.

EXAMPLE:

```
int x = 5;
```

inline *res.* A C++ keyword that suggests to the compiler that the contents of the following (short) function be copied to every place that it is called, rather than incur the overhead associated with a function call. The inline keyword gives programmers some control over the optimization of the compiled code. If a function is short but called from part(s) of the code that must be executed efficiently, the function call can be avoided. There is a trade-off here, however, in that the more often that function is called, the more copies there will be of its code in ROM.

The C99 update to ISO C adds support for this useful keyword to that more popular language.

inline assembly *n.* The inclusion of mnemonics in a program written in a high-level language. Some compilers support inline assembly, whereas others do not. Those that do allow it have proprietary means of doing so, since there is no standard for this. One way is to have the compiler recognize an `asm { ... }` block as containing lines of code that should be passed to the assembler and ignored by the compiler.

Inline assembly is very useful for disabling interrupts and including processor-specific code in C programs, though the resulting code is generally nonportable.

`inport()` (in port) *fn.* An x86-specific C library function for reading data from a port in the I/O space. The prototype for this function can generally be found in the `dos.h` header file. *See also* `outport()`.

input *n.* An analog or digital signal presented to an embedded system and that has a value that affects the operation of that system.

input capture timer *n.* A timer circuit with a latch register connected to the count register for easily capturing the count at a specific time. The timer is run at a constant clock rate (usually a derivative of the processor clock) so that the count register is constantly incrementing (or decrementing, for a down counter). An external signal latches the value of the free-running timer into the processor-visible register and generates an output signal (typically an interrupt).

One use for an input capture timer is to measure the time between the leading edge of two pulses.

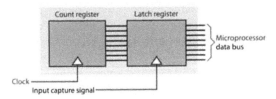

A simple input capture timer.

By reading the value in the latch and comparing it with a previous reading, the software can determine how many clock cycles elapsed. In some cases, the timer's count register might be automatically reset just after its value is latched. If so, the software can directly interpret the value it reads as the number of clock ticks elapsed.

An input capture pin can usually be programmed to capture on either the rising or falling edge of its input signal.

input impedance *n.* The resistance of a sensor's or instrument's input at a particular frequency. It's important to know and control the impedance of devices to ensure that signals are transmitted without distortion. A scope, for instance, can rate its impedance by describing the input circuit—it might be "1 MΩ 13 pF"—so the user can compute the impedance for the frequency of the signal being observed. *See also* impedance.

input protection diode *n.* Commonly found on the inputs of CMOS devices, the input protection diode shorts overvoltage signals to V_{cc}. CMOS parts are vulnerable to SCR latchup: if the input exceeds the power supply level or goes below ground, the semiconductor fails in a spectacular fashion. Input protection diodes help, but only proper circuit design ensures that the system will not experience such failure. *See also* SCR latchup.

input/output *n.* The collection of all external devices and signals connected to an embedded system. Abbreviated I/O.

inspection *See* code inspection.

instance *n.* A run-time realization of a design-time construct such as a class. In C++ and Java, you create an instance of a class with the new operator. *See also* object.

instruction counter *See* instruction pointer.

instruction cycle *n.* The time it takes to fetch and execute a single opcode.

instruction pointer *n.* A register in a processor that contains the address of the next instruction to be executed.

USAGE: The term program counter is often used.

instruction set *n.* The full suite of opcodes recognized by a particular processor or family. This information can generally be found in the databook or programmer's manual provided by the manufacturer.

instruction set architecture *n.* The opcodes common to a processor family. Abbreviated ISA.

EXAMPLE: CPU32 is an instruction set architecture of Motorola. The x86 family uses Intel's most popular ISA. MIPS and ARM are others.

instruction set simulator *n.* A simulator that recognizes a particular processor's instruction set. Sometimes abbreviated ISS. The term is a synonym for simulator, though it does help to distinguish between simulators for verifying hardware and simulators for verifying software, since this term is of the latter type.

insulator *n.* A component or material that does not conduct electricity. *Contrast with* semiconductor, conductor.

INT *See* interrupt.

int (rhymes with hint) *res.* A primitive data type in C and several related languages that declares an integer variable. In C and C++, the size of an int is specified to be whatever is the natural word size of the processor. So an int is 32 bits on a Pentium,

but just 16 bits on a 186. By definition, an int can be no smaller than a short and no larger than a long for a given platform. In Java, however, an int is always 32 bits.

INT 21h (int twenty-one) *n.* The software interrupt used by DOS programs to make system calls. Information about the type of OS request is first loaded into the AH register. Parameters, if any, are placed into other registers according to the rules of DOS, then the INT 21h instruction is executed, which hands control to the operating system. When the request is complete, DOS uses the x86's IRET instruction to return control to the caller.

int8_t (int 8) *res.* A processor-independent typedef for declaring 8-bit signed integers. To declare variables of this type, simply use a C99-compliant compiler and include the stdint.h header file. If you don't have a C99-compliant compiler, mimic the definitions at typedef.

int16_t (int 16) *res.* A processor-independent typedef for declaring 16-bit signed integers. To declare variables of this type, simply use a C99-compliant compiler and include the stdint.h header file. If you don't have a C99-compliant compiler, mimic the definitions at typedef.

int32_t (int 32) *res.* A processor-independent typedef for declaring 32-bit signed integers. To declare variables of this type, simply use a C99-compliant compiler and include the stdint.h header file. If you don't have a C99-compliant compiler, mimic the definitions at typedef.

int64_t (int 64) *res.* A processor-independent typedef for declaring 64-bit signed integers. To declare variables of this type, simply use a C99-compliant compiler and include the stdint.h header file. If you don't have a C99-compliant compiler, mimic the definitions at typedef. *See also* long long.

integer 1. *n.* Any whole number.

2. *n.* A signed or unsigned integer variable. In C, there are four primitive integer data types: `char`, `short`, `int`, and `long`.

integral control *n.* A form of closed-loop control in which each adjustment that is made to the drive signal is a function of accumulated errors in the plant's state. Integral control is not often used on its own. Rather, it is typically used alongside proportional or proportional and derivative (PD) control.

The need for integral control arises because neither proportional nor PD control will always settle exactly to the desired state. In fact, depending on the proportional gain, it's altogether possible that a PD controller will ultimately settle to a state that is far from that desired.

The problem occurs if each individual error remains below the threshold for action by the proportional term. (Say the error is 3; $p = 1/8$, and integer math is used.) The derivative term won't eliminate the error unless the plant's state is still changing. Something else needs to drive the plant toward the set point. That something is an integral term.

An integral is a sum over time, in this case the sum of all past errors in the plant output.

$$change = I \sum_i (desired_i - current_i)$$

Even though the integral gain factor, I, is typically small, a persistent error will eventually cause the sum to grow large and the integral term to force a change in the drive signal. In practice, the accumulated error is usually capped at some maximum and minimum values, which can be set as part of the PID tuning process. *See also* PID.

integrated circuit *n.* A semiconductor that includes a complete circuit, mostly made up of transistors and resistors. Abbreviated IC. ICs can be made of silicon, germanium, or gallium arsenide, but the vast majority are of silicon. A single chip, measuring just a few millimeters on a side, contains dozens to millions of components. Various impurities are diffused into the silicon to create transistors, which are connected by sputtered metallized layers.

Kilby's first IC—an invention that changed the world.

HISTORY: Invented independently by Jack Kilby and Robert Noyce in 1959. Patents awarded to each led to the usual pointless and lengthy litigation. Kilby was awarded the 2000 Nobel Prize in physics for work that included the IC.

integrated development environment *n.* A front end for a set of development tools that typically includes an editor, a compiler, and a debugger, at least. Abbreviated IDE. Some programmer's editors, such as CodeWright, can be made to work as IDEs for any compiler and debugger. Others, such as Microsoft's VisualStudio, are included with and supported by the compiler vendor. Many IDEs also support version control via integrated check-in and check-out commands and instruction set simulation.

The beauty of an IDE is that it combines all of the tools required for the typical edit–compile–test cycle into one integrated user experience. The alternative is using your favorite text editor, switching to a command-line compiler, then launching a stand-alone debugger.

integrator *n.* A circuit that sums or averages inputs.

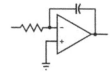

An analog integrator.

Intel *n.* As of this writing, the world's largest chip vendor. Founded in 1968, Intel invented the DRAM; their earliest parts stored a breathtaking 256 bits. They also created large serial shift registers, which were, for a time, a type of computer memory.

In 1971 Intel introduced the 4004, the first microprocessor, followed a year later by the 8008, arguably the first useful micro. When IBM selected their 8088 over Motorola's long-delayed 68000 as the basis for the PC, Intel started its long domination of the desktop processor market.

Intel argument convention *n.* The order in which arguments appear in instructions for Intel processors. Assemblers for Intel processors (e.g., 186) expect the first argument to be the destination; the second is the source. *Contrast with* Motorola argument convention.

EXAMPLE: The x86 instruction

```
MOV [BX], DX
```

moves the contents of register DX to the location pointed to by register BX.

Intel Extended Hex format *n.* A variation of Intel Hex that supports larger address ranges.

Extended Hex has four additional record types over Intel Hex.

- 02—Extended Segment Address Record
- 03—Start Segment Address Record
- 04—Extended Linear Address Record
- 05—Start Linear Address Record

See also Intel Hex format.

Intel Hex format *n.* An ASCII file format devised by Intel for storing and downloading binary images. Sometimes called a .hex file. Most device programmers can read .hex files to import the binary image to be loaded into a ROM, a flash, or another memory device. Similarly, many debug monitors can accept data in Hex format over a serial port, though the ASCII encoding is admittedly a waste of communications bandwidth.

Each line in a .hex file is a record. Records always begin with a colon, followed by the number of data bytes in each record. This value must be between 0x00 and 0xFF. The next pair of numbers in each record represents the 16-bit starting address for the data in the record.

The starting address is followed by a byte representing the record type. If the record type is 0x00, the next bytes will be the data. 0x01 indicates that this is the last record in the file.

Following the record type are the parameters for that record type. In the case of a data record, this is the hex representation of the data to be stored at the previously indicated offset.

The last byte is a two's complement checksum of all of the bytes in the record, not including the colon. Note that this value is derived from the binary values of the bytes, not their ASCII representations. A CR/LF pair terminates each record. *See also* Intel Extended Hex format. *Compare to* Motorola S-record format.

EXAMPLE: A sample Intel Hex record.

```
:1001700070717273747576777879 7A7B7C7D7E7F07
```

- :—start of record
- 10—number of data bytes to follow (in hex)
- 0170—starting address for this record (in hex)
- 00—record type (data, in this case)
- 707172 ... 7F—the 16 (0x10) bytes of data
- 07—two's complement checksum

FURTHER READING: To find out more about these and other record types, visit http://www.wotsit.org/search.asp?page=2&s=binary

intellectual property *n.* A logic core (aka, hardware object) that has been made part of a library for possible inclusion in system-on-chip designs. Abbreviated IP. Most of the FPGA vendors have IP libraries.

interarrival time *n.* The length of time between consecutive occurrences of the same signal, event, or interrupt. *See* arrival time.

intercept *n.* The place where a line crosses the vertical axis. The equation of a line is $y = mx + b$. The intercept occurs where $x = 0$, or b. *See also* slope.

interface 1. *n.* The meeting point of two entities.

EXAMPLE: The hardware/software interface defines one such meeting point. A user interface is another.

2. *v.* To connect components or systems.

interference 1. *See* electromagnetic interference.

2. *See* radio frequency interference.

3. *n.* The amount of time for which a task may be preempted by other tasks.

$$I_i = \sum_k (R_i/T_k)C_k$$

where R_i is the worst-case response time, T_i is the deadline, and C_i is the worst-case execution time of task i.

When performing deadline-monotonic analysis, it is useful to calculate the number of possible preemptions (and the maximum length of each) by each higher priority task. The interference aggregates this information.

interlock *n.* A restriction placed on the user by a device, typically for safety reasons. The interlock condition must be met before some operation can be performed. The implementation can be in hardware or software. A hardware example would be a device that prevented a user from opening the box while the power is still connected. The power cable plug could latch onto the lid of the device to force the user to remove the power cable before opening the box. Interlocks often make devices more difficult to use, but in return, the device might be safer. Also known as a forcing function. *See also* lock-in, lock-out.

internal *adj.* On the inside.

EXAMPLE: An internal peripheral is in the same IC as the CPU.

internal documentation *n.* Documentation, like the comments in a program or on a schematic, that exists within the work product. *See also* external documentation.

internal fragmentation *n.* Wasted space within dynamically allocated objects. Internal fragmentation is less dangerous than external fragmentation, though a larger amount of space can be wasted.

EXAMPLE: Disk drives are subdivided into sectors. Each of these sectors is the same size, typically measured in kibibytes. If the sector size is 4 KiB and a 14-KiB file is to be stored on the disk, it will consume four full sectors, or 16 KiB of space. The other 2 KiB is wasted space within the last sector of the file.

EXAMPLE: Fixed-sized memory pools also suffer internal fragmentation.

internationalization *n.* The process by which a product is made useful to speakers of more than one language. For example, many embedded systems with LCDs and soft keys can supply a user interface in two or more human languages. Internationalization is a de facto requirement for products sold or used in Europe.

Internet appliance *n.* An Internet-connected embedded system for the consumer market.

EXAMPLE: Net-connected MP3 rippers download song lyrics and titles, 3G cell phones surf and exchange email, and Internet-connected toasters, well, toast even better.

Internet checksum *n.* The name of the additive checksum used by the TCP/IP stack. Many protocol stacks include some sort of a checksum within each protocol layer. The TCP/IP suite of protocols is no exception in this regard. In addition to a checksum at the lowest layer (within

Ethernet packets, for example, where the chosen form is a CRC-32), checksums also exist within each IP, UDP, and TCP header. All the fields of the IP header are summed to generate the 16-bit IP checksum. The data, fields of the UDP header, and select fields from the IP header (termed the pseudoheader) are summed to generate the 16-bit UDP checksum. The TCP checksum is generated similarly.

Internet layer *See* network layer.

Internet protocol *See* IP.

interpolation *n.* The process of estimating a value that lies between two known points. Software often must interpolate data to conserve memory and to model incomplete data sets. For instance, it's common for integer trig functions to extract two values from a table that surround the desired parameter and then interpolate to get a more precise approximation. Although linear interpolations are the most common, given some a priori knowledge about the data being modeled, other interpolation methods that better fit a curve to the data might be more appropriate. *See also* linear interpolation.

interpreted language *n.* A programming language that is never compiled to native opcodes. Sometimes BASIC is interpreted. Java is a semi-interpreted language: the Java program is compiled into a portable executable format called a class file (which contains bytecodes); the bytecodes must be converted to native opcodes to be run. If the translation to native opcodes is done at run time by a JVM, the bytecodes are said to be interpreted.

interpreter *n.* A program that executes either a high-level language directly or an intermediate form of a high-level language.

BASIC was the first language to use an interpreter. Forth is another interpreted language. Java

has features of both compiled and interpreted languages; it is called a semicompiled language.

interprocess communication *n.* The passing of data between processes running on the same operating system, typically by means of message queues.

`interrupt` *res.* A reserved word recognized by some C compilers a programmer can use to indicate that a particular function is an interrupt service routine. A mechanism is needed for functions that service interrupts so that they can save the processor flags and additional CPU registers on entry and restore them on exit. The keyword `interrupt`, which is a common feature of compilers for the 80x86 processor family, lets the compiler know about these special requirements.

interrupt *n.* An asynchronous electrical signal from a peripheral to the processor. When the peripheral asserts this signal, an interrupt is said to occur. When an interrupt occurs, the current context is saved and an interrupt service routine is executed. When the interrupt service routine exits, control of the processor is returned to whatever part of the software was previously running.

interrupt acknowledge *n.* The signal generated by a processor or interrupt controller that tells an interrupting device its interrupt has been queued for processing. Some poor designs simply send a pulse to the CPU's interrupt input, the pulse length carefully tuned to ensure the CPU will see the signal. Much better is to keep the interrupt asserted until the CPU or controller responds with an interrupt acknowledge—only at that point is it truly safe to de-assert the signal.

interrupt controller *n.* A hardware device that accepts and prioritizes multiple interrupts, generating a single interrupt request to the processor. Interrupt controllers also produce a vector, which tells the processor which ISR to invoke. Most require extensive and complex initialization by the host processor.

EXAMPLE: Intel's 8259 was an early interrupt controller of great popularity. It still lives as an on-chip component in many microcontrollers.

interrupt enable *n.* A bit in a processor or peripheral control register that enables one or more interrupts. *See also* global interrupt enable.

interrupt handler *See* interrupt service routine.

interrupt latency *n.* The amount of time between the assertion of an interrupt signal and the start of the associated interrupt service routine. Factors that affect interrupt latency include the length of time that interrupts are disabled during normal program execution, processor speed, and preemption of the processor by higher priority interrupts.

interrupt level *n.* The 68000 way of saying "interrupt priority." *See* interrupt priority.

interrupt priority *n.* The execution order of one or a series of pending interrupts. When more than one interrupt is pending, the priority associated with that interrupt determines which gets executed.

Several interrupts can share the same priority; if so, the first executed remains in control until its ISR reenables interrupts at that level.

Interrupt priority can be set by the hardware design (e.g., wiring the daisy chain on Z80s or tying interrupts to inputs on CPU32 machines) or can be programmed into an interrupt controller.

interrupt service routine *n.* A small piece of software executed in response to a particular interrupt. Abbreviated ISR.

USAGE: The term interrupt handler is equivalent.

interrupt sharing *n.* A hardware design that essentially ORs interrupt requests from two or more peripherals onto a single interrupt line input to the CPU or interrupt controller.

interrupt type *n.* A unique number associated with each interrupt. The interrupt type is typically the processor's index into the interrupt vector table.

interrupt vector *n.* The address of an interrupt service routine.

USAGE: This term is sometimes used incorrectly to refer to either the interrupt type or the address of the interrupt vector.

interrupt vector table *n.* A table containing interrupt vectors, indexed by interrupt type, that maps interrupts and interrupt service routines. The interrupt vector table must be initialized before interrupts are enabled.

interrupt, daisy chain *n.* A Z80-specific way to associate priorities with multiple interrupt sources. All Z80 peripherals had a daisy chain signal pair wired through each peripheral chip. When the CPU recognized an interrupt, it sent an acknowledgment down the daisy chain; the first peripheral with a pending interrupt supplied a vector but also blocked the distribution of the acknowledge to devices further down the chain. Devices located upstream on the daisy chain, closest to the CPU, automatically had the highest priority.

interrupt, edge-sensitive *n.* An interrupt input that responds to transitions on the pin. Asserting a constant 1 or 0 does not create an interrupt; only a transition from 1 to 0 (or its reverse, depending on the hardware) initiates interrupt processing. *Contrast with* interrupt, level-sensitive.

interrupt, level-sensitive *n.* An input to a microprocessor that initiates interrupt processing when at a 0 or 1 (depending on the hardware). *Contrast with* interrupt, edge-sensitive.

interrupt, nested *n.* A state where more than one interrupt is being processed, that with the highest priority having suspended those at lower priorities. Nested interrupts can also occur at a single priority level when an ISR reenables that priority before it finishes. At that point, other equal interrupts can suspend the running ISR. This decreases latency at the risk of stack overflow.

interrupt-driven *adj.* Pertains to a system or subsystem design that uses interrupts to indicate that peripherals are ready for service. *Contrast with* polling.

intertask communication *n.* The passing of data between tasks in a multitasking system. Although perverse programmers can accomplish this communication with global variables, all decent RTOSes include extensive resources (mailboxes, queues, etc.) to safely transfer data without risk of race conditions.

intertask synchronization *n.* The coordination of timing and ordering between tasks in a multitasking environment. All decent RTOSes include resources (semaphores, monitors, etc.) to safely synchronize without the risk of race conditions.

`intmax_t` *res.* In C99, the widest integer data type available on the target platform. The `intmax_t` type is typedef'd in header file *stdint.h*.

`intptr_t` (int pointer) *res.* In C99, the smallest integer data type that can contain a pointer.

intranet *n.* A private TCP/IP network, such as a LAN or WAN, operated by a single business. At the office, many engineers have seamless access to their employer's intranet and the global Internet from their desktop computers. Because the intranet typically resides behind a firewall, it might be impossible to access files and computers on the intranet from nodes on the Internet. VPN software is sometimes used to authenticate corporate users for remote access to the intranet from their laptops and home computers.

inverter 1. *n.* A logic device that translates 1s to 0s and vice versa. Also called a NOT gate.

2. *n.* A device that converts DC to AC.

The schematic symbol for an inverter.

`ioctl()` (eye octal) *fn.* A common name for a system call used to perform complex functions above and beyond the simple `read()` and `write()`. Short for I/O ConTroL. Common examples of I/O control functions include seeking to a new location in an open file and changing the baud rate of a serial I/O device. *See also* `seek()`.

IP (as letters) 1. *abbr.* The network layer protocol used on the Internet (and other TCP/IP networks) to route packets. Short for Internet Protocol.

2. *abbr. See* intellectual property.

3. *abbr. See* instruction pointer.

USAGE: Because this abbreviation has so many different meanings in the embedded domain, it is important to ensure that you only use it in a context that is self-explanatory. For example, if you're talking about adding a network connection to your system, you'd probably want to consider the TCP/IP's Internet protocol. On the other hand, if it's 10/100 Ethernet controller logic you need to add to your SoC design, then you're talking about acquiring a piece of intellectual property from a third-party IP library.

IP address *n.* A unique address assigned to each node on an IP network. In IPv4, the address is a 32-bit value. In its human-readable form, it is written in a dotted decimal format (e.g., 192.168.1.1).

IPv6 extends the IP address space to support a far larger number of nodes on the Internet, which was never envisioned as being so widely used back in its DARPA days.

IP pseudoheader *n.* A subset of the standard IP packet header that's used when computing the UDP or TCP checksum. In TCP/IP, there are checksums at both the transport and network layers. However, not all of the fields of the network layer's header are available to the transport layer to compute its checksum, so rather than include all of them, a standardized pseudoheader is formed at the transport layer and included in the checksum. The fields of the IP header that are not included must be zeroed or ignored on the receiving end before validating the received checksum.

IP spoofing *See* NAT.

IPC (as letters) *abbr. See* interprocess communication.

IPsec (eye pee seck) *abbr.* An encrypted version of the Internet protocol largely associated with IPv6. Short for IP Security protocol. With IPv4, it's only possible to encrypt the payload of a TCP or UDP packet; all of the headers travel in the clear, and the encryption and decryption must be done at a higher layer at the two endpoints. With IPsec, virtually everything is encrypted—including not only the payload (even if the protocol used at the level is plaintext), but also much of the header information. Support for IPsec is provided in modern routers and network equipment.

IPv4 (eye pee vee four) *abbr.* IPv4 is the standard on which the Internet and most intranets are built. Short for Internet Protocol Version 4. In the early days of the Internet's popularity, even through the mid-1990s, there were plenty of 32-bit IP addresses to go around. However, a looming address shortage and increased demand for secure communications led the IETF to propose and then standardize an updated version of the Internet protocol called IPv6.

IPv6 (eye pee vee six) *abbr.* An update to the Internet protocol that addresses some of the shortcomings of the widely used IPv4. The four principal changes make the address space larger (64 bits from 32), simplify the packet header to streamline routing, support quality of service route selection, and strengthen authentication and privacy.

HISTORY: There was never a deployed IPv5.

IR (as letters) *abbr. See* infrared.

IRQ (as letters) *abbr.* The name for interrupt type on the PC. Short for Interrupt ReQuest.

irrational number *n.* Any number that cannot be expressed as a ratio of two integers.

EXAMPLE: e, π, and $\sqrt{2}$ are all irrational numbers.

ISA 1. *See* ISA bus.

2. *See* instruction set architecture.

ISA bus *n.* A 16-bit expansion bus popular in older PCs. *Compare to* PCI bus.

ISM (as letters) *abbr. See* Industrial, Scientific, and Medical band.

ISO (eye so) *abbr.* An international network of national standards institutes from over 100 countries. Short for the French equivalent of International Standards Organization. In the U.S., ANSI is an affiliate of ISO.

FURTHER READING: http://www.iso.org

ISO C *N.* The international standard version of the C programming language. Also called ANSI C in the U.S. *Contrast with* K&R C.

ISP (as letters) *abbr. See* in-system programming.

ISR (as letters) *abbr. See* interrupt service routine.

ISS (as letters) *abbr. See* instruction set simulator.

iterative development *See* incremental release.

ITU (as letters) *abbr.* An international organization where governments and the private sector coordinate global telecom networks and services. Short for International Telecommunication Union. The ITU is essentially a telecom standards body based in Geneva, Switzerland. *See also* CCITT.

FURTHER READING: http://www.itu.int

J

J2ME (as letters) *abbr. See* Java 2 Micro Edition.

J2SE (as letters) *abbr. See* Java 2 Standard Edition.

JAR (rhymes with car) *abbr.* A file containing one or more Java class files in a compressed format. Short for Java ARchive. The class loader in a Java virtual machine is capable of reading .jar files and dynamically linking and loading the classes within.

Java *N.* A high-level language created by James Gosling at Sun Microsystems. The Java programming language was originally envisioned for use in high-end embedded systems like PDAs and set-top boxes. However, its introduction coincided closely with the widespread adoption of the Internet. The language was quickly adopted by website designers, where it remains popular. The influence of the Web community can be felt in the current size of the class libraries, which have been subsetted to make their use possible in resource-constrained environments.

Java 2 Micro Edition *N.* A standardized set of Java class libraries and virtual machine features that provides a consistent programming platform for third-party developers targeting Java-enabled embedded systems. Abbreviated J2ME. Unlike desktop-oriented Java 2 Standard Edition, the components of J2ME were selected with consideration for the more limited resources common on typical embedded devices. Many components are optional, so that total memory space can be reduced, as required, to fit a particular platform. Still, J2ME is not exactly small by embedded systems standards. The smallest acceptable implemen-

tation of J2ME, called the Connected Limited Device Configuration, is on the order of 128 KB.

Java 2 Standard Edition *N.* A marketing name for a desktop-friendly set of standard class libraries for a standard Java virtual machine. Abbreviated J2SE. The Java 2 Micro Edition class libraries and virtual machine features are a (not quite proper) subset of the J2SE features. Today's J2SE can be thought of as an extension of the pre-1998 JDK (Java Development Kit) from Sun.

Java processor *N.* A piece of silicon, or IP, capable of executing Java bytecodes natively. When the Java programming language was created, there were no such processors. Therefore, the only way to execute Java code was with a Java virtual machine. Java processors, like those from aJile, make it possible to execute Java bytecodes without a JVM. An interesting side note: compilers exist to translate programs written in other languages, like C and C++, to Java bytecodes. So a Java processor—or a Java virtual machine—can execute code written in any high-level language.

Java virtual machine *N.* A piece of software that translates Java bytecodes into native opcodes and executes them. Abbreviated JVM. The bytecodes act as a portable binary format. In order to execute them on any platform, though, a JVM must be first be ported to the platform. However, the Java program need not be recompiled, thus making the Java executable highly portable.

JDK (as letters) *abbr.* A suite of tools and class libraries for developing Java programs. Short for Java Development Kit. The tool suite includes the Java class compiler (javac), the Java archiver (jar), and a virtual machine and set of class libraries compatible with the Java 2 Standard Edition spec. Versions of the JDK are available for Windows and Unix hosts.

Jeode　(like geode) *N.* An embeddable Java virtual machine from Insignia.

Jini　(genie) *N.* A layer of middleware that resides above a Java virtual machine and makes dynamic network structuring possible. With Jini, devices on the network can learn of existence and capability of services (such as printing) provided by other devices through a discovery protocol. Jini-enabled devices also provide their own drivers in the form of a set of Java bytecodes, which another device can run to use the services they provide. *See also* HAVi, UPnP.

JIT　(like the end of legit) *abbr. See* just-in-time compiler.

jitter　*n.* A dithering in time of a pulse or pulse train. Clock jitter is a tremendous problem in high-speed systems, where even 1 ns of jitter in a signal propagated all over a PCB can cause crashes.

An example of pulse jitter. The interarrival times are supposed to be the same; instead, they differ slightly from one pulse to the next.

JNI　(as letters) *abbr.* A standard way of interfacing Java and other high-level languages. Short for Java Native Interface. JNI is a set of calling conventions and parameter passing rules that makes it possible to declare so-called *native methods*, which are written in another language but called from Java. The full complement of JNI features also allows C or C++ code to create Java objects, invoke Java methods, and so on.

FURTHER READING: Liang, Sheng. *The Java Native Interface: Programmer's Guide and Specification.* Addison-Wesley, 1999.

job　*n.* Work to be done, in the scheduling context.

Johnson noise　*n.* Noise generated by thermal agitation of electrons in a conductor. Also called thermal noise.

The noise power is given as

$$P = kT\Delta f$$

where k is Boltzmann's constant, T is temperature in degrees Kelvin, and Δf is the bandwidth in hertz.

HISTORY: Named for J.B. Johnson who discovered thermal noise in resistors in 1928.

join pseudostate　*n.* A notational shorthand used in UML statecharts to combine two or more incoming state transitions into a single transition. Shown as a vertical bar with two or more transitions going into it and one coming out. Because a system can only be in one state within a given orthogonal region at any point in time, the transitions coming into the join pseudostate must each begin in distinct orthogonal regions. *Compare to* fork pseudostate.

Joint Test Access Group　*N.* A consortium of European electronics companies formed in 1985 to find a solution to the difficulty and expense of applying traditional bed-of-nails testing techniques to surface-mount ICs. Abbreviated JTAG. The result of this effort was the IEEE 1149.1 standard, which defined the so-called JTAG port. Their solution uses a testing technique called boundary scan.

Jolt　*N.* A highly caffeinated soft drink popular among programmers, particularly in their nocturnal formative years at university.

joule　*n.* A standard unit of work. Abbreviated J. One joule of work is a force of 1 newton acting over a distance of 1 meter.

HISTORY: Named for James Prescott Joule (1818–1889).

JRE (as letters) *abbr.* The JVM, class libraries, and supporting native methods required to run a Java program. Short for Java Runtime Environment. The JRE is what might be included in a Java-enabled browser. Compare to JDK.

JTAG (jay tag) *abbr.* A standard for providing external test access to integrated circuits serially, via a four- or five-pin external interface. Short for Joint Test Action Group, which developed the standard. The JTAG standard has been adopted as an IEEE standard (IEEE 1149 Standard Test Access Port and Boundary-Scan Architecture). JTAG ports have been widely embraced by processor manufacturers. Debug monitors and in-circuit emulators increasingly leverage the capabilities inherent in JTAG.

JTAG port *n.* A common name for the test access point defined in IEEE 1149.1.

jump *n.* A machine instruction that causes a transfer of control. Analogous to a goto statement in a high-level language. Also called a branch. Jumps are either conditional (taken if a flag is set or cleared) or unconditional (always taken).

EXAMPLE: Typical x86 jumps.

```
jmp  destination       : unconditional
jr   z, destination    : conditional
                       : (zero result?)
```

jump table *n.* An array of pointers to functions. A jump table is an efficient way to call one of several functions based on some input parameter. The input parameter is typically turned into an integer first, then used as an index into the array of function pointers. The address found there is the destination for the function call.

jumper *n.* A small piece of metal, usually within a plastic sheath, that is placed over a pair of pins to connect them electronically. By closing or open-

ing this electrical circuit, the jumper acts as a switch. Embedded software can make run-time decisions based on the user's attachment or removal of each jumper on a circuit board.

junction 1. *n.* The interface between an N- and a P-type of silicon on a diode, transistor, or other semiconductor.

2. *n.* The connection between two nodes on a schematic or in an electrical circuit.

junction pseudostate *n.* A notational shorthand for a grab-bag of miscellaneous transitions in a UML statechart. Drawn as a black dot. When all other pseudostates won't do what you want, use this one. With it, you can join two transitions from within the same concurrent region, which the join pseudostate doesn't allow. You can also use a junction to split one transition into two or more, assigning each to a different guard condition.

junction transistor *n.* A transistor made by growing P- and N-type material together on a single substrate. The junctions are the P–N interfaces. Junction transistors are thus named to differentiate them from point-contact transistors, the first type of transistor ever made. *See also* bipolar transistor.

just-in-time compiler *n.* An alternative execution engine for Java bytecodes that trades memory for increased efficiency. Abbreviated JIT. The concept behind a JIT is simple: instead of translating each bytecode into a native opcode again and again at each fetch (as an interpreter would), it translates whole methods the first time they are called and saves the results in RAM. Once the compile step is complete, the method will run more quickly. And any subsequent calls to that method won't even require the compile overhead.

There are a couple of noteworthy points to consider before choosing to replace your interpreter with a JIT. First, a JIT engine is a lot like a compiler and so needs RAM to run. Second, you'll wind up with most or all of your code stored both in ROM (as bytecodes) and RAM (as native opcodes). Third, if precompiled code is what you seek, you'd be far better off with an ahead-of-time compiler, which can make better code optimizations. And finally, a JIT is far less portable than an interpreter, so few JITs are commercially available.

That said, it has been shown that a JIT can improve the efficiency of executing Java bytecodes by a factor of 10 to 100, depending on properties of the code itself. That's certainly nothing to sneeze at, if you need additional performance.

JVM (as letters) *abbr. See* Java virtual machine.

k *See* kilo-.

K *n.* An old-style prefix or suffix meaning 1,024. As in, "This system has 128KB of memory." *See also* binary prefixes.

USAGE: We recommend against continued use of K, in favor of Ki.

kΩ (key-low-ohm) *abbr. See* kiloohm.

K&R (kay and aar) 1. *abbr.* Brian Kernighan and Dennis Ritchie, authors of the classic book, *The C Programming Language* (Prentice-Hall, 1978). 2. *N.* A common nickname for the book, *The C Programming Language.*

K&R C (K and R see) *N.* An early, pre-ANSI standard for the C programming language.

Kalman filter *n.* A tool for estimating the states of a linear system. Of all possible filters, it is the one that minimizes the variance of the estimation error.

A Kalman filter estimates the states **x** of a linear dynamic system defined by the equations

$$\mathbf{x}_{k+1} = A\mathbf{x}_k + B\mathbf{u}_k + \mathbf{w}_k$$

$$\mathbf{y}_k = C\mathbf{x}_k + \mathbf{z}_k$$

where A, B, and C are known matrices; $\mathbf{x}_k$ is the state of the system (a vector of quantities, unavailable for measurement) at time k; $\mathbf{u}_k$ is the known input vector to the system; $\mathbf{y}_k$ is the measured output vector; and $\mathbf{w}_k$ and $\mathbf{z}_k$ are noise vectors.

The filter equations are

$$K_k = AP_k C^T (CP_k C^T + S_z)^{-1}$$

$$\hat{x}_{k+1} = (A\hat{x}_k + Bu_k) + K_k(y_{k+1} - C\hat{x}_k)$$

$$P_{k+1} = AP_k A^T + S_w - AP_k C^T S_z CP_k A^T$$

where S_w and S_z are the covariance matrices of **w** and **z**, K is the Kalman gain, and P is the variance of the estimation error.

Kalman filters are often used in control systems where some or all of the desired feedback parameters are not observable by the processor. (In the equations, **y** is observable but **x** is not.) The Kalman filter is used to estimate those parameters mathematically so that the most appropriate control adjustments can be made. *See also* H-infinity filter.

HISTORY: Invented by Rudolf Kalman (1930–) circa 1959. Later used for spacecraft navigation and control in, among others, the Apollo missions.

FURTHER READING: Simon, Dan. "Kalman Filtering", *Embedded Systems Programming*, June 2001.

Karnaugh map *n.* A graphical method to simplify logic equations. *Contrast with* DeMorgan's theorem.

A Karnaugh map for the equation /abc + a/bc + ab/c + abc. Each 1 indicates a logical truth. This map helps us reduce the equation to bc + ac + ab.

		bc			
		00	01	11	10
a	0			1	
	1		1	1	1

kB (kilo-byte) *abbr. See* kilobyte.

kbit (kilobit) *abbr. See* kilobit.

kbps (as letters) *abbr.* One thousand bits per second.

kelvin *n.* A standard unit of temperature with a zero point of absolute zero. Abbreviated K. To convert a temperature in degrees Celsius to kelvin, simply add 273.15.

HISTORY: Named after William Thomson, Lord Kelvin (1824–1907).

kernel 1. *n.* A minimalist operating system.

2. *n.* The core of a microkernel architecture operating system like Mach.

3. *n.* An essential part of any real-time operating system, the kernel consists of the scheduler and context switch routine.

kernel mode *n.* A privileged CPU mode. Sometimes called supervisor mode. Parts of the operating system, such as the scheduler, device drivers, and the memory manager, usually execute in kernel mode, whereas application code executes in user mode. The transition from user mode to kernel mode is typically made somewhere inside an OS system call when a software interrupt instruction is executed.

Many of the statically linked single–memory space RTOSes used in embedded systems never place the processor into user mode. Thus, the threads running on top of such an RTOS can execute any CPU instruction, even those, such as disable interrupts, that could bring the RTOS to its knees.

Note that some processors support multiple levels of privilege, in what are then typically called protection rings. *Contrast with* user mode.

keyboard *n.* An input device typically arranged for the user to type alphanumeric strings. The keys can be arranged QWERTY-style or in some other layout. *Contrast with* keypad.

keypad *n.* Similar to a keyboard, but with fewer keys. Keypads are often function-driven, rather than alphabetic.

EXAMPLE: The input portion of a point-of-sale device like those commonly found at a gas station or grocery store.

keypress *n.* The user action that results in an event at the output of a keyboard or keypad. Individual keypresses are typically debounced within such an input device itself.

kHz (key-low-hurts) *abbr. See* kilohertz.

Ki (kay bee) *abbr. See* kibi-.

KiB (kay bee byte) *abbr. See* kibibyte.

kibi- (kay bee) *pre.* The prefix meaning 2^{10}. Abbreviated Ki. 1 kibibit:

- 1 Kibit = 1,024 bits
- 1 kibibyte: 1 KiB = 1,024 bytes

Note the arcane use of the lower case "k" in the name "kibi," but the use of capital "K" in the abbreviations. *See also* binary prefixes, kilo-.

kibibit (kay bee bit) *n.* 1,024 bits. Abbreviated Kibit. *See also* binary prefixes.

kibibyte (kay bee byte) *n.* 1,024 bytes. Abbreviated KiB. *See also* binary prefixes.

Kibit (kay bee bit) *abbr. See* kibibit.

kill *v.* To prematurely terminate a thread of execution. In Unix, any authorized user can kill any process by executing the `kill` command and providing the process ID as an argument. This translates into the POSIX system call `kill(pid, ...)`.

kilo- (key low) *pre.* The prefix meaning 10^3. Abbreviated k. 1 kilobit:

- 1 kbit = 1,000 bits
- 1 kilobyte: 1 kB = 1,000 bytes

The nearest power of two is 2^{10} (1,024), which is more correctly associated with prefix kibi-. *See also* decimal prefixes.

kilobit *n.* 1,000 bits. Abbreviated kbit. *See also* decimal prefixes.

kilobyte *n.* 1,000 bytes. Abbreviated kB. *See also* decimal prefixes.

kilogram *n.* A standard unit of mass. Abbreviated kg. As the only base unit with a prefix, note that this is the one case where the SI units differ from the standard form. (Perhaps it's the exception that proves the rule?) For consistency with other SI units, the gram would be the standard unit and 1 kg would be defined as 1,000 g.

kilohertz *n.* One thousand cycles per second. Abbreviated kHz.

kiloohm *n.* One thousand ohms. Abbreviated kΩ.

kilovolt *n.* One thousand volts. Abbreviated kV.

kilowatt *n.* One thousand watts. Abbreviated kW.

Kirchhoff's law *N.* Kirchhoff had two laws:

- Kirchhoff's Current Law: The current flowing into a node is the same as the current flowing out of that node.
- Kirchhoff's Voltage Law: The sum of all voltage drops around a closed circuit is zero.

These laws are used to analyze series and parallel circuits.

HISTORY: Named after Gustav Kirchhoff (1824–1887).

KLOCs (kay locks) *abbr.* A unit of measure of code complexity. Short for Thousand Lines Of Code. *See also* lines of code.

knob *n.* A round piece of plastic or metal on the shaft of a control (potentiometer, encoder, variable capacitor, etc.) used to spin the control.

Knuth, Donald *N.* An influential computer scientist, revered mostly for his five-volume opus, *The Art of Computer Programming*. Begun in 1962, volumes 1–3 have been out for a generation. The last two volumes are expected in 2007 and 2009, respectively. Also known for his inventions of TeX and Literate Programming.

kOhm *See* kiloohm.

kV (kilovolt) *abbr. See* kilovolt.

KVM (as letters) *abbr.* A modular, highly portable Java virtual machine designed for use in J2ME systems of the CLDC sort. Short for K Virtual Machine.

HISTORY: Some folks think the K stands for kilobyte; however, it actually stands for Kauai. We haven't been to the island of Java in the South Pacific but can highly recommend Hawaii's garden island Kauai.

FURTHER READING: http://www.netrino.com/Articles/SmallerJava/

kWh (kilo-watt-hour) *abbr.* 1000 watts of power for 1 hour. Kilowatt hours are the standard billing units for electricity delivery in the U.S.

L

L1 cache *n.* A zero–wait state cache located onboard the microprocessor. *See also* cache memory, L2 cache.

L2 cache *n.* A cache that requires a few wait states, located between the L1 cache and main memory (or L3 cache, if any). The sad fact is that processors are much faster than memory; main memory accesses in a PC require 50 to 100 wait states or more. Zero-wait cache is hugely expensive, so most desktop systems have a mix of L1, slower L2, and sometimes even slower L3 cache. *See also* cache memory, L1 cache.

LA (as letters) *abbr. See* logic analyzer.

label *n.* A human-readable alias for an address in memory. Labels are frequently used in assembly language programming, though they can also be used in higher level languages. For example, C supports direct branches to labels through its goto keyword.

In this code snippet, loop is a label. Note that the conditional branch on the second line refers to loop by name, not by the cryptic machine address of the prior instruction.

```
loop:  add  ax,  bx
       jr   z,   loop
```

lamp *n.* A device that illuminates. Sometimes broadly used to include semiconductors like LEDs, but more often it refers specifically to incandescent and fluorescent devices.

Schematic symbol of a lamp.

LAN (like man) *abbr. See* local area network.

language *n.* A way of expressing one's ideas in a way a computer can understand. Languages run from machine language—the 1s and 0s spoken by a processor's hardware—to assembly language—a human-readable form of the machine's dialect—to a vast number of high-level languages like C, C++, Java, Fortran, and hundreds more. *See also* high-level language, machine language, assembly language.

large-scale integration *n.* A qualitative description of the complexity of an IC. Abbreviated LSI. Typically refers to parts with thousands to billions of transistors. *Contrast with* small-scale integration, medium-scale integration.

latch 1. *n.* A logic device that remembers its input at the time clock transitions. Latches can handle a single bit or a group of bits in parallel.

2. *v.* To capture the logical state of a bit or bits for later reference, via any hardware mechanism.

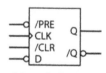

Schematic diagram of the ubiquitous 7474 latch.

latchup *See* SCR latchup.

latency *n.* The time between an event occurring and the beginning of a response.

EXAMPLE: Software people frequently use this term to denote the time between an interrupt arriving and the associated ISR starting. Chip vendors prefer to define interrupt latency as the longest instruction that cannot be interrupted.

layout *n.* The design of a printed circuit board expressed in the placement of it parts, tracks, and vias. The layout consists of many pages, each representing one part of the board. These include: top side tracks; bottom side tracks; silkscreen; drill drawing; various inner layers including tracks, ground, power; and more.

LCD (as letters) *abbr. See* liquid crystal display.

LCD controller *n.* An integrated circuit that drives LCD displays. LCD controllers come in many varieties, from those that handle a few discrete digits, as on a digital voltmeter, to drivers for graphics panels. All LCD displays are arranged in a matrix configuration, which the LCD controller refreshes by constantly cycling its outputs.

LCD controllers also generally create the bias voltages required by the displays and include internal character generators to convert applied ASCII data to the bit pattern that yields a readable character.

ld *See* binutils.

lead pitch *n.* The distance between adjacent pins on a surface-mount IC. A lead pitch of .025 inches or smaller means that anyone who drinks coffee cannot probe the part.

The p dimension is the lead pitch of the part.

lead-acid battery *n.* A type of rechargeable battery used in applications that can tolerate their heavy weight and liquid chemicals. Lead–acid batteries offer an attractive discharge curve (a knee where the voltage stays almost constant until the battery reaches deep levels of discharge) and are easily recharged. Available in massive amp-hour ratings, but even small versions are very heavy. Sealed lead–acid batteries will not drip or leak and can be mounted in any position.

leakage current *n.* Any unwanted current flow in a semiconductor. For instance, although the gate-to-drain impedance on a CMOS part is extremely high, tiny leakage currents do exist. When multiplied by millions of transistors on one die, these currents generate harmful amounts of waste heat.

least significant bit *n.* The bit at the rightmost end of a binary value. Abbreviated LSb. In an unsigned value, the LSb represents the 2^0 term. In a signed representation like two's complement, the LSb is that same bit (in the zeroth position), though its meaning will differ based on the sign of the larger word.

least significant byte *n.* The low-order byte of a multibyte field. Abbreviated LSB. The least significant byte comprises the two hexadecimal digits at the right end of the value. The content of that byte can be extracted, in C, by performing either `% 256` or `& 0x00FF`.

least squares curve fitting *n.* A way of fitting a polynomial to observed data. Suppose you want to build a device to measure the amount of protein in a sample of grain. There's a complicated relationship between protein content and the amount of IR light reflected from the grain at dozens of frequencies. Unfortunately, the relationship isn't well understood, so no simple algorithm exists to predict protein content. Instead, instrumentation vendors calibrate each machine by reading hundreds of grain samples with known protein levels, then doing a least squares curve fit to determine the coefficients of a polynomial that matches the observed IR radiation to known protein contents. The resulting polynomial can then predict the protein content of unknown samples.

least squares error *n.* One of a number of methods of qualifying a system's errors.

The least squares error for a data series is

$$\frac{\Sigma(X_m - X_a)^2}{n}$$

where X_m is the measured data and X_a is its actual value. The number of data points is n.

LED (as letters) *abbr. See* light-emitting diode.

LED blinker *n.* Firmware that turns an LED on and off at some steady rate, such as 1 Hz. Also called das blinkenlights.

FURTHER READING: Barr, Michael. *Programming Embedded Systems in C and C++*. O'Reilly & Associates, 1999.

LED display 1. *n.* A 7-segment display or other output device based on LED technology.

2. *n.* A visual output device comprising a rectangular grid of LEDs, some of which are on and others off. You've almost certainly seen these used to create scrolling news or stock tickers, though those are generally much larger than the ones used in most embedded systems.

LED driver *n.* A small electrical circuit, typically consisting of a DC voltage source and a resistor, that drives an LED.

left justify *v.* To shift the contents of a byte, word, or other storage unit all the way to the left. *Contrast with* right justify.

EXAMPLE: If you left justify the ASCII character A (0x41) in a word, you get 0x4100.

left shift *v.* To move or rotate the bits in a byte or word from LSb to MSb. *See also* <<.

left-hand rule *n.* What an electromagnetics professor inevitably sees one student applying with gusto during the final exam. *See* right hand rule.

legacy code *n.* Software from a prior product or era that is made part of a new design.

level 7 interrupt *n.* Motorola's name for a non-maskable interrupt on 68k-series processors. So named because it was the highest level interrupt of a possible eight, numbered 0 through 7.

level-sensitive input *n.* A processor input that responds only to a logic 1 signal level. *Contrast with* edge-sensitive input.

lex 1. *N.* A tool for generating lexical scanners that is provided standard with most Unix installations. The programmer provides a text file containing rules for recognizing tokens in an input stream of ASCII characters. The lex tool reads that file and outputs C or C++ code that implements such a scanner. When the scanner is run on an input stream, the series of tokens it finds are output to the application for parsing. *See also* yacc.

2. *v.* To scan input data lexically, turning it into a series of tokens.

LFSR (as letters) *abbr. See* linear feedback shift register.

LGPL (as letters) *abbr. See* GNU Lesser General Public License.

library *n.* Any package of software routines. The most commonly used library is the run-time library supplied with the compiler, along with a collection of object modules created by the programmer and bound together with a library manager. A tool called an archiver can be used to create and examine libraries, which constitute a set of individual object files. *See also* dynamically linked library.

life cycle *n.* The entire time domain, use, application, and management of a software product. Unfortunately often neglected by programmers, a product's life cycle can involve costs far outstripping the original development investments. Maintenance and feature enhancements can go on for decades, especially for embedded projects.

LIFO (lie-foe) *abbr.* A type of queue that is sorted so that the latest addition will be the next item removed. In that sense, it is similar to a stack. Short for Last In, First Out. *Contrast with* FIFO.

light-emitting diode *n.* A semiconductor device that radiates light when activated. Abbreviated LED. When a voltage is applied to the LED, electrons can move easily in only one direction across the junction between the P and N regions.

In the P region, there are many more positive than negative charges, whereas in the N region, the electrons are more numerous than the positive electric charges. When a voltage is applied, electrons in the N region have sufficient energy to move across the

Schematic symbol for an LED.

junction into the P region. Once in the P region, the electrons are immediately attracted to the positive charges because of the mutual coulomb forces of attraction between opposite electric charges. When an electron moves sufficiently close to a positive charge in the P region, the two charges recombine.

Each time an electron recombines with a positive charge, electric potential energy is converted into electromagnetic energy. For each recombination of a negative and a positive charge, a quantum of electromagnetic energy is emitted in the form of a photon of light, with a frequency characteristic of the semiconductor material.

lightweight process 1. *n.* A process with a thread of execution but no separate memory space. Abbreviated LWP in Solaris. *See also* thread.

2. *n.* A software development process that's easy to implement, not onerous. Some process changes, such as those mandated by ISO 9000, are difficult to implement within an organization. The Personal Software Process, on the other hand, is lightweight. Both can lead to better software.

limit switch *n.* A switch activated when a moving mechanism reaches its end of travel. The switch tells the software (or hardware in high-reliability systems) to stop moving the device.

line driver *n.* A hardware component—generally an IC—that transmits digital signals over long distances. Without line drivers, digital signals from logic components are reliable over distances of mere inches. Conventional components cannot drive the highly capacitive cables used in connecting different systems. Often it makes sense to send this data differentially to reduce noise susceptibility; only a specialized part can do this.

line feed *n.* An ASCII character that, in the era of the mechanical Teletype, advanced the platen one line without causing a carriage return. Abbreviated LF. ASCII 0x0A.

linear 1. *n.* A polynomial equation of the first degree. Linear equations combine constants and variables without exponents. The equation of a line ($y = mx + b$) is the quintessential linear function.

2. *adj.* A term used to describe analog parts and circuits, such as op-amps.

linear amplifier *n.* Any amplifier that multiplies its input by a constant. Although linear amplifiers might seem to be distortionless, in fact, only class A amplifiers are. Other variants can, for efficiency's sake, drastically alter the signal. Class B amplifiers, for example, essentially clip off all negative excursions of the signal.

linear circuit 1. *n.* An analog circuit with output of the form

$$output = offset + constant \times input$$

2. *n.* Often used to mean any analog circuit, whether it has a linear transfer function or not.

linear feedback shift register *n.* A hardware device used to implement modulo 2 binary division, generally to create CRCs. *See also* modulo-2 binary division, cyclic redundancy code.

linear interpolation *n.* A way to estimate a data point that lies between two known values by drawing a straight line through all three points. *See also* piecewise linear interpolation.

An example of linear interpolation.

EXAMPLE: In the figure, suppose you know data pairs (x_1, y_1), and (x_2, y_2). To find (x, y):

$$(y - y_1)/(y_2 - y_1) = (x - x_1)/(x_2 - x_1)$$

Solving for y gives

$$y = y_1 + (x - x_1)(y_2 - y_1)/(x_2 - x_1)$$

linear predictive coding *n.* A powerful speech analysis technique, and one of the most useful methods for encoding good quality speech at a low bit rate. Abbreviated LPC. LPC provides extremely accurate estimates of speech parameters and is relatively efficient computationally.

LPC assumes that the speech signal is produced by a buzzer at the end of a tube. The glottis (the space between the vocal cords) produces the buzz, which is characterized by its intensity (loudness) and frequency (pitch). The vocal tract (the throat and mouth) forms the tube, which is characterized by its resonances, called formants.

LPC analyzes the speech signal by estimating the formants, removing their effects from the speech signal, and estimating the intensity and frequency of the remaining buzz. The process of removing the formants is called inverse filtering, and the remaining signal is called the residue.

The numbers that describe the formants and the residue can be stored or transmitted somewhere else. LPC synthesizes the speech signal by reversing the process: use the residue to create a source signal, use the formants to create a filter (which represents the tube), and run the source through the filter, resulting in speech.

Because speech signals vary with time, this process is done on short chunks of the speech signal, which are called frames. Usually 30 to 50 frames per second give intelligible speech with good compression.

linear regulator *n.* A DC-DC converter that produces an output voltage smaller than the input voltage. The LM78xx series is one of the most popular choices. For example, the three-pin LM7805 can produce a 5-V output from any DC input in the 7- to 25-V range, and it is easy to use.

linear system *n.* Any system with the transfer function

$$\text{output} = \text{offset} + \text{constant} \times \text{input}$$

The constant multiplier is the system's gain.

lines of code *n.* The total number of lines in all the source code files that make up a module or application of interest. Abbreviated LOCs. The number of lines of code provides some rough information about the relative complexity of one piece of software versus another and is, therefore, used by technical managers for planning and analysis purposes. The cost of a project per LOC is another controversial metric. *See also* KLOCs, significant lines of code.

link layer *See* data link layer.

linker *n.* A software development tool that accepts one or more object files as input and outputs a relocatable program. The linker is thus run after all of the source files have been compiled and assembled into object files. See figure.

linker/locator *n.* A single tool that includes the functions of both a linker and a locator.

lint 1. *n.* A software development tool used to check C and C++ programs for error-prone syntactical constructs. The C and C++ language standards are loosely written. Plenty of run-time details, such as the actual size of an int, are left up to compiler implementers. Lint can help you find dangerous and nonportable constructs in your

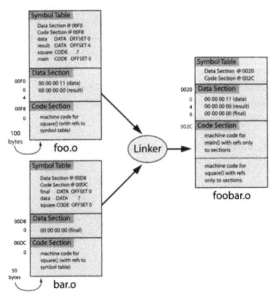

linker A simplified example of how the linker resolves references across symbol tables and combines the code and data sections.

code before a compiler turns them into run-time bugs.

2. *n.* The error-prone syntactical constructs that the lint tool finds in C and C++ programs. A program that passes through the lint tool without generating any warnings is termed "lint-free."

Linux *n.* A GNU-based Unix-like open source operating system, the kernel for which was developed by Linus Torvalds.

Linux/RT *n.* A real-time operating system based on Linux. A trademark of TimeSys.

Linux/RT is somewhat different from the typical real-time Linux, because it's not based on a small real-time kernel running below a standard Linux kernel. Instead, the Linux kernel has been modified to support higher timer resolutions, priority inheritance, and preemptive priority-based scheduling. These modifications are collectively termed the "resource kernel." *Contrast with* RTAI.

liquid crystal display *n.* A graphical or numerical display made from liquid crystals. Abbreviated LCD. Liquid crystals are in a state somewhere between a pure liquid and a pure solid. The crystals are nematic, or twisted around each other. A display has these crystals held in suspension between two pieces of polarized glass. In their nematic state, the crystals block light transmission. Applying an electric field untwists the crystals, blocking the transmitted light.

Small LCDs are cheap, reliable, and require almost no power, making them ideal for a wide range of embedded applications. They are quite sensitive to temperature and, being polarized, lead to problems in some applications. As you pump gas while wearing polarized sunglasses, twist your head as you view the pump's LCD display—the numbers will disappear unless the polarization angles of the sunglasses and LCD line up.

FURTHER READING: http://www.howstuffworks.com/lcd1.htm

Liskov substitution principle *n.* One of the most general laws of generalization. Abbreviated LSP. In its traditional formulation for classes, LSP requires that a subclass can be freely substituted for its superclass. This means that every instance of the subclass should be compatible with the instance of the superclass and that any code designed to work with the instance of the superclass should continue to work correctly if an instance of the subclass is used instead. LSP can be naturally extended to apply to hierarchical states in hierarchical state machines.

LSP is a general law applicable to any specialization/generalization hierarchy, including the hierarchy of states in hierarchical state machines (HSMs). LSP generalized for hierarchical states means that the behavior of a substate should be consistent with the superstate. For example, all states nested inside the heating state of the toaster oven, (e.g., toasting or baking) should share the same basic characteristics of the heating state. In particular, if being in the heating state means that the heater is turned on, then none of the substates should turn the heater off (without transitioning out of the heating state). Turning the heater off and staying in the toasting or baking states would be inconsistent with being in the heating state and would indicate poor design (violation of the LSP).

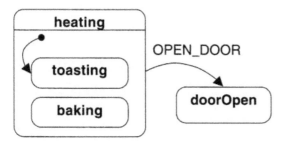

The state model of a simple toaster-oven in which states toasting and baking share the common transition from state heating to doorOpen.

Compliance with the LSP allows you to build better (more correct) state hierarchies and make efficient use of abstraction. For example, in an LSP-compliant state hierarchy, you can safely zoom out and work at the higher level of the heating state (thus abstracting away the specifics of toasting and baking). As long as all the substates are consistent with their superstate, such abstraction is meaningful. On the other hand, if the substates violate basic assumptions of being in the superstate, zooming out and ignoring specifics of the substates will be incorrect.

listen-before-transmit *adj*. Said of a communications protocol that demands that all transmitters check for ongoing transmissions before seizing the channel for themselves. Of course, even if all transmitters listen before starting, there is still a chance that multiple transmitters will collide—just as two humans might both begin to fill a silence simultaneously during a phone call. Collision detection and a backoff strategy must also be employed to work around that problem.

lithium battery *n*. A type of battery often found in embedded systems that offers high energy density and extraordinary shelf life. Lithium batteries work well over an extreme of temperatures and are lightweight. They come in a variety of chemical formulations, each offering its own trade-offs. Lithium batteries are often used as backups for RAM memories, a la NVRAM.

little-endian *adj*. A data representation for a multi-byte value that has the least significant byte stored at the lowest memory address. Note that only the bytes are reordered, never the nibbles or bits that comprise them. Every processor stores its data in either big-endian or little-endian format. Intel's 80x86 family is little-endian.

EXAMPLE: If the 32-bit value 0x12345678 is located at address 1000 in memory, its least significant byte, 0x78, would be found at location 1000. Location 1001 would contain the next least significant byte, 0x56; location 1002 would contain 0x34; and location 1003 would contain the most significant byte, 0x12.

```
char    c1=1;                Offset:    Memory dump
char    c2=2;                0x0000:    01 02 FF 00
short   s=255;   //0x00FF    0x0004:    11 22 33 44
long    l=0x44332211;
```

A little-endian memory dump.

ln (natural log) *abbr*. The natural logarithm, $\log_e$. *See also* log.

load 1. *v*. To move data from memory into a processor register.

USAGE: Use of this term tends to be restricted to RISC processors, on which the only way to read memory is to execute a load instruction.

2. *v*. To download a relocatable or executable module to a target system. If the downloaded code is relocatable, the receiver must be capable of assigning fixed addresses like a locator tool. In this case, the term loader is used. 3. *n*. A component or circuit that dissipates power. Loads are resistive

and/or reactive devices through which current flows. *See also* capacitive load.

load–store architecture *n.* A computer design that manipulates data via registers, and not directly in memory. Load–store machines avoid instructions like

```
add    [mem1], [mem2]   ; [mem2]<-[mem1]+[mem2]
```

in favor of

```
load   [mem1], r1        ; r1<-[mem1]
load   [mem2], r2        ; r2<-[mem2]
add    r1, r2, r2        ; r2<-r1+r2
store  r2, [mem2]        ; [mem2]<-r2
```

Typical of RISC machines, the load–store architecture leads to simpler (therefore faster) hardware designs, but larger program sizes.

loader *n.* A piece of software—often part of the operating system—that relocates code as a new thread is spawned. In most embedded systems, the application threads and the OS are statically linked together and assigned physical addresses via a locator instead.

local *See* local variable.

local area network *n.* A network that connects together individual computers and networked embedded systems within a room, floor, or building. Abbreviated LAN. An entire LAN will typically run the same physical layer protocol, such as Ethernet, Token Ring, or 802.11b. These are then connected together via devices called gateways. *See also* personal area network.

local variable *n.* A variable declared within a function and having a lifetime equal to the length of the function call. Also called an automatic variable, since its storage is created automatically on the call stack as the function is invoked. *Contrast with* global variable.

localhost *n.* A shorthand name for the system on which a TCP/IP protocol stack is running. The localhost name is automatically mapped to reserved IP address 127.0.0.1. Inside the IP layer of the protocol stack, this address should be recognized as a fake destination. Rather than send the packet out over the network interface, it is simply routed back up the stack on the local system. The intended receiver is assumed to be a port on the localhost.

locality of reference *n.* An observation that the very next code or data needed by a system is highly likely to be close to the code or data most recently accessed. Think of locality of reference as the 80/20 rule for running software. It's the reason that caches work so well to reduce average memory access times. If there were no locality of reference and the location of the next access was completely random, the likelihood of a cache hit would be directly proportional to the cache size divided by total memory size.

locator *n.* A software development tool that assigns physical addresses to a relocatable program. This is the last step in preparing software for execution by an embedded system. The resulting file is called an executable. In some cases, the locator's functionality is built into the linker. In others, the operating system might include a loader, which performs the location step. See figure.

lock-in *n.* An interlock placed on a mode of operation that makes it difficult for the user to change the mode of the system. Often used when there is a risk involved in leaving that mode of operation. Once a life-critical lung ventilator has accepted settings and started to deliver breaths, it is good practice to provide no user settings or menus that allow the device to leave breathing mode. If the user wants to start over, or enter another mode (e.g., for service), then the user is forced to turn the device off first. *See also* lock-out.

lock-out *n.* An interlock that makes it difficult to return to a certain mode once the user has left that mode of operation. Some pneumatic systems

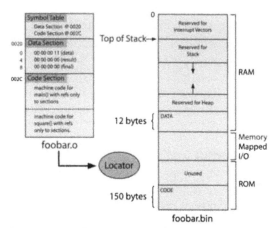

locator A simplified example of how the locator assigns code and data to specific physical memory ranges and adds (uninitialized) stack and heap sections. Not shown is that the initialized data must be stored in ROM and copied out into RAM by the startup code.

have a safety valve that opens if the pressure exceeds the expected limits. To ensure that continued operation is safe, the device will not attempt to pressurize again until a user has pressed a reset key. In more extreme cases, a set of diagnostic self-tests are required before the device can be returned to service. *See also* lock-in.

LOCs (locks) *abbr. See* lines of code.

log (where a bump belongs) *abbr.* Short for logarithm. If b = 10ª, then a is the log base 10 of b. More generally,

$$\log_x b = a \text{ if } b = x^a$$

Base 10 and base 2 logs are common in the computer world. Any $\log_{10}$ is abbreviated simply "log." A $\log_2$ (or any other base) is never abbreviated. The natural log, $\log_e$, is abbreviated "ln."

Before there were calculators, logs and the related tables and slide rules were important mathematical tools. Today, they're used in embedded systems to compress input data ranges, among other things.

logarithmic scale *n.* A graph or other method of mensuration that has one or more of its axes calibrated logarithmically. Log scales compress data that grows rapidly.

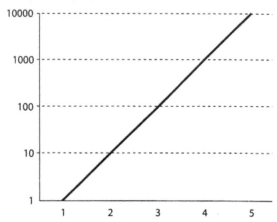

A graph with a log scale on the vertical axis. On this scale, the data is a straight line, which shows that it grows logarithmically. On a linear scale, the same data would produce a very steep curve.

logging *v.* The act of recording data for later analysis. An entire class of instruments called data loggers do nothing more than record data (e.g., temperature data in the Arctic). Wise developers put logging routines in their code to record program behavior; the log is then a clear record of what happened when.

logic 1. *n.* The underpinnings of Vulcan culture.

2. *n.* A set of rules defining the behavior of digital systems.

3. *n.* A group of interconnected digital components.

4. *n.* The workings of an algorithm.

logic 0 *n.* The maximum voltage representing a binary 0 for a particular logic family.

EXAMPLE: Five-volt TTL logic (including most CMOS variants) define a logic 0 (for inputs) as a signal under 0.8 V.

logic 1 *n.* The minimum voltage representing a binary 1 for a particular logic family.

EXAMPLE: Five-volt TTL logic (including most CMOS variants) define a logic 1 (for inputs) as a signal greater than 2 V. RCA's CD4000 family used 4 V.

logic analyzer *n.* A hardware debugging tool that can capture and display the logic levels (0 or 1) of dozens, or even hundreds, of electrical signals as they occur. Logic analyzers can be quite helpful for debugging hardware problems and complex processor–peripheral interactions. They are primarily characterized by their capture memory depth and width and by their acquisition speed.

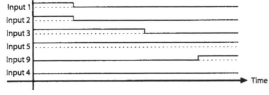

A typical logic analyzer display showing the logic levels of a selected set of inputs over time.

logic error *n.* A bug resulting from a mistake in (typically complex) binary logic.

logic family *n.* A group of digital components with similar electrical parameters. Members of a particular logic family have common logic levels and interconnect with minimal electrical issues.

EXAMPLE: All members of the 74LS family are bipolar and have similar fan-in and fan-out characteristics. 74HC components, however, are CMOS and electrically quite different.

logic gate *n.* Any combinatorial logic component, such as an AND, OR, NOT or XOR gate. *See also* combinatorial logic.

logic levels *n.* The voltage levels that define a 1 and a 0 for a particular logic family.

EXAMPLE: Five-volt TTL logic (including most CMOS variants) define a logic 1 (for inputs) as a

signal greater than 2 V. A logic 0 is a signal under 0.8 V. However, gates generally do better than this to increase noise margins; bipolar gates produce 2.4 V or more for logic 1.

logic minimization *n.* The process of simplifying a digital circuit or other manifestation of a Boolean equation. The easiest way to create a logic circuit is to extract all TRUE values from a truth table and write Boolean terms for them, ORing each. This is also the least efficient, leading to a circuit that works but wastes gates. Karnaugh maps, DeMorgan's theorem, and other strategies can minimize the logic, giving a more cost-effective solution. *See also* Karnaugh map, DeMorgan's theorem.

logic probe *n.* A simple and inexpensive piece of test equipment that senses logic states. Features of logic probes vary, but most indicate steady 1s and 0s, as well as pulse trains. Generally, a visual or audible output will qualitatively indicate a pulse train's duty cycle.

logical address *n.* An address generated by the processor before translation by virtual memory or memory management units. *Contrast with* physical address.

lone guru *n.* A programming wizard, perhaps with a foot-long beard, Harley-Davidson shirt stretched over an ample pot belly, and attitude to match. Sometimes respected, always feared, and never managed, these are the folks destined to destroy huge software projects by their lack of design rigor or implementation discipline. *See also* bus.

long *res.* A primitive data type for declaring large integers in C and several related languages. In C and C++, the size of a long varies across processors and compilers. The only requirement is that a long be at least 32 bits wide. In Java, a long is always 64 bits.

long double *res.* An extended precision floating-point data type. *See also* double.

long long *res.* An integer type at least 64 bits in width.

lookup table *n.* A program construct used to translate an input to an output. Abbreviated LUT. Lookup tables are usually organized as lists of entries in successive memory locations. An associated driver routine takes an input and hashes into the table, extracting the translated output.

Lookup tables are fast to code and execute quickly. They tend to burn up a lot of table space, though, and hence ROM memory. *See also* interpolation. See listing.

lookup table A lookup table and driver that returns elements of the Fibonacci series.

```
; Lookup table of part of the
; Fibonacci Series
table:   db   1
         db   1
         db   2
         db   3
         db   5
         db   8
         db   13
;
; Return Fibonacci series element n,
; where n is passed in de.
; Result comes back in a.
get_fib:
   ld   hl,table
   add  hl, de  ; index into the table
   ld   a, (hl) ; get Fibonacci entry
   ret
```

EXAMPLE: One way to compute an integer cosine is to store every possible value of $\cos(x)$ in a lookup table. A driver takes x and indexes into the table to find $\cos(x)$. An alternative that saves memory is to store a subset of all possible values of $\cos(x)$ and to interpolate between adjacent values.

loop *n.* A portion of a program that repeats. Two general classes of loops are those that loop forever (infinite loops) and those that complete after some period of time.

A busy-waiting loop that idles until some other task sets busy true.

```
while (busy);
```

loop combining *n.* A compiler optimization that detects whether two nested loops use the same number of iterations and, if so, combines them into a single loop. By combining them, loop start/end code can be eliminated. This is a rare example of an optimization that both reduces code size and execution time. *See also* loop unwinding.

loop unrolling *See* loop unwinding.

loop unwinding *n.* A compiler optimization that replaces code loops with the same number of copies of the code inside the loop. The optimization is based on the observation that loops, such as C's for() construct, have tremendous overhead at the start and end of each pass. Many of the comparisons and/or conditional jumps can be eliminated by substituting a sequence of copies of the loop's internal code.

Of course, this can only be done if the loop will execute a fixed number of times (known at compile time), such as

```
for (i = 0; i < 4; i++)
```

It also might not be practical to unwind loops that are executed more than a handful of times because of the increased code size that results.

low *n.* The voltage, typically zero, associated with a logic 0. A signal is typically pulled low via connection to ground through a pulldown resistor. *Contrast with* high.

low-level language *n.* A programming language that lacks some or all of the features of high-level languages.

USAGE: Technically speaking, there is no such thing as a low-level language. You can program in either a high-level language or assembly.

HISTORY: In the introduction to their book, K&R termed C "a relatively 'low-level' high-level language." They went on to state this meant "that C deals with the same sort of objects that most computers do, namely characters, numbers, and addresses."

low-order *adj.* Least significant.

EXAMPLE: The low-order byte of a word is the least significant byte. The low-order bit is the least significant bit.

low-power *adj.* A qualitative term that indicates a device or circuit uses very little electrical power. This term is vague. Today's MP3 players run for 48 hours on two batteries and are considered low power, as are vibration analyzers that run for 2 years from a single AA cell. Generally speaking, low-power circuits are CMOS based and run at low voltages (1 to 3 V).

low-skew routing resources *n.* Special routes in an FPGA that offer a guaranteed maximum skew between any two flip-flops within a certain domain inside the chip. For a design that requires many different clock sources, low-skew routing resources can become precious commodities.

lowpass filter *n.* A digital or analog filter that allows only low-frequency components of the input sig-nal to pass to the output. In theory, a lowpass filter removes frequency components above some threshold frequency completely and allows the components below that threshold to pass through unchanged. In practice, however, the high-frequency components are merely highly attenuated, the low-frequency components might have their magnitude or phase slightly changed, and the cut-off occurs more gradually over a range of threshold frequencies. *Compare to* highpass filter, bandpass filter.

LPC (as letters) *abbr. See* linear predictive coding.

LSB (as letters) *abbr. See* least significant byte.

LSb (as letters) *abbr. See* least significant bit.

LSI (as letters) *abbr. See* large-scale integration.

LUT (rhymes with nut) 1. *abbr. See* lookup table.

2. *n.* A logic block within certain FPGA architectures. Each LUT acts like a mini-ROM, performing a set logic function like an AND, OR, NAND, etc. *See also* configurable logic block.

LynxOS *N.* A popular POSIX-compliant real-time operating system. Prior to the emergence of embedded Linux, LynxOS was the closest thing to a real-time embeddable Unix.

M *See* mega-.

mΩ (milliohm) *abbr. See* milliohm.

MΩ (megaohm) *abbr. See* megaohm.

M/M/1 queue (em em one cue) *n.* The simplest statistical queueing model. The first M is for memoryless arrival time. The second M is for memoryless service time. The 1 refers to the fact that there is just one queue and one servicer of messages. In plain English then, this model describes queues that see messages arrive at times independent of each other and receive messages that have processing times independent of those previously processed. Such queues are the easiest to analyze.

FURTHER READING: Kalinsky, David. "How to Size Message Queues," *Embedded Systems Programming,* May 2003.

mA (milliamp) *abbr. See* milliamp.

MAC (like the truck) 1. *abbr. See* multiply-and-accumulate.

2. *See* MAC address.

MAC address *n.* A globally unique 48-bit hardware address assigned to each device on a network. Every system on a physical network, like Ethernet or Token Ring, includes a peripheral called a network controller. This chip is the processor's interface to the physical communications medium. As part of its initialization, the network controller must be fed a unique hardware address to use when communicating over the network. In the case of Ethernet, the hardware address is a 48-bit value. To guarantee global uniqueness, the upper 24 bits are controlled by the IEEE, which allocates them to individual device manufacturers. See OUI for more information about obtaining a block of Ethernet addresses for your company.

FURTHER READING: http://www.netrino.com/Connecting/2000-06/

machine language *n.* The very low level native language of a computer. Machine language is mostly incomprehensible to humans. Assemblers convert people-friendly (or at least, friendlier) mnemonics (like ADD) into the appropriate binary equivalent. Compilers convert a high-level language program into machine code so that it can be executed on a specific target processor.

macro 1. *n.* A set of assembler or high-level language statements that can be invoked by a single word or phrase in the source code. Macros reduce typing and usually increase readability by expressing commonly used ideas in a single statement. An assembler, preprocessor, or compiler expands each macro invocation into the proper source statements via string substitution and then converts these to machine language.

Macros always allow the user to substitute parameters that pass data to the macro that is then included in the macro expansion.

2. *n.* In C and C++, any specific macro created with the #define and expanded by the preprocessor.

```
#define SQUARE(x) ((x) * (x))   // square x

int main()
{
  return (SQUARE(13));
}
```

macro assembler *n.* A program that translates assembly language mnemonics to machine language and handles user-defined macros.

HISTORY: Today, the term "macro assembler" is redundant, since all assemblers support macros. But in the dawn of the embedded age, during the 1970s and early 1980s, assemblers were limited, often error-ridden products that could barely translate a standard mnemonic to hex. It's hard to believe, but the earliest microprocessor assemblers punched paper tape as mass storage at the breathtaking rate of 10 cps.

macrocell *n.* A subunit of a programmable logic device that can be configured in many different ways. Macrocells are common in FPGAs, PLDs, and GALs. On a GAL, a macrocell is the output block, which can be programmed to be either registered or unregistered. More complex devices are often an array of macrocells with characteristics that are set by the developer. The macrocells are interconnected by a vast matrix of gates. *See also* generic array logic, field-programmable gate array.

magic number 1. *n.* A numerical value saved in memory to provide an additional integrity check. Many checksum algorithms will find a valid checksum for a set of data that consists entirely of zeros. Confirming that a nonzero magic number is present in the data in the proper location and that the checksum is valid provides an additional assurance that the data set has not been corrupted or erased.

2. *n.* A seemingly arbitrary number that's needed to initialize a peripheral. This kind of magic number often has its origin in the tendency of programmers, as a group, not to document their work. The proper practice is to make the meaning of the number (or its subparts) clear through the code or comments, referring to a databook if necessary.

magnet *n.* A device that has a magnetic field. Usually used to describe a device that is specifically used to attract or repel ferrous substances or other magnetically charged devices. However, many electronic components are magnetic, from the ferrous oxide that coats a disk platter to inductors and transformers.

Because all electromagnetic fields have orthogonal electric and magnetic components, even signals radiated from a circuit board are magnetic. To protect very sensitive analog front ends from interference from these fields, designers often enclose the analog portion in a mu-metal box that is mostly impervious to the magnetic field.

magnetic field *n.* A field of energy radiating from any moving charge or magnetic dipole. Electricity and magnetism do not exist in isolation; they are intrinsically coupled by the laws of physics described by Maxwell's equations. The magnetic field is oriented 90 degrees to the electrical field. *See also* magnet, electromagnetics.

magnetic lines of force *n.* A convenient way to visualize magnetic field patterns. There are no actual lines of force; Maxwell's laws show that field strength varies continuously, not discretely. Still, it's convenient to draw lines of force to show the direction of the field. The direction of the magnetic field is tangent to the line of force at a particular point.

To observe something approximating these lines, many high school science students experiment with bar magnets and iron filings. You probably did this yourself. If not, check out the simulation at http://micro.magnet.fsu.edu/electromag/java/magneticlines/.

magnitude response *See* amplitude response.

mailbox *See* message queue.

main( ) *fn.* The nominal starting point for a C/C++ program. Of course, embedded systems programmers realize that additional code, such as hardware initialization and C startup code, must be executed prior to the call to main. main( ) is where the C code itself begins.

main+ISR *See* foreground/background system.

mainframe *n.* The quintessential computer of science fiction movies, the mainframe is a physically large computer that traditionally offered vast computational power. Sometimes called big iron. Although modern computing relies on distributed networks of workstations, each of which far outstrips old mainframes in power, mainframes are still sold by outfits like IBM and are still used for some gigantic applications like airline reservation systems. Some of today's embedded systems have more computing power than the mainframes of the 1960s and 1970s.

mainline code *n.* Software executed from main( ) or a thread. The term is used to distinguish such code from an interrupt service routine, as in, "The PID controller's outputs are recalculated within the mainline code."

make 1. *adj.* Describes a program that uses a text file to designate the relationships between all source and object files in a project and compiles, assembles, links, and locates the final product. A make utility checks the time stamp of each input file to see which have changed since the last build and then reassembles/recompiles only the changed modules.

2. *n.* The process that is the result of running a makefile. *See also* makefile.

3. *v.* To perform a build using a make utility.

makefile *n.* A file containing build instructions for a make. The filenames `makefile` and `Makefile` are common defaults. However, other files can generally hold instructions if the `-f` command line flag is used.

male *n.* The end of a connector or cable with the, um, more pronounced protuberance.

EXAMPLE: In the U.S. and most other countries, any power cable that plugs into the wall is a male. The wall socket is the female, since it, um, receives the male.

`malloc()` (mal ock) *fn.* A function from the C standard library used to allocate memory dynamically from a heap storage area. Many embedded systems programmers who use C avoid `malloc()` like the plague—and with good reason. The use of dynamically allocated memory is associated with memory leaks, dangling pointers (if there are bugs in the program), and external fragmentation (even if there aren't). These are dangers best avoided whenever possible in a system that must run for a long time between resets or is safety critical. *See also* `free()`. *Compare to* new. *See also* memory pool, garbage collector.

MAN (like Adam's gender) *abbr. See* metropolitan area network.

man month *n.* A unit of work representing the output of one typical person in one typical month.

Used in schedule management. *See also* mythical man month.

management 1. *n.* The process of helping workers achieve their maximum productivity. Management means getting the right people for a job, allocating them sufficient resources, instituting the proper processes, empowering them, and monitoring their progress. Enlightened managers remove obstacles to progress.

2. *n.* In the real world, management is often a process of overpromising, underdelivering, making excuses, and delegating the blame.

3. *n.* A generic term meaning the boss and his or her bosses. Upper-level management has access to the executive washroom. Middle management are managers of managers who don't have such corporate privileges. If you're an engineer, your manager is probably a leaf node on the org chart.

mangled name *n.* The symbolic representation of a C++ function name after it has been made unique by the compiler. In order to support function name overloading, the C++ language mangles the names of each function so that even those with the same name will have unique symbolic representations. Information about the types of return and parameters is added to the name in the mangling process. No two functions may have both the same name and the same return and parameter types.

Note that this can cause linkage problems when C functions are called from C++ code. By default, the prototypes for the C functions will also be mangled, though the actual C function implementations will not be. *See also* `extern "C"`.

mantissa *n.* The fractional part of a floating-point number. *See also* IEEE 754.

map 1. *See* memory map.

2. *n.* In the olden days, the name for the linker that bound relocatables into an executable program.

map file *n.* A file produced by the linker or locator, giving the size of the resulting executable along with the address of the text, data, and other segments and possibly the location of each function within those segments. Map file generation is typically off by default and must be turned on via a command-line option.

mapper *n.* A mainframe-era name for a linker/locator still used by some practictioners.

mark *n.* A logic 1 on an RS-232 link. A voltage between −3 and −25 V.

Mars Pathfinder *N.* A NASA mission that was successful, but still instructive.

Sojourner, the Mars Pathfinder rover.

On July 4, 1997, the Mars Pathfinder spacecraft hard-landed on the surface of the planet Mars with an autonomous robotic rover, Sojourner. Designed to last 30 days, the lander and rover operated 83 days, collecting scientific information on the geology, climate, and atmosphere of the red planet.

However, several days after landing, a puzzling problem appeared. Software executing on the lander's flight computer began to miss deadlines while collecting data from the atmospheric/meteorological instrument (ASI/MET).

The lander's flight computer was connected to the ASI/MET through a standard 1553 bus implemented over RS-232. Every 125 ms, the Bus Scheduler task ran to program the bus controller hardware to perform transactions during the next 125-ms period. While this occurred, the bus controller hardware executed the transactions programmed during the prior 125-ms period. When all of the transactions completed, the bus controller alerted the flight computer via interrupt.

The interrupt from the bus controller awoke a Bus Distribution task, which retrieved the transactions from the bus controller hardware and distributed them to other tasks in the system. The Bus Distribution task was a critical task with hard deadlines; it had to distribute the data from the bus controller hardware before it was programmed for the next 125-ms period by the Bus Scheduler task.

Data from the ASI/MET instrument was sent to a low-priority ASI/MET task. This low-priority task processed the data in non–real time and prepared it for transmission to Earth. The information was passed through the operating system's select()-able pipe facility. The ASI/MET task used the select() mechanism to wait for message arrival. When messages arrived, the ASI/MET task would be scheduled by the operating system and process the data.

The RTOS maintained information about the pipe for use by select(). This information was protected by a mutual exclusion semaphore that was not priority inversion aware. Occasionally, the ASI/MET task, inside select(), was preempted by the operating system while in the process of releasing the mutex. When the Bus Distribution task attempted to send the newest ASI/MET data via the pipe, it became blocked trying to acquire the mutex. Several medium-priority tasks ran then, keeping the ASI/MET task (and thereby the high-priority Bus Distribution task) from running.

Finally, the Bus Scheduler task awoke to program the bus controller for the next 125-ms period. It immediately determined that the Bus Distribution task had not completed its previous cycle (a hard deadline in the system) and declared an error that initiated a reset as part of the system's recovery strategy.

Fortunately, flight controllers on Earth were able to debug this problem remotely and reconfigure the RTOS so that the mutexes used by the pipe mechanism were inversion safe.

Besides classically illustrating priority inversion, the lesson of the Mars Pathfinder reminds developers to always code software defensively to check to see whether real-time deadlines are violated. It also argues that remotely located critical systems should always have mechanisms to provide visibility for debugging complex problems and for updating firmware. In this case, controllers updated software on a system located 40 million miles away, which saved the day.

mask 1. *See* bitmask.

2. *v.* To apply a bitmask to a register or variable to check whether certain bits are set or clear or to set or clear them.

3. *See* photomask.

masked ROM *n.* A read-only memory device that is created at the factory with its contents already in place. The mask for the part is created once and then used to create hundreds of thousands or millions of copies. Masked parts are increasingly rare, having been replaced by a variety of less expensive and more versatile ROMs, including OTP, PROM, EPROM, EEPROM, and flash parts.

mass storage *n.* High-density, slow-access, and low—cost-per-bit memory. Mass storage includes CD-ROMs and hard disks. All offer huge amounts of memory at a very low cost but are far slower than the computer.

mass terminators 1. *n.* A device that matches the impedance of a computer bus. Mass terminators are usually plug-in cards that insert into a bus backplane. Every mass terminator is, at heart, a collection of individual terminators.

2. *n.* A connector used primarily in digital systems that handles tens to hundreds of wires. Mass terminations use a single crimp operation to connect all of the wires to the connector's pins.

matched impedance *n.* The condition when both a driver and receiver have the same impedance. *See also* impedance matching.

matrix *n.* An m by n two-dimensional array, where m and n might or might not be equal. The addition and multiplication of matrices form the basis of linear algebra.

EXAMPLE: The identity matrix I_n is an n by n matrix containing all 0s except along the diagonal from upper left to bottom right, where there are 1s. The result of multiplying any m by n matrix M by I_n is M itself.

MAX232 *N.* An IC that converts RS-232 voltage levels to and from TTL levels. The MAX232 replaced the aging 1488/1489 line since it contained both drivers and receivers; it also included a charge pump circuit that made RS-232 voltages from a single +5-V supply. *See also* 1488, 1489.

maximum transfer unit *n.* The largest number of bytes that can be sent in a network packet. Abbreviated MTU. Larger packets of information must be subdivided into smaller fragments before they can be sent over the interface. *See also* fragmentation and reassembly, physical layer.

EXAMPLE: The MTU of Ethernet is 1500 bytes.

Maxwell's equations 1. *N.* A set of four equations discovered by others but recognized by James Maxwell as most concisely expressing the full relationship between electrical and magnetic fields.

In their integral form, the four equations are:

$\varepsilon_0 \int E dS = q$ (Gauss' law for electricity)

$\int B dS = 0$ (Gauss' law for magnetism)

$\int B dL = \mu_0 \left(\varepsilon_0 \left(\frac{d\Phi}{dt} \right) + i \right)$ (Ampere's law, extended by Maxwell)

$$\int EdL = \frac{-d\Phi_b}{dt} \quad \text{(Faraday's law)}$$

where

- E is the electric field vector,
- S is the area of a surface over which the field acts,
- ε_0 is the permittivity constant,
- q is the charge,
- B is the magnetic field vector,
- L is the line over which the magnetic field acts, and
- i is the current.

2. *N.* A particularly geeky thing to know and value.

Maxwell, James *N.* James Clerk Maxwell (1831–1879) put the laws of electromagnetics into the form used today. Maxwell relied heavily on his predecessors but also made vital contributions himself. He deduced that light is electromagnetic in nature and showed how optics and electromagnetics are intimately related. *See also* Maxwell's equations.

MB (meg-uh-byte) *abbr. See* megabyte.

Mbit (meg-uh-bit) *abbr. See* megabit.

Mbps (as letters) *abbr.* One million bits per second.

MCU (as letters) *abbr. See* microcontroller.

Mealy automaton *N.* One of the classical interpretations of the finite state automaton, which associates actions with state transitions. In a Mealy automaton, actions are assumed to take no time to execute (zero-time assumption) to avoid the conceptual difficulty of an ill-defined state during a state transition. Because actions necessarily take a finite amount of time, a Mealy automaton causes a conceptual difficulty: although a system is executing actions, it is not in any state (it is "between" two states). In other words, the state of a Mealy automaton is not well defined at all times. *See also* Moore automaton.

Mealy–Moore state machine *N.* The formal name for a finite state automaton. Mealy and Moore automata are mathematically equivalent (i.e., one always can be transformed into the other). In general, however, a Moore automaton requires more states to model the same system because a Mealy automaton can use different transitions (transitions with different triggers) to the same state and can execute different actions. A Moore automaton must use different states to represent conditions in which different actions are performed.

mean *n.* A mathematical average. *Contrast with* median.

> **EXAMPLE:** The mean of the set { a, b, c } is
> $$\frac{(a + b + c)}{3}$$

mebi- (meh bee) *pre.* The prefix meaning 2^{20}. Abbreviated Mi. 1 mebibit:

- 1 Mibit = 1,048,576 bits
- 1 mebibyte: 1 MiB = 1,048,576 bytes

See also binary prefixes, mega-.

mebibit (meh bee bit) *n.* 1,048,576 bits. Abbreviated Mibit. *See also* binary prefixes.

mebibyte (meh bee byte) *n.* 1,048,576 bytes. Abbreviated MiB. *See also* binary prefixes.

median *n.* The middle value in a set of numbers. In other words, the value for which there are an equal number of smaller and larger values in the set.

The median is useful for filtering out extreme values. For example, the mean income in the U.S. is much higher than the median income simply because of a few overpaid Fortune 500 CEOs. The median income, like the median home value, is far more representative of the norm than the mean could ever be.

median filter *n.* A filter that finds the median value from a set of inputs. Most filters compute means or weighted means of the most recent input values. But if you're building a robot to find and put out fires, you'll want to use a median filter to process the raw data from its light sensor(s). Fires are generally much brighter than their surroundings, so a strong average reading in one direction can be used to direct the robot to the fire. But a single stroke of lightning will max out all of the input values. Such data should be ignored, as can be done easily by applying a median filter.

medium-scale integration *n.* A vague term that describes the complexity of chips between SSI and LSI. Abbreviated MSI. MSI circuits typically comprise adders, ALUs, shifters, and the like. They make use of multiple gates, yet offer far less functionality than the more complex LSI parts. *See also* large-scale integration, small-scale integration.

mega- (meg-uh) *pre.* The prefix meaning 10^6. Abbreviated M. 1 megabit:

- 1 Mbit = 1,000,000 bits
- 1 megabyte: 1 MB = 1,000,000 bytes

See also decimal prefixes.

megabit *n.* 1,000,000 bits. Abbreviated Mbit. *See also* decimal prefixes.

megabyte *n.* 1,000,000 bytes. Abbreviated MB. *See also* decimal prefixes.

USAGE: In some contexts, notably disk drive sizes, the term megabyte is used when mebibyte is meant. This should be avoided.

megahertz *n.* One million cycles per second. Abbreviated MHz.

megaohm *n.* One million ohms. Abbreviated MΩ.

megavolt *n.* One million volts. Abbreviated MV.

memcmp() (mem compare) *fn.* A function in the C standard library for comparing the contents of two blocks of memory.

memcpy() (mem copy) *fn.* A function in the C standard library for copying blocks of data from one location to another.

memory access time *n.* The interval between supplying a memory with a valid address and control signals and either storing write data or extracting read data from the memory. *Contrast with* cycle time, memory.

memory address decoding *See* address decoder.

memory bank *n.* A complete section of memory. A memory bank is a logically distinct section of memory. It might be physically separate from other memory (e.g., ROM vs. RAM) or merely separated by use or by the configuration of a memory management unit. One RAM array can have dozens of banks within it, if an MMU treats each bank as an independently addressable unit. *See also* memory management unit.

memory cell *n.* One bit of memory. Memory cell usually refers to the physical configuration of a memory bit. In DRAM, one cell is one transistor. SRAM uses four to six transistors per cell, which is a big reason it's more expensive.

memory dump *See* core dump.

memory fragmentation *See* fragmentation.

memory image 1. *n.* The binary representation of executable code and data to be loaded into a processor's nonvolatile memory, usually via a download or device programmer.

2. *n.* An exact copy of all or much of the content of the system's volatile memory. A memory image is usually generated after a system crash. This "postmortem dump" can be used as a forensic aid when determining the cause of the crash.

memory leak *n.* A condition that occurs when software creates storage dynamically on the heap but doesn't properly free that storage when it is no longer being used. Over time, as more and more dead objects are left on the heap, the total amount of free space drops. Eventually, an out-of-memory condition can result. Garbage collection is designed to prevent memory leaks by automating the reclamation of dead heap objects. *See also* dangling pointer, dangling reference.

memory location *n.* A particular address in a processor's memory space. *See also* memory-mapped I/O.

memory management unit *n.* A quite complex circuit that translates logical addresses to physical addresses. Abbreviated MMU. An MMU is used to manage the memory needs of multiple processes in a single physical memory. The MMU segments physical memory into many frames, each of which has its own (read/write/execute) access rights. A particular process can run only within its own frames; any attempt to access other frames results in a fault. The OS captures the fault and takes appropriate action.

MMUs create debugging problems because the link map addresses do not correspond to those actually on the bus.

EXAMPLE: Windows 3.1 ran most programs within a single memory partition; frequent crashes resulted. Developers do remain somewhat astonished that later versions of the OS exhibit the same behavior, since the use of the Pentium's MMU should limit crashes to single applications only—but then, those crashes are mostly bugs inside the kernel or drivers, which have access to all of memory.

memory map *n.* A table or diagram containing the name and address range of each peripheral and memory device within a processor's memory space. Memory maps are a helpful aid in getting to know one's target.

memory-mapped I/O *n.* A common hardware design methodology in which peripheral control and status registers are mapped into the memory space

EPROM (128K)	FFFFFh
	E0000h
Flash Memory (128K)	
	C0000h
Unused	
	7200h
Zilog SCC	70000h
Unused	
	20000h
SRAM (128K)	
	00000h

A memory map for a real-mode x86 processor with memory-mapped I/O.

rather than the I/O space. From the software developer's point of view, memory-mapped I/O devices look very much like memory devices. Their registers can even be accessed via ordinary pointers and data structures, greatly simplifying device driver implementation. *Contrast with* ported I/O.

memory page *n.* A single chunk of contiguous memory locations referenced via a virtual memory system. Virtual memory systems (a.k.a., paging) extend the concept of memory management units to permit portions of the program to not be resident in physical memory. They're swapped in from mass storage as needed. *See also* memory management unit, virtual memory.

memory pool *n.* A dynamic memory area, such as the heap.

USAGE: The term "memory pool" is generally used when the allocation units within that pool are all of a fixed size. So to say that a particular RTOS "supports memory pools" indicates that it has a way to manage the risks of external fragmentation and make dynamic memory allocation useful in a real-time system.

memory space   *n.* A processor's standard address space. *Contrast with* I/O space.

memory test   *n.* A piece of software that tests a memory bus (or individual device on that bus) to confirm that it is working properly. *See* checkerboard test, walking 1s test, walking 0s test.

FURTHER READING: For a portable public domain memory test suite designed for isolating and testing the data bus, address bus, and memory chip, visit http://www.netrino.com/Articles/MemoryTesting/.

memory, backup   *n.* Memory used to store data even when system power is removed. Backup memory is nonvolatile, though it might use RAM with battery backup. *See also* battery backup, NVRAM.

memory, byte-wide   *n.* An IC memory device that stores data in chunks 8 bits wide (instead of single bits). Byte-wide memories store and read back an entire byte of memory in a single write or read cycle.

The JEDEC 21-C standard (http://www.jedec.org) for memory configuration defines pin arrangements for byte-wide memories to ensure compatability between vendors' products.

memory, cache   *n.* Very high speed memory used to implement a cache. Cache memory generally offers one or two cycle access times. *See* cache memory.

memory, shadow   *n.* A type of memory used in some in-circuit emulators to log data. Every time the target code writes to a variable, the write goes to normal RAM as well as the ICE's hidden shadow RAM. This memory is multiport and can be read by the debugger without slowing the target code, so the user gets real-time access to system variables.

MEMS   (rhymes with hems) *abbr.* The integration of electronics, microsensors/actuators, and micromechanical elements on a common silicon substrate.

Short for Micro-Electro-Mechanical Systems. Tiny mechanical and electromechanical components are fabricated using processes that etch away existing silicon or add new structural layers.

The ultimate goal for MEMS, which is still an area of developing technology, is to give standard ICs the ability to interact with their environments on a molecular level. Chips, which today can only "think," could soon "smell," "touch," and so on. This would bring a revolution in capability and scale that would surely have a large effect on the role of embedded systems in the universe.

EXAMPLE: As of this writing, the most successful commercial applications of MEMS have been accelerometers for airbag-deployment sensors and inkjet printer micronozzles. Many more successes are sure to come.

message passing   *n.* The technique of using message queues to send and receive data between threads. One nice thing about a software architecture based on message passing is that it adapts easily to reimplementation as a distributed system. Some microkernel operating systems even use message passing between subsystems.

message queue   *n.* An operating system data structure for passing arbitrary data values or buffers between two or more threads. Generally speaking, each would-be receiver thread creates a message queue of a particular size. Thereafter, threads that want to send messages to the receiver (the sender and receiver must typically agree about what these messages will contain) can simply make a system call and be guaranteed an uncorrupted delivery. If the queue is full, however, the caller may block (depending on the specifics of the API), so sizing the queues becomes a critical issue in real-time systems.

If you're using an operating system that doesn't support message queues directly, it's possible to create your own at the application level using semaphores or a monitor.

metadata (meh tuh data) *n*. Data about data. For example, a file containing a database can begin with a header full of metadata describing the record formats.

metastability *n*. A condition that gives random data when a flip-flop's setup or hold times are violated. Every flop has a specified minimum setup time: the number of nanoseconds that data must be present at the device's input before the clock signal transitions. If the data appears inside of this window (say, if the minimum setup time is 2 ns and data changes 1 ns before clock changes), then the output of the flip-flop is undefined. This condition is called metastability and is clearly a profound issue. The same is true for violating the flop's hold time.

Fully synchronous systems don't suffer from metastability issues since, by definition, the data only changes at safe times. Instead, metastability comes into play when data is asynchronous to clock. Suppose a parallel encoder goes into a 12-bit latch that is clocked by the CPU when the processor is ready to read the data. The encoder is asynchronous to the CPU's clock, so there's no reasonable way to ensure that the changing encoder data will meet the latch's setup time. Occasionally—not often—the latched data will be corrupt.

Other than making things synchronous, so the setup and hold times are never violated, there is no solution to the metastability problem. Various partial approaches can reduce the chance of a problem to a very low, always nonzero, probability. These solutions always involve using two stages of flip-flops, both toggled from the same clock state.

meter *n*. A standard unit of length. Abbreviated m.

method 1. *n*. In object-oriented languages, a function that is part of a class. Also called a member function.

2. *n*. A technique or a way of doing something.

metropolitan area network *n*. A network linking the buildings within a city or metro area. Abbreviated MAN. A MAN is basically a localized (geographically) wide area network. However, a MAN is normally managed by a service provider and connects the LANs of multiple corporations and governments together.

mF (millifarad) *abbr. See* millifarad.

MHz (meg-uh-hurts) *abbr. See* megahertz.

Mi (meh bee) *abbr. See* mebi-.

MiB (meh bee byte) *abbr. See* mebibyte.

Mibit (meh bee bit) *abbr. See* mebibit.

micro (mike row) *abbr. See* microcontroller.

micro- 1. *pre.* The prefix representing a numerical multiplier of 10^{-6}. Abbreviated μ.

2. *pre.* Small or miniature. As in a microclip probe.

microamp *n*. A millionth of an ampere. Abbreviated μA.

microcode *n*. The "software" that implements machine instructions. On many computers, the machine instructions are implemented by software-like routines; that is, if you execute a machine ADD instruction, it might actually invoke a series of microcode instructions, each of which specifies at the register level how data moves around inside the processor.

On some early computers, especially in the minicomputer era, gutsy developers could change the microcode, which allowed them to create instructions optimized for specialized applications. Modern microcode is buried within the processor itself, is programmed by the chip vendor when the part is initially designed, and cannot be changed.

microcontroller *n*. A microcontroller is very similar to a microprocessor, except that it is designed specifically for use in embedded systems. Microcontrollers typically include an integrated CPU, memory (a small amount of RAM, ROM, or both), and other peripherals on the same chip. Common examples are Microchip's PIC, the 8051, Intel's 80196, and Motorola's 68HCxx series.

microfarad *n.* A millionth of a farad. Abbreviated µF.

microkernel *n.* An utterly simple operating system; one that can live in the limited address space of even a minimal processor like low-end PICs and Z8s. *See also* kernel.

microphone *n.* A transducer that converts spoken audio to electrical impulses.

microphonics *n.* An analog circuit sensitive to mechanical vibration. Microphonics are the unwanted by-products of the mechanical effects on circuits. Bang a capacitor and its shape, and therefore its capacitance, changes. Wiring that moves with vibration can change impedance as it gets closer and farther from the chassis and other components. All of these effects can get coupled into an analog system's transfer function, corrupting the desired data.

microprocessor *n.* A piece of silicon containing a general-purpose CPU. The most common examples are Intel's 80x86 and Motorola's 680x0 families.

microprocessor development system *n.* A computer plus specialized accessories used primarily to create firmware. Sometimes abbreviated MDS.

HISTORY: The MDS originally referred to an ICE with an integrated development station, such as Intel's circa 1975 Blue Box. These sorts of devices included the emulator plus a complete computer system, with monitor, keyboard, disks, and a rudimentary OS. Intel's systems used either CP/M or ISIS, a proprietary Intel OS that fortunately died.

microsecond *n.* A millionth of a second. Abbreviated µs. A microsecond is the length of a clock cycle at a 1 MHz rate. If your processor runs faster than 1 MHz, it will be able to execute at least a few instructions every microsecond and will respond to interrupts (when enabled) about that fast.

Microsoft *n.* The largest microprocessor software company. Sometimes abbreviated M$. Microsoft is a highly profitable, cash-rich company that completely dominates the desktop PC OS and office software market. Their primary embedded offerings are various versions of Windows CE: a stripped down version of Windows designed for ROMable and somewhat resource-constrained applications.

HISTORY: Microsoft was there at the dawn of the desktop computer age, originally offering a BASIC interpreter that ran in only 4 KiB of RAM on the Apple II. When IBM offered the first PC, it came with a version of Microsoft's DOS. With the advent of the 386, the PC had enough power to run Windows—and Microsoft had been through enough versions to make a saleable product.

microvolt *n.* A millionth of a volt. Abbreviated µV.

middleware *n.* Third-party software that runs on top of the operating system but is not itself a part of the application code. TCP/IP stacks and GUIs are common pieces of middleware.

MIDP (mid pee) *abbr.* A profile describing a set of class libraries for PDAs and cell phones compatible with Java 2 Micro Edition. Short for Mobile Information Device Profile. The MIDP profile is based on the CLDC configuration.

midpoint *n.* A point halfway between the two ends of a line segment.

mil-spec *adj.* Refers to components that meet the military's much more stringent environmental requirements than those of commercial products. Short for Military Specifications. Whereas a commercial IC might be guaranteed for correct operation between 0 and 70°C, the mil-spec version could run from −40 to +120°C.

Interestingly, many commercial apps now need mil-spec components: a car radio, for example, must operate over an astonishing temperature range.

mil-std (mill-standard) *adj.* Refers to hardware components that meet one or more of a huge range of DoD specifications, such as operating temperature ranges and ability to withstand vibrations. Short for Military Standard.

milestone *n.* An important date on a project's schedule. Typical milestones are associated with the completion of deliverables, such as the requirements, design, and implementation of each subsystem.

milli- *pre.* The prefix representing a numerical multiplier of 10^{-3}. Abbreviated m.

milliamp *n.* A thousandth of an ampere. Abbreviated mA.

millifarad *n.* A thousandth of a farad. Abbreviated mF.

USAGE: Rarely used; capacitances in the millifarad range are more frequently expressed using microfarads (e.g., 2,000 µF).

milliohm *n.* A thousandth of an ohm. Abbreviated mΩ.

millions of instructions per second *n.* A technically deficient but widely quoted benchmarking measure. Abbreviated MIPS. The problem with MIPS is it doesn't take real-world effects (caching, interrupts, or memory latency) and applications into account when comparing processors.

millisecond *n.* A thousandth of a second. Abbreviated ms. From the perspective of software and electronics, a millisecond is a very, very long time. A

processor running at just 1 MHz might be able to execute as many as a thousand instructions in what is to humans a very short period of time. (And, of course, most processors run much faster than that.) Most real-time operating systems have a 1- or 10-ms clock tick.

millivolt *n.* A thousandth of a volt. Abbreviated mV. A millivolt is a very small amount of voltage. Signals sensed from the human body (e.g., via EKG electrodes) are in the millivolt range.

milliwatt *n.* A thousandth of a watt. Abbreviated mW.

Mims III, Forrest M. *N.* A widely published amateur scientist whose interests include encouraging students to participate in long-term projects to measure haze, solar ultraviolet, photosynthetically active sunlight, polarization of the sky, and total column ozone and water vapor in the atmosphere. He is currently director of the Sun Photometer Atmospheric Network in Texas. He is author of numerous books on electronics, including *The Forrest Mims Engineer's Notebook* and *The Forrest Mims Circuit Scrapbook,* which many engineers first encountered in Radio Shack.

minimize *v.* To reduce a circuit or algorithm to a very compact form. *See also* logic minimization, Karnaugh map.

minimum laxity first *n.* A preemptive scheduling algorithm in which thread priorities are changed on the fly so that the thread with the least laxity remaining before its next deadline is selected to run. Abbreviated MLF. The laxity of each thread is defined as the difference between the time until its next deadline and the remaining processor time required (worst-case) to meet that deadline. *Compare to* earliest-deadline-first.

minterm *n.* The Boolean AND of all variables (either complemented or uncomplemented), such that the AND results in a logic 1. Every AND has one minterm (that product for which the result is 1) and $2^n - 1$ cases where the product is 0.

When used for a NAND, it's the NAND that includes each variable such that the output is a 0. *Contrast with* product term.

EXAMPLE: In the equation /a/b/c, the minterm is inputs 000 (a = 0, b = 0, c = 0), since that's the only condition that yields a 1.

MIPS (rhymes with tips) 1. *abbr. See* millions of instructions per second.

USAGE: Many engineers use the term MIPS as shorthand for processing power. They'll say, for example, that their algorithm will consume 10 MIPS. This vague characterization should be taken as a sign that the speaker has done no testing of the algorithm on any specific processor and likely has made only a back-of-napkin analysis that could be insufficient to effect a successful processor selection.

2. *n.* A RISC processor family developed by MIPS Computer Systems. Short for Microprocessor without Interlocked Pipeline Stages. Used in Nintendo's N64 and Sony's PlayStation and PS2, the MIPS architecture has come to dominate the video game market. This, though, perhaps had more to do with its successful inclusion in SGI workstations and later availability as a licensable IP than any unique technical ability.

mismatch *n.* Generally used in referring to impedance mismatching, this is a condition where a driver and the receiver do not have the same impedance. Mismatched impedances result in signal degradation or even total loss of the signal. As signals transition faster between 0s and 1s, PCB tracks behave less like simple wires and more like complex LC circuits. *See also* impedance matching.

MISRA (miz-rah) *abbr.* A U.K.-based software reliability association concerned with the risks of using C to develop firmware for automotive applications.

Short for Motor Industry Software Reliability Association. *See* MISRA C.

MISRA C (miz-rah see) *n.* A set of 127 guidelines for the use of C in safety-critical software. Although widely used in automotive systems, for example, ISO standard C is not itself properly suited to the development of safety-critical software. The MISRA C guidelines attempt to shore up weaknesses in the programming language standard so that something very like C can be used to reliably develop safe software.

MISRA C can be considered a subset of ISO C; the discarded language constructs are those deemed most prone to error. For example, rule 35 prohibits the use of assignments within Boolean expressions; thus, simple if (x = 1) typos can't cause run-time errors that are difficult to detect and debug. If enforced by a code-checking tool as part of the build process, these rules can be complied with selectively and easily.

FURTHER READING: *Guidelines for the Use of the C Language in Vehicle Based Software.* Motor Industry Software Reliability Association, April 1998. Available for purchase at http://www.misra.org.uk.

miss rate *n.* In a system with a cache, the percentage of time that the cache does not contain the memory location of interest. It is desirable to design the cache in such a way that the miss rate is minimized across the vast majority of programs that will be run on the system. *Contrast with* hit rate.

missed interrupt *n.* An interrupt that occurred but was never processed. One way this can happen is if interrupts are disabled temporarily at the CPU. If an interrupt occurs during that time, it won't be processed until interrupts are enabled again. The interrupt will be missed, though, if the same interrupt occurs again before interrupts are enabled. The ISR only runs once, even though more than one interrupt has occurred at that source.

mission-critical *adj.* Said of a system that must work in order for its larger mission to succeed. For example, the lander on a spacecraft on its way to another planet must work properly the first time, or the mission will be a disaster and the responsible agency will have its funding cut and its engineering scrutinized by politicians.

mixed-signal *adj.* A system or subsystem that comprises both analog and digital components. Although any analog/digital circuit is mixed-signal, today it's possible to put both linear and digital components on a single IC, leading to classes of mixed-signal integrated devices.

EXAMPLE: Tektronix's and Agilent's mixed-signal scopes combine both scope and logic analyzer. These devices are ideal for troubleshooting mixed-signal systems because the scope can trigger the analyzer and vice versa; as a result, the user can capture system operation in either the analog or digital domain.

MLF (as letters) *abbr. See* minimum laxity first.

MMU (as letters) *abbr. See* memory management unit.

mnemonic *n.* The human-readable representation of an opcode input to an assembler or output by a disassembler or debugger. The opcode is a binary sequence that would be difficult to encode or decipher, so the programmer uses mnemonics and the assembler converts them into bit patterns the CPU will understand.

mod *See* modulo.

model-view controller *n.* A design pattern or partitioning strategy commonly used in programs with modern graphical user interfaces. Abbreviated MVC. The MVC pattern separates the display of information (the view), the internal representation of that information (the model), and the logic that translates user actions into state changes (the controller) into three distinct modules.

Any modern graphical application involves a great deal of state information: the state of the various visual components, modal information collected from earlier user actions, and information that has been extracted from or is destined for the more abstract portions of the program. Because there are strong connections between some of these elements of state (e.g., the visual state of a checkbox and the logical value to be entered into a Boolean field in some associated database), programmers often attempt to intertwine the code related to the visual components with the code related to the more abstract portions of the application. The result is usually overly complex and difficult to change.

In a well-done MVC design, each aspect of the program's behavior can be revised by changing just one component. Changes to the "look and feel" will be confined to the view. Changes in how the data is stored, processed, or represented will affect only the model. Changes in how the two interact (e.g., allowing both "Y" and "yes" for a particular answer) will be confined to the controller.

MVC designs aren't just conveniently partitioned code, though. By encouraging the programmer to focus on subtle role-related differences in closely related state information, MVC analysis encourages cleaner, better informed designs.

EXAMPLE: Consider a program to graphically simulate a number of bouncing balls. The model might be a collection of objects, where each object manages information about one ball—say its initial position, size, color, rebound characteristics, and velocity—and knows how to compute new position and velocity values for arbitrary points in time. The model, however, should not know anything about how the balls are currently displayed. Symmetrically, the view might be an object that knows how to draw balls of a given size and color at particular coordinates on a viewport but would know nothing about the ball's history or future. The controller would coordinate the two. Based on some timer or sampling rate, the controller would request new position information from the model and translate that information into drawBall() operations on the view.

An initial draft of this application might always display some fixed number of balls with fixed initial attributes. By revising only the controller, the application could be enhanced to display a randomly chosen number of balls, each with randomly chosen initial conditions. Initially, the application might render balls as flat circles. Later, by changing only the view, the application could draw the balls with 3D shading. Initially, the simulation might assume earth-normal gravity in a frictionless atmosphere, but by changing only the model, it could be used to simulate other gravities, and even bouncing in a fluid.

modem (moe dem) *n.* A device that encodes a serial bitstream onto a communications line or decodes them at the receiving end. Short for MOdulator–DEModulator. Examples include cable modems (which generally convert 100Base-T to a wideband RF signal appropriate for a cable) and dial-up modems (which convert RS-232 or logic levels to tones suitable for transmission over plain old telephone lines).

modular 1. *adj.* Pertains to a type of software architecture where the program is broken into many smaller parts, each of which is a module or function. One hopes that all programs are modular, though it's not always the case. The use of object-oriented programming concepts encourages the practice through encapsulation. 2. *adj.* Said of a hardware or software design that uses purchased or reused pieces.

modulation 1. *n.* The information component of a signal.

2. *n.* Modulation is the process of modifying a base signal (a carrier) by the information. AM, for example, consists of a carrier that's multiplied by

the data. *See also* demodulation, frequency modulation, pulse width modulation.

module *n.* A hardware or software component that is easily added to or removed from a system.

modulo *n.* A mathematical operation that divides two numbers and returns the remainder. Usually abbreviated MOD. *See also* %.

EXAMPLE: 18 MOD 4 is 2, since 18/4 is 4 with a remainder of 2.

EXAMPLE: Modulo-2 arithmetic uses a divisor of 2; therefore, the result is 1 if the dividend is odd and 0 if the dividend is even.

modulo-2 binary division *n.* A style of division involving binary sequences that is most often used for computing CRCs. Implementing modulo-2 binary division is much more straightforward in hardware than it is in software. In hardware, you simply need to shift the message bits through a linear feedback shift register as they are received. The bits of the divisor are represented by physical connections in the feedback paths. Because of the greater simplicity and efficiency of this approach, CRCs are usually implemented in hardware whenever possible.

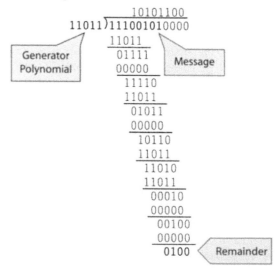

An example of modulo-2 binary division in a CRC calculation.

modulo-*n* counter *n.* A counter that rolls over to zero automatically when it reaches the value *n.*

MOhm *See* megaohm.

mole *n.* A standard unit of quantity. Abbreviated mol. A mole is the amount of a substance that contains 6.02×10^{23} (Avogadro's number) atoms, molecules, ions, or other elementary units. Also called gram molecule.

monitor 1. *n.* A language-level intertask synchronization primitive. Java is the only language in the embedded systems space that supports monitors. 2. *n.* The CRT or LCD display attached to a computer. 3. *See* debug monitor.

monostable 1. *adj.* Having only one stable state. 2. *See* monostable multivibrator.

monostable multivibrator *n.* A type of logic device that normally produces either a 0 or a 1 but that, when triggered by a logic pulse, momentarily goes to the other state. Also called a one-shot. Monostable multivibrators use an external resistor and capacitor to set how long the device will be in its unstable state. If the RC combination gives a dwell time of, say, 50 ms, then when the activation pulse comes along, the output will go from a 0 to a 1, stay at a 1 for 50 ms, then transition back to 0.

Monostable multivibrators are useful in many sorts of timing applications. Unskilled or lazy designers will sometimes overuse these, using a monostable where a better design might employ a counter. The dwell time of any monostable is greatly affected by temperature and the characteristics of the external resistor and capacitor. It's important to note that caps have very large tolerances, so it's hard to guarantee precise or repeatable timing. *Contrast with* astable multivibrator.

monotonic *adj.* Having a consistent trend, either continually increasing or decreasing. For example, when using RMA, priorities are assigned monotonically with rate. That is, the shorter the period of a thread, the higher its assigned priority. If you plot the period versus the priority on a graph, you'll see that the curve is monotonic.

Moore automaton *N.* One of the classical interpretations of the finite state automaton, which associates actions with states rather than transitions. The output of a Moore automaton depends only on the current state, whereas the output of a Mealy automaton depends on both the current state and the current input. The state of a system is always well defined in a Moore automaton (even without the zero-time assumption) because actionless transitions can be considered instantaneous (actions might take time but are executed in a well-defined state context). *See also* Mealy automaton.

Moore's Law *N.* An observation by Intel founder Gordon Moore that integrated circuits double in transistor count about every 12 months. Although the observation was made in 1965, when Intel was a memory supplier, this simple rule of thumb has held up as an approximation for almost four decades. However, there has been some slowing in the rate of doubling, first to 18 months and then to 24 months.

FURTHER READING: http://www.njtu.edu.cn/depart/xydzxx/ec/spectrum/moore/mlaw.html

Morse code *n.* A signaling technique that uses short and long pulses (called dots and dashes, respectively) in a standard way to indicate letters (upper case only), numbers, and many symbols. Morse code is a very efficient way to transmit data. It needs only a very narrowband channel (on the order of 100 Hz). Speeds of 60+ words per minute are possible with skilled operators.

Morse code, though, is all but dead, used today primarily by ham radio operators. Even there, its demise is certain; in 2000 the FCC eliminated all high-speed Morse requirements from ham tests;

today hams need learn it at only five words per minute, a very easy thing to master.

Properly, though, no one uses Morse code. Today all Morse is International Morse code, which is very different from the character coding devised by Samuel Morse (now called American Morse code).

Morse code is a good example of a compact coding scheme. Frequently used characters are short; for example, E is represented by a single dot and T by a single dash. Z, on the other hand, is dash dash dot dot.

HISTORY: Named for its creator, Samuel Morse (1791–1872), who also patented the telegraph.

MOSFET (moss-fet, ryhmes with bet) *abbr.* A type of FET in which the gate is insulated from the channel by a layer of oxide. Short for Metal-Oxide Silicon Field Effect Transistor. FETs and MOSFETs are both three-terminal devices. They both have a channel: a continuous piece of silicon through which current moves. The electric field on the gate modulates this flow. The current flows from the source to the drain. However, because the MOSFET's gate is truly not connected to the channel, its input impedance is on the order of 10^{12} ohms; essentially no current flows into the gate.

MOSFETs come in two flavors: depletion-mode devices conduct when the gate voltage is zero—the channel's resistance increases as the gate's voltage increases—and enhancement-mode MOSFETs are normally off and start conducting as the gate voltage goes up.

Because of their high impedances and fast response, MOSFETs are the basic element of most large digital ICs, like processors and memories.

most significant bit *n.* The bit at the leftmost end of a binary value. Abbreviated MSb.

EXAMPLE: In an unsigned 16-bit word, position 2^{15} is the MSb. For example, only the most significant bit in binary 1000 0000 0000 0000 is set.

Contrast with least significant bit.

most significant byte *n.* The byte of a multibyte value that contains the most significant part of the numerical value. Abbreviated MSB. For example, the most significant byte of the 32-bit value 0x12345678 is 0x12. The most significant byte is always at the left of the value when it is written on paper. However, in a computer, it can be at either the highest or lowest memory offset. *See also* endianness.

motherboard *n.* A printed circuit board that contains connectors into which other cards (daughterboards) can be inserted. A motherboard/daughterboard design makes sense when a computer system can be expanded by the user.

EXAMPLE: The main PCB in a PC is its motherboard, since it accepts a variety of plug-in boards. The old S-100 computers, which mostly ran CP/M, used a motherboard with no active electronics; it was just a row of connectors into which a processor board, memory cards, and I/O boards were inserted.

motor *n.* A device that turns electrical energy into rotational or linear motion. *See also* DC motor, step motor, induction motor, brush motor, brushless motor.

motor drive *n.* A circuit that controls an electric motor. Motors are high-power devices that no processor can drive directly. A variety of amplifier circuits boosts the output of the processor to levels appropriate for a motor. The simplest is a relay, though that offers nothing other than on/off control. Thyristors and high-power transistors support variable speed designs; stepper motors use multiple transistors to control the field windings.

motor, stepping *See* step motor.

Motorola *N.* An important vendor of microprocessors and other ICs for the embedded space.

HISTORY: Founded in 1928 as the Galvin Manufacturing Corporation of Chicago, Illinois, the company was renamed Motorola in the 1930s as it became very successful building car radios (the name suggests moving radios). Their 68HC05 and CPU32 families of processors are found in embedded systems everywhere. Today the company is heavily focused on cell phones.

Motorola argument convention *n.* The order in which arguments appear in instructions for Motorola processors. Assemblers for Motorola processors (e.g., CPU32) expect the first argument to be the source; the second is the destination. *Contrast with* Intel argument convention.

EXAMPLE: The 68000 instruction

```
MOVE.W #$55AA, D0
```

moves the immediate data 0x55AA to register D0.

Motorola S-record format *N.* An ASCII file format created by Motorola and used to store and download binary images. Like the competing Intel Hex format, many device programmers are capable of importing and exporting files in this format.

Motorola S-records are a text representation of hexadecimal-coded binary data. All data uses only ASCII characters, so the format is portable across virtually all computer platforms.

Each line in a Motorola S-record file is a record. Records always begin with the letter S, followed by a 1 if the record contains data or a 9 if it is the last record in the file.

The next byte represents the number of bytes in the record, including the starting address, data bytes, and the checksum. The next pair of numbers represent the 16-bit absolute starting address of the data in the record. Following the address

are the hex representations of the data to be stored.

The last byte is an 8-bit 1s complement checksum of all of the bytes in the record (except the first two). Note that this value is derived from the binary values of the bytes, not their ASCII representations. A CR/LF pair terminates each record.

EXAMPLE: An example of a data record.

```
S11301707071727374757677778797A7B7C7D7E7F03
```

- 1—record type (data)
- 13—19 (0x13) bytes follow, including address and checksum
- 0170—starting address of this record
- 707172 ... 7F—the data bytes
- 03—a checksum

FURTHER READING: For more information see http://www.wotsit.org/search.asp?page=4&s=binary.

mount *v.* To logically connect a disk or other I/O device to a computer system. Not often done in the embedded world, mounting is a mostly Unix convention of opening a connection to a mass storage device. *Contrast with* unmount.

HISTORY: In the bad old days, mounting referred to putting a specific magnetic tape on a drive, something the operator did in response to a request by a user (users had no direct access to computers).

mouse *n.* A computer input device that translates motion on a desk to motion on the screen. Not often used on embedded systems, though it can be considered one itself (to its designers).

HISTORY: Invented about 1964 by Douglas Engelbart at Stanford. In 1973 Zerox PARC produced their Alto personal computer (never turned into a product), which was the first computer to use a mouse and a GUI.

mouse pointer *n.* On a GUI, a visual indication of the current location on the screen pointed to by the pointing device. *See also* cursor.

moving average *n.* A mean calculated only over the most recent data available. Moving averages are often used to filter input samples from an A/D to reduce fluctuations. They are also a popular tool for technical analysis of stocks and stock markets. *See also* finite impulse response.

MPSD (as letters) *abbr.* The name for the proprietary on-chip debug capability included in TI DSPs. Short for Modular Port Scan Device. MPSD is based on a standard JTAG boundary scan and is, therefore, tied to TI debuggers. The debugger must know which revision of the silicon is in your system in order to drive the debugging functions in the chip through this interface.

MPU (as letters) *abbr. See* microprocessor.

ms (mill-ee-second) *abbr. See* millisecond.

MSb (as letters) *abbr. See* most significant bit.

MSB (as letters) *abbr. See* most significant byte.

msec (mill-ee-second) *abbr. See* millisecond.

USAGE: The preferred abbreviation is ms, which is recommended by NIST and IEEE Computer Society.

MSI (as letters) *abbr. See* medium-scale integration.

MTBF (as letters) *abbr.* The average length of time until a component or system can be expected to fail. Short for Mean Time Between Failures.

MTU (as letters) *abbr. See* maximum transfer unit.

multibit error *n.* A sequential burst of more than one incorrect bit in a transmission. Single-bit errors are fairly easy to detect by adding a parity bit to each transmitted byte or word. More complex errors, often spawned by a noise burst that briefly corrupts the data stream, require additional detection bits. CRCs can detect many multibit errors at the expense of computing and transmitting the

CRC of the data packet. *See also* cyclic redundancy code.

multicast *n.* The broadcast of a data steam to multiple receivers on a network. Multicast is different from general broadcast in that a specific list of intended receivers is explicitly specified in the packet. *See also* IGMP.

multidrop *adj.* Said of any communications link where more than two devices can be tied to the same cables.

EXAMPLE: The I^2C interface widely included in smaller microcontrollers uses two wires in a multi-drop configuration to connect many devices.

multilayer *adj.* Describes a printed circuit board that uses more than two copper layers. Dense boards require more interconnects than is possible on two layers; for this reason most modern digital boards use four or more. Noise problems also make it unwise, in most cases, to mix power, ground, and signal tracks on the same layer. Multilayer PCBs generally allocate one layer to each power supply, one or more to ground, and the rest to interconnects between component pins.

One- and two-sided PCBs are fabricated by etching copper from the top and bottom of a generally fiberglass board. Multilayer boards are built from stacks of double-sided boards glued together after the appropriate etching takes place.

multimeter *n.* A piece of electrical test equipment capable of measuring many quantities, including at least voltage and resistance.

multiplex *v.* Putting two or more signals on a wire or bus at different times. Multiplexing saves pin counts on ICs because a single pin or group of pins can carry more than one kind of data. *See also* multiplexed bus.

multiplexed bus *n.* A group of wires that holds more than one set of signals, each set appearing at different points in time. IC pins are expensive. Vendors minimize pin counts by using multiplexed buses to bring many signals out using a minimum of pins.

EXAMPLE: Intel's 186 microprocessor uses a multiplexed bus that combines both address and data on the same set of 16 pins. During the first part of a memory cycle, the address is driven out of the pins, and ALE (address latch enable) is high. ALE clocks the address information into external latches provided by the designer.

During the next T-state the processor de-asserts the address and either drives (for a write cycle) or accepts (for a read cycle) data over the same set of pins.

See also address latch enable, address strobe.

multiplexed display *n.* A display unit that minimizes pin count by grouping display elements in a bus. Multiplexed displays greatly reduce both pin and driver requirements. Generally, they bus segments of the display (e.g., individual characters) together. A controller turns on one character at a time, at a very fast rate. Like a television, such displays rely on the persistence of the eye to fool the user into thinking the device is showing data all of the time.

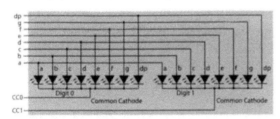

Typical LED multiplexed display. Note how the anodes are bused together. A single 8-bit-wide driver can drive these, with one additional driver per digit that turns on the appropriate digit when its data is on the bus.

multiplexer *n.* A device that selects one input from many. One of a number of inputs are selected by a binary code. *See also* analog multiplexer, digital multiplexer.

multiplexing 1. *n.* The process of selecting one of a number of inputs.

2. *n.* The process of using a single bus to handle several types of data. *See also* multiplexed bus, analog multiplexer, digital multiplexer. *Contrast with* demultiplexing.

multiplier *n.* A circuit that computes the product of two numbers. There are many types of multipliers: floating-point multipliers require a vast number of transistors and are thus sometimes implemented in coprocessors; integer multipliers in smaller processors are often only 16 × 16 bits, so they require additional software help to handler larger numbers.

HISTORY: Although multiplication requires a lot of electronics, even some of the earliest computers included hardware support. IBM's 704 (circa 1955) had a hardware floating-point unit. The 1620, a smaller and much cheaper ($85k) machine that followed in 1959 had an integer multiply that used hardware lookup tables. Early computers were used largely for scientific and accounting applications, where fast multiplication was essential.

multiply-and-accumulate *adj.* Describes a special CPU instruction, common on digital signal processors, that performs both a multiplication and an addition in a single instruction cycle. The result of the multiplication is typically added to a sum kept in a register. Abbreviated MAC. A multiply-and-accumulate instruction is helpful for speeding up the execution of the many digital filters and transforms required in signal processing applications. In recent years, many microprocessor and microcontroller makers have included a MAC instruction on their products as well.

multiprocessing *n.* The use of more than one processor in a single computer system. So-called multiprocessor systems usually have a common memory space through which all of the processors can communicate and share data. In addition, some multiprocessor systems support parallel processing.

multiprocessor *adj.* Describes a system that uses more than one CPU. Multiprocessor systems are usually tightly coupled, sharing data over a multiport bus or via a high-speed message-passing scheme. It's common to find two or more processors on a single chip today: one is often a DSP for number crunching and the other a conventional CISC machine that handles routine housekeeping.

multitasking *n.* The execution of multiple software routines in pseudoparallel. Each routine represents a separate thread of execution. The operating system is responsible for simulating parallelism by parceling out the processor's time to the individual threads.

multithreading *See* multitasking.

mutex (mew tex) *n.* An operating system data structure used by threads to ensure exclusive access to shared variables or hardware registers. Short for MUTual EXclusion. A mutex is a multitasking-aware binary flag that can be used to synchronize the activities of multiple tasks. As such, it can protect critical sections from interruption and shared resources from simultaneous accesses.

USAGE: The term "mutex" is best reserved only for binary semaphores that are aware of the potential for priority inversions and implement an appropriate workaround. But beware that many RTOS vendors do not make such distinctions.

mutual exclusion *n.* A guarantee of exclusive access to a shared resource. In embedded systems, the shared resource is typically a block of memory, a global variable, a peripheral, or a set of registers. Mutual exclusion is typically achieved with the use of a mutex.

mux (rhymes with tux) *abbr. See* multiplexer.

mV (mill-ee-volt) *abbr. See* millivolt.

MV (meg-uh-volt) *abbr. See* megavolt.

MVC (as letters) *abbr. See* model-view controller.

mW (mill-ee-watt) *abbr. See* milliwatt.

mythical man month *n.* To the dismay of managers, it is often impossible to complete a problem that will take nine man months more quickly by throwing nine engineers at it for one month. Like pregnancy, some tasks simply can't be divided up in that way. In fact, the mere introduction of additional developers can increase the total workload.

HISTORY: Frederick P. Brooks noted this phenomenon in his seminal book *The Mythical Man Month*. Decades of experience since confirm his observation.

FURTHER READING: Brooks, Frederick P. *The Mythical Man-Month: Essays on Software Engineering*, 2nd ed. (Anniversary Edition). Addison-Wesley, 1995.

N-m *See* joule.

N-version programming *n.* A means of achieving high availability in software, in which *N* pieces of software, all of which are designed to meet the very same requirements, are developed by separate development teams. Abbreviated NVP. Run in parallel and combined with a voting algorithm of some sort, the decisions of each of the *N* pieces of software can be weighed to make the final decision. Although having multiple teams implement the same spec might result in fewer bugs in the final decision, there is a big flaw in N-version programming: an error in the spec can be replicated in all *N* implementations! For that reason (and the high cost), the technique is little used.

nA (nan-oh-amp) *abbr. See* nanoamp.

NAK (knack) *n.* A response that something was not received properly. Short for Not AcKnowledged. Ironically, the mere fact that there's a NAK implies that the packet or command was received. It could be that there was some sort of an error (checksum related?) or that the requested command was not supported.

naming convention *n.* A standard way of creating variable and function names. Naming conventions promise to ease code readability by eliminating difficult-to-decipher names. Unfortunately, however, everyone has their own idea about the best conventions; worse, few programmers seem to follow whatever conventions are established for their project or company. *See also* Hungarian notation, foo, coding standard.

EXAMPLE: Without conventions, it's common to see loop variables named i, and ii, and (this author's personal favorite) iii as the nesting level increases. The casual use of names led one compiler team to emit errors on any profane name (the RALPH Fortran compiler); this feature backfired when the agriculture department ran a program designed to study male chickens.

NaN (rhymes with man) *abbr. See* not-a-number.

NAND (rhymes with Rand) *n.* A Boolean operator that performs an inverted AND. Short for NOT AND.

$$A \text{ NAND } B = \text{NOT } (A \text{ AND } B)$$

Put another way, a NAND produces false if all inputs are true.

NAND gate *n.* A logic device that computes the NAND of two or more inputs.

The schematic symbol for a NAND gate.

nano- (nan-oh) *pre.* The prefix representing a numerical multiplier of 10^{-9}. Abbreviated n.

nanoamp *n.* A billionth of an ampere. Abbreviated nA.

nanofarad *n.* A billionth of a farad. Abbreviated nF.

nanosecond *n.* A billionth of a second. Abbreviated ns. A nanosecond is the length of one clock cycle at a 1 GHz rate. In that sense, it is a relatively short interval of time in which the software in a more typical MHz/kHz embedded system cannot even begin to respond to events around it.

nanovolt *n.* A billionth of a volt. Abbreviated nV.

NASA (nass-uh) *abbr.* The U.S. government's civilian space and aviation research department. Short for National Aeronautics and Space Administration. NASA's mission is to understand and protect our home planet, to explore the universe and search for life, and to inspire the next generation of explorers.

NASA is primarily known for its work in space, but $2.8 billion of its 2003 $15 billion budget was set aside for work on aviation.

NAT (gnat) *abbr.* An IP routing hack used by DSL/cable routers and other gateways to make all traffic to and from a LAN of computers behind them appear as if it refers to a single IP address on the WAN. Short for Network Address Translation. Formerly called IP spoofing. RFC 1631.

The technique basically revolves around having the router modify all of the packets from a client on the LAN to a server on the WAN so they appear to come directly from the router's WAN IP address. Each such transaction results in the creation of a fake port number. When the response arrives at the router from the server, the port number is used to decode the true destination and to route the packet onto the LAN properly.

National Semiconductor *N.* An important semiconductor company that caters to both the digital and linear markets.

HISTORY: Founded in Danbury, Connecticut, in 1959 by eight former engineers of Sperry Rand Corporation. Not a major player in microprocessors, though their 1984 NS32032 was an early high-performance 32-bit CPU that was perhaps too much processor too early in the microprocessor revolution.

native method *n.* A function written in C or C++ but linked to a Java program and called from there. The Java keyword `native` is used to declare the method in the Java class it belongs to. However, the implementation of that method is outside the Java program and, once compiled, must typically be statically linked to the JVM.

NC (as letters) *abbr. See* no connect.

near *res.* A special non-standard reserved word recognized by some x86-specific C compilers. Used to declare functions or data near.

NEAR (rhymes with fear) *abbr.* A NASA spacecraft that almost failed its mission as a result of a multitude of software bugs. Short for Near Earth Asteroid Rendezvous. *See also* Clementine, Ariane 5, Therac-25.

near *n.* In real-mode x86 code, a function or data that is in the current segment. *Contrast with* far.

negation *n.* The process of inverting a bit, state, or word. Expressed by a variety of symbols, including NOT, /, and ~. Some CPUs that lack an explicit negation instruction implement this important construct by XORing the data with all 1s.

negative feedback *n.* A type of feedback in which the system's output is inverted and then coupled to the system's input. Negative feedback stabilizes systems. It reduces the overall gain, since a part of the inverted output bucks the signal being processed, but in so doing, minimizes the chances of oscillation. Feedback is also used in op-amps to control the amplifier's transfer function. *Contrast with* positive feedback.

negative logic *n.* A design where a logic 0 represents the asserted state.

EXAMPLE: A NAND gate produces 0 only if both inputs are 1; the 0 is the asserted, or TRUE, state.

negative temperature coefficient *n.* A device that exhibits a decrease in some parameter as the temperature goes up. *Contrast with* positive temperature coefficient. *See also* temperature coefficient.

EXAMPLE: The input leakage current of the 741 op-amp has a negative temperature coefficient as it goes from about 200,000 picoamp at −50°C to 100,000 picoamp at 100°C.

negative true *See* active low.

nested breakpoint *n.* A debugging resource that stops program execution after a number of specified events occur. Nested breakpoints let the developer zero in on the typical sort of bug that occurs only within some combination of events. If function A( ) works when called from B( ) but not from C( ), then a nested breakpoint that breaks on A( ) after C( ) will let the developer see the system state only at that time. Nested breakpoints are invariably a part of the resources provided by complex breakpoints.

nested interrupt *See* interrupt, nested.

net *n.* On a schematic, an interconnection between components. *See also* netlist.

net label *n.* The name given to a net on a schematic.

netlist *n.* A computer file that lists all of the connections needed to produce a printed circuit board. The netlist is an ASCII text file that lists the characteristics of each component and what each pin of every component connects to. Each of these connections is called a node.

Netlists are produced by schematic capture programs and are sometimes used as inputs to autorouters.

network *n.* A system that transmits any combination of voice, video, and data between users. The network includes the network operating system in the client and server machines, the cables connecting them, and all supporting hardware in between such as bridges, routers, and switches. In wireless systems, antennas and towers are also part of the network. *See* local area network, wide area network, personal area network.

A portion of a netlist. Note that node N00002 is found under both the resistor and the diode; these two components thus connect together.

```
'M RC20.RESISTOR.LIB.10.059FF410.R2,.GR1
(1 N00001 PA A1)
(2 N00002 PA A1)
;

'M DO-7.DIODE.LIB.Diode.059FF6A4.D1,.GR1
(1 N00002 PA A1)
(2 N00000 PA A1)
;
```

network byte order *n.* The endianness of a network protocol. For example, TCP/IP's network byte order is big-endian. *Contrast with* host byte order.

network layer *n.* The protocol layer responsible for the routing of packets between source and destination via zero or more intermediary nodes. Layer 3 of the OSI reference model. In the TCP/IP protocol suite, details of the network layer are defined almost entirely by the IP software, though ICMP (ping) and IGMP (multidrop) are also network layer protocols. Each packet that goes out on the network is either an IP packet or an ICMP packet or an IGMP packet but never more than one of these types. *See also* data link layer, transport layer, data plane.

network processor *n.* A device that is similar to a microprocessor, except that it has been optimized for use in applications involving network routing and packet processing. Abbreviated NPU. There is no standard architecture, but many network processors feature multiple RISC CPUs running in parallel. In this configuration, one central processor typically receives and handles network control packets while the others pass data packets through the system at network speeds. *See also* control plane, data plane.

FURTHER READING: http://www.netrino.com/Articles/NetworkProcessors/

Never-Never Land 1. *N.* Where the processor is said to have wandered off to after a crash or hang. This characterization is particularly apropos if the cause of the crash is an unhandled interrupt or chasing a null pointer, since these often result in the processor executing whatever code or data is at logical address 0x00000.

2. *N.* Peter Pan's 'hood.

new *res.* A C++ and Java keyword for creating a new object on the heap. In function, this keyword is essentially equivalent to C's malloc(). However, the syntax of use is a bit different, and what's actually returned is a reference for the new object rather than a pointer to its memory location. *See also* delete.

newbie *n.* Someone with very little experience. Embedded systems newbies tend to make the same mistakes—such as kicking a watchdog timer from a timer ISR—on their way to learning, through the hard knocks of experience.

newton *n.* A standard unit of force. Abbreviated N. One newton is the force required to give a 1-kilogram mass an acceleration of 1 meter per second[2].

HISTORY: Named for Sir Isaac Newton (1642–1727).

Newton's method *n.* An iterative way to approximate the roots of equations.

To find the roots of $f(x) = 0$, for example, take a guess at the solution and call that x_n. Then compute

$$x_{n+1} = x_n - \frac{f(x_n)}{f'(x_n)}$$

where x_{n+1} is a better estimate of the solution than x_n. Iterate this equation until the solution converges to the required accuracy.

Although Newton's method is simple, it's not an optimal solution. Convergence can require many iterations. A bad initial guess can slow convergence; worse, for a function with many minima, a

bad guess can cause the method to return at a local minimum.

HISTORY: An early version of the method was invented by Isaac Newton (1643–1727) in 1669. In 1690, Joseph Raphson (1678–1715) simplified Newton's approach. Simpson (1710–1761), Mourraille (1720–1808), Cauchy (1789–1857), and Kantorovich (1912–1986) all improved the approach. Today, though, it's called either Newton's method or the Newton–Raphson algorithm.

Newton-Raphson algorithm *See* Newton's method.

next significant bit *n.* When examining a word, the next significant bit is the one immediately to the left or right of the one just processed. Abbreviated NSb.

EXAMPLE: If the word contains 0x4000 and you've just looked at the MSb while working your way to the right, the NSb is a 1.

Nexus *N.* Properly called Nexus 5001, an IEEE effort to define a standard debugging interface for microprocessors. Increasing processor speeds and difficult-to-probe packages, along with advanced processor features like pipelines and caches, all make traditional ICE and logic analyzer tools either very expensive or nearly useless. Chip vendors have developed a variety of on-chip debugging resources (BDM, various JTAG interfaces, etc.) that address these problems. Nexus 5001 is an attempt to standardize these debug solutions, hopefully leading to cheaper tools.

FURTHER READING: http://www.nexus5001.org

nF (nan-oh-farad) *abbr. See* nanofarad.

NFS (as letters) *abbr.* A network protocol that operates above TCP and allows for local mounting of filesystems physically located on other network nodes. Short for Network FileSystem. RFC 1094. NFS is handy when developing software for embedded systems, which typically don't have a local filesystem, because the host workstation's

filesystem can be mounted and accessed locally.
For example, this model is often used by developers using the VxWorks shell to load and run individual object modules during development and testing.

EXAMPLE: The NFS model is often used by developers using the VxWorks shell to load and run individual object modules during development and testing.

nibble *n.* A 4-bit chunk of data. Any byte consists of an upper nibble and a lower nibble. This is a convenient unit of data precisely because it can represent one of 16 values. A single hexadecimal digit (0 through F) can represent the nibble in a data dump.

nickel-cadmium battery *n.* A type of rechargeable battery that is often seen as a replacement for dry-cell or alkaline disposable units. Abbreviate Ni-Cad. Ni-Cads have a reasonable discharge knee (though not as flat as a lead-acid battery), moderate energy densities, and moderate weights.

NIH (as letters) *abbr.* Short for Not Invented Here. Some corporate cultures and engineering design teams are said to suffer from a syndrome in which they cannot accept any technology that was "not invented here."

nines complement *See* 9s complement.

NIST (rhymes with mist) *abbr.* A U.S. agency that sets standards for units of measure and other technologies that facilitate trade. Short for National Institute for Standards and Technology.

FURTHER READING: http://www.nist.gov

nm (nan-oh-meter) *abbr.* 10^{-9} meters. *See also* angstrom.

NMI (as letters) *abbr. See* nonmaskable interrupt.

no connect *n.* A pin that is not to be connected to any other part of a circuit board.

USAGE: The abbreviation NC is often used on schematics.

no parity *n.* A type of serial communications in which no parity bit is transmitted. *See also* 8N1, parity, even parity, odd parity.

no-op *See* nop.

node *n.* A junction where two or more signals come together. *See also* netlist.

noise *n.* Any undesirable component of a received signal. Noise is like pornography: it's difficult to define precisely what it is, yet you know it when you see it. *See also* white noise, pink noise, shot noise, Johnson noise.

noise reduction *n.* Any of a number of methods to smooth data. Raw data read from the real world tends to be noisy; noise reduction techniques remove some or all of the noise to make the data more closely resemble the real signal. Methods include averaging, boxcars, curve fits, and many more. *See also* noise, average, boxcar integrator, least squares curve fitting.

nominal 1. *adj.* According to plan, or meeting expectations.
EXAMPLE: "The inputs appear nominal" is often heard in a lab.
2. *adj.* Of a trifling amount.
EXAMPLE: "A nominal sum" means very little.

nominal value *n.* The expected data. *See also* nominal.

nonce *n.* A number that is only used once, as in a security protocol.

nonintrusive *adj.* Said of a debugging tool that does not change the functioning of the embedded system being tested. Nonintrusive debug is by and large a myth for most tools. Single-stepping and breakpointing, after all, halt the program's execution, which has a very intrusive effect. Vendors often use the term to designate tools that don't require resources on the target (extra memory, interrupts, etc.) and that don't substantially change the system's electrical parameters.

nonlinear distortion *n.* Any undesired signal alteration that is more than a simple offset or gain change.

EXAMPLE: A class C amplifier clips negative excursions of the signal, inducing a nonlinear distortion.

nonlinear system *n.* Any system with a transfer function more complicated than that defining a straight line.

EXAMPLE: Nonlinear transfer functions include exponentials like $y = mx^2$ and more complex functions like $y = \tan(x)$.

nonmaskable interrupt *n.* An interrupt that cannot be disabled. Known as a trap (on some Intel processors), as a level 7 interrupt (Motorola), or by other names.

nonpreemptive scheduling *n.* A type of multithreading that does not have the ability to stop the running thread. *Contrast with* preemptive scheduling. *See also* scheduling point, shortest-job-first, run-to-completion.

EXAMPLE: DOS uses a nonpreemptive run-to-completion scheduler. Once a program starts running, no other program can use the processor until the first terminates.

Of course even in DOS, hardware interrupts may still fire, and those can be handled by ISRs written in software. That's the concept behind terminate-and-stay-resident (TSR) programs.

nonrecurring engineering cost *n.* The cost of designing and implementing a new or updated product. *See also* nonrecurring expense.

nonrecurring expense *n.* A business investment in the development of a new product. Abbreviated NRE. Unlike parts and manufacturing costs, which recur for each unit sold, nonrecurring costs, such as engineering time, occur just once and can be amortized over the life of the product.

nonreentrant *adj.* Said of a function that cannot be safely called by parallel tasks. *Contrast with* reentrant.

nonvolatile *adj.* Pertains to a C variable not declared with the `volatile` keyword. Nonvolatile variables are altered only by the program, not by things done by the hardware. *Contrast with* volatile.

nonvolatile memory *n.* A memory device that will not lose the data it contains when power is removed. Popular nonvolatile memory devices include the various flavors of ROM (PROM, EPROM, etc.), flash, and NVRAM. FRAM is another nonvolatile RAM, but it is little used.

nop (no-op) *n.* An opcode that forces the CPU to do nothing for a complete cycle. Short for No OPeration. Often used to implement brief timing delays.

NOR *n.* A Boolean operator that returns a true if and only if all inputs are false. Short for NOT OR.

$$A \text{ NOR } B = \text{NOT } (A \text{ OR } B)$$

Put another way, a NOR produces false if any input is true.

NOR gate *n.* A logic device that computes the NOR of two or more inputs.

The schematic symbol for a NOR gate.

normal distribution *n.* The normal distribution is a ubiquitous and extremely important probability distribution used in statistics. Often called the Gaussian distribution and illustrated by its representative plot (the bell curve). The probability density function of the normal distribution with mean μ and standard deviation σ is

$$\frac{1}{\sigma\sqrt{2\pi}}e^{-\sqrt{\frac{\sigma-\mu}{\sigma}}}$$

About 68% of the area under the curve is within one standard deviation of the mean, 95.5% within two standard deviations, and 99.7% within three standard deviations (the 67–95.5–99.7 rule).

HISTORY: The normal curve was developed mathematically in 1733 by DeMoivre (1667–1754) as an approximation to the binomial distribution. Subsequently, Gauss (1777–1855) used the normal curve to analyze astronomical data in 1809.

NOT *n.* A Boolean operator that returns the inverse of its input. NOT is often denoted by a preceding forward slash (/) or tilde (~), or by a trailing single quote ('). If the input is true, NOT returns false. If the input is false, it returns true.

NOT gate *n.* A logic circuit that computes the NOT of the input. Also called an inverter.

The schematic symbol of a NOT gate.

not-a-number *adj.* Describes a flag that indicates a result held in a variable isn't a legal number. Abbreviated NaN. Floating-point packages often use a NaN flag to designate results that are illegal.

EXAMPLE: $\log(x) = $ NaN when $x < 0$.

notch filter *n.* A filter that passes or blocks a narrow range of frequencies.

NP-complete (en pee complete) *adj.* Said of a problem that is calculable on a computer via a polynomial-time algorithm. Short for Nondeterministic Polynomial-time–complete. Sometimes abbreviated NPC. Polynomial-time algorithms are O(n), O(n^2), etc.

NP-incomplete *adj.* Said of a problem that is not NP-complete.

NPN transistor *n.* A bipolar transistor that is constructed by diffusing N regions on either side of a P region. NPN transistors are on when the base-emitter junction is forward biased. *Contrast with* PNP transistor.

The schematic symbol of an NPN transistor.

NRC (as letters) *abbr.* Short for Non-Recurring Costs. *See* NRE.

NRE (as letters) *abbr.* The one-time, fixed, up-front costs associated with the development of a piece of hardware, a piece of software, or an entire system. Short for NonRecurring Engineering costs. These costs are nonrecurring because they do not directly affect the per-unit manufacturing cost of the product. However, from an accounting point of view, they should be amortized over the cost of all units ultimately produced.

NRZ encoding (as letters) *n.* A coding scheme used in transmitting data, where the signal's 1s and 0s are sent unaltered. Short for NonReturn to Zero. Using NRZ, a logic 1 bit is sent as a high value and a logic 0 bit is sent as a low value (the driver chip might invert these signals).

Nonreturn to zero encoding is commonly used in slow-speed communication interfaces for both synchronous and asynchronous transmission.

Because NRZ transmissions might have long runs of 0s or 1s, the receiving circuit, if based on a phase-locked loop, can drift out of synchronization with the data. For this reason, Ethernet transmissions use Manchester encoding. *Contrast with* NRZI encoding.

NRZI encoding *n.* A recording method used for nine-track magnetic tapes and USB, where a 0 is represented by a change in the signal and a 0 by no change. *Contrast with* NRZ encoding.

ns (nan-oh-second) *abbr. See* nanosecond.

NSb *See* next significant bit.

nsec (nan-oh-second) *abbr. See* nanosecond.

> **USAGE:** The preferred abbreviation is ns, which is recommended by NIST and the IEEE Computer Society.

`ntohl()` (network-to-host long) *fn.* A function or macro for converting a 32-bit value from network to host byte order. See code listing.

`ntohs()` (network-to-host short) *fn.* A function or macro for converting a 16-bit value from network to host byte order. See code listing.

Nucleus *N.* A popular family of RTOSes from Accelerated Technology (now part of Mentor Graphics).

`NULL` *lit.* A constant used in checking for a destination before dereferencing a pointer. Generally `#defined` as `((void *) 0)` in C. *See also* null pointer.

null modem *See* null modem cable.

null modem cable *n.* A cable used to connect two RS-232 devices of the same type (e.g., DTE to DTE).

Because all DTE devices transmit on pin 2 (on a 25-pin connector), a null modem cable must swap pins so that each DTE device sends data to the receive pin (3) on the other DTE. Useful null modem cables also swap the handshaking signals or, in some cases, loop them back, since not all devices properly drive the handshakes.

FURTHER READING: See *The Art of Electronics* (Paul Horowitz and Winfield Hill, 2nd ed., Cambridge University Press, 1989) for drawings of various kinds of null modem cables.

null pointer *n.* A pointer to address zero. Pointers are generally null until they are assigned something to point to. They should not be dereferenced while they are in this state; if they are, the CPU might wander off into Never-Never Land.

number, normalized *n.* A floating-point number stored in its correct form. Normalized numbers always have the mantissa adjusted so its most significant bit is a 1. Typical intermediate products of math operations (addition, subtraction) destroy the number's normalization, so the final step in such an operation is to readjust the mantissa. *See also* IEEE 754.

`ntohl()`   If the network protocol is TCP/IP, which uses a big endian representation, this C macro will perform the byte reordering.

```
#if defined(BIG_ENDIAN)
#define ntohl(A)  (A)
#elif defined(LITTLE_ENDIAN)
#define ntohl(A)  ((((uint32_t) (A) & 0xff000000) >> 24) | \
                   (((uint32_t) (A) & 0x00ff0000) >> 8)  | \
                   (((uint32_t) (A) & 0x0000ff00) << 8)  | \
                   (((uint32_t) (A) & 0x000000ff) << 24))
#endif
```

`ntohs()`   If the network protocol is TCP/IP, which uses a big endian representation, this C macro will perform the byte reordering.

```
#if defined(BIG_ENDIAN)
#define ntohs(A)  (A)
#elif defined(LITTLE_ENDIAN)
#define ntohs(A)  ((((uint16_t) (A) & 0xff00) >> 8) | \
                   (((uint16_t) (A) & 0x00ff) << 8))
#endif
```

numerical integration *n.* The process of computing the integral of a function, or the area under a curve, by summing many discrete values. Numerical integration is the opposite of analytical integration, wherein one derives an equation that is the integral of a function.

numerical methods *n.* A huge class of techniques for solving equations using approximations on computers.

FURTHER READING: http://www.numerical-methods.com.

Numerical Recipes *N.* A series of books that contain algorithms for various numerical methods. The most recent, *Numerical Recipes in C++* (Cambridge University Press, 2002), contains more than 350 such recipes.

FURTHER READING: The *Numerical Recipes* books are now online at http://www.nr.com.

nV (nan-oh-volt) *abbr. See* nanovolt.

NVP (as letters) *abbr. See* N-version programming.

NVRAM (en-vee ram) *abbr.* A type of RAM that retains its data even when the system is powered down. Short for NonVolatile Random Access Memory. NVRAM frequently consists of an SRAM and a long-life battery.

Nyquist rate *N.* The rate at which a signal must be sampled to reconstruct it. *See also* Nyquist theorem.

Nyquist theorem *N.* When reading a signal, the highest frequency that can be accurately represented is less than one half of the sampling rate. More precisely: the discrete time sequence of a sampled continuous function contains enough information to reproduce the function exactly, provided the sampling rate is at least twice that of the highest frequency contained in the original signal.

HISTORY: Proposed by Harry Nyquist (1889–1976) in 1927.

O() (oh of) *fn.* A computer science notation for describing the computational complexity of an algorithm in shorthand. Many algorithms are $O(n)$, meaning they require a number of CPU cycles in proportion to the number, n, of data elements to be manipulated. For example, algorithms that require $2n + 4$ and $45n + 340$, respectively, are both $O(n)$. Any algorithm that is polynomial in nature is $O(n^d)$ where d is the degree of the polynomial. Many algorithms are $O(\log_2 n)$, $O(\ln n)$, or $O(n^2)$; others, by contrast, are NP-incomplete.

obfuscated C *n.* A yearly contest in which the goal is to write the cutest, most confusing, least expected, and most bizarre C code. Ironically, the contest has guidelines, rather like the standards they seem to disavow. The official goals are

- to write the most obscure/obfuscated C program using the guidelines,
- to show the importance of programming style in an ironic way,
- to stress C compilers with unusual code,
- to illustrate some of the subtleties of C, and
- to provide a safe forum for poor C code.

Some pundits suggest that the very existence of this contest is a condemnation of C, the programmers who embrace obfuscation, or both.

FURTHER READING: The contest website is http://www.ioccc.org.

objdump *See* binutils.

object *n.* A run-time realization of a class. Though there may be more than one object of the same type, all generally share the same code. Each object has its own unique data, on which that code operates.

object code *n.* A set of processor-readable opcodes and data. The output of compilers and assemblers and the input and output of a linker are files containing object code. However, there are a variety of standardized and proprietary object file formats, meaning that development tools from one vendor can only rarely read the object code produced by those of another.

object file *n.* A file containing object code; in particular, the output of a compiler or assembler. Most object files begin with a symbol table, which is followed by intermixed segments of code and data.

object file format *n.* The proprietary or standard format of an object file. Standard object file formats include a.out, COFF, and ELF.

FURTHER READING: A good source for information about these files is http://www.wotsit.org.

object lifelines *n.* The dotted lines associated with actors, objects, and roles in a sequence diagram.

object-oriented *adj.* A design that partitions a system into objects—combinations of methods (code) and the data the method works on. Abbreviated OO. OO designs exploit encapsulation, polymorphism, and inheritance.

object-oriented programming *n.* A method of implementation in which programs are organized as cooperative collections of objects, each of which represents an instance of some class, which have classes that are all members of a hierarchy of classes united by inheritance relationships. In such programs, classes are generally viewed as static, whereas objects typically have a much more dynamic nature, which is encouraged by the existence of polymorphism.

octal *n.* A number in base-8 notation. Because there are only eight values to represent, only the digits 0–7 are necessary. Octal notation is useful for representing 3-bit values. In C and various related languages, an integer constant will be assumed octal when it begins with a 0. Be aware that leading a decimal number with a 0 is a sure way to create a bug, since the compiler will only warn you if an 8 or 9 follows.

octave *n.* A factor of two. From music theory, where the 880-Hz note, A, is one octave above its 440-Hz brother. *See also* decade.

odd parity *n.* A type of parity in which a bit is appended to data to make an odd number of 1s. Used by the receiver to ensure correct data transmission. *Contrast with* even parity.

EXAMPLE: ASCII character 'A' (0x41), if transmitted with odd parity, would be sent as 0100 0001 1b. The LSb is the parity bit and is set, since the character has an even number of 1s. By contrast, lowercase 'a' (0x61) would be sent as 0110 0001 0b with odd parity.

OEM (as letters) *abbr. See* original equipment manufacturer.

off-by-1 error *n.* An implementation error resulting from an end condition being set to one less or one more than the appropriate value. The symptoms of bugs resulting from such errors can sometimes be subtle and hard to detect.

EXAMPLE: A loop needs to execute five times and is constructed as follows.

```
for (x = 0; x <= 5; x++) {...}
```

Because of the <= (instead of <), this loop actually executes six times. The end-of-loop condition is off by one.

offset 1. *n*. On an x86 processor, the less significant half of a segment:offset address pair. Registers that hold offsets include IP, SP, SI, and DI. *See also* segment:offset.

2. *n*. The difference between a specific address and a base address. *See also* base-plus-offset addressing.

3. *n*. A constant added to any circuit that transforms a signal. *See also* gain.

EXAMPLE: Consider a simple op-amp used as a linear amplifier. Its transfer function will be

$$output = gain \times input + O,$$

where O is the offset.

offset error *n*. Any error that is a constant added to the input signal. Analog electronics suffer from many error sources; of these, offset error is the most common and easiest to fix. In op-amps, for instance, it's common to eliminate offset errors by using a potentiometer. Proper design includes balancing the input impedances of both inputs to minimize this error.

ohm (like the mantra) *n*. The unit of resistance. Abbreviated Ω. One ohm is the resistance that will allow 1 ampere of current to flow when 1 volt of EMF is impressed across the resistance.

HISTORY: Named for Georg Simon Ohm (1789–1854).

Ohm's Law *N*. The basic rule that relates voltage, current, and resistance.

$$V = I \times R$$

V is voltage in volts, *I* is current in amps, and *R* is resistance in ohms.

ohmmeter *n*. A piece of electrical test equipment that measures resistance. Usually an ohmmeter will measure other parameters as well, such as voltage, current, and more.

on-board *adj*. Said of a feature or peripheral that's included on the same PCB as the CPU. On-board peripherals are also called external peripherals, since they are external to the silicon in which the CPU is located. *Contrast with* on-chip.

on-chip *adj*. Said of a feature or peripheral that's included within the same silicon as the CPU. Microcontrollers generally can have lots of on-chip peripherals, such as timer/counter units and interrupt controllers. *Contrast with* on-board.

on-chip debug *n*. A technology-agnostic name for the variety of techniques (like BDM) that include software debug capability within the processor hardware. Sometimes abbreviated OCD. The connection to the host-based debugger is generally over a standard JTAG port or a proprietary header. *See also* background debug mode, OnCE, MPSD, Nexus.

on–off control *n*. A simple way to manage an analog system. The on–off approach controls a system by measuring an input and then turning the output on or off as needed. Also called bang-bang control. The on–off technique is distinct from more sophisticated control algorithms that measure how much error there is in the input and then apply just enough correction to the output to bring the system to the desired state. *Contrast with* proportional control. See figure.

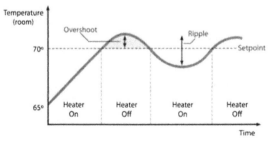

The mechanical thermostat is a simple on–off control system. When the room's temperature is lower than the preset value, the furnace comes on, staying on full blast until the temperature of the room reaches the set point.

OnCE (once) *abbr.* An on-chip debug solution used in Motorola DSPs. Short for On-Chip Emulation. Similar to BDM in features, but more complex in that its internal state machine is driven by the remote debugger. Connection is via dedicated processor pins (old) or JTAG (newer parts).

one *See* logic 1.

one's complement *n.* The binary representation of a particular integer value in one's complement notation.

one's complement notation *n.* A way of encoding positive and negative integer values in binary. One's complement notation creates negative numbers by inverting each bit in the number. Thus, the one's complement of 1101b is 0010b. Both positive (0000b) and negative zeroes (1111b) are defined. One's complement notation is rarely used by modern computers. *Compare to* two's complement notation, sign magnitude notation.

one-shot *See* monostable multivibrator.

one-shot timer *n.* A timer that fires just once after a prespecified interval. A one-shot timer can be implemented in hardware or software and is most often used to implement a timeout.

Hardware "one-shots" are sometimes called monostable multivibrators and are usually implemented as an IC (e.g., 74LS121) using a capacitor and resistor to set the "on" time. *Contrast with* periodic timer.

one-time programmable *adj.* Describes any programmable device, like a PROM or a PLD, that can be programmed just once by the end user. Abbreviated OTP.

USAGE: The term OTP is used most commonly to describe a microcontroller with an on-chip PROM.

HISTORY: In the olden days several vendors sold EPROMs without windows. These could be programmed but not erased. Removing the windows meant the parts could be packaged in plastic instead of ceramic, greatly reducing their price.

OOP (rhymes with goop) *abbr. See* object-oriented programming.

op-amp *See* amplifier, operational.

op-amp, chopper-stabilized *n.* An analog circuit that offers almost perfectly low offset outputs. Op-amps are physical devices suffering from thermal and component drift over time. One error resulting from these drifts is the output offset, which should be zero but rarely is. Certain very high precision applications cannot tolerate the small drifting offsets typical of an op-amp, so the chopper-stabilized design is sometimes used instead.

Chopper-stabilized circuits use two op-amps connected together. One maintains a null voltage, which corrects the other. An oscillator periodically drives the devices into an auto-zeroing mode.

opcode *n.* A binary value that is recognized by a processor as one of the instructions in its instruction set.

open *adj.* Said of an electrical connection that is supposed to be connected but isn't. *Compare to* no connect. *See also* short circuit.

open loop *n.* A system that controls something without using a feedback path. Open loop systems tend to run wildly out of control. Driving down a narrow street with your eyes closed is one example of open loop control, though the screams of pedestrians on either side of the road might induce some level of feedback. *Contrast with* closed-loop control. *See also* feedback.

open source *adj.* A vague term describing any software that comes with source code, no matter how its use is or is not restricted.

Unfortunately, there is no clear definition for "open source software" and no standard license. Many companies are using the term open source these days, but in far different ways. Although the idea is similar to that of free software (you can generally still use, modify, and redistribute the software), there is far less emphasis on the right of the source code to be free.

Although not as true with respect to Linux, many open source companies seem to be unwilling to give up central control of their software. (Free software, on the other hand, has no owner.)

What's important about open source software, particularly for embedded systems developers, is that its licensing terms are more like LGPL than GPL. In other words, you are typically free to add your own proprietary software to the open source code and produce a proprietary result. The free software movement doesn't much like this but is otherwise more in alignment with the newer open source movement than in opposition to it. *Contrast with* free software, proprietary software.

FURTHER READING: http://www.netrino.com/Articles/LinuxLaw/

FURTHER READING: http://www.netrino.com/Articles/OpenSource/

`open()` *fn.* A common name for a system call that opens (and creates new) files, given only the path/name and a list of requested (read/write/execute) permissions. A part of the standard Unix API for files and I/O devices, once a file has been `open()`ed successfully, it can be read or written via the file descriptor returned to the caller. *See also* `read()`, `write()`, `close()`, `ioctl()`.

open-collector *adj.* Describes a type of output on some ICs that allows many chips to drive a single node. Open-collector outputs have a transistor in which the collector is connected to the output pin but has no other attached components inside the chip. Although once commonly used for multiplexed buses, the invention of tristate logic displaced open-collector drivers from this role.

Open-collector parts are still useful for driving LEDs, relays, and other devices.

open-loop control *n.* The realization of a control system without feedback. *Contrast with* closed-loop control.

open-loop gain *n.* A characteristic of op-amps, the open-loop gain expresses the device's maximum gain with no components in the feedback loop. An ideal op-amp's open-loop gain is infinite; practical devices' open-loop gains run in the millions.

operand 1. *n.* An argument in an assembly language instruction.

2. *n.* An operator's argument.

operand stack *n.* A special stack dedicated to the manipulation of data. A Java virtual machine uses an operand stack to perform arithmetic and to dereference objects. Rather than load a value from RAM into a general-purpose register, as you might in x86 assembly if you wanted to increment it, the Java bytecodes push that value onto the top of the operand stack, then push a 1, then apply the "+" operator to pop both off the stack and push their result. *See also* reverse Polish notation.

operating system *n.* A piece of software that makes multitasking possible. An operating system typically consists of a set of system calls and a periodic clock tick ISR. The operating system is responsible for deciding which task should be using the processor at any given time and for controlling access to shared resources. *See also* real-time operating system, multitasking.

operator 1. *n.* A mathematical construct that transforms input arguments. Operators can be unary (one input argument), binary (two arguments), or more complex.

EXAMPLE: The binary "+" operator takes two inputs and produces their sum as output.

2. *n.* That infuriating person using your product who is never satisfied with your brilliant design.

operator overloading *n.* The process of creating distinct behaviors for a single operator so that it will perform differently based on the data types involved. A handy feature of C++, it is just like function overloading, except that it affects operators like +, −, &, etc.

Operator overloading allows you to do things like create a `ComplexNumber` class along with the knowledge of how to add/subtract/multiply/divide two complex numbers. The addition operator can be implemented as the `ComplexNumber::operator+()` method. The C++ compiler will call that method whenever two `ComplexNumbers` are combined by a "+".

operator precedence *n.* A set of rules that defines the order of execution of the various operators in an equation or statement of program code. Mostly, these rules derive from math and logic. For instance, multiplication takes precedence over addition. ANDs and ORs have a similar precedence relationship.

If you're not sure of the precedence in your programming language/environment, you can always use parentheses to group operators and operands to enforce the desired order of execution.

optical fiber *See* fiber optic cable.

optical isolator *n.* An IC that provides extremely high levels of isolation by coupling signals via light. Also called an optoisolator. Used in many applications, including isolating high voltages from logic levels, and in reducing the coupling of noise between circuits (since the optical isolator allows designers to couple systems with no connected grounds).

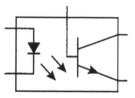

An optical isolator. The LED illuminates the light-sensitive transistor.

optical spectrum *n.* That part of the electromagnetic spectrum that's visible to the human eye. The visible spectrum runs from about violet (400 nm) to red (700 nm), though the exact limits are vague because of the different responses among individual eyes. *See also* electromagnetic spectrum.

optimization *n.* A step in the compilation of a program that reduces memory needs, increases execution speed, or some combination of the two. Compilers use a wide range of optimization techniques. Unfortunately, increasing speed usually comes at the expense of more code, and vice versa. *See also* common subexpression elimination, loop combining, loop unwinding.

optimizer *n.* The part of the compiler that optimizes the code. Often the optimizer is really a collection of tools spread throughout compile phases: portions examine the source; other parts tune the compiled code. *See also* optimization.

option *n.* One of a group of boss management techniques. Wise developers never confront their boss with problems; better, show him the problem along with a variety of potential solutions (options).

optoisolator *See* optical isolator.

OR *n.* A Boolean operator that returns a true if any input is true. Symbolically, the addition sign (+). A + B is the OR of inputs A and B.

OR gate *n.* A logic device that computes the OR of two or more inputs.

Schematic symbol of an OR gate.

or-state *n.* States that are mutually exclusive. An object is either in state A or B at any given time. *See also* and-state.

original equipment manufacturer *n.* A vendor who supplies equipment to another manufacturer for inclusion in a product. Abbreviated OEM.

EXAMPLE: IC vendors are OEMs since their products go into other products.

orthogonal 1. *adj.* Perpendicular.

2. *adj.* Two vectors are orthogonal if their dot product is zero.

3. *adj.* Said of instruction sets where most instructions can use any addressing mode.

EXAMPLE: The 68000 was much admired when it first came out, largely because of its very orthogonal instruction set.

OS (as letters) *abbr. See* operating system.

oscillator *n.* A circuit that employs feedback to autonomously change states. Most oscillators produce either sine or square waves.

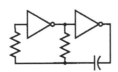

A simple oscillator that produces square waves.

oscillator, free-running *n.* An oscillator that runs forever; it's never gated on and off. *See also* oscillator.

oscilloscope *n.* A hardware debugging tool that allows you to view the voltage on one or more electrical signals. A scope for short. An embedded software developer might use an oscilloscope to determine whether a particular interrupt is currently asserted or to confirm the duty cycle of a PWM output. *See also* analog oscilloscope, digital storage oscilloscope.

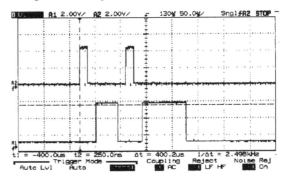

A scope trace showing two channels.

OSGi (as letters) *abbr.* A way for network-enabled devices that don't speak Internet protocol directly to communicate over IP networks using Java. Short for Open Systems Gateway Initiative.

Developed by a consortium including Ericsson, IBM, Lucent, and others, OSGi supports protocols like LONWorks and HomeRF by providing devices on those networks' virtual IP addresses.

FURTHER READING: http://www.osgi.org

OSI reference model (as letters) *n.* A seven-layer breakdown of network functionality that is commonly referenced during protocol design. Short for Open Systems Interconnection. The OSI reference model defines the following seven layers.

1. *physical*—bit-level transmission
2. *data link*—packet-level error control, data framing, and physical addressing
3. *network*—logical addressing and traffic management
4. *transport*—error checking, segmentation, and reassembly
5. *session*—conversation setup, coordination, and termination
6. *presentation*—data transmission, compression, and encryption

7. *application*—quality of service and authentication

The underlying idea is that once you've defined the functionality that should exist at each level, it's possible to, for example, substitute one Layer 1 electrical/mechanical interface for another and still have the other layers operate unchanged over the new layer.

OTP (as letters) *abbr. See* one-time programmable.

OTPROM (oh-tee-pee ROM) *abbr.* A memory device with contents that are initially empty (e.g., all bits are set to 1) that can be programmed exactly once. Short for One-Time Programmable Read-Only Memory. Once an OTPROM has been programmed it cannot be erased and reprogrammed. *Contrast with* EPROM.

USAGE: The term PROM is equivalent in meaning and is preferred for clarity. OTP is a bit more generic, since it might also apply to a PLD.

OUI (as letters) *abbr.* An identifier that can be used to create unique MAC addresses. Short for Organizationally Unique Identifier. The relevant standard is ANSI/IEEE Std 802-1990.

To obtain an OUI for your organization, first register with the IEEE (http://standards.ieee.org/regauth/oui/). You start by filling out some paperwork and sending them a check for US$1,650 (in 2002). In return, your organization becomes the proud owner of a unique 24-bit number and the 16,777,216 unique MAC addresses it is capable of identifying. You must manage those 16 million-plus subaddresses yourself.

out of memory *n.* An exception or error condition that occurs when the heap is empty and a requested dynamic memory allocation cannot be made as a result. In Java, an exception will be thrown. In C and C++, there will be no exception, so it is important always to check the return value from `malloc()` or `new` to ensure that the allocation request is fulfilled.

out-of-order reception *n.* The arrival of packets in a data stream in an order other than that in which they were transmitted.

EXAMPLE: TCP/IP packets are serialized and can individually transit any route between transmitter and receiver. No guarantees are made that the packets will arrive in their original order. Some might even be lost and require retransmittal.

outport() (out port) *fn.* An x86-specific C library function for writing data to a port in the I/O space. The prototype for this function can generally be found in the `dos.h` header file. *See also* `inport()`.

output enable *n.* A control signal on chips that sends data to a shared bus, which, when asserted, turns on the chip's output drivers. When off, the drivers are tristated so other chips can drive the bus.

The G pin on this 74244 is the output enable. Assert it and the data on the A inputs go to the Y outputs.

overclocking *n.* A really dumb way to gain marginal performance increases from a computer system. Overclocking means cranking the CPU's clock rate to frequencies not supported by the chip vendor. Overclocking works (sometimes) because the chips are specified to run over a wide temperature range; this requires the vendor to put a bit of margin in the clock spec. But because data is a lot more valuable than computer hardware, it makes little sense to run the risk of erratic crashes just to save a few bucks.

overflow *See* arithmetic overflow.

overlay *n.* In the mainframe era, the linker (at that time, usually called a mapper) could segment a large executable into multiple pieces called overlays, which were loaded one at a time at the same memory address as needed. Some modern embedded systems still use overlays, especially for local variables on small non-stack microcontrollers like the PIC.

overlay RAM *See* emulation RAM.

overload 1. *n.* A condition where an electrical circuit attempts to drive more than it can. Overloads range from too much fan-out on a logic gate, which corrupts the signal, to burning up components by stressing them too much.

2. *n.* A condition in which the computational demands placed on the system exceed available CPU cycles. Sometimes called a transient overload. Overloads cause deadlines to be missed. The Apollo 11 landing was nearly aborted when its guidance computer experienced a series of overloads.

oversample *v.* To increase the resolution of an A/D converter by sampling many times and averaging the results. Most analog signals have some inherent noise. The noise corrupts the data when read via a single sample of the A/D, but is erased by oversampling.

Oversampling both minimizes the noise and increases the effective resolution of the A/D. The resolution goes up because small signal changes below the A/D's normal resolution, which normally would not be detectable, are dithered up and down by the noise to a level the A/D can see. Averaging essentially converts the probability of the signal's being seen to new bits of resolution.

overshoot *n.* A characteristic of a signal, where positive-going transitions go momentarily to a level above the desired voltage. In embedded systems, overshoot comes mostly from mismatched impedances between the driver and receiver. It can lead to erratic data, or even the complete destruction of a circuit from SCR latchup.

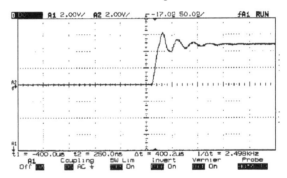

Note the overshoot on the leading edge of this signal.

P

P() *fn.* Dijkstra's name for the semaphore acquisition primitive. P is short for *proberen*, which is the Dutch word for test.

p-p (pee-to-pee) *abbr. See* peak-to-peak.

package 1. *n.* The plastic, metal, or ceramic container that encloses an IC. Packages protect the chip and bring the leads from the outside world to the chip.

2. *n.* In Java, a collection of classes.

EXAMPLE: `java.awt.*`, `java.io.*`, and `java.math.*` are packages in the standard class libraries.

3. *n.* In UML, a model element that contains other model elements.

A variety of chip packages.

packet *n.* The unit of data transfer on a network. For example, each TCP/IP packet on the Internet contains information coming from a sending node and destined for one or more receiving nodes. There is generally some upper limit, such as the MTU, on the size of a packet.

pad *n.* A copper-ringed hole in a printed circuit board into which one of the pins of an IC will be inserted. For surface mount components, the pad consists only of a contact point.

page fault *n.* An exception that's taken when a virtual memory page is off on disk, and not in main memory. The operating system captures the fault and reads the appropriate page in from disk. *See also* virtual memory.

pair programming *n.* One of the 12 practices of eXtreme Programming that has two programmers working together at a single workstation. Pair programming's promise is that two sets of eyes looking at the code results in better software. That opinion is certainly backed up by 25 years of history with code inspections. Some might consider pair programming to be too intimate, whereas others may cherish the intimacy.

PAL (pal) *abbr.* A type of logic chip in which functionality can be set by a device programmer. Short for Programmable Array Logic. A PAL consists of a fixed number of inputs and outputs. Each output is the OR of a large number of product terms, which the user programs.

HISTORY: First promulgated by Monolithic Memories (MMI), PALs include both unregistered (e.g., 20L8) and registered (20R6) versions.

PalmOS (palm oh ess) *N.* An operating system developed for use in the Palm series of personal digital assistants but now used in some other types of systems as well. PalmOS is actually more of an API than an OS. In fact, the earliest release was a set of libraries running on top of a small commercial RTOS (Kadak's AMX). Today, PalmOS is used in some hybrid PDA/cell phones and devices like barcode readers from Symbol, among other things. It can usually be recognized by the unique look and feel of its GUI.

PAN (rhymes with man) *abbr. See* personal area network.

parabola *n.* A line representing the equation $y = ax^2$.

parallel I/O *n.* A way of simultaneously moving more than 1 bit of data in and out of a computer. Abbreviated PIO. *Contrast with* serial I/O.

parallel port *n.* An I/O channel that moves more than 1 bit at a time in or out of a computer. Usually implemented (for outputs) as a latch connected to the data bus, enabled by a strobe decoded from the address and control buses. Input parallel ports are made from a tristate buffer connected in a similar manner. *Contrast with* serial port.

EXAMPLE: A bank of LEDs connected to a computer generally interface on one or more parallel ports.

parallel processing *n.* The capability to apply two or more processors to a single computation.

paralleled capacitances *n.* The process of combining two or more capacitors in parallel to create a new value. The total capacitance of a circuit with n capacitors in parallel is

$$C = C_1 + C_2 + C_3 + C_4 + \ldots + C_n.$$

Contrast with series capacitances.

paralleled resistances *n.* The process of combining two or more resistors in parallel to create a new value. For n resistors in parallel, the total effective value of the circuit is

$$R = \frac{1}{(1/R_1 + 1/R_2 + \ldots + 1/R_n)}$$

For two resistors, this simplifies to

$$R = \frac{R_1 \times R_2}{R_1 + R_2}$$

Contrast with series resistances.

Two paralleled resistors yielding an effective *R* of 3333 ohms.

parallelism *n.* The execution of two or more software units (tasks, threads, or processes) on an equivalent number of processors, all of which are running at the same time. *Contrast with* pseudoparallelism.

parameter 1. *n.* A data value or object passed during a function call.

2. *n.* Any value that changes the behavior of a system or function.

parent directory *n.* In a filesystem, the directory in which the current directory is stored. Only the root directory has no parent.

parent state *See* composite state.

parity 1. *n.* An extra bit appended to data to ensure correct transmission. Often used with RS-232 data transmission. *See also* even parity, odd parity, no parity.

2. *adj.* Describes a type of memory device with an extra parity bit in each storage word.

parity bit *n.* An extra bit of redundant data sent or stored alongside a larger binary value as a primitive checksum. So-called parity memory devices associate a parity bit with each stored byte, making them 9 bits wide.

parse tree *n.* An intermediate form of code representation generated by a compiler. The first step in any compilation is to convert the raw text into a series of tokens—a process called lexical analysis. Once the individual tokens, such as variable names, keywords, and operators, are identified, they must be grouped into grammatically correct expressions in a process called parsing. The result of this syntactical analysis is called a parse tree.

The information in a parse tree can be used for semantic analysis, which finds programming errors, and to identify potential optimizations.

Pascal *N.* A once-popular programming language that is now rarely used outside Computer Science 101 courses.

pascal *n.* A standard unit of pressure. Abbreviated Pa. One pascal is the pressure of a force of 1 newton acting over an area of 1 square meter.

HISTORY: Named for Blaise Pascal (1623–1662).

pASIC (pee ay sick) *N.* The name of a family of FPGAs from QuickLogic. A registered trademark.

path *n.* The complete address of a file, including directories.

EXAMPLE: On a Unix system, a file path might look as follows.

```
/users/mbarr/.forward
```

Windows paths have drive letters and use backslashes.

```
C:\Windows\system.ini
```

pattern sensitivity *n.* An error condition in RAMs, where complex patterns of data cause the chip to return bad information. In the bad old days, DRAMs were likely to exhibit pattern sensitivity, leading to the creation of tedious memory tests containing all possible patterns. Today, pattern sensitivity is rarely seen.

payload *n.* The part of a network packet or transmission that contains the application-level data. The payload is generally surrounded by one or more headers, and possibly a trailer, too, before it is sent to the receiver.

PC (as letters) 1. *abbr. See* personal computer.

2. *abbr.* Short for Program Counter.

PC-relative addressing *n.* An addressing mode in which the instruction's arguments are added to the program counter (PC) to form the effective address.

EXAMPLE: The x86 instruction

```
JZ address
```

is PC-relative. Although to the untrained eye `address` looks like the destination location, the assembler stores this as the difference between the current PC and the destination. At run time, the CPU adds the PC to this stored number and then branches.

PC/104 *N.* A standardized line of computer boards that all interconnect. Based on PC architecture, PC/104 systems can run most PC software. Unlike the PC, though, these boards do not require a motherboard since they stack.

Stacked PC/104 boards.

They're more robust than the ISA cards found in a PC; thus, they are more suited for certain embedded applications.

HISTORY: The name comes from "PC," for IBM PC, and "104," for the number of interconnection pins on the boards. Invented by Ampro, who published the spec in 1992. Today, more than 150 vendors provide PC/104 boards.

FURTHER READING: http://www.pc104.org

PCB (as letters) 1. *abbr. See* printed circuit board.

2. *See* process table entry.

PCB, multilayer *n.* A printed circuit board with more than two layers of copper. Many multilayer boards will provide separate layers for ground and power. These are then called the ground plane and power plane, respectively. Tracks on individual layers are then connected by vias as required.

PCI *See* PCI bus.

PCI bus *n.* A 47-pin high-speed bus used in PCs to provide direct access to memory and peripherals. Short for Peripheral Component Interconnect.

HISTORY: Introduced by Intel in 1991, though not generally adopted until the 1995 introduction of Windows 95, which brought Plug and Play into the mainstream.

FURTHER READING: http://www.pcisig.com

PCP (as letters) *abbr. See* priority ceiling protocol.

PCP emulation *See* priority ceiling emulation.

PDU (as letters) *abbr.* A payload of information to be sent by some packet network protocol. Short for Protocol Data Unit. This term is most often encountered when reading the spec for the given protocol. The protocol's header information will be prefixed to the PDU and the PDU's contents might be checksummed as well; otherwise, the PDU is just data.

PE (as letters) 1. *abbr. See* processing element.

2. *abbr.* Short for Professional Engineer, it designates a state-issued certification more popular with practitioners of civil and mechanical than electrical engineering.

peak 1. *adj.* Maximum.

USAGE: "The signal's peak value is 10 V."

2. *v.* The point at which a signal reaches a maximum value.

USAGE: "The signal peaks 27 μs into the datastream."

peak-to-peak *adj.* Describes the maximum extent of a signal, measured from the signal's most negative to most positive excursion. *See also* root mean square.

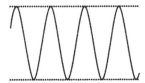

The peak-to-peak value of this sine wave is the range between the two dotted lines.

peek *v.* To read a register or memory location.

Peltier thermoelectric device (pelty-er) *n.* A device that functions as a heat pump, using electricity to move heat from one side of the device to the

other. Thus, a powered Peltier device is cold on one side and hot on the other. Sometimes called Peltier plates. The devices are a sandwich of two ceramic plates with an array of small bismuth telluride cubes in between.

The devices are not at all efficient, sucking many amps for any appreciable amount of heat transfer. Yet, they require no moving parts and are quite small, so they are often used to cool electronic components.

HISTORY: Named for Jean Peltier (1785–1845).

FURTHER READING: http://www.peltier-info.com

Pentium *N.* A class of 32-bit processors sold by Intel primarily for the PC market. The devices range from the Pentium to the current Pentium IV. Intel's roadmap to higher end processors departs the Pentium in favor of their 64-bit Itanium architecture.

Pentium bug *n.* A flaw in Intel's first-generation Pentium processor that produced incorrect results for certain floating-point division operations. The reduced accuracy was first reported by mathematician Thomas R. Nicely of Lynchburg College in Virginia in 1994, who happened upon the only 1 in 9,000,000,000 possible calculations (and recognized the error!) while researching prime numbers. The problem was corrected in a subsequent release of the chip, proving that at Intel, quality is job 0.998.

FURTHER READING: Ivars Peterson has a very approachable description of the details at http://www.maa.org/mathland/mathland_5_12.html.

Peopleware *N.* A seminal book that showed how interruptions reduce programming efficiency by a factor of three. Demarco and Lister conducted "code wars" for 10 years; they found a 300% difference in productivity between teams and correlated the difference to interruptions and the lack thereof.

FURTHER READING: Demarco, Tom and Timothy Lister. *Peopleware: Productive Projects and Teams*, 2nd ed. Dorset House, 1999.

performance analyzer *n.* A tool that determines how much time is spent in each part of a program. Used to identify slow sections needing optimization.

Performance analyzers for embedded systems were traditionally logic analyzer–like devices that monitored the address bus to see where the program spent its time. Modern processors translate logical to physical addresses in such complex ways that this is no longer a practical approach. Most now instrument the code, seeding in commands that give the tool clues about where the program is executing. *Compare to* profiler.

period *n.* The interval of time over which something (e.g., a signal or a task) repeats. The period is the inverse of frequency ($T = 1/f$).

EXAMPLE: A 2-Hz square wave has a $1/2$-second period.

periodic *adj.* Having a fixed period of repetition. Periodic threads become ready to run at regular intervals. *Contrast with* aperiodic.

periodic task *n.* A task that restarts automatically at regular intervals. Generally scheduled only once and then regularly placed in the ready queue by the RTOS.

periodic timer *n.* A timer that expires at a regular interval. Periodic timers can be implemented in hardware, via a counter/timer unit, or in software, as a derivative of a hardware-driver timer tick. *Contrast with* one-shot timer.

peripheral *n.* A piece of hardware other than the processor, usually an I/O device. A peripheral can reside within the same chip as the processor; in which case, it can be called an integrated or on-chip peripheral.

personal area network *n.* A short-range wireless network of gadgetry on or around an individual. Abbreviated PAN. *See also* local area network.

personal computer *n.* A low-cost general-purpose computer targeted at the mass market. Abbreviated PC. The PC has come to mean, in general, either a Wintel or Apple machine. A few other types (Amiga) exist but have zero percent of the market. Recently, Linux for the x86 market is challenging Windows, though the vast majority of users still run in a Microsoft environment.

Personal Software Process *N.* A development methodology invented by Watts Humphrey for individual programmers rather than teams. Abbreviated PSP. Humphrey, an architect of the Capability Maturity Model, realized most organizations cannot realistically ever adopt the stringent requirements of the CMM. He developed the PSP as an alternative that requires no corporate buy-in, only the commitment of individual programmers. *See also* Capability Maturity Model.

FURTHER READING: Humphrey, Watts S. *A Discipline for Software Engineering.* Addison-Wesley, 1994.

peta- *pre.* The prefix meaning 10^{15}. Abbreviated P.

phase *n.* The fraction of a complete cycle elapsed as measured from a specified reference point. Often expressed as an angle, 0 to 360 degrees.

Two signals 90 degrees out of phase.

EXAMPLE: In reactive AC circuits, the voltage and current lead or lag each other and are thus out of phase.

phase distortion *n.* Unwanted corruption of a signal's phase by a circuit.

EXAMPLE: An op-amp used in its simplest config-uration is inverting; thus, it distorts the signal's phase by 180 degrees.

phase response *n.* The effect of a filter on the phase of the individual frequency components passed through it to the output signal. The degree of phase shift can vary by frequency. This phase shift can be thought of as a time delay, and the effect is very similar to what happens to the half of a beam of light that's reflected through a series of prisms, only to rejoin the other half at a point just after it was split off. *See also* amplitude response.

phase shift keying *n.* A modulation method that shifts the carrier's phase to represent data bits. Abbrevi-ated PSK. Often a 0 is represented by no phase shift and a 1 by 180 degrees. One advantage of PSK is that using different phase shifts (e.g., 0, 90, 180, and 270 degrees) results in encoding more data in the same bandwidth.

phase-locked loop *n.* A circuit that includes an oscilla-tor with a phase that is maintained constant com-pared to a reference signal. Abbreviated PLL. Used for a multitude of applications, such as recovering a clock from self-timed data streams like NRZI, multiplying clock frequencies (which is how some processors derive a high-frequency clock from a cheap 32,768-Hz watch crystal), and demodulating frequency shift–keying modulation.

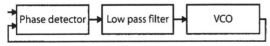

Block diagram of a PLL.

photocell *n.* A component in which resistance varies depending on the intensity of applied light. Typi-cal photocells have a minimum resistance in bright light of a few kiloohms (kΩ), varying to a maxi-mum resistance of a few hundred kiloohms when in the dark.

photomask *n.* An opaque image on a transluscent plate that is used as a light filter in manufacturing integrated circuits. Called a mask for short. A photomask is a high-purity quartz or glass plate containing precision images of integrated circuits. The photomask is used as a master by chip makers to optically transfer these images onto semicon-ductor wafers. The chips contained on the wafer are manufactured layer by layer, each requiring a unique photomask. The current generation of advanced chips has 25 or more layers.

photon (faux tahn) *n.* A particle associated with elec-tromagnetic radiation. Abbreviated γ. Photons are energy particles that travel at the speed of light; they have no mass. The amount of energy is in direct proportion to the frequency, where the constant of proportionality is Planck's constant, h.

photoresistor *See* photocell.

phototransistor *n.* A transistor that is sensitive to light and turns on in the presence of light. Phototrans-istors typically show a collector–emitter leakage of 100 µA or so when off; when illuminated, the device turns on, conducting a couple of milli-amps.

Phototransistors are used less often than photocells for sensing low light levels but are an important part of optical isolators. *See also* optical isolator.

PHY (feye) *abbr.* An IC that includes physical layer functionality. Short for PHYsical.

physical address *n.* The address that is placed on the address bus when accessing a memory location or register.

physical layer *n.* The protocol layer that defines the physical communications medium, including such details as the encoding of 0s and 1s, the frame for-mat, and the protocol for gaining access to the channel. Layer 1 of the OSI reference model. The physical layer lies below and outside the TCP/IP protocol suite. Any of several physical layers, such as Ethernet, Token Ring, or wireless 802.11, can be used with no effect that would requiring changes in the layers above. *See also* data link layer.

pi *See* π.

PIC (pick) 1. *N.* A member of any of several micro-controller families from Microchip, formally termed PICmicro microcontrollers.

HISTORY: Back in 1975, General Instruments needed a way to compensate for the poor I/O performance of its 16-bit CP1600 CPU. Their solution was to dedicate a simpler CPU called a Peripheral Interface Controller (PIC) to the task. Around 1985, Arizona Microchip Technology spun out of General Instruments to focus on the PIC business, which continues to thrive. More than 2 billion PICs had been sold by 2002.

2. *abbr.* Short for Position-Independent Code. *See* relocatable.

pico- (pee-coe) *pre.* The prefix representing a numerical multiplier of 10^{-12}. Abbreviated p.

picoamp *n.* One trillionth of an ampere. Abbreviated pA. Op-amp bias currents are on the order of picoamps.

picofarad *n.* One trillionth of a farad. Abbreviated pF. Capacitors used to pad crystal oscillators are on the order of 10 pF.

HISTORY: Formerly called a micromicrofarad.

picosecond *n.* A trillionth of a second. Abbreviated ps. A picosecond is a unit of time not yet in the reach of software. Even today's fastest 2-GHz PCs have instruction cycles of at least 500 ps.

PID (rhymes with lid) 1. *abbr.* A three-part technique for designing control systems that use feedback. Short for Proportional–Integral–Derivative. The individual proportional (to the current error), integral (of all past errors), and derivative (predictor) terms work in conjunction to drive the system to its desired state quickly and with only minor overshoot.

PID controllers have been used for over a century in various mechanical, pneumatic, and electronic forms. A digital PID controller is implemented as firmware running on a processor.

FURTHER READING: http://www.netrino.com/Publications/Glossary/PID.html

2. *abbr. See* process ID.

PID tuning *n.* The mathematical or empirical process of selecting appropriate values for the proportional, integral, and derivative gain constants in a PID controller. Generally speaking, the best empirical approach is to set the proportional gain way too high and disable the integral term altogether to first tune the derivative gain. Once a desirable value for the derivative gain is found, the proportional gain should be tuned. At that point the system should work but be extremely sluggish. Adding back in and then tuning the integral gain should speed the response time.

piecewise linear interpolation *n.* A way of estimating the shape of a curve by breaking it into many short linear segments. *See also* linear interpolation.

piezo element (pee-eh-zo) *n.* A small piece of quartz or other material that flexes when electricity is applied to it.

piezoelectric buzzer *n.* A device for creating sounds that requires little power. When a DC voltage is applied to the device, a piece of quartz (or other piezo element) flexes. If a signal in the audible frequency range is applied, a tone can be heard.

pin count *n.* The number of pins on an IC.

ping *v.* To send a small data packet and wait for an acknowledgment to see whether a node on a network is reachable. The name comes from the pinging technique used in submarines. *See also* ICMP.

ping-pong buffers *See* double buffer.

pink noise *n.* A type of noise in which power density decreases 3 dB per octave with increasing frequency (density proportional to $^1/f$) over a finite frequency range. *See also* white noise.

pinout *n.* The correspondence between signals and pins on an IC or other device. Pinouts on common parts largely have been standardized; JEDEC, for instance, set the rules for byte-wide memory parts many years ago.

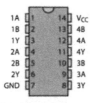

The pinout of the 7400 quad NAND chip.

PIO (as letters) *abbr. See* parallel I/O.

PIP (rhymes with hip) *abbr. See* priority inheritance protocol.

pipe *n.* An operating system data structure that is basically a byte-oriented message queue. Think of pipes as serial ports linking processes or tasks.

pitch *See* lead pitch.

pixel *n.* The smallest controllable unit of a graphical display. On-screen, each pixel can have its own color from the available palette. The net effect of all the pixel's chosen colors is of the larger desired image. In GUI applications, many drawing objects are measured in pixel widths.

place-and-route *adj.* Describes a type of software that designs printed circuit boards. Place-and-route software automates most of the PCB design process. It decides where to put components on the board to minimize track lengths and maximize routability. It then routes the board; that is, it connects all of the nodes in a manner prescribed by the netlist provided by the schematic capture software. *See also* netlist, printed circuit board.

plant 1. *n.* The physical device manipulated by a control system.

EXAMPLE: A heating element is the plant driven by a thermostat.

2. *n.* The buildings, equipment, and fixtures of an institution or facility, often controlled by a mix of embedded systems.

plastic leadless chip carrier *n.* A type of surface-mounted IC package with large lead pitch and relatively low lead density. Abbreviated PLCC. PLCC packages predate the ultra-fine pitch parts like TQFP. They're still widely used because, unlike most SMT devices, these parts work well in sockets.

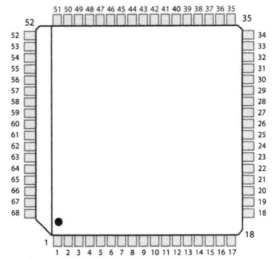

The schematic symbol for a 68-pin PLCC part.

platform FPGA *n.* A hybrid microprocessor plus programmable logic product that can be used instead of an ASIC to implement a system-on-chip hardware design. In contrast to the alternative of purchasing a standard, blank-slate, FPGA and building or buying a microprocessor core to program into it, platform FPGAs (like Xilinx's Virtex-II, which sports a PowerPC) already have a fixed-logic processor included on-chip. This maximizes the programmable area of the chip, making the price of the combination cheaper per unit than competing alternatives.

USAGE: This term should be reserved for silicon products that already include a processor when they ship from the vendor, to distinguish them from systems in which a processor is bought or created to be downloaded into an ordinary FPGA. Although both of these are SoC situations, the first involves the use of a "hard core"; the second a "soft core."

platter *n.* A rotating circular storage layer in a disk drive. Modern drives have multiple platters, each with its own read/write head. Each platter is logically subdivided into concentric circular tracks, each of which contains the same number of sectors. Data is read or written a sector at a time.

PLC (as letters) *abbr. See* programmable logic controller.

PLCC (as letters) *abbr. See* plastic leadless chip carrier.

PLD (as letters) *abbr. See* programmable logic device.

PLL (as letters) *abbr. See* phase-locked loop.

plug pack *n.* An AC-to-DC power converter that plugs into a wall outlet.

USAGE: This term is regional, being used mostly in Australia and New Zealand. The term AC-to-DC converter or wall transformer is preferred in the U.S.

PMC (as letters) *abbr.* A standard form factor for daughter cards that uses PCI bus technology. Short for PCI Mezzanine Card.

PNP transistor *n.* A way of constructing bipolar transistors by diffusing P regions on either side of an N region. PNP transistors are on when the base–emitter junction is reverse biased. *Contrast with* NPN transistor.

The schematic symbol of a PNP transistor.

pod *n.* The part of an in-circuit emulator that connects to the target system. Many ICEs are a box or a PCB that plugs into the devel-opment station's bus with a cable that goes to the target system. The end of the cable invariably has a small board, the pod, that matches impedances and provides some buffering to help drive the cable.

The trend is to put more of the emulator's logic on the pod, which simplifies the propagation of high-speed signals and reduces delays. Some emulators are entirely contained on the pod. *See also* in-circuit emulator.

pointer *n.* A variable that contains an address. In C, a pointer can contain the address of any memory location. There can be stack, heap, or some other kind of data at that location, or the pointer can contain the address of code to be executed. Using memory-mapped I/O, the pointer can even be assigned an address that's decoded by the glue logic as a peripheral register. *Compare to* reference.

pointer arithmetic *n.* An incredibly powerful, and also dangerous, way of changing a pointer's value. In C and some other languages, all manner of pointer arithmetic is possible.

This implementation of `strlen()` uses a simple form of pointer arithmetic.

```
int
strlen(char const *  str)
{
    int     len = 0;
    char *  p = (char *) str;

    /*
     * Count characters in the string.
     */
    while (*(p++) != '\0') len++;

    /*
     * Return the length.
     */
    return (len);

} /* strlen() */
```

poke *v.* To write a register or memory location.

poll (like toll) *v.* To repeatedly read a status bit or register to determine when an I/O operation has completed. A preferred alternative is to use interrupts.

polling *n.* A method of interfacing to a peripheral that involves repeatedly reading a status register until the device has reached the awaited state. Device drivers are either polling or interrupt-driven, with the latter being more generally preferred.

polymorphism *n.* A way of designing software so that objects with the same interface can be interchanged at run time. Along with inheritance and encapsulation, polymorphism is one of three pillars of object-oriented programming.

polynomial *n.* A mathematical function consisting of a sum of products of a single variable. All polynomials have the form

$$f(x) = a_n x^n + a_{n-1} x^{n-1} + \dots + a_1 x^1 + a_0 x^0$$

EXAMPLE: $f(x) = 4x^3 + x^2 + 16$

polynomial approximation *n.* The most widely used method to compute floating-point approximations to, for example, square-roots and trig functions. A Taylor series approximation can be derived for any differentiable function, which tells us that any such function can be approximated by a polynomial of sufficient degree. In practice, Taylor series converge slowly, so a wide range of other techniques are used.

Developers use either the approximations contained in the run-time library or precomputed approximations provided by authors of algorithm books. Each involves a trade-off of precision versus execution time versus range.

EXAMPLE: This polynomial approximates $\cos(x)$, accurate to about 14.7 decimal digits over the range $[0, \pi/2]$.

$c1 = 0.99999999999999806767$
$c2 = -0.4999999999998996568$
$c3 = 0.04166666666581174292$
$c4 = -0.001388888886113613522$
$c5 = 0.000024801582876042427$
$c6 = -0.0000002755693576863181$
$c7 = 0.0000000020858327958707$
$c8 = -0.000000000011080716368$
$\cos(x) = c1 + x^2(c2 + x^2(c3 + x^2(c4 + x^2(c5 + x^2(c6 + x^2(c7 + x^2(c8)))))))$

polynomial degree *n.* The exponent of the largest term in a polynomial. Also called the polynomial order. *See also* O().

EXAMPLE: The polynomial $4x^3 + x^2 + 16$ has degree 3. It is termed a third-order polynomial.

polynomial order *See* polynomial degree.

pop *v.* To remove the top value from a stack, typically copying it into a register.

port 1. *n.* A location in the I/O space.

2. *n.* A label on a schematic that marks a connection to another part of the circuit on another sheet.

3. *v.* To modify a piece of software so that it will run on a platform other than the one for which it was originally written. If you're lucky, the platform-dependent parts of the code have already been separated out into a board support package by the original author(s).

portability *n.* A property of software. The more easily it can be moved to new platforms, the more portable the software is said to be.

ported I/O *n.* A convenient name for the alternative to memory-mapped I/O, utilizing a processor's I/O space for peripheral connections. Separate I/O spaces are not common on modern processors (with the notable exception of the x86 family), so memory-mapped I/O is the norm.

porting *n.* The process of modifying software with the intention of moving it to a new platform.

position-independent code *See* relocatable.

positive feedback *n.* A type of feedback in which the system's output is coupled directly to the system's input. Positive feedback tends to create unstable systems. *See also* negative feedback.

EXAMPLE: Although an unstable system seems undesirable, it can be used to create an oscillator. Feed an AND gate's output back to its input and the gate will output a square wave with a frequency that is a function of the various component's parameters.

positive temperature coefficient *n.* A device that exhibits an increase in some parameter as the temperature goes up. *Contrast with* negative temperature coefficient. *See also* temperature coefficient.

EXAMPLE: Thermistors are resistors in which resistance increases as the temperature increases.

positive true *See* active high.

POSIX (pahz-icks) *abbr.* An IEEE standard describing the API of a Unix-like process model operating system. Short for Portable Operating System Interface, with an X added at the end to make it sound like yet another variant of Unix (which it essentially was when first written down). IEEE Std 1003.1-1990. In the early days of Unix, flavors from AT&T, HP, and many others coexisted. Each had its own set of system calls. The POSIX standard was an attempt to bring these APIs into conformance so that applications could be developed that would run on all of these platforms. It worked for the Unix side, and even Windows and Macintosh platforms (and some real-time operating systems, like QNX, VxWorks, and LynxOS) can today run applications written to the basic POSIX API. *See also* pthreads.

POSIX threads *See* pthreads.

POST (rhymes with most) *abbr. See* power-on self-test.

postdecrement 1. *adj.* Describes an addressing mode that uses the contents of a register as the argument's address, but with the computer subtracting 1 from the register after fetching the data. *Compare to* postincrement.

EXAMPLE: This 68000 instruction pulls data from the memory location addressed by A5 and then subtracts 1 from A5.

```
MOVE.W D0,(A5)-
```

2. *v.* In C and several related languages, applying the -- operator after the operand name. *Contrast with* predecrement.

EXAMPLE: To decrement x after assigning its current value to y:

```
y = x--;
```

postincrement 1. *adj.* Describes an addressing mode that uses the contents of a register as the argument's address, but with the computer adding 1 to the register after fetching the data. *Compare to* postdecrement.

EXAMPLE: This 68000 instruction pulls data from the memory location addressed by A5 and then adds 1 to A5.

```
MOVE.W D0,(A5)+
```

2. *v.* In C and several related languages, applying the ++ operator after the operand name. *Contrast with* preincrement.

EXAMPLE: To increment x after assigning its current value to y:

```
y = x++;
```

postmortem *n.* The process of analyzing the successes and failures associated with an engineering project recently completed so that the development team might gain knowledge that will help improve future projects and scheduling.

pot (rhymes with hot) *abbr. See* potentiometer.

potentiometer *n.* A resistor with resistance that varies as a user turns a knob. Also called a pot or variable resistor. Pots are often used to set the gain of a circuit; before computers, a radio's volume control was a pot. Today, it's most likely an optical encoder feeding a digital signal to the computer.

The schematic symbol of a potentiometer.

There are now a class of pots controlled by computers, not users, called digital pots. These provide a resistance determined by the digital input signals.

POTS (like kitchen pots) *abbr.* An ordinary analog phone line and the PSTN equipment that supports it. Short for Plain Old Telephone System. The developers of modem standards, such as V.90, must be intimately familiar with the worst-case electrical properties of POTS communication channels.

power 1. *n.* The electricity applied to a circuit to make it run.

2. *n.* The product of voltage and current, expressed in watts. Computable two ways.

$$P = V \times I$$
$$P = I^2 \times R$$

power cycle 1. *v.* To restart a system, by temporarily disrupting its power supply.

2. *v.* A common way for users to deal with firmware bugs.

power plane *n.* A layer of a printed circuit board devoted to propagating one kind of power to all components needing that voltage. A board can have multiple power planes, especially when there's more than one power source (say, a digital and an analog power).

FCC and CE rules require low emitted RF radiation. Many designers achieve this by putting ground and/or power planes on the outside layers of their circuit boards. These layers act as a poor man's Faraday shield.

power supply 1. *n.* A circuit or device that converts electricity in one form to another form that can power a system. A power supply is often connected to the AC mains, converting, say, 110 VAC to 5 VDC for logic circuits.

2. *n.* A piece of test equipment that converts the AC mains to a voltage and frequency that can be applied to a circuit being tested. Also called a switcher. *See* power supply, switching.

power supply, linear *n.* A device that provides power to a circuit, regulating it by transforming the unwanted part to heat. Linear power supplies use a series pass transistor that reduces the input voltage to the desired output. The transistor is in a partially on state, its series resistance controlled by a regulating circuit. It thus heats up.

Although simple, linear supplies are not efficient and more and more are being replaced by switching supplies.

power supply, switching *n.* A device that supplies power to a circuit, transforming the input in a highly efficient manner. Also known as switchers. Switchers, like linear supplies, have a series pass transistor between the input and output nodes. In the case of a switcher, it is either on or off, infinite or 0 ohms; thus, it does not dissipate power. Smart logic turns the transistor on at a high rate (kHz to hundreds of kHz), and capacitors and/or inductors smooth the pulse train to a clean DC level. *Contrast with* power supply, linear.

power-on self-test *n.* Any hardware diagnostic run at power-up. Abbreviated POST.

power-up 1. *n.* The time at which power is first applied to a system.

2. *v.* To apply power to a system.

PowerPC (power pee see) *N.* A popular 32-bit RISC microprocessor family developed by a consortium, including IBM and Motorola. PowerPC chips have been used to power Macs as well as many, many embedded systems. They are particularly common in telecom equipment and have even been used to power video game systems. Motorola's QUICC family is among several highly integrated microcontroller variants of the basic processor.

PPC (as letters) *abbr. See* PowerPC.

ppm (as letters) *abbr.* A measure of concentration or tolerance. Short for Parts Per Million.

PPP (as letters) *abbr.* An alternative to traditional physical networks, like Ethernet and Token Ring, that can provide network access over a serial port. Short for Point-to-Point Protocol. RFC 1134. In a typical arrangement, the target communicates via TCP/IP over PPP to another TCP/IP-enabled system that is on the network. The other system thereby provides a gateway for the embedded system to access a larger intranet or the Internet. *See also* SLIP.

pragma *See* #pragma.

preamble *n.* A pattern of synchronization bits sent over an asynchronous communications channel to allow the receiver to prepare to properly receive a packet of information that follows.

preamplifier *n.* An amplification stage that occurs on the raw sensor data. Sometimes called a preamp. It's very difficult to build stable high-gain amplifiers; it's much easier to cascade multiple amplifier stages, each with a reasonable gain. The first of these is the preamplifier.

Preamps are often used in situations where low-level signals must be transmitted to another instrument. Instead of sending a signal that's not much above the noise and is likely to be corrupted by more noise in the transmission, it's better to amplify it a bit before transmission.

precision *n.* A measure of how well a signal matches its expected value. High-precision signals have low error; they're very close to the real value. Thus, an analog circuit that erroneously adds an offset is not precise. Often confused with accuracy.

predecrement 1. *adj.* Describes an addressing mode that uses the contents of a register as the argument's address, but with the computer subtracting 1 from the register before forming the address. Used in handling stacks and queues and in processing strings. *Compare to* preincrement.

EXAMPLE: On the 68000, the following instruction pulls data from the address in A5-1,

```
MOVE.W D0,-(A5)
```

2. *v.* In C and several related languages, applying the -- operator before the operand name. *Contrast with* postdecrement.

EXAMPLE: To decrement x before assigning its value to y:

```
y = --x;
```

preemption *n.* The process of stopping or suspending running software. Preemption occurs when an interrupt fires and the corresponding ISR "interrupts" whatever software is running at the time. It can also occur in an RTOS when a task becomes ready to run; if the newly ready task has a priority higher than the running task, the running task is preempted. *See also* scheduling point.

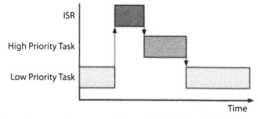

Nested preemption can occur in a variety of ways. In this example, the execution of the ISR causes an event that readies the high-priority task. When the ISR completes, it is that task that runs next, before the preempted low-priority task resumes.

preemptive *adj.* An operating system is said to be preemptive if it allows the running task to be suspended when a task of higher priority becomes ready (or a task of equal priority is granted a turn). Nonpreemptive schedulers are easier to implement but less appropriate for embedded systems, which must be responsive to external events.

preemptive scheduling *n.* A type of multithreading that supports interruption of the running thread so that another thread that is ready to run can use the processor immediately. Priority-based preemptive schedulers are common in commercial real-time operating systems. In those, the highest priority thread that is ready to run is guaranteed to be running. *Contrast with* nonpreemptive scheduling. *See also* scheduling point.

prefetcher *n.* A part of most 16- and 32-bit processors that tries to maximize memory bandwidth by reading a few instructions ahead and queueing the instructions for the processor.

Modern CPUs separate the processor from the bus interface unit (BIU). The BIU grabs instructions from memory and transfers them to the processor via a small queue. If the processor is busy executing an instruction, the BIU will fill the idle time by guessing that the next instruction needed is at the next sequential address in memory and will read that into the queue.

Every branch and interrupt defeats this by flushing the queue and restarting the BIU's sequential fetching. Intel introduced a technique called branch prediction in the Pentium to try to avoid these nasty flushes as often as possible.

preincrement 1. *adj.* Describes an addressing mode that uses the contents of a register as the argument's address, but with the computer adding 1 to the register before forming the address. Used in handling stacks and strings. *Compare to* predecrement.

EXAMPLE: On the 68000, the following instruction pulls data from the memory location in A5+1.

```
MOVE.W D0,+(A5)
```

2. *v.* In C and several related languages, applying the ++ operator before the operand name. *Contrast with* postincrement.

EXAMPLE: To increment x before assigning its value to y:

```
y = ++x;
```

preprocessor *n.* A development tool, typically associated with and run before a particular compiler, that performs substitutions based on constants, expands macros, incorporates header files, and makes language extension possible.

The C preprocessor is often abbreviated cpp. It processes #define, #include, #if, #pragma, and other related statements, which the C compiler does not even know exist. Some languages, such as Java, have no preprocessor.

prescaler *n.* A divider that reduces the clock frequency before it's applied to a peripheral. Prescalers are common on counter/timer units and baud rate generators. The CPU clock, which often drives these devices, might be far too fast to be useful. The prescaler divides the clock by a power of two, typically ranging from 16 to 256, before sending it to the peripheral. In most cases, the prescaler feeds another divider, this one programmable.

printed circuit board *n.* The substrate on which circuits are assembled. Abbreviated PCB. PCBs are usually fiberglass with layers of copper. Acid etches parts of the copper away, leaving connections for the components. In embedded systems, there are usually 2 to 10 copper layers in the board.

printf() *fn.* A commonly used output function from the C standard library that is often unavailable in embedded systems. Most embedded systems lack displays, so the only possible remaining meaning for a `printf()` would be to send the text string over a serial port. To do that requires a rewrite of the standard `printf()` library routine—and a serial port and software to control it.

Printing "Hello, World" turns out to be a lousy first program for a book on embedded programming. In fact, that example appears only at the end of Michael Barr's *Programming Embedded Systems in C and C++*. And even that example doesn't use `printf()`.

priority *n.* The relative urgency of one task or interrupt compared to another. In the case of tasks, the priority is an integer and the scheduler in a preemptive priority-based scheduler compares the priorities of all that are ready to run and selects the one with the highest urgency to run.

priority ceiling *n.* The priority assigned to a shared resource. The priority ceiling is generally set to a level just slightly higher than the priority of the highest locker. This may or may not be easy to determine a priori. *See also* priority ceiling emulation.

priority ceiling emulation *n.* A practical approximation to the priority ceiling protocol. Also called highest locker protocol. In priority ceiling emulation, each shared resource is assigned a priority equal to that of the highest priority thread that ever uses it. Subsequently, when any thread acquires the mutex protecting that resource, the thread's priority is raised to the resource's ceiling. Only threads of priority higher than the set that shares that resource can preempt the running thread while it has that resource.

A very cool thing about this technique is that it can be implemented without help from the operating system. In fact, it suggests a technique for sharing resources without mutexes. Rather than try to acquire the mutex for a resource of interest, any thread wanting to use that resource can simply ask the OS to raise its priority to the ceiling. While it holds that resource, only threads of such importance that they outrank all users of the held resource can preempt the holder. Once done with the resource, of course, the thread must lower its priority back to its own nominal level. *Compare to* priority inheritance protocol.

priority ceiling protocol *n.* A formal but impractical solution to the problem of priority inversion. Abbreviated PCP. Rather than being implemented in operating systems, this protocol is approximated instead. *See* priority ceiling emulation.

FURTHER READING: Sha, L., J. P. Lehoczky, and R. Rajkumar. "Priority Inheritance Protocols: An Approach To Real-Time Synchronisation." Computer Science Department, Carnegie-Mellon University, 1987.

priority inheritance protocol *n.* One solution to the problem of priority inversion. Abbreviated PIP. To use this technique, the operating system must be modified so that when a higher priority thread blocks, waiting for a needed resource, the priority of the thread that currently holds that resource is raised to the priority of the blocked thread. This prevents a thread of medium priority from preempting the lower priority thread before it finishes with the needed resource. The lower priority thread is said to inherit the priority of the blocked thread. *Compare to* priority ceiling protocol.

priority inversion *n.* An unwanted software situation in which a high-priority task is delayed while waiting for access to a shared resource that is not even being used at the time. For all practical purposes, the priority of this task has been lowered during the delay period. Priority inversion arises when a medium-priority task preempts a lower priority task using a shared resource on which the higher priority task is pending. If the higher priority task is otherwise ready to run, but a medium-priority task is currently running instead, a priority inversion is said to occur.

Anytime you use a mutex in a preemptive operating system environment, priority inversion is a possible result. A workaround, such as priority inheritance protocol, can be used to bound the length of this inversion but not eliminate it entirely.

FURTHER READING: http://www.netrino.com/Publications/Glossary/PriorityInversion.html

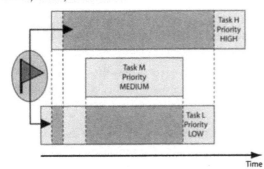

A priority inversion timeline. The inversion begins when Task M starts to run with Task H still waiting for Task L.

priority queue *n.* A queue ordered by the priority of its thread members, rather than in FIFO or LIFO order. For example, the threads blocked in mutex wait queues in real-time operating systems are generally ordered by their individual priorities, regardless of when they began waiting. The highest priority thread blocked on that mutex will gain access to it first. *See also* priority inversion.

private *adj.* Describes any variable or function of a C++ or Java class that cannot be accessed by users of the class.

probe 1. *n.* A device used to sense signals in a system under test that transfers those signals back to other test equipment. The scope probe is at heart nothing but a piece of wire. In

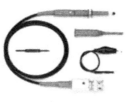

A scope probe.

reality, it must be more complex; it's a coax lead, to avoid induced noise, with a tip designed to clip onto test points and with reactive characteristics that can be tuned out using the compensator.

2. *v.* To connect a piece of test equipment to a node in a circuit, for the purpose of examining a signal.

probe effect *n.* The alteration of the behavior of a system when it is connected to test equipment. A scope probe is designed to be (electrically) invisible to the device under test, but it will exhibit some reactive and resistive effects. These sometimes alter the operation of sensitive circuits. There's nothing quite so infuriating as a device that starts working perfectly as soon as it's connected to the scope.

A similar effect is also seen when developing firmware. Adding test code will sometimes break or fix a system. Performance analyzers that seed instructions into the code, by their nature, change the system's timing—the very thing they desire to measure.

procedure *n.* In formal computer science, a function that doesn't return anything to the caller. In everyday use, however, the term is equivalent to function.

process 1. *n.* A word that is often confused with thread. The crucial distinction is that processes have their own private virtual memory spaces. One or more threads can run in the memory space of each process.

Processes are more common in multiuser systems than in embedded systems, where the added security and reliability outweigh the overhead costs. *See also* task.

2. *n.* A sequenced set of activities performed by a collaborating set of workers resulting in a coherent set of project artifacts, one of which is the desired system.

process control block *See* process table entry.

process ID *n.* A unique identifier for a process. The process ID is a handle that is typically returned by the OS when the process is created.

process table *n.* An operating system data structure that tracks the state and properties of individual processes. The process ID is often used by the OS to index into this table to find the process table entry of an individual process.

process table entry *n.* An individual entry in an operating system's process table that describes a specific process. Abbreviated PTE. Sometimes called a process control block (PCB) or a task control block (TCB). Each PTE will typically contain at least the following: the state of the process (ready, running, blocked, etc.), a pointer to its last saved context, a pointer to the associated page table, and handles for open files.

processing element *n.* Any CPU in a multiprocessor system. Abbreviated PE. In many network processors, there are multiple processing elements. All but one of these generally focus solely on data path processing, whereas one control path PE handles the more complicated exchanges.

processor *n.* A generic term that does not distinguish between microprocessor, microcontroller, network processor, or digital signal processor.

processor bandwidth *n.* The throughput capability of a particular processor at 100% utilization.

processor clock *See* clock.

processor core *n.* The processor part of an SoC design or platform FPGA. A processor core can be either soft (downloaded) or hard (in silicon). There also can be more than one of them, as is common in network processors.

processor family *n.* A set of related processors, usually successive generations from the same manufacturer. For example, Intel's 80x86 family began with the 8086 and now includes the 80186, 286, 386, 486, Pentium, and many others. The later models in a family are typically backward-compatible with the ones that came before.

processor speed *n.* A CPU's clock frequency. Ideally, doubling the clock doubles performance. In the real world, that's seldom true, since memories can't keep up with very fast processors. For example, a 2-GHz Pentium IV runs fast when executing out of cache but then might suffer 50 wait states for any memory access that results in a cache miss. As a result, PC users have noticed surprisingly small performance increases in recent years despite the availability of much faster CPUs.

Vendors generally select CPUs for speed by culling fast parts from a manufacturing batch and selling them for a premium price.

processor-independent *adj.* Said of a piece of software that is independent of the processor on which it will be run. Most programs that can be written in a high-level language are processor independent. *Contrast with* processor-specific.

processor-specific *adj.* A piece of software that is highly dependent on the processor on which it will be run. Such code must usually be written in assembly language. Poor design can make an HLL program very processor specific; careless assumptions about the size of longs and ints in C, for example, or explicit accesses to memory that create a particular endianness limit portability. *Contrast with* processor-independent.

product term *n.* The AND or NAND of all of a Boolean equation's variables. *Contrast with* minterm.

EXAMPLE: There are three product terms in the formula /A/B/C + ABC + /ABC.

profiler *n.* A software development tool that collects and reports execution statistics for your programs. These statistics include the number of calls to each subroutine and the total amount of time spent within each. This data can be used to learn which subroutines are the most critical and, therefore, demand the greatest code efficiency. Unfortunately, such technology is not often available in the remote debugging environment typical of embedded systems development.

program 1. *n.* A complete piece of software, either in source code or binary form.

2. *v.* To write software. 3. *v.* To (re)write the contents of a chip, such as an EPROM via a device programmer.

program counter *See* instruction pointer.

programmable *adj.* Capable of having its behavior controlled by software, like a processor, or its contents rewritten, like an EEPROM.

programmable logic *n.* Any IC used to create a circuit in which the internal design is not defined until after it has been programmed by the engineer. Programmable logic offers higher densities than possible with discrete logic and allows designers to change their designs even after the PCBs are built.

An alphabet soup of varieties exist, including PALs, PLDs, GALs, CPLDs, and FPGAs. These parts are programmed in a number of different ways. Some must be inserted into a device programmer, others load their equations at boot time from a small external ROM, and some FPGAs can be partly or fully reprogrammed on the fly.

programmable logic controller *n.* The brain of an industrial manufacturing process. Abbreviated PLC. A PLC is nothing more than a ruggedized computer that controls a portion of a factory. PLCs are programmed using ladder logic or in a conventional language like C.

In the olden days, they were mechanical devices using rotating cams and relays.

programmable logic device *n.* An integrated circuit that can be used to implement a digital logic design in hardware. Abbreviated PLD. PLDs

require far less board area, power, and wiring than several equivalent 7400-series TTL parts. And their internal structure can be reprogrammed if the logic later changes. For these reasons, inexpensive programmable logic devices like PLAs (programmable logic arrays), PALs (programmable array logic), and GALs (generic array logic) are commonly used for address decoding and other "glue" logic on circuit boards. PLDs are not as large or as flexible as FPGAs.

FURTHER READING: http://www.netrino.com/Articles/ProgrammableLogic/

programmer 1. *n.* A person who develops software.

2. *See* device programmer.

programmer's editor *n.* An editor with special features for software developers.

programmer's model *n.* A particular processor's internal accumulators, registers, and flags.

The programmer's model of the Rabbit 2000, a Z80 derivative of the late 1990s.

project management *n.* Are you kidding? You're reading a dictionary for hints about project management? Just start coding the silly thing and pray.

PROM (like the senior prom) *abbr.* A type of ROM that can be written (programmed) with a device programmer. Short for Programmable Read-Only Memory. These memory devices can be programmed only once, so they are sometimes referred to as write-once or one-time programmable. *See also* one-time programmable. *Compare to* EPROM.

promiscuous mode *n.* A mode common in network interface controllers that receives all incoming data frames on the physical interface, not just those destined for the local MAC address. Promiscuous mode is useful in debugging and also in making products, like network analyzers, that snoop the network. However, it can be a security concern if you're sending any data unencrypted across an insecure network.

proportional control *n.* A form of closed-loop control in which each adjustment that is made to the drive signal is a function only of the error between the desired and the sampled state of the plant. If the difference between the current plant output and its desired value (the current error) is large, the controller should probably change the drive signal a lot. If the error is small, it should change it only a little. In other words, you always want

$$change = P \times (desired - current)$$

where P is a constant proportional gain set by the system's designer.

For example, if the drive signal uses PWM, it can take any value between 0% and 100% duty cycle. If the signal on the drive is currently 20% duty cycle and the error remaining at the output is small, it might need to be tweaked to 18% or 21% to achieve the desired output at the plant.

If the proportional gain is well chosen, the time the plant takes to reach a new set point will be as short as possible, with overshoot (or undershoot) and oscillation minimized. However, proportional control alone is not sufficient in all control applications. One or more of the requirements for response time, overshoot, and oscillation might be impossible to fulfill at any proportional gain setting. *Contrast with* on–off control. *See also* PID.

proprietary *adj.* Describes technology that belongs to its inventor and generally is protected as a trade secret.

proprietary software *n.* In this most traditional licensing model for commercial software, no customer is allowed to examine the source code for the product. The exception is a customer willing to pay an additional, often exorbitant, source code licensing fee. But even if you do buy the source code for such a product, you cannot generally publish that code or otherwise cause it to fall into the possession of anyone outside the licensed group. Your right to modify the source code you've bought might even be restricted. *Contrast with* free software, open source.

protected mode *n.* An addressing mode of 286, 386, 486, and Pentium processors that allows programs to access memory beyond real mode's restrictive 1 MB limit. In order to provide for a full 32-bit (4-GB) address space, protected mode uses so-called selectors instead of the real mode's 16-bit segment registers. A selector selects one of 8192 entries in either of two descriptor tables (called global and local).

Each entry in a descriptor table (called a descriptor) is 8 bytes long and contains metainformation about a particular segment of memory. On the 386 and up, each descriptor contains a 32-bit base address for the segment, up to a 20-bit length (formally, limit), and access rights. *See also* real mode.

protection bit *n.* A bit that prevents a sector in a flash memory device from being erased or reprogrammed. Sometimes such a bit can be cleared in software so that the sector can again be made programmable.

protocol analyzer *n.* A piece of test equipment much like a logic analyzer, but with protocol-specific knowledge and features. Also called a bus analyzer. The underlying technology is just simultaneous logic-level capture from a small or large number of pins. However, the knowledge of the bus or communications protocol being used on the channel, such as PCI, USB, or TCP/IP, makes the human interface much more accessible. The protocol analyzer automatically decodes the bits and bytes of the raw packet and displays the higher layer information of most interest to the user.

protocol of interaction *n.* In UML, the allowable sequences of interactions between actors and a system. Protocols of interaction are often captured in sequence diagrams.

protocol stack *n.* Any set of communication protocols, such as TCP/IP, that consists of two or more layers of software and hardware. It's called a stack because each layer builds on the functionality in the layer below.

For example, in TCP/IP parlance, the lowest layer is called the physical layer. That's where the rubber meets the road; or, more accurately, the bits meet the communications medium at the network interface. Above that is the data link layer, which gives each device on the network its unique address. These first two layers of the TCP/IP protocol stack are typically implemented in hardware. Once the networked devices have addresses, they can communicate. That's where layer three, the network layer, comes in. IP is just one of the protocols that exists at this level in a TCP/IP stack; TCP and UDP are competing protocols at the transport layer.

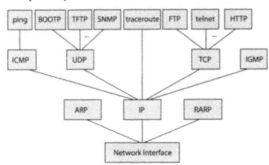

Some of the protocols in the TCP/IP protocol suite.

Three more layers of software (session, presentation, and application) are defined above those, thus completing the seven-layer OSI reference model. When data is sent across the network, it generally begins at layer 4 or above, travels down through the protocol stack on the sending system, out onto the network, then back up the stack on the receiving system.

protocol suite *n.* A complement of protocols that processes outgoing and/or incoming communications data. *See also* protocol stack.

EXAMPLE: TCP/IP

prototype *See* software prototype, hardware prototype.

pseudocode *n.* A partial code listing used in teaching and design that could not necessarily be compiled directly. Pseudocode is used to simplify the actual code to make the logic clear in as few lines and words as possible. These days, pseudocode is almost always C-like. In the past, Pascal-like syntax was more dominant (and it still is in some academic settings).

pseudoparallelism *n.* The appearance of parallel execution of software, such as tasks, when in reality there is just one processor. Such pseudoparallelism is often created with the use of an operating system, which allocates use of the processor to one particular task at a time. Because such decisions can take place over a short period of time, though, the system appears to be running all those behaviors simultaneously.

pseudorandom number generator *n.* A function that produces a nearly random string of numbers. In computers, there are no random number generators. Because computers are deterministic, starting the sequence with the same seed always results in the same string of numbers. The trick is to get as random of a seed as possible, perhaps by reading a user delay or the contents of a free-running counter.

Most are implemented as linear feedback shift registers.

pseudostate *n.* A transient node in a state machine diagram that is not drawn as a state proper. *See also* initial pseudostate, shallow-history pseudostate, deep-history pseudostate, join pseudostate, fork pseudostate, junction pseudostate, choice pseudostate.

PSK (as letters) *abbr. See* phase shift keying.

PSK31 (as letters and number) *abbr.* A modulation method used for over-air keyboard-to-keyboard chats via PC sound card (sender) and microphone (receiver), increasingly popular among ham radio enthusiasts. Short for Phase Shift Keying, 31 baud.

pSOS (pee sauce) *N.* A once-popular commercial RTOS from Integrated Systems. Also called pSO-System. The company was acquired by Wind River Systems in 1999, where pSOS was later deprecated in favor of rival VxWorks.

PSP (as letters) *abbr. See* Personal Software Process.

PSTN (as letters) *abbr.* A nickname for the entire telephone system of the U.S. Short for Public Switched Telephone Network.

PTE (as letters) *abbr. See* process table entry.

pthreads (pee threads) *n.* A standard API for multithreading that leaves many of the implementation details up to the operating system implementer. Short for POSIX Threads. IEEE Std 1003.1c-1995. All of the system calls begin with the `pthread_` prefix. For example, use `pthread_create()` to spawn a new thread.

`public` *res.* In C and C++, the reserved word `public` means a variable's storage information is declared in the current module. The linker then assigns absolute or near-absolute addresses to the `public`s and digs through all other modules to insert this address information into other uses of the variable. *See also* global variable.

public domain *n.* A software licensing scheme that makes the source code free for any use. Software that's in the public domain can be modified and the results made proprietary. It can also be incorporated unchanged into proprietary code. In these ways, software in the public domain is far more free than so-called *free software*.

pulldown *n.* A resistor used to drive an input to a logic 0. Pulldown resistors are used on unconnected inputs. Why not tie them directly to ground? Well, automatic test equipment might have to drive these nodes during manufacturing test. Also used on inputs driven by devices that might go to a high-impedance state.

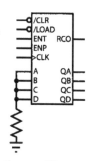

Here, a pulldown resistor drives four inputs to 0.

pullup *n.* A resistor used to drive an input to a logic 1 state. Pullups are used on unconnected inputs, or on inputs that source no current (see figure).

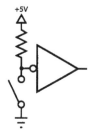

A pullup used to supply current for a switch input.

Why not tie an unconnected input directly to V_{cc}? Automatic test equipment might need to drive the pin during manufacturing test. Also, some logic families have very odd input specs. 74LS logic, for instance, allows a maximum of 5.5V on any input, yet V_{cc} can go to 7V without destroying the part. If you tie an input directly to V_{cc}, a glitch on the supply line could destroy the device. Run it through a pullup, and the resistor acts as a current limiter.

pulse *n.* A transition from a 0 to 1 and back again (or the reverse for negative logic).

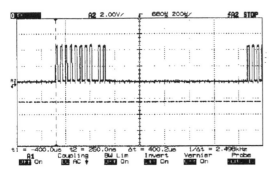

A sequence of pulses.

pulse width modulation *n.* A digital control technique wherein the processor adjusts the duty cycle of a sequence of fixed-width pulses. Abbreviated PWM. Unlike other modulation techniques, PWM is used more to control external analog signals or mechanical devices than to transmit data.

Consider driving a motor: a simple analog approach is to bias a transistor by varying amounts to control the motor's speed. This is very inefficient because the transistor dissipates considerable amounts of heat. PWM offers an alternative: connect the same transistor to a digital output pin and control the duty cycle of a train of pulses. Now the transistor is either on or off, so there's little power ($P = I^2 \times R$) loss.

Other applications abound. Passing the digital output through a lowpass filter converts the pulses to analog—the voltage a function of duty cycle. In effect, it's a cheap D/A converter.

Many processors have built-in PWM controllers that generate the pulse stream for a programmable duty cycle.

FURTHER READING: http://www.netrino.com/Publications/Glossary/PWM.html

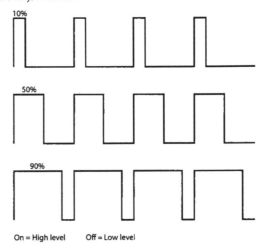

On = High level   Off = Low level

PWM signals of various duty cycles.

push *v.* To add a new value to the top of a stack.

PWM (as letters) *abbr. See* pulse width modulation.

Q

Q factor *n.* Short for quality, the Q of an inductor, capacitor, or circuit made from these components is the ratio of its ability to store energy to the total of all energy losses in the component.

$$Q = \frac{X}{R}$$

where X is reactance and R is resistance.

QA (as letters) *abbr. See* quality assurance.

QNX (cue-nix) 1. *N.* A popular Unix-like real-time operating system that has been widely used to develop real-time systems based on PC-like x86 platforms. The latest versions of QNX are well-known for their ability to run on any standard PC and for their nifty Linux ABI compatibility features, though other processors and platforms are also supported.

2. *N.* The company that makes the QNX RTOS. Short for QNX Software Systems.

quadrature *adj.* The condition when two signals are 90 degrees out of phase. *See also* phase.

quadrature encoder *n.* A type of rotary encoder. A mechanical device, the quadrature encoder produces two outputs 90 degrees out of phase. By counting transitions of these outputs, a computer can decode the shaft's position and its direction of motion. *Contrast with* binary encoder, Gray code encoder.

The optical path of a quadrature encoder showing its two out-of-phase rings, each of which blocks a light source as the device rotates.

quality *n.* An oxymoron when applied to software of any sort. Software quality is an important and elusive issue. A hot topic today, debates rage about its meaning. Does quality imply bug-free code? On large systems, zero bugs is pretty much impossible. And even bug-free code can be of horrible quality if the spec is flawed.

One reverse definition: if you have a reasonable customer who is unhappy with your product, there's a quality issue.

quality assurance *n.* A department or group in an organization primarily concerned with the quality of the finished product, and sometimes also with the processes used to create that product.

Quantum Framework *N.* A particular realization of an active object–based application framework that has been specialized for real-time systems. The Quantum Framework is a publish–subscribe architecture based on the author's Quantum Programming.

FURTHER READING: http://www.quantum-leaps.com

quantum programming *n.* Any programming involving a quantum computer. Quantum computers are devices that compute using superpositions of quantum states. Small quantum computers have recently been built, and progress is continuing. It is widely suspected that if large-scale quantum computers can be built, they will be able to solve certain kinds of problems far faster than any classical computer.

EXAMPLE: Quantum programming attacks problems like finding a password. The problem has these four properties. The only way to solve it is to guess answers repeatedly and check them. There are n possible answers to check. Every possible answer takes the same amount of time to check. There are no clues about which answers might be better; generating possibilities randomly is just as good as checking them in some special order. For problems with all four properties, it will take an average of $n/2$ guesses to find the answer using a classical computer. The time for a quantum computer to solve this will instead be proportional to the square root of n.

Quantum Programming *N.* A programming paradigm that extends traditional object-oriented programming with two additional fundamental concepts: hierarchical state machines and computing based on active objects. Abbreviated QP. These two concepts complement encapsulation, inheritance, and polymorphism—the famous tripartite mantra of OOP—and are just as fundamental. *See also* Quantum Framework.

FURTHER READING: Miro Samek. *Practical State-charts in C and C++: Quantum Programming for Embedded Systems.* CMP Books, 2002.

R

R/~W (read/not write) A signal that indicates the type of transfer on a bidirectional bus. If the signal is set, the transfer will be a read. If the signal is reset, the transfer will be a write. Short for Read/Not Write. The read and write signal need not be combined in this way, though it is a common way to reduce a processor's pin count by one. The write signal is active low—hence, the "not write" in its name.

Rabbit 2000 *num.* A modern microcontroller variant of the now ancient Z80 architecture.

race condition 1. *n.* A situation in which the combined effects of two or more programmatic threads (or a single thread and an ISR) varies depending on the precise order in which the instructions of each are executed.

Race conditions can be eliminated by surrounding critical code sections that must be executed without interruption with a pair of mutex take and release system calls. To prevent race conditions

involving ISRs, interrupts must be disabled for the duration of the critical section.

EXAMPLE: If two threads both try to increment a shared global variable ($x = x + 1$;) and they race, the result of both threads incrementing the variable once from an initial value ($x = 0$;) can be either 2 (correct) or 1 (incorrect).

This race condition exists if either increment step is not executed atomically. If a context switch occurs in the middle of an increment (which is typically a sequence of three CPU instructions to read the old value into a register, increment the content of the register, then write the new value), an incorrect value can result. The error might not always occur, making tracking down such bugs incredibly difficult.

The outcome (final value of x) in this case is dependent on the precise order in which the instructions of the two threads are executed. The shared data and random nature of preemptive context switches are the culprits that cause the race condition.

2. *n.* A situation in digital logic where timing errors cause erratic outputs.

radian   *n.* A measure of angles. A circle, or 360 degrees, comprises 2π radians; thus, one radian is about 57 degrees.

radio frequency   *n.* That portion of the electromagnetic spectrum used to transmit radio signals. Abbreviated RF. Although there are no precise limits to the RF band, it's generally from about 100 kHz to 10 gHz. *See also* electromagnetic spectrum.

radio frequency interference   *n.* Unwanted signals in the RF band that are radiated or received. Abbreviated RFI. Embedded systems are a big source of undesired RFI. Digital switching radiates across a broad range of frequencies, causing annoying and even dangerous interference on other systems. FCC and European CE rules now limit the amount of RFI any electronic device may emit.

RAM   (rhymes with ham) *abbr. See* random access memory.

random   *See* pseudorandom number generator.

random access memory   *n.* A broad classification of memory devices that includes all devices in which individual memory locations can be read or written in any order required by the application. Misused to mean memory that can be both read and written, but the term is so broadly (mis)used in this fashion that nearly everyone assumes random access is the same as read–write.

random number generator   *n.* A mythical piece of hardware or software that generates a random stream of numbers. *See* pseudorandom number generator.

RARP   (rhymes with harp) *abbr.* A reverse-lookup service related to ARP. Short for Reverse Address Resolution Protocol. Using RARP, a system can obtain the IP address of a machine given only its hardware address. ARP is used by every machine on the Internet; the use of RARP is more limited.

RAS   (raz) *abbr. See* row address select.

rate monotonic algorithm   *n.* A priority assignment algorithm for use with a real-time operating system that uses fixed-priority preemptive scheduling. Abbreviated RMA. RMA is a technique for setting the priorities of each thread relative to the others. The periods of the thread are calculated and compared; the shorter the period of a thread, the higher its assigned priority (hence: "rate" monotonic). RMA is the optimal fixed-priority scheduling algorithm. Only dynamic-priority scheduling can achieve higher CPU utilization without missed deadlines. *See also* deadline-monotonic algorithm.

rate monotonic analysis   *n.* The process of analyzing a real-time system to assign individual thread priorities according to the rate monotonic algorithm.

RC   (as letters) *abbr.* A circuit made of a resistor and a capacitor in series. *See also* RC time constant.

An RC circuit.

RC time constant   *n.* The time required to charge the capacitor in an RC circuit to 63.2% of the applied voltage.

The time constant is

$$\tau = RC$$

where τ is the time to charge to 63.2%, *R* is the resistance in ohms, and *C* is the capacitance in farads.

After τ seconds elapse, the capacitor is at 63.2% of the applied voltage; after another τ seconds, it charges another 63.2% of the difference between the capacitor's voltage at τ and the applied voltage.

A lot of embedded systems use an RC circuit to drive the CPU's reset input. When power is applied to the circuit, the voltage across the capacitor takes time to build, holding reset low for a while. Although simple, this is a less than ideal approach, since brownouts can result in partial resets.

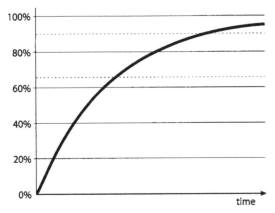

The RC time constant curve. Dotted lines show the 1τ and 2τ times.

RCS *N.* An open source version control system from GNU. Short for Revision Control System.

FURTHER READING: http://www.gnu.org/software/rcs/

re-spin *v.* The act of producing another version of a PCB or ASIC, invariably to fix design bugs. PCB re-spins are common and accepted; the first version is always a prototype that gets covered with modifications. ASIC re-spins are less acceptable because of the costs involved, which can approach $1 million for parts made with 0.13-micron geometry.

reactance *n.* Resistance to AC current flow caused by the energy storage in a magnetic field (for inductors) or by that stored in an electric field (for capacitors).

The reactance of a capacitor is

$$X_C = \frac{1}{2\pi f C}$$

and of an inductor is

$$X_L = 2\pi f L$$

where C is capacitance in farads, L is inductance in henries, and f is frequency in hertz.

Reactance is essentially AC resistance. The total resistance of a circuit is called "impedance" and is the combination of DC resistance and reactance. *See also* resistance, impedance.

reactive system *n.* A system in which the primary function is constant interaction with its environment by sending and receiving events. The main difficulty in building reactive systems is the unpredictable order, type, and timing of the events that the system must handle. A graphical user interface (GUI) is an example of a reactive system.

read cycle *n.* A memory or I/O bus cycle used for reading data.

read() *fn.* A common name for a system call that reads data from an open file and stores it into the specified memory buffer. A part of the standard Unix API for files and I/O devices, once a file has been open()ed successfully, it can be read() via the file descriptor held by the caller. *See also* write(), seek().

read–modify–write *adj.* Describes a common software behavior in which the contents of a variable or peripheral register are read into an accumulator, modified in some way, and then written back to the original location outside the processor. If this cannot be done in a single instruction cycle, there is a risk of a race condition if that variable or register is shared with an ISR or another thread. To prevent race conditions, read–modify–write sequences must be made atomic, either by disabling interrupts or by acquiring a mutex. *See also* swap, test-and-set.

read-only memory *n.* A broad classification of memory devices that includes all devices in which memory locations cannot be modified. Misused to mean any nonvolatile memory, including flash and EEPROM, that can be modified in-system. *See also* random access memory.

readelf *See* binutils.

ready 1. *adj.* Describes a task state that indicates the task is ready to run. Many tasks can be in the ready state simultaneously, but only one of them will be selected by the scheduler to run. *See also* running.

2. *n.* A bus signal used to indicate the processor does not need to wait for memory or a peripheral. Used on some processors (e.g., x86), ready is essentially ~wait.

ready list *n.* An operating system data structure that tracks the set of tasks in the ready state. Despite the name, the data structure need not be a linked list.

ready queue *See* ready list.

real estate *n.* The amount of PCB surface area consumed by a component. Like the land under your house, the space under an IC is in short supply.

real mode *n.* A mode of the x86 processor family in which all physical addresses are 20 bits. In real mode, each 20-bit address is built from a 16-bit segment and a 16-bit offset. (The segment is shifted left 4 bits, then the offset is added to it.) The total addressable memory space in this mode is, therefore, 1 MB. *See also* protected mode, flat real mode.

real-fast *adj.* Describes a property that's often confused with real time but is independent of deadlines. A real-fast system does not have to also be a real-time system. More importantly, a real-time system can have deadlines days apart and, so, run quite slow.

real-time *adj.* Having timeliness requirements, typically in the form of deadlines that can't be missed. *See also* hard real time, soft real time.

real-time clock *n.* A hardware device that maintains time-of-day information. Abbreviated RTC. A real-time clock is distinct from the CPU's clock signal, which is merely an oscillator, though it is possible to use a counter and software to track the time of day.

Real-time clocks are generally addressed as peripherals and will typically provide both time and date information. They are usually battery-backed to maintain time even when the system is shut down. Like a VCR with a flashing 12:00 that reminds you to initialize the device, the embedded system must get the time and date from the user or some other source to initialize the RTC, generally at the factory. The system clock is often based on a real-time clock, but need not be.

real-time Java *See* Real-Time Specification for Java.

real-time Linux *n.* Any Linux distribution that has been customized to meet the needs of real-time system designers. *See also* Linux/RT, RTAI.

real-time operating system *n.* An operating system designed specifically for use in real-time systems. Abbreviated RTOS.

Real-Time Specification for Java *N.* An update to the Java virtual machine specification that adds priority-based scheduling to Java threads (along with ways to deal with garbage collection's inherent lack of determinism), handles interrupts, and interfaces directly to hardware from Java. Abbreviated RTSJ.

FURTHER READING: http://www.rtj.org

real-time system *n.* Any computer system, embedded or otherwise, that has timeliness requirements. The following question can be used to distinguish real-time systems from the rest: "Is a late answer as bad, or even worse, than a wrong answer?" In other words, what happens if the computation doesn't finish in time? If nothing bad happens, it's not a real-time system. If someone dies or the mission fails, it's generally considered "hard" real-time, which is meant to imply that the system has hard deadlines. Everything in between is "soft" real-time.

EXAMPLE: Most industrial automation equipment has deadlines. If the bottle doesn't get a cap applied properly as it passes by on the production line, there is a failure. However, the consequences of that failure would not be as severe as the consequences of a failure in an airplane, a pacemaker, or any of a thousand other hard real-time systems.

FURTHER READING: Stewart, Dave. "Introduction to Real-Time." *Embedded Systems Programming,* October 2001.

real-time trace *n.* An execution history collected by a debugging tool like an in-circuit emulator. Sometimes called a trace for short. Breakpointing and single-stepping are incredibly powerful tools for debugging, but they necessarily corrupt the program's timing. The hardest bugs, especially those related to interrupts and tasking, are rendered undebuggable unless tested at full speed.

A trace capability is essentially a built-in logic analyzer. The tool captures program execution into a history buffer. The developer later views this history using tools that correlate the binary addresses to C or C++ source files.

```
>> main(): Module: tc_demo.c  Line: 18  Addr: F800:008E
void        main (void)
000    0.0uS  0100  111  0F808E  PUSH    BP
003    0.7uS  0110  111  00083C          00  Memory WR
004    1.0uS  0110  111  00083D          00  Memory WR
001    0.2uS  0100  111  0F808F  MOV     BP.SP
005    1.2uS  0100  111  0F8091  SUBSX   SP.04
008    2.0uS  0100  111  0F8094  PUSH    SI
00B    2.7uS  0110  111  000836          00  Memory WR
00C    3.0uS  0110  111  000837          00  Memory WR
009    2.2uS  0100  111  0F8095  PUSH    DI
00E    3.6uS  0110  111  000834          00  Memory WR
00F    3.8uS  0110  111  000835          00  Memory WR
      str = ""           /* Clear variables  */
00A    2.5uS  0100  111  0F8096  MOV     DI.0017
    num_words = 0;
011    4.3uS  0100  111  0F8099  MOVW    [BP+FE].0000
017    6.2uS  0110  111  00083A          00  Memory WR
018    6.4uS  0110  111  00083B          00  Memory WR
```

Example real-time trace, showing intermixed C source and disassembled machine instructions, with timing information.

When selecting a tool with trace, important features are the depth of the history buffer (how many machine cycles can it capture), triggering flexibility (how it starts and stops collecting the data), width (how much of the bus is collected),

and time stamps (it's nice to have a tool that tags each frame with the actual time).

Real-time trace is an important feature that differentiates ICEs from most BDMs and similar tools. *See also* in-circuit emulator.

real-world benchmark *n.* A benchmark or suite of benchmarks that uses actual algorithms and application code to compare the performance of different processors or systems objectively. *Contrast with* synthetic benchmark.

reboot *v.* To restart a software-run system. *See* cold boot, warm boot. *See also* reset.

receive buffer *n.* A hardware or software buffer into which incoming data is placed as it arrives. For example, within a serial controller, there is typically an 8-bit receive buffer into which the individual bits are shifted. Once an entire byte of data has arrived, all 8 bits in the receive buffer are written in parallel into a latch that the processor can read when it is ready. Meanwhile, the next incoming byte begins shifting into the receive buffer. Other receive buffers might consist of multiple or even hundreds or thousands of bytes.

received signal strength indicator *n.* A feature of many RF transceiver chips that indicates the strength of the current signal activity at a particular frequency. Abbreviated RSSI. An RSSI can be useful in implementing listen-before-transmit functionality and determining link quality.

reconfigurable computing *n.* The use of dynamically reprogrammable FPGAs or other techniques to implement hardware that varies in form and function over time. In a sense, FPGA(s) can be thought of as a hardware computing fabric on which one set of computing primitives might execute for a while, then another set.

Computing of this sort could well be the future of hardware design, or maybe not. Although dynamically reprogrammable FPGAs exist, many of the practical details (including scheduling and hardware object interfacing) remain to be worked out. Meanwhile, the cost savings are not yet apparent, given that transistors are more or less free (and increasingly so). *Contrast with* configurable computing.

FURTHER READING: http://www.netrino.com/Articles/RCPrimer/

reconfigurable processing unit *n.* An array of programmable logic that can be used as an execution platform for one or more hardware objects. For example, an FPGA. *See also* reconfigurable computing.

rectifier *n.* An electronic component that passes electricity in only one direction. Rectifiers are widely used in circuits to convert AC to DC, to reduce unwanted transients from coils and other

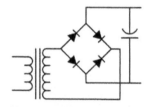

Here, four diodes and a capacitor convert AC to DC.

devices, and for many other uses. Rectifiers include silicon diodes, vacuum tube diodes, "cat's whisker" crystals, and selenium devices, for example.

recursion *n.* A way of specifying a function in terms of itself. In software, recursive functions call themselves. Classic situations where this makes sense are in computing Fibonacci sequences, computing factorials, and sorting.

Recursion is a powerful though dangerous technique. You must ensure that the recursive function will complete its nested set of calls without stack overflow, which can be a problem in memory-constrained embedded systems. Debugging such routines can be tricky.

recursive *adj.* Said of software that calls itself. Recursion should generally be avoided in an embedded system, since it frequently requires a large stack.

A recursive function that computes the factorial of the input.

```
int
factorial(int n)
{
    if (n == 1)
    {
        /*
         * Final step: multiply by 1.
         *
         * Every recursive function must
         * have a final step that does not
         * involve recursion.
         */
        return (1);
    }
    else
    {
        /*
         * n! = n * (n-1)!
         *
         * Recursion occurs when the
         * function calls itself. The nested
         * calls to factorial() will return
         * "up" the stack until we finally
         * get back here in this call.
         */
        return (factorial(n-1) * n);
    }
}
```

reduced instruction set computer *n.* The architecture of a processor family. Abbreviated RISC. So-called *RISC processors* generally feature fixed-length opcodes, a load–store memory architecture, and a large number of general-purpose registers and/or register windows. The MIPS processor family is an excellent example. *Contrast with* complex instruction set computer.

reentrant *adj.* Said of software that can be executed multiple times simultaneously. A reentrant function can be safely called recursively or from multiple tasks. The key to making code reentrant is to ensure mutual exclusion whenever accessing global variables or shared registers.

reference 1. *n.* In C++ and Java, a handle for an object on the heap. Although a pointer could be used to make reference to such an object in C++, a reference is generally safer. Java doesn't allow the use of pointers at all. *Compare to* pointer.

2. *See* reference voltage.

reference counting *n.* A technique for preventing memory leaks and dangling references. The number of references to an object is tracked so that when it falls to zero the object can be freed. Otherwise, memory leaks result from not deleting objects that have no more references to them, and dangling references result when an object is deleted while one or more references to it remain.

Reference counting is also used in Windows to track the number of installed applications dependent on a particular DLL. In theory, once you uninstall the last application that uses that DLL, the DLL will be removed from the system folder.

The same technique can be used to implement automatic garbage collection, simply by moving the object deletion inside the run-time environment.

reference voltage *n.* A precise low-noise voltage applied to an analog device to set the device's full range scale. In the past, reference voltages were created mostly by resistor dividers from an analog supply. Today's high-resolution devices (like 24-bit A/Ds) need much more accuracy and stability, so designers use a reference voltage chip.

EXAMPLE: Analog Device's ADR01 provides a reference voltage that's very stable over temperature (low tempco), time, and changing loads.

EXAMPLE: All A/D converters require a reference voltage (though in some devices this is built in and not explicitly supplied by the designer). Apply 2.5 V to the reference input of an 8-bit A/D, and each bit is then worth about 9.77 mV (2.5 V/256).

refresh *v.* The act of regularly updating something to maintain its state. Despite a world of cheap tran-

sistors, there are still a couple of applications where it makes sense to minimize transistor counts via smart logic. The first is memories. An SRAM requires four to six transistors per cell, compared to one for DRAMs. The downside of DRAMs is that the charge that holds the 1 or 0 leaks away quickly and must be updated every 2 to 4 ms with a "refresh cycle." A controller, sometimes on the processor chip, does this refreshing automatically.

The second area is displays. LCD units in particular can display lots of bits. Building a driver that latches each bit individually would eat up too much logic and require too many connections. It's cheaper to build a circuit that drives the display in an x–y pattern, cycling the displayed bits on the screen over and over, relying on the eye's persistence to give the illusion of a steady-state display. *See also* DRAM refresh.

refresh cycle *See* DRAM refresh.

refresh rate *n.* The interval between refresh cycles. For DRAMs, typical refresh rates are on the order of tens of microseconds. *See also* refresh.

register *res.* A storage class specifier in C and C++ that can be used to suggest that the compiler place a particular automatic variable into a processor register. On its own, the compiler might not recognize the speedup that could be possible by keeping a particular, frequently accessed automatic variable in a register. With a hint from the programmer, the compiler can properly allocate the item to a register.

Beware, though, that tagging more than one or two variables in a function with register might result in compiler confusion. Also be aware that a good optimizing compiler might do a better job of deciding how to use registers than you, and you won't be able to take the address of any register variable.

register *n.* A memory-like location that is part of a processor or an I/O device. The reference to the register is encoded as part of the instruction, not as a discrete address. A processor register is much faster to read or write than a location in memory. Generally, each bit or set of bits within a peripheral register controls or tracks some behavior of the larger device.

register allocation *n.* A process the compiler goes through, on a function-by-function basis, to assign automatic variables to particular general-purpose processor registers.

register window 1. *n.* A set of processor registers, typically including at least the flags and general-purpose registers, as well as the program counter and stack pointer. Processors that have register windows have multiple such sets. If desired, the operating system can assign each register window to one thread. This makes the process of performing a context switch much faster, since only one instruction (to set the new active register window) need be executed and an otherwise large number of memory writes and reads can be avoided.

Of course, most processors that support register windows do not have an unlimited supply (four or eight sets is typical), so some context switches will still require memory accesses if there is a larger number of threads than windows.

2. *n.* A window in a simulator, emulator, or remote debugger that shows the contents of all of the processor's flags and other internal registers.

register-indirect addressing *n.* An addressing mode in which the argument's address is contained in a register.

EXAMPLE: The 68000 instruction

```
MOVE.B (A0),D0
```

gets the data from the memory location specified in A0.

regression testing *n.* The process of going back and testing that bugs previously fixed have not recurred. Each regression test in a suite represents a test that the system previously passed (or failed and then passed). When changes are made to any system, such old tests ought to be run as a group to ensure that the system is now at least as reliable as it was before those changes. Your customers will thank you for it.

Unhappily, regression testing is problematic for many embedded systems since it's hard to automate button presses and interactions with other systems and the real world.

relocatable *n.* A file containing object code that is almost ready for execution on the target. The final remaining step is to use a locator or loader to fix the remaining relocatable addresses within the code. The result of that process is an executable.

remote debugger *n.* A software program that runs on a host computer and controls a small debug monitor in the target to help programmers find bugs. Remote debuggers typically send commands to the monitor over a serial or Ethernet communications link to the target. Most such commands are quite simple: read memory or register contents, alter same, start execution. The debug monitor, occupying just a kilobyte or two of target program space, executes these commands. Remote debuggers are inexpensive and relatively powerful but often crash when the target program crashes and offer little support for real-time trace.

Sometimes the monitor program is really a BDM or JTAG interface inside the target processor.

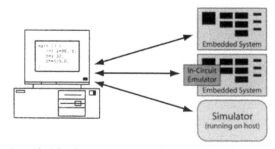

In an ideal development environment, the same remote debugger front end can be connected to a variety of back-end debugging tools.

reprogrammable *adj.* Capable of being erased and rewritten. UV-erasable EPROMs are reprogrammable, as are EEPROM and flash memories and FPGAs.

request to send *n.* A flow control signal, popular in serial communications, asserted by a sending device when it has data to send. *See also* clear to send, hardware flow control.

requirements document *n.* In an ideal world, the document that specifies the system's intended behavior. In the real world, the requirements document is usually abbreviated, incomplete, and wrong. It's not unusual for it to be a verbal order from the boss, like: "Uh, make another colorimeter, kinda like the last one, but smaller and better … dude."

reserved *adj.* Said of a bit or group of bits in CPU and peripheral control registers in which the function is currently undefined but that the vendor wants left available for possible future enhancements. A basic firmware rule is: never, ever, alter any reserved bit. Sometimes these bits will do strange and unexpected things, and future silicon releases might appropriate them for new functions.

reset 1. *v.* To make a bit or a pin a logic 0.

2. *v.* To restart a system.

3. *n.* The state through which a system goes when it is restarted.

reset address *n.* The address from which the first instruction will be fetched after a processor is powered on or reset; usually in ROM.

reset code *n.* A small piece of code that is placed at the reset address. The reset code is usually written in assembly language and might simply be the equivalent of "jump to the startup code."

reset vector *See* reset address.

resistance *n.* The inverse of a material's ability to conduct electricity.

$$R = \frac{V}{I}$$

where R is resistance in ohms, V is voltage in volts, and I is current in amperes.

Resistance is a property of materials and varies widely for different substances. Copper is one of the best conductors, so it's common to compare materials to it. Aluminum, for instance, has 1.6 times the resistance of copper; lead 5.1 times. Other materials are more complex: the resistance of a semiconductor changes depending on how it is used.

resistance temperature detector *n.* A temperature-sensitive wire, often made of copper, nickel, or platinum, that's used to measure temperature. Abbreviated RTD. An RTD can be constructed on a ceramic part. Common RTD materials are copper, platinum, or nickel.

resistor *n.* An electronic component that opposes current flow, generating heat in the process. Resistors are characterized by their resistance, measured in ohms, according to Ohm's Law:

The schematic symbol for a resistor.

$$R = \frac{V}{I}$$

where R is resistance in ohms, V is voltage in volts, and I is current in amps.

Resistors used in embedded systems typically range in value from a few to several million ohms.

resistor color code *n.* A system of colored bands placed on resistors to indicate their rated resistance (in ohms) and tolerance (percentage error). See table on page 290.

resistor pack *n.* A single component that contains a number of resistors—generally between 4 and 16. Resistor packs increase the density of components on a PCB and reduce costs. Three types are common:

- pullup—one node of each resistor is connected together, the other left free. The common node is connected to V_{cc} and the others to various signals requiring pullups.
- series—both sides of each resistor are brought out.
- termination—groups of resistor pairs, each pair wired in series and all tied to common nodes. Used to terminate high-speed signals.

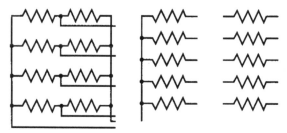

Three types of resistor packs. From left to right: termination, pullup, and series.

resistor–transistor logic *n.* An obsolete type of logic chip, pioneered by Fairchild in the 1960s. Abbreviated RTL. RTL logic was slow but cheap. It used a very simple design, with a transistor organized in a common-emitter configuration. More linear than digital, RTL was very sensitive to getting the logic voltages right.

resolution *n.* The level of precision to which a measurement can be made. In embedded systems, resolution usually refers to the ability of a system to distinguish small differences in analog inputs. *See also* oversample.

EXAMPLE: An 8-bit A/D that measures over a 5-V range resolves to 5/256, or 19.5 mV. A change in the LSb corresponds to 19.5 mV; no finer resolution is available.

resonance *n.* The condition when both inductive and capacitive reactances in a circuit are equal. Because reactance is a function of frequency as well as the components' values, a circuit with

inductors and capacitors is resonant only at certain frequencies. Depending on the circuit's design, it either effectively passes or blocks the resonant frequency.

retransmission *n.* A command or response re-sent because the intended receiver of the previous try either did not acknowledge receipt in time or reported an error in communication.

return *v.* To leave a function, possibly returning data to the caller in the process. The function's stack frame is effectively deleted and the return address is popped from the call stack as part of this process. The compiler handles all of these details for the programmer, though if you are combining code in a high-level language and assembly, you will need to implement these steps in your public assembly routines.

return address *n.* The address to return to after a function call completes.

return from interrupt *n.* A special opcode for returning from an interrupt service routine. On the x86, an IRET. Because of the asynchronous nature of interrupts, entering and exiting interrupt service routines requires saving registers and other processor states. In particular, the flags (carry, zero, etc.) set by the previously executed instruction must be restored when the ISR exits. The return from interrupt instruction typically takes care of this, then resumes execution from where the program was interrupted.

return value *n.* The data returned by a function call. In C and C++, the term applies only to data specifically sent back to the caller via a return statement, not to other global data or parameters changed while the function executed.

reuse *v.* To incorporate a hardware or software module or subsystem from a previous project. In the ideal case, the reused component will require no changes, although that experience is rare in practice.

It has been observed that reuse fails until a module or function has been reused three times. When attempting to reuse a generic routine in a new application, unanticipated factors often pop up that require recoding. But after about three reuses, modules tend to become truly generic.

rev (as in rev up) *abbr.* A hardware version number. Short for revision.

EXAMPLE: As in, "There's a new rev of the board available. Do you know if the software will be affected by the changes?"

reverse engineer 1. *v.* To try to figure out how a something works. For example, although they rarely admit it, many engineering organizations attempt to reverse-engineer their competitor's products in the hopes of learning something that might improve their own design.

reverse Polish notation *n.* A stack-based alternative to algebraic notation, most often associated with HP calculators. Abbreviated RPN. The key difference involves the order of operand and operator entry. In RPN, a binary operator is preceded by its two operands.

The beautiful thing about RPN is that there's never a need to write down an intermediate value. Prior results can be left on the stack until a new operator brings them back into the calculation. Michael Barr finds it inefficient and nearly impossible to do math on a calculator that doesn't work this way.

EXAMPLE: To compute 80% of $221,000, you could either use an algebraic calculator (221000 × 80 / 100 =) or an RPN calculator (221000 ENTER 80 ENTER 100 / ×).

rewind *v.* To return the read/write pointer to the top of an open file. In some operating systems, there is a dedicated rewind() system call; in others, seek() must be used.

rework station *n.* A tool or group of tools used to change surface mount devices and to fix the PCB on which the devices are mounted. Changing SMT parts requires much more sophisticated tools than a soldering iron. The rework station has hot-air soldering tools, vacuum pickup devices, and the like. *See also* surface mount.

RF (as letters) *abbr.* Short for Radio Frequency.

RFC (as letters) *abbr.* A public memo describing how a piece of Internet technology works. Short for Request For Comments. For example, RFC 951 is the original spec for the Bootstrap Protocol (aka BOOTP).

FURTHER READING: http://www.rfc.net

RFI (as letters) *abbr. See* radio frequency interference.

ribbon cable *See* flat ribbon cable.

right hand rule *n.* A mnemonic device to help remember the direction of the result from the cross product of two vectors.

The cross product of two vectors produces a third vector that is perpendicular to the plane in which the first two lie. That is, for the cross of two vectors, A and B, you place A and B so that their tails are at a common point. Then, their cross product, $A \times B$, gives a third vector, C, with a tail that is also at the same point as those of A and B. The vector C points in a direction perpendicular to both A and B.

The right hand rule tells you the direction of C. If you curl the fingers of your right hand from vector A to B, then your thumb points in the direction of C.

The cross product of $B \times A$ causes you to instead curl your fingers from B to A, so the direction of result C is now opposite that of $A \times B$.

During electromagnetics and physics exams, many students can be seen performing various gyrations of the hand to try to get their directions right. If all goes well, they remember to use their right hand instead of their left.

right justify *v.* To shift a value all the way to the right in a byte, word, or other storage unit. *Contrast with* left justify.

EXAMPLE: The number 0x10 right justified in a word is 0x0010.

right shift *v.* To move or rotate the bits in a byte or word from MSb to LSb. *See also* >>, >>>.

ring buffer *See* circular buffer.

ripple counter *n.* A digital counter made up of a cascaded series of flip-flops. As an input stream of alternating 1s and 0s enters the counter at one end, each 1 causes the flip-flop at that end to change. The second flip-flop changes only every other leading edge. The third only every fourth. The net effect is that of a divider that provides many possible derivatives of the input signal. As such, it is useful for deriving many different clock signals from a single frequency input clock signal, all related to the first by a power of two. Ripple counters are slow, since after each clock the signals "ripple" through every flip-flop. *Contrast with* synchronous counter.

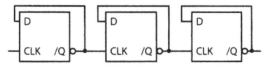

A ripple counter made from 7474 parts.

RISC (like risk) *abbr. See* reduced instruction set computer.

rise time *n.* The length of time for a logic signal to transition from a 0 to a 1. Perfect digital signals would need no time to rise, but in the real (capacitive) world, these times can run to the tens of nanoseconds. *See also* fall time.

rising edge *n.* The portion of a logic signal that transitions from a 0 to a 1.

Ritchie, Dennis *N.* Designer of C while at Bell Labs about 1972.

RMA (as letters) 1. *abbr. See* rate monotonic algorithm.

2. *abbr. See* rate monotonic analysis.

RMS (as letters) *abbr. See* root mean square.

robot *n.* An embedded system that moves or physically manipulates its environment or nearby objects. Some robots are made to move only via remote control; others are fully automatic. Both kinds are used in space exploration, factory automation, and a variety of other settings.

Many dream of a future in which automated robots will make life easier, whereas equal numbers worry about robots later becoming sentient and banding together to overthrow their human masters. A variety of books and movies have explored these possibilities.

roll back *v.* To restore the state of a single thread or entire system to its state at the last checkpoint. For example, if something goes wrong in the middle of a complex banking transaction, the bank's computer should roll back to the state of the involved accounts before that transaction began; otherwise, an inconsistency could result.

roll your own *See* buy versus build.

ROM (rhymes with mom) *abbr.* Any of several memory devices that can be read but not written. Short for Read-Only Memory. *See* masked ROM, PROM, EPROM. *Compare to* EEPROM, flash.

ROM emulator *n.* A debugging tool that plugs into the target system's ROM sockets (or that attaches to the SMT ROM parts). ROM emulators link the target system to a host

A ROM emultator from TechTools.

computer. A plug either inserts into the target ROM sockets, clips over SMT ROM chips, or is soldered down in place of the ROM parts. The emulator then links this connection to the host computer over RS-232, Ethernet, or USB.

A ROM emulator lets the developer examine and change memory, I/O, and registers. It will support breakpoints (usually software-only), and single stepping. The biggest advantage of a ROM emulator is that it doesn't require a dedicated target comm port, as a ROM monitor would.

ROM monitor *See* debug monitor.

ROM, fusible-link *n.* A mostly obsolete type of non-volatile memory that stored data in polysilicon fuses that were selectively burned out to represent 0s. Fusible-link ROMs were designed as write-once devices. However, clever developers learned to patch code by burning new instructions on top of old ones, as long as the new instructions added 0s. It was never possible to turn a 0 into a 1.

ROM-DOS *n.* A variant of DOS that is ROMable and used in embedded PCs.

ROMable *adj.* Able to be placed in ROM. Software is ROMable if it has been statically linked and assigned fixed physical addresses and data can be separated from code to be located in RAM. A development tool called a locator is typically employed as the final step in building a ROM image. Once the software is ROMable, it can be programmed into a ROM or flash memory chip.

ROMize *v.* To make a Java program ROMable. Because Java is normally dynamically linked and interpreted by a Java virtual machine, specialized tools are required. A typical ROMizer strips out unneeded classes, methods, and data from the class libraries; precompiles the Java bytecodes to native opcodes; and statically links the resulting program to the garbage collector and other run-time checking routines.

root 1. *n.* A solution of an equation.

 EXAMPLE: The roots of the equation

$$x^2 - 4 = 0$$

 are 2 and −2.

2. *n.* Another name for the superuser in Unix.

3. *n.* The owner of files created by a Unix superuser.

4. *n.* The highest level directory in a filesystem.

root directory *n.* The top-level directory in a filesystem.

root finder *n.* An algorithm or program that finds the solutions of equations. *See also* root, Newtons-method.'

root mean square *n.* A measure of the amplitude of an AC signal. Abbreviated RMS. For sine waves, the RMS of an AC input is 0.707 times the signal's peak-to-peak values. An AC signal's RMS is the voltage or current that will produce the same heating effect.

ROPES (rhymes with hopes) *abbr.* An iterative development process. Short for Rapid Object-oriented Process for Embedded Systems.

 FURTHER READING: Douglass, Bruce Powel. "On the ROPES," *Embedded Systems Programming*, December 2000.

rotary encoder *n.* A device that generates a pulse stream as its input shaft is rotated. Also called an angular encoder. Rotary encoders might produce a simple set of pulses, say 256 per revolution, or a pair of quadrature streams that helps the processor determine which way the shaft is turning. Often used as digital substitutes for analog potentiometers or variable capacitors as controls on instruments and consumer appliances. *See also* binary encoder, Gray code encoder, quadrature encoder.

round-robin *n.* A secondary scheduling algorithm commonly used by RTOSes. Scheduling by round-robin gives all ready tasks within a particular priority level more or less equal time to run. When the time quantum elapses, the scheduler gives the next ready task of the same priority control of the CPU, switching between these tasks until a higher priority event occurs.

row address select *n.* A signal from a DRAM controller that tells DRAMs the current address information is the row address. Abbreviated RAS. DRAMs don't take a normal binary address; the DRAM controller breaks addresses into rows and columns, dumping first one then the other into the chip. *See also* refresh, DRAM, DRAM controller.

royalty *n.* A licensing fee paid to a supplier for each copy of a piece of software resold. For example, some RTOSes require payment of royalties. Every system manufactured with one of those in ROM generates a royalty payment to the RTOS developer. In that way, the inclusion of the RTOS in the final product incurs per-unit production costs similar to the inclusion of any hardware component.

RPM (as letters) *abbr.* A measure of velocity. Short for Revolutions Per Minute.

RPN (as letters) *abbr. See* reverse Polish notation.

RPU (as letters) *abbr. See* reconfigurable processing unit.

RS-232 *See* RS-232C.

RS-232C *N.* An EIA standard that defines a commonly used serial communications scheme. RS-232C is widely used to transfer data between computers or other devices using an asynchronous serial link at speeds ranging from 110 to 115,200 baud. The standard defines connectors, signals, signal levels, and typical handshake.

A "space" (logic 0) ranges from +3 to +25 V; "marks" (1s) are −3 to −25 V.

Unfortunately, the standard permits a wide range of connections and handshaking. As a result, the two RS-232C devices you're trying to connect might may not plug and play. *See also* serial cable, null modem cable.

FURTHER READING: http://www.epl.co.uk/info16.htm

RS-422 *N.* An EIA standard that defines a serial communications scheme designed for sending data over long distances in noisy environments. RS-422 defines a serial, asynchronous, four-wire communications link using differential signals. Two wires each are used for transmission and reception. Polarity of the signal defines 1s and 0s: a voltage of +200 mV to +6V is 1 ("mark"); −200 mV to −6 V is a 0 ("space").

RS-422 supports data rates to 10 Mbps over cables up to 1200 meters long.

RS-485 *N.* An EIA standard that defines a serial communications scheme designed for sending data over long distances in noisy environments in multidrop (or "party line") applications with as many as 32 connected devices. RS-485 defines a serial, asynchronous, four-wire communications link using differential signals. Two wires each are used for transmission and reception. Polarity of the signal defines 1s and 0s: a voltage of +200 mV to +12V is a 1 ("mark"); −200 mV to −V is a 0 ("space").

Although the electrical parameters are similar to RS-422, the slightly extended voltage range might not be compatible with all 422 ICs.

RS-485 supports data rates to 10 Mbps over cables up to 1200 meters long.

RTAI (as letters) *abbr.* An open source kernel for running real-time tasks alongside Linux and non–real-time Linux processes. Short for Real-Time Applications Interface. *Contrast with* Linux/RT.

FURTHER READING: http://www.rtai.org

RTC (as letters) 1. *abbr. See* real-time clock.

2. *abbr. See* run-to-completion.

RTCA *See* DO-178B.

RTD (as letters) *abbr. See* resistance temperature detector.

RTL (as letters) *abbr. See* resistor–transistor logic.

RTOS (are-toss) *abbr. See* real-time operating system.

> **USAGE:** Pluralization of RTOS is difficult, as is writing out "real-time operating systems" every time it's needed. There is no easy solution to this dilemma. Reasonable possibilities, listed in order of increasing popularity, include RTOS's, RTOSes, and RTOSs. Note, however, that RTOSes seems to be the form preferred by those most in the know. RTOSen is another cute possibility. RTOS's is frowned upon for its false suggestion of a possessive property.

RTS (as letters) *abbr. See* request to send.

RTSJ (as letters) *abbr. See* Real-Time Specification for Java.

RTXC (as letters) *abbr.* A popular RTOS for a wide range of 8- to 32-bit processors. RTXC was originally produced by the AT Barrett company, which morphed into Embedded Systems Products, then to Embedded Power, which was bought by Lineo and is now sold and supported by Quadros.

rule of thumb *n.* A rough and easy-to-apply engineering rule that most often leads to a correct solution. Rules of thumb are used by engineers to quickly sense the appropriateness of a particular solution.

> **EXAMPLE:** In firmware, a rule of thumb is: Be suspicious of code that leaves interrupts disabled a lot.

run-time check *n.* A validation that takes place automatically via the run-time system.

> **EXAMPLE:** In Java, the virtual machine checks all divisions beforehand to ensure they won't result in a divide-by-zero and checks all array accesses to ensure they aren't outside the bounds of the array. These are software run-time checks, which spend CPU cycles to avoid problems.

run-time library *n.* The prepackaged set of routines that comes with a compiler to support a program's execution. The run-time library contains everything at all complicated that cannot be efficiently turned into inline code, like floating-point, 32-bit math (on smaller processors), string handling, `printf()`, and much, much more. The compiler, when it encounters a statement like

```
a = b * tan(sin(x));
```

generates at least two calls to the run-time library.

run-time system *n.* Generally the same as the run-time library, but sometimes includes other packages like the RTOS and protocol suite.

run-to-completion *adj.* Said of a nonpreemptive scheduling algorithm that runs each thread until it is completed. Abbreviated RTC. The only scheduling point in an RTC operating system occurs when the running thread exits. *Compare to* shortest-job-first.

run-to-completion step *n.* A piece of code that will be run without an intervening context switch.

running *adj.* Describes a task state that indicates the task is currently executing on a processor. No more than one task can be in the running state at a give time on a single-processor system. In a multiprocessor system, each processor can run one task. *See also* ready.

running task *n.* A task that is currently in the running state. In a single-processor system, there can only be one running task at any instant of time. If no user tasks are ready to run, then the idle task is the running task.

S

S-record *See* Motorola S-record format.

S/H (as letters) *abbr. See* sample-and-hold.

s/w (software) *abbr. See* software.

safety ground *n.* A ground connection designed to divert leakages from failed components. Usually also the frame ground, the safety ensures that a loose wire inside the device will cause a short circuit, blowing a fuse or circuit breaker.

Older readers will remember the glory days of beautifully engineered power tools with aluminum cases. Those case were all tied to the AC mains ground. Any internal failure would short to the conductive case, and thus to the mains ground, blowing the fuse. Today these tools are all encased in plastic and often have no ground connection to the mains. The nonconductive case will not conduct a short circuit to the user, so although there's no safety ground, the user is already protected.

safety-critical *adj.* Said of a system that could or would cause a human or financial catastrophe if it failed.

sample-and-hold *adj.* Said of a circuit that memorizes an analog input. Sometimes abbreviated S&H or S/H. A sample-and-hold circuit stores an analog input in a capacitor when a digital input is asserted. A high-impedance op-amp ensures the cap's voltage remains stable for a reasonable period (milliseconds to seconds, depending on the circuit).

Sample-and-hold behavior is a basic part of most A/D converters.

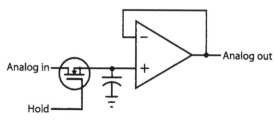

A typical sample-and-hold circuit. The capacitor latches the analog input.

sampling rate *n.* The rate at which a system reads an input (usually analog). The sampling rate largely determines the ability of a system to accurately represent the input. *See also* Nyquist theorem.

sanity check *n.* A crude but quick approximation that gives one a sense of the correctness of a system or solution. Sanity checks are part of what differentiates engineers and scientists. Engineers often build systems that are simply good enough. Sanity checks offer a quick sense of the "goodness."

EXAMPLE: Watchdog timers are an example of a sanity check. Their lack of firing doesn't prove absolutely that the system is running properly, but they require enough proper operation to suggest that the software is muddling along, at least to a first approximation.

SBC (as letters) *abbr. See* single-board computer.

scan code *n.* The numeric value associated with a particular key on a keypad or keyboard. Software generally reads scan codes one at a time or out of a FIFO buffer, figures out what to do in response to a particular scan code, and behaves accordingly.

scanning 1. *n.* Parsing an input stream to identify lexical tokens.

2. *n.* A way of reading multiplexed input data. Keyboards, for instance, would eat vast numbers of input lines if each key were tied to an input line. Instead, they are arranged in an *x–y* matrix; smart software samples these by shifting an asserted bit into the *x*-axis of the array and reading the *y* to see that asserted bit, which would indicate that the key at that $x = y$ junction was asserted. *See also* switch matrix.

SCC (as letters) *abbr.* A common name for a UART or DUART IC. Short for Serial Communications Controller.

schedulability analysis *n.* The process of determining whether a particular set of real-time tasks can be scheduled such that all deadlines will be met.

schedulable *adj.* Said of a set of real-time threads that can share the same processor and still meet all of their deadlines. *See also* rate monotonic algorithm.

schedulable bound *n.* The maximum achievable processor utilization, W, as a percentage, for a set of *n* threads prioritized by applying the rate monotonic algorithm.

$$W_n = n(2^{1/n} - 1)$$

If there's only one thread to be run, the schedulable bound is 100%. If there are two threads, the worst-case schedulable bound drops to 82.8%. The formula approaches a limit of 69.3% (ln 2, to be precise) as the number of threads grows larger.

It is important to realize, however, that a particular set of *n* threads with their combination of specific periods, deadlines, and worst-case execution times might be able to achieve a higher overall utilization with RMA. The formula above gives only the schedulable bound for the worst possible combination of any *n* threads.

schedule *v.* To select the next thread to run.

scheduler *n.* The part of a multitasking operating system that decides which task to run next. The scheduler's decision is based on the state of each task, the relative priorities of those that are ready to run, and the specific scheduling algorithm implemented.

scheduling *n.* The process of selecting the next thread to run.

scheduling algorithm *n.* The way in which the operating system decides which thread to run next. Most commercial RTOSes use a preemptive priority-based scheduling algorithm, which guarantees that the highest priority ready task is run every time. Some possible scheduling algorithms, among many, include run-to-completion, shortest-job-first, and earliest-deadline-first.

scheduling overhead *n.* The percentage of processor utilization that is consumed by the operating system. The operating system is just a facilitator, so any CPU cycles it consumes in the process of performing context switching or making scheduling decisions are wasted.

scheduling point *n.* An opportunity for the scheduler to execute and select a new task to run. Operating systems are just collections of system calls—invoked by application programs to perform work on their behalf—and interrupt service routines. Depending on the type of scheduler employed in the operating system, there will be one or more system calls that result in scheduler invocation.

Every operating system has a scheduling point at the time a task completes its work and exits. At that time, there would be no running task, so the scheduler must select a new task to run. Run-to-completion and shortest-job-first schedulers might have only this one scheduling point.

Most modern operating systems also have a scheduling point at the time that the running task blocks to wait for some event, and preemptive operating systems can additionally stop the running task and select a new one whenever a new task is created (always by the running task, by definition) or a previously blocked task unblocks.

scheduling policy *See* scheduling algorithm.

schematic *n.* In electronics, a drawing comprising standardized symbols to represent all of a circuit's components and its connections.

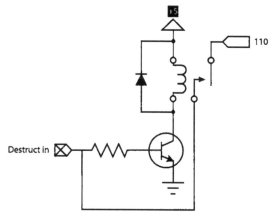

A circuit that destroys itself and connected components when the Destruct in signal is asserted. Can be used to implement a processor's SD (self destruct) instruction, which should not be executable in user mode.

Schmitt trigger *N.* A type of logic gate input that exhibits hysteresis. A gate with a Schmitt trigger input flips its output state only when the input exceeds some specified level; when the input falls back to that level, the gate does not flip back to the previous state. Instead, the input must fall to a level lower than that which set the original transition.

The use of a Schmitt trigger increases an input's noise immunity.

EXAMPLE: The 7414 hex inverter was the classic Schmitt trigger device.

scientific notation *See* exponential notation.

scope 1. *n.* The region of code in which a particular variable is recognized.

EXAMPLE: The scope of an automatic variable is limited to the function in which it is declared.

2. *abbr. See* oscilloscope.

SCR latchup *n.* A situation in which a CMOS device conducts power to ground because its safe input voltage levels were exceeded, usually resulting in the device's failure.

SCR latchup happens when the input to a gate or other CMOS device goes above the part's V_{cc} or below ground. This might seem unlikely in the benign environment of a digital circuit, but fast edges sent over even a few inches of PCB track can generate overshoot or undershoot from impedance mismatches. Sometimes there's enough over- or undershoot to drive the part into latchup. It's also a problem when plugging an unpowered board into a hot socket; if the input pins get signals before power and ground make a connection, SCR latchup can result.

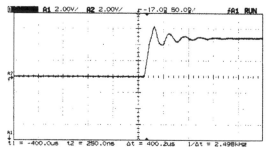

This signal exhibits the sort of overshoot on its rising edge that can lead to SCR latchup.

A CMOS device is fabricated from diffused regions of N- and P-type dopings onto an N- or P-type substrate, creating an NPNP or PNPN junction, which is an SCR (silicon-controlled rectifier). It stalks the circuit, buried quiescently, until an errant voltage excursion, at which point it turns on and conducts power to ground. Like an SCR, once on, it's on until power is removed.

SCR latchup failures are often dramatic—the IC could quite literally explode as thermal stresses rapidly exceed what the package can contain.

SCRUM *n.* An agile development methodology that stresses an evolutionary approach to developing a product. SCRUM lies between XP and the waterfall approach. It features a defined process for both the planning (architecting) and closure (preparing the product for release) phases. In between, a "sprint" process translates requirements into designs and code. Constant reviews ensure that the product meets customer requirements. The sprint phase is circular; designs and code change to meet new needs and a better understanding of the problems encountered.

second *n.* A standard unit of time. Abbreviated s.

sector 1. *n.* A wholly erasable region of a flash memory device. Like EEPROMs, the contents of flash memories, although nonvolatile, can be rewritten. However, the location(s) to be rewritten must be erased first. In a flash, the erase cycle is only supported at the sector level. Typical sector sizes are in the range 256 bytes to 16 KB.

2. *n.* The smallest unit of storage on a disk drive. Each sector is one part of a circular track on a particular platter. The disk head must be positioned directly over that sector in order to read or write its contents.

Entire sectors are read or written; you cannot read/write a part of a sector. Each sector generally holds 512 bytes.

Also called a block, an individual sector can be addressed by specifying its CHS (cylinder, head, and sector) numbers. The disk controller is often responsible for maintaining a map from each simple linear sector number to the CHS numbers. For example, with IDE drives, the filesystem need know only of sectors by linear number (0 to *n*).

seek( ) *fn.* A common name for a system call that repositions the read/write pointer of an open file.

A part of the standard Unix API for file I/O, most implementations of seek( ) support repositioning relative to the beginning, end, or current position in the file. The three parameters are the file descriptor, starting point, and relative offset. *See also* rewind, EOF.

segment *n.* A piece of a relocatable or an executable that contains part of the code or data for a compiled program. Each source file that's compiled results in an object file. Those object files are organized into separate sections containing code, initialized data, and uninitialized data. The linker combines related sections from each of the linked object files into segments, without yet assigning specific memory locations to any of them. (References between segments can be partially resolved, though, since the offset within the segment is already known.) The locator assigns specific memory locations to each segment and adds new segments for run-time elements like the stack and heap. *See also* BSS segment, text segment, data segment.

segment register *n.* A register used in the x86 processors to extend addressing beyond 64 KB. When Intel introduced the 16-bit 8088, they tried to make it backward compatible—sort of—with the 8-bit 8080. That meant using 16-bit address registers, which offered far too little address space for a real 16-bit processor. The solution was to define four new segment registers, named SS, CS, DS, and ES, and make them part of address calculations.

In the 8088 (and all later x86 processors running in real mode), an address is formed by shifting the appropriate segment register left 4 bits and adding it to the address to form a 20-bit physical address.

Later x86 processors added protected mode, which supports a full 32 bits (4 GB) of address space. A much more complex address translation takes place in protected mode, though it still uses segment registers.

segment:offset *n.* An x86 segment–offset pair. The effective address is formed by shifting the 16-bit segment number left 4 bits and adding the 16-bit offset. The result is a 20-bit physical address. *See also* real mode.

segmented addressing *n.* The process of forming an address using segment registers. *See* segment register.

SEI (as letters) *abbr.* Short for the Software Engineering Institute. The SEI mission is to improve software engineering. Their approach focuses on three themes.

- Move to the left—They believe in working as much as possible on issues in the early life cycle of a product, like up-front design and specification.
- Reuse everything—Reuse is the cheapest way to produce a product.
- Never make the same mistake twice—They advocate employing feedback mechanisms to constantly improve.

The SEI is thus somewhat at odds with those who advocate a focus on the code (e.g., eXtreme Programming).

The SEI is best known for the Capability Maturity Model. They also push the Personal Software Process and the Team Software Process. *See also* Capability Maturity Model, Personal Software Process.

FURTHER READING: http://www.sei.cmu.edu

self-modifying code *n.* An executable that modifies itself at run time. Obviously, code stored in ROM cannot modify itself—which is a good thing!

HISTORY: These days, the most common examples of self-modifying code are viruses. However, in the early days of computing, legitimate uses for self-modifying code were more common.

semaphore *n.* A data structure that is used for inter-task synchronization. Semaphores are usually provided by the operating system and come in two types: binary and counting. The former can be used for mutual exclusion.

semiconductor 1. *n.* A solid-state substance with conductivity that varies with applied voltage or applied light.

2. *n.* A device, like a diode or transistor, made from semiconducting materials. Semiconductors are the basis of all modern electronics. The transistor is a three-terminal semiconductor; all ICs are basically aggregates of connected transistors.

sequential *adj.* Said of something that happens in a particular order. In embedded systems, it usually refers to sequential logic. *See* sequential logic.

sequential logic *n.* A logic circuit in which the next state is affected by previous states. Sequential circuits have memory, typically flip-flops, and a clocking mechanism to advance the circuit's state. Nothing changes until the clock transitions.
Q: Why is there time?
A: So everything doesn't happen all at once.
This old adage is the basis of all computers (with the exception of very preliminary work being done on asynchronous computing). Computers are sequential: a clock drives the computer through its processing. *See also* synchronous counter, synchronous logic. *Compare to* combinatorial logic.

serial cable *n.* A set of wires compatible with RS-232 communications, typically with 9- or 25-pin D-type connectors at each end.

serial EEPROM *n.* An EEPROM that's read and written serially, typically by bit banging a general-purpose I/O pin or via I^2C. Small serial EEPROMs, say 4 KB or less, are sometimes used to store a system's configuration parameters.

serial I/O *n.* Any input or output that comprises a byte, word, or longer stream that's shifted into or out of the system a single bit at a time. Serial I/O is used mostly for data communications. It's cheaper to run a few wires between remote devices than a parallel bus, especially since noise considerations usually mandate level shifters on each line. But even within a computer, some serial I/O is not unusual: the I^2C bus often connects several processors on a single PCB, and serial EEPROMs are widely used to store MAC addresses and other nonvolatile data. *See also* RS-232C, RS-422.

serial port *n.* An input or output port that handles serial data. Most serial ports have a UART or other serial/parallel converter. However, it's possible, though painful, to create a serial port entirely with software that, through exquisite timing, shifts data in or out of the machine. *See also* serial I/O.

series capacitances *n.* The process of combining two or more capacitors in series to create a new value. For any number of capacitors in series, the total effective value of the circuit is

0.01uf   0.03 uf

These two series capacitors have an effective value of 0.0075 µF.

$$C = \frac{1}{(1/C_1 + 1/C_2 + 1/C_3 + ... + 1/C_n)}$$

For two capacitors, this simplifies to

$$C = \frac{C_1 \times C_2}{C_1 + C_2}$$

Contrast with paralleled capacitances.

series resistances *n.* The process of combining two or more resistors in series to create a new value. The total resistance of a circuit with n resistors in series is

$$R = R_1 + R_2 + R_3 + ... + R_n$$

Contrast with paralleled resistances.

servo (serve-oh) 1. *abbr. See* servomotor.

2. *v.* To change the position of a device using feedback. *See* servo track.

servo track *n.* A track written to a hard disk that is used to help control the position of the disk's read/write heads. Hard disks position their heads using a servo track written on the disk; the disk reads this track and moves the heads to maximize the returned signal.

servomotor *n.* A motor with a shaft that can be positioned to specific angular positions. Called a servo for short. As long as the coded signal exists on the input line, the servo will maintain the angular position of the shaft. As the coded signal changes, the angular position of the shaft changes. In practice, servos are used in radio-controlled airplanes to position control surfaces like the elevators and rudders. They are also used in radio-controlled cars, puppets, and of course, robots.

Servomotors use a variable pulse–length input to control their position.

set *v.* To make a bit or a pin a logic 1.

setup time *n.* The time data must remain stable before clock transitions on a flip-flop. Violating the setup time parameter will create a metastable state. *See also* hold time, metastability.

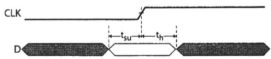

Clock is the top graph; the flip-flop's input data is the bottom graph. Setup time (t_{su}) is the time the input data must be stable before clock transitions.

seven-segment display *See* 7-segment display.

shadow memory *n.* Memory inside of some debugging tools that maintains a copy of all program write cycles. Shadow memory is most often found on in-circuit emulators. It's essentially a dual-ported memory. Logging all memory writes, it provides a real-time record of the contents of variables, which the user can view without slowing program execution.

shallow-history pseudostate *n.* A visual shorthand for the complicated idea of having a parent state remember which child state was last active. Shown as a circled letter "H" in UML. On any transition to a state's shallow history, the last active child state is reentered. If the parent has never been active prior to that time (and so has no history), the transition shown from the shallow-history pseudostate should be used as default. *Compare to* deep-history pseudostate.

shared interrupt   *See* interrupt sharing.

shared library   *n.* A dynamically linked library that is loaded into memory just once, though can be used by multiple processes. The challenging part about implementing shared libraries is that processes are supposed to have distinct logical memory spaces. Yet the shared library needs to exist in all of these spaces at once. Help from the operating system is in order.

In simpler single-process systems, typically with no MMU, all libraries are "shared," although usually by static linking. This is not really the same thing at all.

shared memory   *n.* A range of physical memory that is capable of being read and/or written by two or more processes. Ordinarily, processes cannot access the physical memory assigned to each of them for its code, data, stack, and so on. However, some operating systems will allow shared memory areas to be created so that an interested set of processes can share or pass data. Data in shared memory must be protected from race conditions, typically via a mutex.

shared resource   *n.* Data, registers, or other items of interest to more than one thread. Shared resources are often the source of race conditions. In order for such resources to be shared safely, access to

them must be coordinated via a mutual exclusion primitive, such as a mutex. *See also* priority inversion.

shift   *n.* A basic computer operation that moves the bits of a binary value to the left or right. Shifts come in many flavors, including the following.

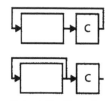

Top: rotation through the carry. Bottom: a circular shift.

- left shift—multiply the data by 2
- right shift—divide by 2
- arithmetic shift—shift the data, but preserve the state of the sign bit
- circular shift—shift the data so the overflow (from the MSb or LSb) goes around to the other side of the data (generally the bit that shifts out of the register also appears in the carry)
- rotate—shifts through the carry
- barrel shift—a one-cycle shift of more than 1 bit.

See also >>, <<, >>>.

`short`   *res.* A primitive data type for declaring small integers in C and several related languages. In C and C++, the size of a `short` varies by processor and compiler. The only requirement is that it be no smaller than an `int`. In Java, a short is always a 16-bit value.

short   *See* short circuit.

short circuit   *n.* An unwanted connection that diverts current from its intended path.

shortest-job-first   *adj.* Describes a nonpreemptive scheduling algorithm in which the thread with the least work to do is run first. Once selected to run, a thread runs to completion or until it blocks. Abbreviated SJF.

The principal advantage of SJF scheduling is that it achieves the maximum number of satisfied customers. For that reason, it was popular in the early days of computing when users submitted their jobs to an operator. The longest jobs were typically run at night or at other times when there were no shorter jobs in the queue. SJF scheduling is not typically used in embedded systems. *Compare to* run-to-completion.

shot noise *n.* The noise caused by random fluctuations in the motion of charge carriers in a conductor. The electrical current through a point contact is not constant in time, but fluctuates. The conductance determines only the time-averaged current; shot noise is the variations in the current.

shunt 1. *n.* Any component placed in parallel with another. Typically used in reference to a resistor.

2. *v.* To place a component in parallel with another.

SI (as letters) *abbr. See* Système international d'unités.

side effect *n.* An unintended consequence. For example, modifying the implementation of one function might have the side effect of causing another function to fail. Software side effects can best be eliminated by separating the interface from the implementation so that the latter can be changed without negative effects. *See also* coupling.

sideband *n.* A band of frequencies higher or lower than the carrier frequency. AM modulation adds the input signal (voice, typically) to the carrier. The result is three frequencies: the carrier and two sidebands. One sideband is at the carrier + modulation frequencies, the other at the carrier − modulation. These sidebands contain all of the information.

Double sideband and SSB are techniques that suppress the unneeded carrier and, in the case of SSB, one of the sidebands. *See also* single-sideband modulation, amplitude modulation, double-sideband modulation.

sign magnitude notation *n.* A way of encoding positive and negative integer values in binary. In sign magnitude notation, a sign bit denotes a positive or negative value and the magnitude is stored as an absolute value. For a number of reasons, sign magnitude representations are rarely used in modern computers. *Compare to* one's complement notation, two's complement notation.

EXAMPLE: The integer value 17 expressed in 16-bit sign magnitude notation is 0000 0000 0001 0001b. Its negative (−17) is 1000 0000 0001 0001b.

signal ground *n.* The negative reference for low-level logic and analog signals in a system. Signal ground is always tied in some way to the power supply.

Systems with a mix of analog and digital often have separate analog and digital grounds. Digital logic is inherently noisy; it's undesirable to couple that noise to the sensitive analog. The digital and analog grounds are then connected at a single point designed to reduce ground loops.

signal-to-noise ratio *n.* The ratio between the desired signal and unwanted noise. Abbreviated SNR.

$$SNR = 10\log\left(\frac{V_s^2}{V_n^2}\right)$$

where V_s is the signal in volts and V_n is the noise in volts.

SNR is measured in decibels. *See also* noise reduction.

signed *res.* Used with `char`, `short`, `int`, or `long` to declare a signed integer.

signed integer *n.* A variable that can store any whole number. *Contrast with* unsigned integer.

significant lines of code *n.* The number of lines of code that contain actual code, not just white space or comments. Abbreviated SLOCs. Plain old lines of code is a poor comparative metric, since lines of white space and comments are included.

SLOCs are more meaningful, though still of questionable comparative value.

silicon 1. *n.* The element with atomic number 14. Abbreviated Si. Silicon is the main ingredient of glass and a critical building block for integrated circuits.

2. *n.* An integrated circuit.

EXAMPLE: "Once we get silicon for our ASIC, we can start testing the new firmware."

silkscreen layer *n.* On a PCB, the set of painted-on signal and component labels. Such labels are helpful during assembly and debugging.

SIMM (rhymes with hymn) *abbr.* A form factor for RAM banks that was once widely used in PCs. Short for Single Inline Memory Module. SIMMs were eventually replaced by DIMMs.

simple state *n.* A state that does not contain any other states. Also called a child state. If the child doesn't handle a given event, it inherits the action of its parent on that event. In that way, the child is a special case of the parent, much as a class uses inheritance to extend the behaviors of another. *See also* composite state.

simplex *adj.* A type of communications channel in which transmission occurs in one and only one preassigned direction. *Contrast with* duplex.

simulator *n.* A debugging tool that runs on the host and pretends to be the target processor. A simulator can be used to test pieces of the embedded software before the embedded hardware is available. Unfortunately, attempts to simulate interactions with complex peripherals are often more trouble than they are worth.

sine 1. *n.* A trigonometric function that is the ratio of the side of a triangle opposite the angle of interest to the hypotenuse. Abbreviated sin.

$$\sin(\alpha) = \frac{opposite}{hypotenuse}$$

2. *n.* Any signal with a shape that resembles a sine wave. *See also* sinusoid.

single sideband *See* single-sideband modulation.

single step *v.* To execute the next instruction or line of code then break again. If you're single-stepping in a source-level debugger, you'll need to know the difference between stepping into and stepping over. If you step into, and the next line of code is a function call, then the break will occur inside that function. If you step over, the entire function call will run before the break.

single-board computer *n.* A COTS hardware platform that can be used for prototyping or to realize an embedded product. Abbreviated SBC. Most embedded systems designers create their own specialized hardware. But there are some markets, particularly those in which NRE costs matter more than COGS, in which SBCs thrive as the implementation hardware of choice. The most successful SBC designs tend to be based around popular backplanes and bus architectures, such as VME and PC/104, since multicard designs are popular in those spaces and special-purpose SBCs can be inserted with ease on the bus alongside the required custom hardware.

single-precision *adj.* Generally refers to a 32-bit floating-point number. *Contrast with* double-precision. *See also* IEEE 754.

single-sideband modulation *n.* A highly efficient way to transmit primarily voice signals over a radio. Abbreviated SSB. Ordinary AM uses a carrier with an amplitude that is modulated. This results in a central high-power carrier signal, which carries no information, and two weaker sidebands positioned on either side of the carrier, which each hold identical copies of the information. SSB suppresses the carrier and one sideband.

SSB is widely used in ham radio transmissions. *Compare to* double-sideband modulation.

sink *See* current sink.

sinusoid *n.* A signal with a shape that resembles a sine function. *See also* sine.

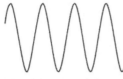
A waveform of sinusoid shape.

SIO (as letters) *abbr. See* serial I/O.

`sizeof()` (size of) *fn.* An operator that returns the size of an object or data type in bytes.

EXAMPLE: The result of `sizeof(uint32_t)` will be 4 if you've typedef'd `uint32_t` properly for your target platform.

skew 1. *n.* Any unwanted shift in data.

USAGE: "Skewed data" suggests information that is basically correct but shifted in time, amplitude, or other dimension.

2. *n.* A digital signal's unwanted shift in time.

SLD (as letters) *abbr. See* source-level debugger.

sleep *v.* To yield the processor to other threads for a set length of time, typically via a system call of the form `sleep(interval)`, where *interval* is some small fraction of a second.

sleep mode *n.* A low-power mode supported by many microprocessors that shuts down most on-chip functions. In sleep mode, though the chip has stopped executing code, it is still somewhat aware of the outside world. Usually it responds to an interrupt by coming back into normal mode.

Sleep mode reduces power needs by orders of magnitude. Some embedded systems live in sleep mode nearly all of the time, coming to life only when a user presses a key or takes some other action—for example, the TV remote control. *See also* low-power.

slide rule *n.* An ultra–low-power calculating machine, requiring neither batteries nor the manipulation of complicated keys. A "2 banger" slide rule uses a combination of linear and logarithmic scales to compute the two basic math operations (multiplication and division). More sophisticated ("full function") units provide trig functions, logs, and more.

Once upon a time, engineers were readily identified by a slide rule hanging from a belt. See figure.

SLIP (slip) *abbr.* A de facto standard for encapsulating TCP/IP packets over serial connections. Short for Serial Line Internet Protocol. RFC 1055. SLIP defines a sequence of characters that frame IP packets on a serial line. Prior to its introduction, a variety of proprietary means were used to do this, since TCP/IP was primarily envisioned to run over Ethernet and Token Ring networks; it was never supposed to run on serial lines.

C/SLIP and PPP offer better throughput characteristics; PPP has largely supplanted SLIP and C/SLIP these days.

SLOCs (slocks) *abbr. See* significant lines of code.

slope *n.* The rise over run of a line or tangent to a point on a curve. Any line can be described by an equation $y = mx + b$, where m is the slope. *See also* intercept.

slide rule A typical slide rule.

small-scale integration *n.* A type of logic IC that comprises dozens to a hundred or so transistors. Abbreviated SSI. SSI parts include small gates and flip-flop parts like the venerable 7400 and 7474.

smart card *n.* A credit card–sized product with a microcontroller inside. Smart cards have several visible electrical contacts on the underside. When the card is inserted into a smart card reader (typically at some point of sale) the processor is powered up and the firmware stored there runs. Applications include debit and credit cards, electronic voting, digital security, and a myriad of other things.

Astonishingly, although they seem pretty simple (8-bit microcontrollers with just a few kibibytes of ROM and RAM), the amount of memory and processing power is similar to that available in the original IBM PC.

smart sensor *n.* A sensor plus microprocessor combo. Most sensors are prone to nonlinearities, gain, and offset errors. In addition, their output signals typically have a small dynamic range and high impedance, making them susceptible to electrical noise as well. As a result, ordinary sensors typically require dedicated signal conditioning circuitry for error compensation, filtering, and buffering.

Unlike their plain vanilla brethren, smart sensors integrate the sensor along with the required conditioning circuitry in a single enclosure. Circuitry onboard the smart sensor usually consists of data converters, a processor and firmware, and some form of nonvolatile memory. Because they are processor-based devices, smart sensors can be custom programmed to satisfy specific system requirements and later reprogrammed as these requirements evolve.

On-board data processing and local storage enable added capabilities at the sensor's location, such as the ability to take action without intervention by the main system controller. For example, a smart sensor might use hardware monitors to issue a quick early warning when measured parameters approach critical limits or change at an abnormal rate.

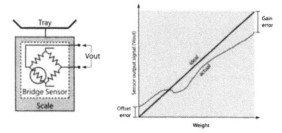

The bridge sensor signal in a butcher's scale requires conditioning to remove gain, offset, and nonlinear errors.

smearing *n.* In the process of curve fitting or noise reduction, an effect where the input data's sharp discontinuities are blurred. *See also* curve fitting, boxcar integrator, noise reduction.

Notice how the raw data (with the sharp discontinuity) has been smeared by a simple boxcar average.

smoke *n.* The part of an electronic component, like a resistor or an IC, that makes it work. Once the smoke has been released, the component becomes useless.

smoothing 1. *n.* Filtering and/or noise removal. *See also* noise reduction.

2. *See* curve fitting.

SMT (as letters) *abbr. See* surface mount.

SNAP (rhymes with nap) *abbr.* Scalable Node Address Protocol.

FURTHER READING: http://www.hth.com/snap/

snoop *n.* To receive or examine all of the packets sent over a network—even those not addressed to that specific system. *See also* promiscuous mode.

SNR (as letters) *abbr. See* signal-to-noise ratio.

SoC *See* system-on-chip.

socket (sock-it) 1. *n.* A TCP (connection-oriented) or UDP (connectionless) communications port.

2. *n.* A physical connector into which something else plugs.

EXAMPLE: You generally get AC power by plugging a cable into a socket in the wall.

EXAMPLE: Many types of ICs, especially DIP microcontrollers and ROMs and PLCC PLDs, can be inserted into a socket for easy removal, rather than directly onto the PCB. Surface mount parts are an obvious exception.

sockets *n.* A popular API for creating TCP connections, sending and receiving data over them, and tearing them down once the connection is no longer needed. Sending and receiving UDP datagrams are also supported through a related API. The general idea is that you can code to the sockets API and be portable to any vendor's TCP/IP stack. In practice, it isn't that easy. In particular, there are two API variations called BSD sockets and Windows sockets.

soft core *n.* A processor that's programmed into an array of programmable logic, such as an FPGA. *See* platform FPGA.

soft deadline *n.* A deadline with consequences that are not dire should it be missed. *See also* hard deadline, soft real time.

soft key *n.* A software-defined input. The meaning of such an input can change depending on the current mode of the system.

EXAMPLE: If you have used an ATM machine, you've probably pressed a generic button on the side of the display. A graphic or text on the display indicates the current meaning of the button. That's a soft key. By contrast, each numeric key on the keypad (used to enter the PIN) is assigned a fixed function.

soft real time 1. *adj.* Pertains to a system with timeliness requirements that are specified stochastically.

Embedded systems run the gamut from having no real-time requirements to having only hard deadlines. In between, there are numerous systems with deadlines of a softer sort. These systems must typically meet the majority of their deadlines to function properly; however, simply missing one deadline will not cause a catastrophe.

Ironically, it's much easier to prove *a priori* that a system will meet all of its deadlines (a la hard real time) than that it will meet a certain percentage of them or never have too long a run of missed deadlines, so the designers of many soft real time systems use hard real time design tools and techniques.

EXAMPLE: A cable or satellite TV set-top box that decodes MPEG video must typically decode 30 frames of data every second to work properly. In that sense, it is a real-time system with a frame deadline every 33.3 ms. However, missing a frame deadline every now and then probably will not result in any discernible (to the human viewer, anyway) change in audio or video quality. Missing a lot of these deadlines, particularly a lot in a row, though, could cause the customer to become dissatisfied with the product and return it.

2. *n.* A deadline that can be missed sometimes.

software *n.* The part of a system that doesn't need to be 100% working until long after the hardware ships, if ever.

software breakpoint *n.* A software debugging resource that stops program execution when a specified event occurs. Debuggers set software breakpoints by changing the target instruction to one that executes a transfer of control, like a software interrupt or call. All BDM and software debuggers use software breakpoints. They are cheap and easy to implement, requiring no hardware. Because the code must be changed, software breakpoints can only be set in RAM memory, so it is not possible to debug a ROMed program with them.

software engineering *n.* The art of using available resources in known ways to solve a programming problem. The "known ways" is important; when they are unknown, the effort is science, not engineering. One might encounter unknown or unexpected problems along the way but then use standard engineering practices to address them as they are encountered.

software flow control *n.* A flow control technique that uses in-band signaling. When a receiver in a bidirectional communications channel is no longer able to process or buffer incoming data, it transmits a special character request to the sender to pause the flow. When it is capable of again receiving new data, it then transmits a different character to the sender to resume the flow. *See also* XON, XOFF. *Contrast with* hardware flow control.

software IC *See* component.

software interrupt *n.* An interruption of a program that is initiated by a software instruction. Software interrupts are commonly used to implement breakpoints and operating system entry points. Unlike true interrupts, they occur synchronously with respect to program execution; that is, software interrupts always occur at the beginning of an instruction execution cycle.

software monitor *See* debug monitor.

software prototype *n.* Code developed just to understand how something works, generally without documentation, comments, or structure. Unfortunately, the prototype still in its undocumented form is too often then included in or is the basis for the final product.

SOIC (as letters) *abbr.* Short for Small Outline Integrated Circuit.

solar cell *n.* A semiconductor that produces a small voltage when light impinges on it. Also called photovoltaic, or PV, cells. Solar cells are highly

inefficient devices (15–20%) but offer the promise of free electricity from the sun.

In embedded systems, they are used either to power small devices or as simple sensors for on–off applications. Photoresistors are preferred for use as sensors that detect subtle variations in light intensities. *See also* photocell.

solder mask *n.* The green (generally speaking) coating on a PCB. This coating prevents solder from flowing between pads during assembly.

solenoid *n.* A device that moves linearly when sufficient voltage is applied. Solenoids are electromagnets that surround a moving iron rod. They require vast amounts of power, so they always have a driver circuit between the processor and the solenoid. A typical use is to release the spring-loaded mechanism locking a cash register's drawer.

source 1. *See* current source

2. *See* source code.

3. *n.* The terminal of a FET that acts as the source of current flow. *See also* drain, gate.

source code *n.* A program (or part of one) in its original, human-readable form. Any file containing C/C++ code or even assembly is made up of source code.

source file *n.* A file containing source code. If it contains just part of a larger program, it is often termed a module or source module.

source-level debugger *n.* A debugger that's capable of interleaving the original code and the individual instructions so that the user can debug at the source code or opcode level or switch back and forth during a session. A typical source-level debugger reads the information in a symbol file that must be specially output by the compiler each time the code is recompiled. The compiler in this case is configured to generate "debug info."

SourceSafe *N.* A popular version control system from Microsoft.

space *n.* A logic 0 on an RS-232 link. Any voltage between +3 and +25 V. *See also* mark.

spaghetti code *n.* Incomprehensible source code, typically including apparently meaningless jumps or gotos or a high degree of unnecessary coupling between modules.

spawn *v.* To create a new thread of execution.

SPDT (as letters) *abbr.* A type of switch that has one actuator (pole) that connects to one of two contacts. Short for Single Pole, Double Throw. Used to select one of two conditions. *Compare to* SPST.

The schematic symbol for an SPDT switch makes its design and purpose clear.

spec (speck) *abbr. See* specification.

SPEC (speck) *abbr.* A nonprofit organization formed to establish a standard set of benchmarks for high-performance computers. Short for Standard Performance Evaluation Corporation.

specification *n.* A description in all its gory technical detail of how something works or will work. Often shortened to spec. The only difference between a spec and a standard is that the latter has been through a formal standardization process. So, for example, the IEEE 1003.1c standard is also a spec.

specification document *n.* A spec that describes how a product works and that is also a deliverable (perhaps to the customer). The spec is essentially the engineer's formal response to a set of requirements.

SPECmark (speck-mark) *n.* The metrics for SPEC's original benchmarks (aka CPU89). According to SPEC itself, the term often is used to refer collectively to the CPU95 ratio speed metrics.

spectrum *See* electromagnetic spectrum.

Spectrum *N.* The name of the IEEE's primary monthly magazine. All active IEEE members receive a subscription to *Spectrum*. Other journal subscriptions are optional and cost extra.

spectrum analyzer *n.* An oscilloscope-like tool that displays signals in the frequency domain.

speed of light *See c.*

SPI (as letters) *abbr.* An inexpensive bus for chip interconnection that is popular on circuit boards. Short for Serial Peripheral Interface. *See also* I²C, 1-Wire.

FURTHER READING: Kalinsky, David and Roee Kalinsky. "Introduction to Serial Peripheral Interface," *Embedded Systems Programming*, January 2002.

spin wheels 1. *See* busy wait.

2. *v.* What young engineers often do when confronted with a confounding problem.

spinlock *n.* A mutex implemented via busy waiting. Busy waiting wastes precious CPU cycles, during which time (on a single-processor system, anyway) the thread that's using the resource is also unable to progress closer to releasing it. The attempted mutex acquisition can't happen until after the other thread runs, so it's desirable to block the thread that must wait immediately rather than waste those CPU cycles.

Spinlocks can be useful on multiprocessor systems when the awaited resource reasonably can be expected to be released in fewer cycles than a pair of context switches would consume.

spiral development model *n.* A class of alternatives to Big Up-Front Design, the spiral development model stresses building many small releases of a product. Virtually all new software development methodologies recognize the difficulty of defining system specs accurately and completely. These new models instead lead to earlier code production in an effort to *provoke* rather than discourage changes. In short cycles (a few weeks), product subsets are released so that customers or their proxies can provide early feedback to the development team. *See also* eXtreme Programming.

spiral model   *See* spiral development model.

sporadic   *adj.* Aperiodic, but recurring only after some minimum amount of time.

spread spectrum   *n.* A general name for the idea of dividing a communications data stream into small chunks and sending successive chunks in different frequencies. Because they offer good protection against both eavesdropping and jamming, spread spectrum techniques were first used by the U.S. military. They have since become more mainstream, particularly in unregulated regions of the frequency spectrum where lots of devices need to communicate in an ad hoc fashion and where interference is high.

SPST   (as letters) *abbr.* A type of switch that has one actuator (pole) that connects to one contact. Short for Single Pole, Single Throw. Used to turn a circuit on or off in the manner most people think of first when they hear that a switch is involved. *Compare to* SPDT.

The schematic symbol for an SPST switch.

square wave   *n.* A waveform that alternates between a high and low state at a regular rate. The rate of change is the signal's period. Perfect square waves are impossible to generate in practice; physical limitations restrict the minimum rise and fall times of the edges. *Contrast with* sinusoid.

A square wave.

SRAM   (ess-RAM) *abbr.* A type of RAM that retains its contents as long as the system is powered on.

Short for Static Random Access Memory. Data stored in SRAM is lost when the system is powered down or reset.

SRD   (as letters) *abbr.* Inexpensive devices that use low–data rate, short-range wireless communications. Short for Short-range Radio Device.

> **EXAMPLE:** A remote keyless entry system for a car.

srec   *See* Motorola S-record format.

SSB   *See* single-sideband modulation.

SSI   (as letters) *abbr. See* small-scale integration.

stack   1. *n.* A list in which elements are always added and removed from the (conceptual) end. A last-in, first-out queue. Stacks are one of the four basic kinds of queues or lists. They are used most frequently to keep track of hierarchically nested processes. They are common in both application- and system-level software. Any processor that implements a call instruction must also support some kind of hardware stack (the run-time stack). Compilers rely on the run-time stack to support function calls and argument passing. Most RTOSes require a separate stack for each thread or task.

> **HISTORY:** A few processors did exist without hardware stacks, though these antiques are never seen today. RCA's 1802, the first really useful CMOS processor—used in many ultra–low-power apps in the 1970s and early 1980s—did not have a hardware stack. Instead, programmers simulated stacks with code that took a return address in a register and added it to a software-implemented stack.

2. *n.* The run-time stack associated with a particular task. In most multiprocessing environments (SSX, SST, and Erika are exceptions), each process or task requires a separate stack area. When the RTOS switches tasks, it saves the current stack pointer as part of the old task's context (usually in a task control block) and then reloads the stack

pointer from the new task control block, making it point to the top of the new task's stack.

stack frame *n.* An area of the stack associated with a particular function call.

stack overflow *n.* What happens when a thread overruns the end of its stack, perhaps corrupting another thread's stack or some code or data located in an adjacent area of RAM. A stack overflow is a most dangerous sort of software fault, which can unfortunately go undetected until the firmware either crashes or wanders off into Never-Never Land.

Two common causes of stack overflow are recursive function calls and nested interrupts.

Some run-time environments, such as Java's virtual machine, can detect stack overflow and raise an exception before any data gets corrupted. That's the ideal environment in which to be running your software when this happens to you.

stack segment *n.* A region of memory reserved for the stack. The startup code may or may not zero the stack memory area before starting the program.

standard deviation *n.* A measure of the spread of a dataset from the mean.

$$\sigma^2 = \frac{\Sigma(x_i - \mu)^2}{n}$$

where σ is the standard deviation, x_i is a data point, μ is the mean of the entire data set, and n is the number of items in the data set. *See also* normal distribution.

standard library *n.* A set of functions or classes that's part of a language standard, and supplied with standards-compliant compilers. The languages C, C++, and Java each have their own standard library. *See also* library.

standoff *n.* A metal or plastic bolt that serves as a "leg" for a circuit board. A set of four standoffs,

attached to the four corners of a circuit board, can be used to keep it safe from static electricity.

start bit *n.* The first bit transmitted in an asynchronous serial character. Asynchronous serial data starts at random points in time. Because the first real data bit could be a 0 or a 1 and thus have the same state as the idle line, a start bit is prefixed to each transmitted character to tell the receiver that data is coming. *See also* stop bits, serial I/O.

startup code *n.* A piece of assembly language code that prepares the way for software written in a high-level language. Most cross-compilers come with startup code that you can modify, compile, and link with your embedded programs. Startup code usually initializes code and data segments, safes I/O, and sets up chip selects and wait states.

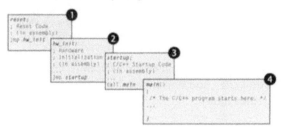

The world before main().

starvation *n.* The failure of a thread to make further progress, generally as the result of a bug in the operating system or the implementation of another thread. Starvation differs from deadlock in that only the one thread is affected and there is no circular wait. With starvation, a resumption of progress is theoretically possible, though not happening.

EXAMPLE: In the Dining Philosopher's Problem, in which a table of philosophers must share eating utensils, the occurrence of starvation is quite literal. If the philosophers on either side of philosopher N alternate eating in just the right way, N will never find a chopstick on both the left and right available simultaneously. Philosopher N will starve.

state *n.* According to the UML specification, "a situation or condition in the life of a system during which some (usually implicit) invariant holds, the system performs some activity, or the system waits for some external event." In less formal terms, a mode of system behavior.

EXAMPLE: When you strike a key on a keyboard, the character code generated will be either an uppercase or a lowercase character, depending on whether the Caps Lock is active. Therefore, the keyboard is in the capsLocked state, or the default state (most keyboards have an LED that indicates when the keyboard is in the capsLocked state). The behavior of a keyboard depends only on certain aspects of its history—namely, whether Caps Lock has been activated, but not, for example, how many and which specific characters have been typed previously. A state can abstract away all possible (but irrelevant) event sequences and capture only the relevant ones.

state diagram *n.* A visual representation of the states, pseudostates, and transitions that make up a finite state machine.

state machine *See* finite state machine.

state transition *n.* Any change from one state to another in a state machine. Every transition has a from state (source) and a to state (destination). It can also have associated actions beyond those associated with exiting the source and entering the destination. If it does have associated actions, those must be executed after the exit actions and before the entrance actions. *See also* state diagram.

state transition diagram *See* state diagram.

statechart *n.* In UML, the formal name for a state diagram. *See also* Harel statechart, UML statechart.

static *res.* The C keyword used to define a static variable. *See also* static variable.

static electricity *n.* A current flow created by mechanically ripping electrons from atoms. Also called "static." Static electricity is familiar as the sudden jolt one encounters when touching a doorknob after shuffling across a carpet. The rug rips electrons from your shoes.

Static is a nightmare for high-integration electronics. With transistor geometries at submicron levels, a tiny bit of overvoltage applied to an IC's pins could destroy devices. Thus, people working with ICs ground themselves to eliminate static buildup. *See also* grounding strap.

static priority *n.* A priority that cannot be changed at run time. *Contrast with* dynamic priority. *See also* rate monotonic algorithm.

static RAM *See* SRAM.

static variable *n.* A variable that is defined either outside the scope of any function or (in a function) with the static keyword. Although the scopes of such variables vary depending on precisely how and where they are declared, their lifetimes are always that of the program itself. Static variables are either placed into the data or BSS segment of the object file.

status *n.* A data structure that holds some part or all of a system's current operating modes and conditions. Most embedded systems run in numerous states. A motor might be on or off; a door open or closed. Generally, status words or bits hold the current state of each of these conditions.

Unfortunately, common practice involves using one or more words to hold all system status information. These are invariably global variables, leading to reentrancy and debugging headaches.

A better approach is to encapsulate status information using drivers ("methods" in OOP-speak). Only the driver can access the status information. *See also* global variable, encapsulation.

status bit *n.* A bit that holds part of a processor's or peripheral's state. *See also* status.

status flag *See* status bit.

status LED *n.* Any LED used to indicate the state of something. The LED can be under hardware or software control. It can flash, as a heartbeat, or simply remain lit while the something is operating properly.

EXAMPLE: Most Ethernet hubs have several status LEDs per port. One will indicate a 10 or 100 Mbps connection, another network activity.

step motor *n.* A four-winding constant-power motor controlled by sequenced signals from a computer. Step motors have constant power, where

$$power = torque \times speed$$

Between steps, the motor holds its position (and its load) without the aid of clutches or brakes. Thus, a step motor can be precisely controlled so that it rotates a certain number of steps, producing mechanical motion through a specific distance, and then holds its load when it stops. Furthermore, it can repeat the operation any prescribed number of times.

FURTHER READING: Simon, Dan. "Get Your Motor Running," *Embedded Systems Programming*, May 2003.

step-down transformer *n.* A transformer with fewer windings in the back end than the front. The transformer reduces the input voltage. Most often used to reduce the AC mains to a lower level in power supplies.

step-up transformer *n.* A transformer with more windings in the back end than the front.

stepper *See* step motor.

stepper motor *See* step motor.

stochastic process *n.* A random function.

EXAMPLE: The distribution of white noise is entirely stochastic.

stop bits *n.* One or more bits appended to each transmitted character in an asynchronous serial stream. The stop bits provide idle time for the receiver to get ready for the next character. This was important in the Teletype days, since time was needed for the wizardry of levels, gears, and motors to print the character. Today, stop bits are sometimes used but rarely needed. *See also* 8N1.

storage class *n.* The segment to which a particular variable is assigned. In C, the recognized storage class specifiers are auto, extern, register, static, and typedef. The first four of these affect the storage and extent of the variable.

By default, variables declared outside any function are global and, therefore, part of the data or BSS segment; variables declared within a function (or sub-block) are local by default and, therefore, located on the stack.

storage duration *n.* The length of time, measured relative to a program's execution, for which a particular variable's storage is guaranteed. *See also* extent.

EXAMPLE: An automatic variable's storage lifetime is the length of time from the call of the surrounding function to its return.

store *v.* To move data into memory, typically from a processor register.

USAGE: Use of this term tends to be restricted to RISC processors, on which the only way to write memory is to execute a store instruction.

strain gauge *n.* A transducer used to measure force. A strain gauge is made of a material that changes its resistance linearly with the strain it experiences as a result of the application of a force. This change in resistance is manifested as a change in the voltage measured across the gauge. When coupled with an A/D converter, a strain gauge can be used as a digital force sensor.

string *n.* An array of character data, commonly in ASCII with a 0 at the end.

strings *See* binutils.

strobe *n.* A signal that clocks data or that indicates data is valid.

EXAMPLE: A chip select that enables memory is a strobe, as is the read signal from a microprocessor.

stub *n.* An empty function. Stubs are common when software is first being developed. Stub functions are generally meant to be filled in later.

stuck at 0 *n.* A condition in which a logic signal is always a 0.

stuck at 1 *n.* A condition in which a logic signal is always a 1.

stuff *v.* To insert a component into a PCB, generally during circuit assembly.

HISTORY: The origins of this term obviously pre-date surface mount parts.

substate *n.* A state within another state.

summing amplifier *n.* An analog circuit that adds two inputs. Specifically,

output = C × (input A + input B) + D,

where C and D are constants and are often 1 and 0, respectively. A summing amplifier is usually an op-amp with both input signals applied through resistors to the same input. A feedback resistor sets the amplifier's gain.

super-loop architecture *See* cyclic executive.

superblock *n.* In Unix, a disk block that contains metadata about the filesystem. If the superblock is corrupted, it might not be possible to reconstruct the data on the disk, so multiple copies are often kept.

superstate *n.* Any state that has substates.

supervisor mode *See* kernel mode.

surface mount *adj.* Describes a type of component that solders on top of a PCB, without using pins inserted in holes in the circuit board. Referred to as SMT for Surface Mount Technology. SMT offers much higher density than traditional thru-hole technology. Today, virtually every component is available in an SMT configuration. *Contrast with* thru-hole technology.

SW (software) *abbr. See* software.

SWAN (like the bird) *abbr.* A description of the major qualifiers for hiring an embedded systems engineer. Short for Smart, Works hard, Ambitious, and Nice.

swap *n.* An atomic CPU instruction to swap the values in two memory locations.

switch *n.* An input device that can take any one of two or more values. Most switches are binary: either open or closed. *See also* dip switch.

switch matrix *n.* An *x–y* grouping of switches used to reduce component count. Switch matrices are commonly used for keyboards and keypads that require lots of switches. Outputs from the processor scan the matrix (typically shifting 0s through one dimension of the matrix) as the CPU monitors the other dimension looking for corresponding 0s, which indicates switch closure.

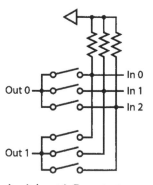

A switch matrix. Two outputs from the CPU scan the matrix; three inputs read it.

switcher *See* power supply, switching.

switching regulator *n.* A type of power supply that achieves very high efficiencies by modulating an output transistor's duty cycle. Also called a switcher. A linear power supply controls its DC output by varying the output transistor's bias, essentially turning the transistor into a variable resistor. That means lots of power is wasted in the part, since $P = I^2R$.

A switcher turns that transistor completely on or off; it's never in a partially conducting state. In a perfect world, then, the transistor's resistance is either zero ($R = 0$) or infinite ($I = 0$).

The output of the transistor is fed to an LC circuit, which turns the pulsed signal into smooth DC. Very smart electronics monitor the output and then modulate the transistor's duty cycle to regulate to the desired voltage.

Switching supplies can take AC or DC as inputs (depending on the design); DC-DC converters are common.

One of the bulkiest and most expensive components in linear power supplies is the transformer; its purpose is to reduce the 110 VAC (in the U.S.) mains to a level just a bit above the desired regulated supply output. Off-line switchers dispense with the transformer, switching the AC mains directly to the desired DC output. Off-line switchers, of course, have no isolation from the mains, so they are not legal in some applications (notably patient monitoring devices).

symbol table *n.* A data structure containing information about each variable and function name in an object file, relocatable, or library. The symbol table is part of the metadata associated with each compiled module. Its contents are used by the linker to resolve variables and functions of the same names across modules and (optionally) by a source-level debugger.

synchronous 1. *adj.* When two or more events occur at the same time. In many cases, the events are locked together so they always occur at the same time; they are then said to be in sync. The clock in a computer synchronizes all events.

EXAMPLE: Whether you call them traps, faults, software interrupts, or exceptions, things that go wrong as part of an instruction's fetch or execution are synchronous events. These contrast with hardware interrupts, which are inherently asynchronous.

2. *adj.* Describes a type of logic design. *Contrast with* asynchronous. *See also* sequential logic.

synchronous bus *n.* A bus that includes a clock in the control lines. Synchronous buses use a fixed protocol for communication that is measured relative to the clock. They need very little logic and can run very fast. However, every device on the bus must run at the same clock rate. *Contrast with* asynchronous bus.

synchronous communication *n.* Generally refers to a serial communications technique that uses two signals: a clock and data. Each transition of the clock indicates another data bit is available. Synchronous communication is faster than asynchronous because neither timing delays nor start/stop bits are needed. *Contrast with* asynchronous communications.

EXAMPLE: Examples include I^{2}C and HDLC.

synchronous counter *n.* A device that counts in a (usually) binary sequence, with all of its outputs changing at clock transitions. Synchronous counters are glitch-free; because all outputs change at the same time, they are always in known and legal states. As synchronous counters grow in size, their complexity grows rapidly; a feed-forward mechanism is required to propagate carries from previous stages to the next. *Contrast with* ripple counter.

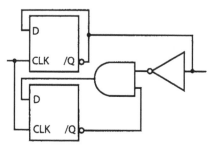

A 2-bit (so to speak) synchronous counter.

synchronous logic *n.* Logic with output that changes only when clocked. Spurious input transitions don't affect the output. Synchronous logic is the solution to many glitches and race conditions.

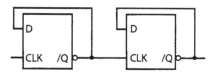

This ripple counter, though it uses a clock, is not synchronous because the outputs all change at different times.

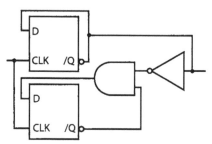

This synchronous counter changes all states at once and is glitch-free.

synthesis *n.* The process of turning design logic represented in an HDL into a physical implementation that can be programmed into an FPGA or ASIC. Synthesis is the hardware design equivalent to compilation.

synthetic benchmark *n.* A benchmark created with the intent to measure one or more features of a given system, processor, or compiler. Synthetic

benchmarks might try to mimic instruction mixes in real-world applications, or they might be entirely artificial. They are useful in measuring a very specific feature, such as the number of floating-point operations that can be performed in a given time unit. However, their artificial nature makes inferences about application performance speculative at best and meaningless at worst. Dhrystone and Whetstone are both completely synthetic benchmark suites, as are Winstone and Winbench in the PC world. *Contrast with* real-world benchmark.

system *n.* A combination of hardware and software.

system call *n.* A request to the operating system. A system call is often effected via a software interrupt, since the processor must be switched to kernel mode before the code inside the OS runs.

EXAMPLE: All of the DOS system calls are executed via the 80x86 instruction INT 21h. The type of OS request is indicated by the value in the AX register.

system clock *n.* The date and time according to the operating system. *Compare to* timer tick.

USAGE: The term system clock is sometimes used to describe the processor clock as well.

system integration *n.* When all or most elements of an embedded system are tied together for testing. Integration is the time when development gets hard. Up to that point, little more than unit testing happens. Modern development strategies stress continuous integration, which means testing full-up systems all the time (or as full-up as is possible).

Experienced developers know that the (generally brief) schedule item named integration really means "abandon all hope ye who enter here."

system partitioning *n.* The process of deciding which parts of a system's function should be implemented in hardware versus software. Although attempts have been made to automate the process, system partitioning remains more of an art than a science.

system status *See* status.

system under test *n.* A system or subsystem currently undergoing testing.

system-on-chip *n.* A highly integrated IC that includes all of the components—such as proces-

sor, memory, and peripherals—required to implement a given hardware design. Abbreviated SoC. An ASIC or FPGA can contain an SoC design, which is generally built of functional blocks from a library of IP. *See also* intellectual property.

Système international d'unités *N.* The international standard for the metric system, which is the most widely used system of units and measures. Abbreviated SI.

T

T-state *n.* What happens in a processor in one clock cycle. Traditional CISC processors require two, three, or more clocks to execute an instruction; each of these is a T-state.

RISC machines execute instructions in a single T-state. However, CISC CPUs increasingly offer one-clock instructions as well.

tangent 1. *n.* A straight line that touches a curve at exactly one point. Also called a tangent line.

2. *n.* A trigonometric function that is the ratio of a triangle's two nonhypotenuse sides. Abbreviated tan.

$$\tan(\alpha) = \frac{opposite}{adjacent} = \frac{\sin(\alpha)}{\cos(\alpha)}$$

tantalum 1. *n.* A material used to make polarized high-capacitance capacitors in a small package.

2. *n.* Short for tantalum capacitor.

TAP (rhymes with map) *abbr. See* test access port.

taps *See* filter taps.

tarball *n.* An archive file produced by the Unix `tar` facility. Such a file usually has a `.tar` filename extension.

target *n.* The embedded system under development.

USAGE: This term is never used to describe a finished product. During development, the embedded system (for which the software is being developed) is normally called the target to distinguish it from the host system (where the software is being developed). This distinction is necessary, in part, because the host might also be capable of executing the software under development—either directly or in a simulator.

target system *See* target.

task *n.* The central abstraction of a real-time operating system. Each task must maintain its own copy of the CPU's instruction pointer and general-purpose registers. Unlike processes, tasks share a common memory space and so programmers must be careful to avoid overwriting other task's code, data, and stack.

USAGE: For most practical purposes, the terms task and thread are interchangeable. However, task is preferred when working with real-time operating systems, which generally have just one memory space, whereas thread is more commonly used on multiuser platforms such as Unix or Windows, where multiple threads of execution can run within the memory space of a single process.

task control block *n.* The equivalent to a process table entry in an operating system that supports tasks but not processes. Abbreviated TCB.

task ID *n.* A unique identifier for a task. The task ID is a handle for the task, which is typically returned by the OS when the task is created. This handle can be used by the application to request that the OS kill the task, among other possibilities.

task states *n.* The states of a task during its lifetime. The most important task states are running, ready (to run), and waiting (for some resource, event, or time). The last is also known as the blocked state.

Task states.

When a task is created, it is added to the ready list; its initial state is ready. It then either cycles through states running, waiting, ready, and running, or it runs, is preempted (and sent back to ready by the OS), and then runs again.

Taylor series *N.* A well-known way to create an approximation to any continuous function.

The Taylor series of a function $f(x)$ around a point, a, is

$$\sum\left(\frac{f^n(a)(x-a)^n}{n!}\right)$$

where the summation runs from $n = 0$ to as many terms as needed for a reasonably accurate approxi-

mation, and $f^n(a)$ is the nth derivative of f at point a.

A Taylor series is a sum of polynomials; increasing the number of terms increases the precision of the approximation at the expense of additional compute time.

In practice, Taylor series usually converge rather slowly, so other approximations are used (e.g., Chebyshev).

TCB (as letters) *abbr. See* task control block.

TCP (as letters) *abbr.* A connection-oriented transport layer protocol. Short for Transmission Control Protocol. RFC 793. When using TCP to send packets over an IP network, a connection must first be established between the sending and receiving nodes. This connection should be torn down once all data has been received.

While the connection is in place, the TCP protocol handles the details of packet fragmentation and reassembly, of retries for lost packets, and of reordering at the receiver. This is why TCP is said to be a reliable protocol compared to its unreliable UDP competitor. However, all this reliability comes at a cost: TCP is 10 times harder to implement (because of all the connection and packet states to be tracked) and generally involves more code and processing at each end even without losses. So if you only need UDP, you can write the protocol stack yourself; if you need TCP, you should buy one instead.

TCP port *n.* A numeric identifier for a TCP endpoint on a particular network node. To reach a particular device, each TCP packet must be addressed to a valid IP address and port number. If no thread is listening on that particular port, the packet will be discarded by the receiver's TCP/IP stack. *See also* socket, well-known port numbers.

TCP/IP (as letters) *abbr.* A suite of networking protocols encompassing the data link, network, and transport layers of the OSI reference stack. Higher layer protocols and applications, such as FTP, HTTP, NFS, and telnet, run on top of the TCP/IP stack.

USAGE: When the term TCP/IP is used, the inclusion of UDP support is assumed. When UDP/IP is used, TCP (and any higher layer software dependent upon it) is assumed excluded.

See also UDP/IP.

TDM (as letters) *abbr.* Digital multiplexing in which two or more apparently simultaneous channels are derived from a given frequency spectrum or bit-stream by interleaving pulses representing bits from different channels. Short for Time-Division Multiplexing. In some TDM systems, successive pulses represent bits from successive channels (e.g., voice channels in a T1 system). In other systems, different channels take turns using the channels for a group of successive pulse times (a "time slot").

TDMA (as letters) *abbr.* A technique for sharing a communications channel across multiple transmitters by granting access to the channel to one device at a time. Short for Time Division Multiple Access. In this way, the full bandwidth is made available to each device for short periods of time. The decision about which transmitter can use the channel at a given time can be made in advance, in which case each transmitter has a dedicated time slot every so often, or dynamically. *Compare to* FDMA.

telecom *adj.* Of or relating to the transfer of telephony data over a communications network. Historically, telecom equipment and networks have been based on circuit-switched technologies. However, telecom data increasingly is sent over the same packet-switched networks as datacom traffic. *Compare to* datacom.

tempco *See* temperature coefficient.

temperature coefficient *n.* The amount by which an electrical parameter increases or decreases with a change in temperature. Often shortened to tempco.

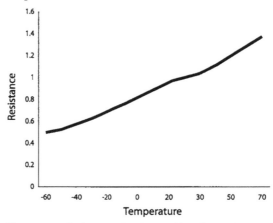

The response of a thermistor's resistance (*y*) to changes in temperature (*x*). The resistance increases as the temperature goes up. This is an example of a positive tempco.

ten commandments *n.* A set of rules, written in the style of the Old Testament, for C programmers to follow to prevent shooting themselves in the foot.

FURTHER READING: http://www.lysator.liu.se/c/ten-commandments.html

tera- (tear uh) *pre.* The prefix meaning 10^{12}. Abbreviated T.

terminate *v.* To add a terminator to a node in order to match the receiver impedance to that of the driver. *See also* termination.

termination *n.* A device that is connected to a receiver to match the impedance of the driver. Most gates produce a low-impedance output but have a high-impedance input. At high speeds when signals are transmitted a long distance (anything more than a few inches!), this mismatch can lead to incorrect data and SCR latchup. A termination eliminates the problem.

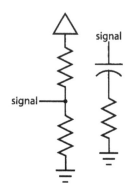

The two most common terminations: on the left, the classic two-resistor version; on the right, the "AC" termination, which uses no power except during transitions.

All kinds of terminations exist, from simple resistive pullups to active circuits.

test access port *n.* The formal name for a JTAG boundary scan interface. Abbreviated TAP. There are four required pins and one optional pin: TCK (clock), TMS (mode select), TDI (data in), TDO (data out), and TRST (reset, optional). These signals drive an internal state machine.

test equipment *n.* Laboratory instruments used to verify and debug hardware and firmware. Test equipment refers specifically to instruments like oscilloscopes, logic analyzers, and emulators—not to software-only tools like debuggers and profilers.

Although vendors tout the almost magical improvement in debugging that their tools offer, the truth is that all tools overpromise and underdeliver. Good tools are essential, but don't count on them to find or fix all (or even most) of your problems.

test point *n.* Any sort of electrical contact included solely for the purpose of attaching test equipment, such as an oscilloscope. Most PCBs have test points for power, clock, and other commonly referenced signals.

test vector *n.* Any pattern of inputs used to verify a hardware design. A set of test vectors is often run on a simulation of the hardware before even the first chip is brought to life. These same vectors can later be used at the factory to verify each system as it comes out of production.

test-and-set *adj.* Said of an atomic CPU operation that reads the value of a memory location and sets it without the possibility of interruption. A test-and-set instruction is a primitive building block for a multitasking OS, particularly for multiprocessor systems. If the target processor doesn't have either a test-and-set instruction or the functionally equivalent swap primitive, the OS must disable interrupts while performing the equivalent functionality across multiple opcodes.

testing *n.* The act of checking a system's operation against a test procedure, spec, or vague sense of how the thing should work. Testing comprises everything from informal debugging to rigorous procedures put in place by a QA department. Sadly, too many development groups focus on early coding instead of careful design (yielding a buggy system that will need a lot of testing) and then shortchange the tests.

Demming showed it's impossible to test quality into a system; yet, it's clear that exhaustive tests are part of building great products. Most agile processes stress continuous integration and detailed tests: two traits that lead to better firmware.

The IT world's reliance on regression tests unfortunately translates poorly to embedded systems because it's hard to automate tests on a system that interacts with its environment. *See also* unit test.

testpoint *See* test point.

Texas Instruments *N.* A pioneering technology company now best known for their DSPs. Abbreviated TI. Founded in 1930 to provide equipment to the

Texas oil industry, the company went on to develop the first commercial silicon transistors, the first integrated circuit, and the first electronic hand-held calculator.

text segment *n.* A segment in an object file that contains the executable code.

TFTP (as letters) *abbr.* A simpler noninteractive variant of the FTP protocol sometimes used to download new firmware during system boot after receiving configuration parameters via BOOTP or DHCP. Short for Trivial File Transfer Protocol. RFC 1350.

Therac-25 *N.* A radiation therapy machine, implemented as an embedded system, that suffered a series of race conditions that killed six people by overdosing between June 1985 and January 1987. The product was made by Atomic Energy of Canada Limited. The flawed software was implemented in PDP-11 assembly language, though that was not specifically the source of the problem. In essence, the race conditions resulted from a poor software design riddled with global variables representing the various modes of the system's operation. Attempts to fix the first of the problems ended up only making matters worse.

HISTORY: A detailed analysis of the events and their causes is found at http://sunnyday.mit.edu/papers/therac.pdf. It is must reading for all software engineers.

FURTHER READING: Leveson, Nancy. *Safeware: System Safety and Computers.* Addison-Wesley, 1995.

FURTHER READING: Leveson, Nancy and Clark S. Turner. "An Investigation of the Therac-25 Accidents," *IEEE Computer,* July 1993.

thermistor *n.* A type of sensor used to measure temperature that is essentially a temperature-sensitive resistor. In conjunction with a reference voltage, an op-amp, and an analog-to-digital converter, a thermistor can be used to measure temperatures

digitally. *Compare to* resistance temperature detector, thermocouple.

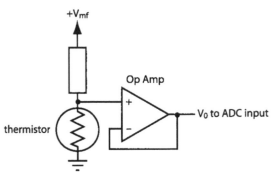

A thermistor circuit.

thermocouple *n.* An electronic component used to sense temperature. A temperature-sensitive junction of two dissimilar materials produces a small voltage (typically 50 $\mu V/°C$).

Thevenin's theorem *N.* A theorem used to simplify complex circuits. It states that any two-terminal network of resistors and voltage sources is equivalent to a single resistor in series with a single voltage source.

HISTORY: The theorem was first published by Herman Von Helmholtz (1821–1894) in 1853, then rediscovered by M. L. Thevenin (1857–1926) in 1883.

thread *n.* Another name for a task. This name is more common in operating systems that support processes. A task is simply a thread in a single-process system.

thread group *n.* A collection of threads that can be controlled as a group. Some operating systems (and the Java programming language) support thread groups for the convenience of programmers. All of the threads in a thread group typically can be started or stopped at the same time. It might also be possible to control a group in other ways.

thread of execution *n.* A chunk of code plus CPU context and stack that can be executed on an operating system. Often called simply a thread (or task). *See also* process.

thread-safe *See* reentrant.

throughput *n.* A qualitative measure of a computer's ability to get work done. Mostly used by the IT industry. In embedded systems, it's more important to complete all required tasks in the required time. Useful measures are scarce; the EEMBC has been formed to evaluate a processor's ability to accomplish typical embedded tasks.

throw *v.* To generate an exception, as a call to a particular function or method might.

thru-hole technology *n.* A type of electronic component that is assembled onto a PCB by inserting and soldering the component's leads into a hole on the board. Thru-hole parts are easy to assemble and repair, requiring no special tools, in contrast with surface mount devices. SMT beats thru-hole for density by a wide margin.

HISTORY: The PCB revolutionized electronics, replacing the point-to-point wiring of chassis-mounted parts common in the vacuum tube era. Until the 1980s, all PCBs were built using thru-hole parts. The pursuit of ever-smaller products spawned SMT, which now dominates.

TI (as letters) *abbr. See* Texas Instruments.

tick *See* timer tick.

time constant *See* RC time constant.

time domain *n.* The function of objects with respect to time. Working in the time domain means thinking about something that changes over time, such as voltage, current, or temperature.

By contrast, one might work in the frequency domain on another problem, or even on another aspect of the same problem. For instance, it's much more enlightening to think about modulation in the frequency domain.

time invariance *n.* A property of a circuit or system that ensures its behavior is independent of the passage of time. Most analog components and circuits decay over their lifetimes, though that kind of variance is not what one is typically concerned with here. More commonly, the term is used to describe filters that generate the same response to a given input signal no matter when that input arrives in time.

time slicing *n.* A type of multitasking in which each thread is assigned a quantum of CPU time and is preempted if it runs so long that all that time is used. A thread that blocks or terminates before its quantum has expired may or may not (typically not) get to use the excess at its next opportunity. This sort of scheduling is often called round-robin.

time to market *n.* The total calendar time required to bring a product from conception to the market. Abbreviated TTM.

timebase *n.* The part of a tool (like a scope) that controls the timing of the acquisition of signals. The timebase on a scope lets the user set the sweep rate, which controls the width of a displayed signal. Double the sweep rate (timebase setting) and a pulse's displayed width will double.

timeout 1. *n.* The length of time something will be idle before software intervention occurs. Timeouts are very common in firmware. A typical application waits for some external event but gives up after a timeout period elapses.

Many timeouts are implemented by simple delay loops that count down while looking for the event. However, more robust software usually results from using a timer.

2. *v.* To give up waiting for something to happen.

timer *n.* A peripheral that measures elapsed time, typically by counting processor cycles or clocks. *See also* input capture timer. *Compare to* counter. *See also* counter/timer.

timer tick *n.* A periodic interrupt from a counter/timer. A timer tick ISR is a part of most preemptive real-time operating systems.

timestamp *n.* An elapsed time that's added to real-time data acquired by a debugging tool or datalogger. The timestamp lets the developer see what happened when and measure the execution time of various program constructs. Generally found only on hardware-based tools like in-circuit emulators.

```
>> main(): Module: tc_demo.c  Line. 18  Addr: F800:008E
void        main (void)
000         0.0uS  0100  111  0F808E  PUSH    BP
003         0.7uS  0110  111  00083C          00   Memory WR
004         1.0uS  0110  111  00083D          00   Memory WR
001         0.2uS  0100  111  0F808F  MOV     BP,SP
005         1.2uS  0100  111  0F8091  SUBSX   SP,04
008         2.0uS  0100  111  0F8094  PUSH    SI
00B         2.7uS  0110  111  000836          00   Memory WR
00C         3.0uS  0110  111  000837          00   Memory WR
009         2.2uS  0100  111  0F8095  PUSH    DI
00E         3.6uS  0110  111  000834          00   Memory WR
00F         3.8uS  0110  111  000835          00   Memory WR
     str = "";              /* Clear variables    */
00A         2.5uS  0100  111  0F8096  MOV     DI,0017
```

An in-circuit emulator's real-time trace display, showing a timestamp in the second column.

timing *n.* The time relationships between digital signals in a system. *See also* timing diagram.

timing diagram *n.* A graphical representation of a circuit's timing, showing time on the horizontal axis and the binary value along the vertical. Timing diagrams are used to design synchronous logic circuits and to ensure that things happen in the proper order.

USAGE: Although it's reasonable to call the similar-looking timing information collected and displayed by a logic analyzer a timing diagram, in practice, this is rarely done.

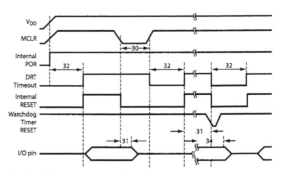

timing diagram A typical timing diagram.

token ring network *n.* A less successful physical network that competes with Ethernet within the intranet. The relevant standards are IEEE 802.5 and ISO/IEC 8802-5.

tolerance *n.* The vendor's guarantee of how well a part's actual parameters will meet its specified values. Everything in the real world has errors and uncertainties; yet, an engineer needs to know the range of possible values associated with a part. Tolerance is specified in parts per million (ppm) or as a percentage.

EXAMPLE: Resistors typically have a 5% tolerance rating, which is specified by a gold fourth color band. Capacitors are much worse: +20%/−80% is common, especially for electrolytics.

tolerance stackup *n.* A condition that occurs out of the perversity of nature, in which all component tolerances combine in the worst possible way, usually leading to a circuit or system failure. *See also* tolerance.

toolchain *n.* The complete set of software tools used to build a product. The toolchain usually refers to the tools used to create firmware, such as compilers, editors, and the like. *See also* tools.

tools *n.* A general term that includes every hardware device and software application used to create a product. Like catalysts, the tools are design aids that are not consumed by the product. Therefore, a purchased protocol stack is not a tool, but the protocol analyzer used to troubleshoot the communications is.

One of the more useful tools for working on frustrating fine-pitch devices.

EXAMPLE: Soldering irons, screwdrivers, in-circuit emulators, software or hardware debuggers, oscilloscopes, logic analyzers, frequency generators, PCB routers, schematic capture packages, compilers, locators, and linkers are just a few of the most common tools used in embedded work.

See also test equipment, development tools.

Tornado *N.* The name of the toolchain that goes with VxWorks. The heart of this toolchain is the open source GNU tools, though they're all wrapped in a pretty bow by a proprietary graphical front end called Tornado.

touchscreen *n.* An LCD or CRT display that is sensitive to touch or the location of a user's finger or stylus. A variety of techniques are used to implement touchscreens.

TQFP (as letters) *abbr.* A high-density surface mount package. Short for Thin Quad Flat Pack.

trace 1. *n.* A log of system, processor, or bus activity. *See also* real-time trace, tracepoint.

A TQFP package.

2. *n.* An electrical connection etched onto a printed circuit board.

3. *n.* A signal displayed on an oscilloscope. Most scopes show two to four distinct traces corre-

sponding to the number of input channels. *See also* oscilloscope.

trace buffer *n.* The part of a debugging tool that stores trace data. Typically high-speed RAM in an in-circuit emulator, the trace buffer is a wide and deep array that stores the address, data, and control buses, as well as a timestamp and external inputs.

Some processors include a small trace buffer on-chip to help support advanced BDM-style debuggers. *See also* in-circuit emulator, real-time trace.

tracepoint *n.* Like a breakpoint except that, rather than stopping the program, a counter is incremented. Tracepoints are not supported by all debugging tools.

track 1. *n.* A path on a printed circuit board.

2. *n.* A circular area of a rotating disk platter. *See also* cylinder.

track width *n.* The width of a track on a printed circuit board. The wider the track, the more current can flow through it.

track-and-hold amplifier *n.* A circuit or component with an output that follows an analog input, but which then latches the input when told to by a hold signal. Track-and-hold amplifiers are used as front ends for A/D converters. *Contrast with* sample-and-hold.

EXAMPLE: Analog Device's HTC-0300A is a track-and-hold amplifier.

trackball *n.* A spherical input device that's rotated on either of two axes to move a cursor on a screen.

EXAMPLE: If you've ever played the arcade classic Centipede, you've used a trackball.

trade show 1. *n.* A gathering of potential customers and tire-kickers in a public meeting place, where vendors display new and old products. Trade shows are a staple of the business travel industry, since they result in huge blocks of room bookings, excessive alcohol consumption, and expense account meals no one would ever buy at home.

2. *n.* An artificial deadline used by management. "It's got to be ready by The Show," is the oldest scheduling ploy around, and the most dysfunctional. Although trade shows can be important to generating business, their dates are set by forces not correlated to a development schedule. When confronted with a show deadline, implement just enough functionality in the product to wow the customer in the 10-second demo typical of any show.

transceiver *n.* A peripheral that provides functions for both receiving and transmitting data over some sort of physical communications medium.

transducer *n.* A device that converts one type of force or energy into another. In an embedded system, most transducers convert to or from electrical energy. A strain gauge, which converts pressure to voltage, is an example of an input transducer. A piezoelectric buzzer, which converts current to sound, is an output transducer.

transfer function *n.* The equation that describes how a circuit changes the input. The transfer function f of any system is: out $= f(\text{in})$.

EXAMPLE: A perfect unary gain amplifier has the transfer function out $=$ in. A more useful amplifier's output might be

$$\text{out} = \text{offset} + \text{in} \times \text{gain}.$$

transformer *n.* An electromagnetic component that changes the voltage of an AC signal. Transformers come in three basic varieties: step-up (the output voltage is greater than the input), step-down (the reverse), and isolation (the input and output voltages are the same). In embedded systems, step-down transformers

The schematic symbol for transformers of all kinds. The input and output voltages are indicated on each side's terminals.

dominate; most are elements of the power supply.

Although transformers increase or reduce voltage, they don't create power. A step-up transformer will reduce the available current. The power into the transformer is the same as the power out, minus efficiency losses (typically 20%).

Switching power supplies often do without a transformer, using smart circuits to work with the AC mains directly. *See also* power supply.

transient 1. *n.* A brief surge on an electrical signal, generally caused by a sudden change elsewhere in the system. Unfortunately, transients can cause errors in systems if the signal is affected long enough to confuse its receiver.

2. *adj.* Said of any short-lived phenomenon.

transistor *n.* A three-terminal (usually) semiconductor device that can amplify input signals. There are many types of transistors. Bipolar and MOS devices dominate. Bipolar transistors consist of two back-to-back diodes. MOS (metal

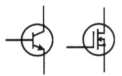

Schematic symbols for two types of transistors: on the left, a bipolar transistor; on the right, a MOS device.

oxide semiconductor) transistors have a channel through which current flows, with a gate not quite connected to the channel; the gate is insulated by a very thin oxide layer.

transistor–transistor logic *n.* The most common type of bipolar logic IC. Abbreviated TTL. TTL devices are characterized by an output stage that has two transistors tied together (or through a diode and/or resistor), with their other terminals going to ground and V_{cc}. One conducts at a time, providing a very low impedance path to ground or power.

TTL devices span the range from SSI to MSI and offer high speeds, high power consumption, and great ease of interface.

Although TTL is still used for glue logic, CMOS families now predominate.

transmission line *n.* A conduction path that has distributed inductance and capacitance. Transmission lines were once the province of RF design; they were mostly the cable connecting a transmitter to its antenna. With the advent of high-speed digital, though, a transmission line now is any conductor that behaves as a tuned circuit rather than a wire.

This means short paths (less than few inches) are wires. Longer ones are transmission lines and act in complex ways on the transmitted signal. *See also* impedance.

transport layer *n.* The protocol layer that provides end-to-end message passing from one network node to another. Layer 4 of the OSI reference model. Connection-oriented TCP and stateless UDP are alternative competing transport layer protocols in the TCP/IP protocol suite. Every application layer packet is either a TCP or a UDP packet but cannot be both. *See also* network layer, application layer.

trap *n.* An interruption of a program that is triggered by the processor's own internal hardware. For example, the processor might trap if an illegal opcode is found within the program. *Compare to* software interrupt. *See also* exception.

FURTHER READING: Russel Massey. "Introduction to Interrupts." *Embedded Systems Programming,* May 2001.

trap handler *See* exception handler.

trig tables *n.* A paper list of the sine, cosine, and tangent of thousands of angles. Once commonly used for accurate trig computations, now almost obsolete since a $10 calculator gives more solutions with high accuracy.

trigger *n.* An event that starts or stops data collection on a piece of test equipment.

EXAMPLE: On a scope, until the trigger event occurs, the beam does not sweep. The trigger starts the sweep going at the rate set by the time base. A trigger level knob sets the analog voltage that must be sensed to qualify as a trigger event; sometimes a pulse of minimum or maximum width can be specified.

Logic analyzers and emulators can have sophisticated triggers, usually letting the user specify digital patterns, or even sequences of patterns, that must occur before the tool starts collecting data.

trigonometry *n.* The mathematics of triangles. Often shortened to "trig."

Some basic trig relationships follow.

$$\sin(\alpha) = \frac{opposite}{hypotenuse}$$

$$\cos(\alpha) = \frac{adjacent}{hypotenuse}$$

$$\tan(\alpha) = \frac{opposite}{adjacent} = \frac{\sin(\alpha)}{\cos(\alpha)}$$

Compiler run-time libraries include extensive math routines that compute all of the basic trig functions. *See also* Taylor series, approximation.

EXAMPLE: Trig functions are critical to many real-world computations. Motion control often ramps speeds up and down—a ramp is a triangle. GPS computes coordinates using spherical trig (trigonometry on the surface of a sphere).

trimming *n.* The act of removing the DC offset from an analog circuit. Offset errors are usually small in modern op-amp circuits, but for some applications, even a few millivolts can be excessive. Some devices include provisions for trimming; the designer adds a potentiometer (those little cube-shaped boxes with an

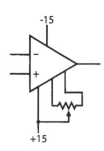

An LF155 op-amp with a trimming pot connected.

adjustable screwhead protruding from the top), which technicians then use to zero out the circuit's offset.

tristate 1. *adj.* Said of the output of a gate when in a high-impedance state. Bus structures abound in computer systems, but a bus is a wire or group of wires that can be driven by many different sources. To avoid bus contention, all of the drivers that are not in control are electrically disconnected from the bus. Each idle driver goes into a tristate condition, where its impedance goes to a very high value.

Thus, an output has three possible states: 1, 0, and tristate. Tristate drivers have an enable input (called output enable, or OE), which selects the high-impedance state. All memory chips have an OE pin, as do many logic components.

2. *adj.* Describes a gate that can have an output of 1, 0, or high impedance.

true *res.* An operator used for comparison and asserting Boolean truth in C++, Java, and several other languages. In C++ or Java, the statement `while (true) { ... }` is an infinite loop.

C99 adds `true` to C's lexicon, in header file std-bool.h. *Contrast with* TRUE.

TRUE *lit.* A popular, but nonstandard, #define indicating a Boolean truth in C programs. An unfortunate oversight in C was the lack of `true` and `false` keywords. By definition, any nonzero result is considered Boolean truth, and 0 is considered a false result. This has all sorts of implications, from the syntactic validity of the usually erroneous statement `if (x = 3)` to the fact that C programmers must define their own truth.

It is generally best to use the following definition pair.

```
#define FALSE 0
#define TRUE (!FALSE)
```

Contrast with `true`.

truth table *n.* A matrix that illustrates all possible inputs and outputs of a Boolean equation or logic circuit. Truth tables are used to both design and minimize circuits. Every combination of inputs is listed with the corresponding output. The designer ignores all outputs of 0 and writes AND terms for those that give a 1. These are then ORed together. *See also* Karnaugh map, minimize.

Consider a circuit that must turn an LED on when two inputs (A and B) are in different states. The truth table looks like the following figure. You can extract equations from it by ORing all of the conditions where a 1 results, yielding A/B + /AB, which is an XOR.

A	B	Out
0	0	0
0	1	1
1	0	1
1	1	0

TTL (as letters) *abbr. See* transistor–transistor logic.

TTM (as letters) *abbr. See* time to market.

Turing machine *N.* A simple machine consisting of a tape, a read/write head, and a table of state changes. The tape is divided into discrete boxes, each of which can have either a 0 or a 1 in it. The head will read or write a 0 or 1, depending on the current state and what is in the current tape square that the head reads.

Despite the simplicity of this idea, it lays down all the foundations for understanding the modern computer and computation in general.

Turing was able to show that the Turing machine was a mechanical process that was able to perform all the operations a person working with a logical system would be able to perform. Alonzo Church, in reference to Turing's work, formulated what is now called the Church–Turing thesis; namely, that all definitions of computability are equivalent. In other words, Turing machines can compute any function that is computable, assuming that both the tape and time are infinite.

History: Named for Alan Turing (1912–1954).

Turing test *n.* A proposed measure of intelligence developed by Alan Turing in 1950. The Turing test assumes an interrogator communicates with a human and a machine but does not know which is which. Turing postulates that if, by asking questions of the computer and the machine, the interrogator cannot determine which is the machine and which is the human, then the machine is intelligent.

Further Reading: Turing's original paper is at http://www.oxy.edu/departments/cog-sci/courses/ 1998/cs101/texts/Computing-machinery.html

Twist'N'Flat *n.* A type of flat ribbon cable that contains pairs of conductors twisted together. Also known as Twist-n-Flat. The cable is designed for propagating high-speed signals. Designers put a ground as one element of each pair: twisting a ground with each signal minimizes radiated energy, reduces coupling from adjacent conductors, and helps control the cable's impedance. Flat (untwisted) sections every 18 inches are included for mass termination connectors. *See also* flat ribbon cable, twisted pair.

twisted pair *n.* Two wires wrapped tightly around each other to minimize radiated energy and coupling with other signals and to control impedance. Twisted pairs are used to propagate high-speed digital signals. Often one conductor is ground. Although not as perfect a transmission medium as coax, twisted pair is a cheap and reasonably effective alternative.

In cases where magnetic effects create problems (say, around a flux gate compass), it's common to twist even the V_{cc} and ground wires together to cancel their magnetic field.

two's complement *n.* The binary representation of a particular integer value in two's complement notation.

two's complement notation *n.* A way of encoding positive and negative integer values in binary. Two's complement notation creates negative numbers by first inverting each bit then adding one to the result. Thus, the negative of 0101b is 1010b + 0001b = 1011b. Note that this results in all positive numbers having an MSb of 0 and all negative numbers having an MSb of 1.

Two's complement notation is the dominant representation of integer values in modern binary computers. *Compare to* one's complement notation, sign magnitude notation.

two-pass *adj.* Said of a compiler or assembler that makes two passes through the source code before producing the final output. The easiest way to implement an assembler, for example, is to first read the file and record all the symbol table entries. Once each variable has had storage defined to it through that process, the file is reread and the individual mnemonics are translated into machine code, complete with those addresses.

typedef *res.* A keyword used to define new data types in C. In C++, typedef is still available but less frequently used. All C++ structs, enums, and classes are automatically defined as new types. Only in C do you need to write

```
typedef struct { ... } myNewType;
```

to later declare myNewType foo;.

Useful for defining platform-specific primitive types, such as int8_t.

A set of typedefs for fixed-sized integer types. The specifics differ by processor/compiler; those shown are for a 16-bit x86 target.

```
typedef signed char      int8_t;
typedef signed short     int16_t;
typedef signed long      int32_t;

typedef unsigned char    uint8_t;
typedef unsigned short   uint16_t;
typedef unsigned long    uint32_t;
```

typedef 1. *n.* Any type created by a `typedef`.
   2. *v.* To define a new type via `typedef`.

USAGE: Right or wrong, the past tense is often written typedef'd.

U

UART (you art) *abbr.* Universal Asynchronous Receiver–Transmitter.

uClinux (you see Linux) *n.* A variant of the popular Linux kernel designed for use in systems without an MMU. A trademark of Lineo. Despite the absence of an MMU, uClinux provides complete and stable support for multitasking, along with a TCP/IP stack, support for popular filesystems such as ext2, NFS, and FAT, and the familiar Linux API. It has been used successfully in commercial products.

FURTHER READING: http://www.uclinux.org

UDM (as letters) *abbr. See* Universal Design Methodology.

UDP (as letters) *abbr.* A connectionless transport layer protocol. Short for User Datagram Protocol. RFC 768. Network packets sent via UDP cannot be larger than the MTU, can get lost in transmission, and could arrive out of order. If your application needs any of these things and can't work around these problems easily, use TCP instead.

UDP port *n.* A numeric identifier for a UDP endpoint on a particular network node. To reach a particular device, each UDP datagram must be addressed to a valid IP address and port number. If no thread is listening on that particular port, the datagram will be discarded by the receiver's

UDP/IP stack. *See also* socket, well-known port numbers.

UDP/IP (as letters) *abbr.* A variant of a TCP/IP stack that supports only the UDP protocol at the transport layer. TCP and UDP are peer protocols, in that they both operate at the same OSI layer and both run on top of IP. In many networked embedded systems, TCP's costs outweigh its benefits. In those, UDP can be used exclusively; hence, the TCP/IP stack becomes a UDP/IP stack. The former is simply a superset of the latter.

`uint8_t` (you int 8) *res.* An unsigned 8-bit integer data type similar to `int8_t`.

`uint16_t` (you int 16) *res.* An unsigned 16-bit integer data type similar to `int16_t`.

`uint32_t` (you int 32) *res.* An unsigned 32-bit integer data type similar to `int32_t`.

`uint64_t` (you int 64) *res.* An unsigned 64-bit integer data type similar to `int64_t`.

ultrawideband *n.* A communications scheme that distributes the signal across an extremely wide frequency band. Abbreviated UWB. Sub-nanosecond pulses spread the energy of the signal across a wide range of frequencies. Because the energy is thus divided, the energy of individual frequency components is extremely low—often below the noise floor of other users of the same spectrum.

Although the basic technique is quite similar to Guglielmo Marconi's transatlantic spark-gap transmission experiments circa 1901, UWB wasn't formalized until the DoD started using it for radar, location, and communication in the late 1980s. Some attractive features of UWB are its ability to penetrate walls and other objects, relative undetectability (because of the low power), and potentially high data rates (because of the wide bandwidth).

At the time of this writing, the FCC had recently allowed limited commercial use of the technology. It remains to be seen what applications it might dominate.

UML (as letters) *abbr. See* Unified Modeling Language.

UML state machine *See* UML statechart.

UML statechart *n.* An object-based variant of the Harel statechart. UML statecharts represent the current state of the art in state machine theory and notation. They are hierarchical state machines that additionally support orthogonal regions.

As hierarchical state machines, UML statecharts support state nesting and behavioral inheritance. In addition, a composite state can be decomposed into two or more orthogonal regions (orthogonal means independent in this context); being in such a composite state entails being in all of its orthogonal regions simultaneously.

In most real-life situations, orthogonal regions are only approximately orthogonal (i.e., they are not quite independent). Therefore, UML statecharts provide a number of ways for orthogonal regions to communicate and synchronize their behaviors. From this rich set of (sometimes complex) mechanisms, perhaps the most important is that orthogonal regions can coordinate their behaviors by sending event instances to each other.

Even though orthogonal regions imply independence of execution (i.e., some kind of concurrency), the UML specification does not require

that a separate thread of execution be assigned to each orthogonal region (although it can be implemented that way). In fact most commonly, orthogonal regions execute within the same thread. The UML specification only requires that the designer not rely on any particular order in which an event instance will be dispatched to the involved orthogonal regions.

EXAMPLE: A computer keyboard has two independent parts: the main keypad and a smaller numeric keypad. The main keypad can be in two states: Default and capsLocked, depending on the state of the Caps Lock key. The numeric keypad also can be in two states: Numbers and Arrows, depending on whether the Num Lock key is active. The complete state space of the keyboard in the standard decomposition is the cross product of the two components (main keypad and numeric keypad) and consists of four states: Default–Numbers, Default–Arrows, capsLocked–Numbers, and capsLocked–Arrows. However, these states are unnatural because behavior of the numeric keypad does not depend on the state of the main keypad and vice versa. Orthogonal regions allow you not to mix the independent behaviors as a cross product, but rather to keep them separate.

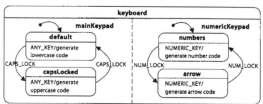

A UML statechart describing a computer keyboard with two orthogonal regions.

unary *adj.* Said of an operator that takes one input. In high-level languages, operators transform one or more input arguments. A unary operator requires exactly one input.

EXAMPLE: The tilde (~) is a unary operator taking one input and returning the bitwise-NOT.

underflow *See* arithmetic underflow.

Unicode (you knee code) *N.* A 16-bit extension of the ASCII character set. The Unicode character set includes some 35,000 characters from numerous languages. Java and C99 both include direct support for this ultimate of character sets. *See also* internationalization.

unidirectional *adj.* A one-way flow of information, as in some communications channels. *Contrast with* bidirectional.

EXAMPLE: The address bus coming out of a processor is generally unidirectional.

Unified Modeling Language *N.* A standardized visual notation for communication about system specifications and design details.

uninitialized data *n.* Static variables that have no initial value assigned to them. Uninitialized data is generally located in the bss segment. *Contrast with* initialized data.

EXAMPLE:

```
int x;
```

unit impulse *See* Dirac impulse function.

unit test *n.* The act of testing a function or module stand-alone. Unit tests use test data and/or test drivers; they don't happen as part of a check of the entire system. A (flawed) belief is that unit testing all of the functions means the system will work. In fact, the unit test is the easy part. *See also* system integration.

unity gain *n.* A constant gain of precisely 1.0.

universal asynchronous receiver–transmitter *n.* A component that receives and transmits asynchronous serial data. Abbreviated UART. The UART accepts a parallel byte from the computer. It serializes the byte, transmitting each bit at the appropriate time. A start bit is added, as are (optionally) stop and parity bits. Reception is the reverse. The UART usually also handles handshaking signals.

Although it's possible to simulate a UART in software (the so-called bit banger), the relatively precise timing needed by asynchronous serial data makes this a headache. *See also* asynchronous communications.

Universal Design Methodology *n.* A process for planning and designing hardware. Abbreviated UDM. UDM is defined in Bob Zeidman's book, *Designing with FPGAs and CPLDs* (CMP Books, 2002), though it is applicable to other kinds of hardware design like PCB and ASICs as well.

Universal Serial Bus *n.* A serial protocol and physical link that transmits all data differentially on a single pair of wires. Abbreviated USB. USB is an increasingly popular replacement for slower serial and parallel ports, especially for connecting to general-purpose computers. In addition to higher throughput, USB also offers the ability to power downstream devices and to connect a much larger number of devices.

The USB 1.0 standard specifies two kinds of cables and two variations of connectors. High-speed cables, for 12 Mbps communication, are better shielded than their less expensive 1.5 Mbps counterparts. Each cable has an "A" connector on one end and a "B" on the other. Since the two types are physically different it's impossible to install a cable incorrectly. See figure.

universal synchronous–asynchronous receiver–transmitter *n.* A peripheral that receives and transmits asynchronous and synchronous serial data. Abbreviated USART. The USART accepts a parallel byte from the computer. It serializes the byte, transmitting each bit at the appropriate time. A start bit is added (for asynchronous transmissions), as are (optionally) stop and parity bits. Reception is the reverse. The USART usually also handles handshaking signals. *See also* universal asynchronous receiver–transmitter, I²C.

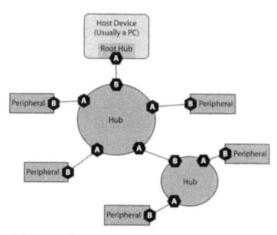

Universal Serial Bus The interconnections of USB devices in a tiered star topology.

Unix (you-nicks) *n.* A multiuser operating system for workstations. The most common use for Unix in the embedded realm is as a host platform for software or hardware development. There are various "flavors" of Unix, including Solaris and Linux. All are multitasking operating systems, but only a few specialized variants support real time.

unmount *n.* To logically disconnect a disk or other I/O device from a computer system. *Contrast with* mount.

unobtanium *n.* A component or subassembly that is no longer available to manufacturing, generally resulting in a new engineering effort. Individual ICs and SBCs often are discontinued, and companies still building products that incorporate these parts must go back to the drawing board. Many product companies attempt to manage this problem by choosing commodified parts that are multisource or by purchasing large inventories of single-source parts that would put them at most risk if no longer available.

unsigned *res.* Used with `char`, `short`, `int`, or `long` to declare an unsigned integer.

unsigned integer *n.* A variable that can store only zero or a positive whole number.

untwisted pair *n.* Two parallel wires used to transmit an analog or digital signal. Sometimes abbreviated UTP Untwisted pairs are fine for very short connections but have widely varying impedances, so they fair poorly with high-speed data. They are susceptible to EMF interference and are therefore problematic for analog signals. *See also* twisted pair.

unused inputs *n.* GPIO pins that are not used in a particular system.

up counter *n.* A counter that counts up from zero toward its maximum value. *Contrast with* down counter.

upgrade 1. *v.* To download or otherwise cause a system to run a newer version of firmware. Some products must be returned to the factory to accomplish this. Others might require that a ROM be replaced. The most flexible solution involves flash memory and a flash-resident piece of software called a bootloader.

2. *n.* A newer firmware version.

upload *v.* To move data or code, generally from a target to a host, over a communications channel such as a serial port. Data or code is uploaded in a direction opposite a download.

EXAMPLE: An embedded system might be connected to a laptop in the field in order to upload a data or error log to the PC for offline analysis.

UPnP (you pee 'n pee) *abbr.* An initiative driven by Microsoft to provide for the discovery and the service APIs for a dynamic network environment. Short for Universal Plug and Play. UPnP is based on IP and other existing protocols. *See also* HAVi, Jini.

FURTHER READING: http://www.upnp.org

UPS (as letters) *abbr.* A stand-alone backup for AC power sources. Short for Uninterruptible Power Supply. If or when the power goes out, a battery in the UPS is switched on and used to power anything plugged into it for as long as possible. Although a UPS won't run forever, it is a critical component for any system that must achieve five nines reliability.

USART (you-sart) *abbr. See* universal synchronous–asynchronous receiver–transmitter.

USB (as letters) *abbr. See* Universal Serial Bus.

user mode *n.* A state in which a processor will not execute some of its instructions. For example, while in user mode, it might not be possible to disable interrupts. *Contrast with* kernel mode.

UTC (as letters) *abbr.* The current time at 0 longitude. Short for the French version of Coordinated Universal Time. *See also* GMT.

utilization *See* CPU utilization.

utilization bound *See* schedulable bound.

utilize *v.* A pretentious way of saying "use." One finds this word sprinkled with abandon throughout technical documents and users' manuals. Don't use it.

UTP (as letters) *abbr. See* untwisted pair.

UV eraser *n.* A device that emits ultraviolet radiation for the purpose of erasing EPROMs.

UWB (as letters) *abbr. See* ultrawideband.

**V() ** *fn.* Dijkstra's name for the semaphore release primitive. V is short for *verhogen*, which is the Dutch word for increment.

V_{cc} (vee see see) *n.* The power pin to an IC. Mostly used to designate digital power, though rarely one sees this used as an analog device's positive power pin. In digital circuits, this was once always 5 V, today V_{cc} is edging to lower values to minimize power dissipation in ICs; 3.3-, 2-, and even 1-V power supplies abound.

V_{dd} (vee dee dee) *n.* Positive rail pin for analog and (rarely) some digital ICs. On digital devices most vendors designate power by V_{cc}; V_{dd} was primarily used on old-style CMOS chips.

V-F converter *See* voltage-controlled oscillator.

vacuum tube *n.* A (usually) glass-encased active element used to amplify or rectify a signal. Vacuum tubes (called valves in the U.K.) were, before the transistor, the only active element in electronics (other than sele-

The schematic symbol for a 12AX7.

nium diodes and a few other oddities). Like a transistor, the tube is basically an amplifying device. Unlike transistors—but similar to FETs—it is based on voltage rather than current.

Tubes have a cathode that emits electrons, one or more grids through which the electrons flow, and a plate to which they are attracted. A small voltage on the grid modulates the current flow. A filament heats the cathode to bake electrons from the cathode's surface.

A dual triode 12AX7, one of the most popular tubes ever made.

HISTORY: The earliest computers all used vast arrays of vacuum tubes; ENIAC used some 18,000. Because tubes have a limited life, technicians pushed shopping carts of tubes around the machine, almost constantly replacing defective devices.

No computer today uses tubes; however, they can still be found in some RF applications and guitar amplifiers; musicians (and audiophiles) like the sound.

valve *See* vacuum tube.

variable *n.* A location in RAM that has a name assigned to it and can be accessed through that name.

VB (as letters) *abbr. See* Visual Basic.

VCO (as letters) *abbr. See* voltage-controlled oscillator.

VCS (as letters) *abbr. See* version control system.

vector 1. *n.* A quantity that has both magnitude and direction. Often drawn as a directed line. *See also* velocity.
EXAMPLE: A force has both a magnitude and a direction.
2. *n.* The address of a destination. Vectors are usually arranged in tables (e.g., an interrupt vector table). An index is formed into the table (by the interrupt controller in the case of interrupt vectors), which selects the appropriate entry. *See also*

reset address. 3. *v.* To call a function through a vector table.

vector table *See* interrupt vector table.

velocity *n.* A vector quantity that gives the direction and amount of motion. Velocity is the integral of acceleration and the derivative of position. Note that speed is the scalar (magnitude only) part of velocity; speed has no direction.
EXAMPLE: A car at 60 miles per hour in a constant turn is accelerating, since the direction part of the velocity vector is changing.

Verilog *N.* A popular hardware description language.

version *n.* A numerical identifier for a particular release of a product, particularly software. Sometimes abbreviated "v", as in Linux v7.2.

version control system *n.* A tool used by programmers to track the changes resulting from enhancements and bug fixes in the history of one or more source files. For a small project with just one or two source files, it might be realistic to keep a version history by keeping copies in distinctly named archive directories or Zip files, but when a project grows larger, and particularly when more than one developer is involved, a version control system can be indispensable.

If you've ever needed to reconstruct the source code for an older deployed version of your firmware or keep separate source trees for new development and bug fixes, you've already seen what a version control system can do for you. So if you aren't using one, why not?
EXAMPLE: SCCS, ClearCase, and Visual Source-Safe are popular version control tools.

very large scale integration *n.* A term associated with ICs that have millions—or more—of transistors. Abbreviated VLSI. *Contrast with* small-scale integration.

very long instruction word *n.* A computer architecture that uses a wide word format to implement instruction-level parallelism. Abbreviated VLIW. Similar to superscalar architectures, VLIW processors have several execution units of the same type (e.g., two multipliers), which enable the CPU to execute several instructions simultaneously (e.g., two multiplications). A wide instruction word is used to select from the available options.

VHDL (as letters) *abbr.* A popular hardware description language. Short for VHSIC Hardware Design Language.

VHSIC (as letters) *abbr.* Short for Very High Speed Integrated Circuit.

via *n.* A copper trace that connects signals on two or more layers of a PCB.

video RAM *n.* A block of RAM dedicated to a graphical display. Video RAM is quite often dual ported so that the processor can write new image data into it in the very same cycle that the graphics controller is drawing the old.

virtual machine *n.* An instruction-level simulator/run-time environment such as those used to execute Java bytecodes. The concept is not exclusive to Java but is strongly associated with that language. *See* Java virtual machine.

virtual memory *n.* A scheme that permits a system to use vast amounts of memory, even exceeding the amount that physically exists on the system. Virtual memory systems use a paging unit, which (like an MMU) translates addresses into physical addresses. The paging unit, though, also tracks the location of a page of virtual memory, which can be in physical memory or off on a hard disk. If not in memory, it's swapped in from the disk.

Virtual memory isn't used often in embedded systems, but as customers' appetites for features grow, this could change. Woe to the poor developers charged with writing all of this code! *See also* memory management unit.

Visual Basic *n.* A modern variant of BASIC developed by Microsoft and used to create and extend Windows applications. Abbreviated VB.

VLIW (as letters) *abbr. See* very long instruction word.

VLSI (as letters) *abbr. See* very large scale integration.

VME (as letters) 1. *abbr.* Short for VersaModule Eurocard. VME is codified in the IEEE-1014-1987 standard.

2. *See* VME bus.

VME bus *n.* A popular backplane used mostly for higher performance systems. Mechanically, VME-compatible cards are 160 × 100 mm (3U), 160 × 233 mm (6U), or 367 × 400 mm (9U). They support 16- to 32-bit addressing, with extensions to 64 bits under the VME64 standard. Boards offer up to 500 MBps transfer rates over the backplane and multiprocessing capabilities.

void *res.* Having no defined type. In function prototypes and definitions, the void keyword is used to indicate the lack of a return value or parameters. In pointer creation and manipulation, it asks the compiler to forgo all possible knowledge of the type of data pointed to.

How not to avoid void.

```
/*
 * A function with no parameters.
 */
int func1(void)
{
    ...
    return (0);
}

/*
 * A function with no return value
 * and a pointer with no defined type.
 */
void func2(int a, int b)
{
    void * p = (void *) &a;
    ...
}
```

VoIP (as letters) *abbr.* A communications protocol for sending real-time voice data over an IP-based packet network. Short for Voice-over Internet Protocol. VoIP can be used to communicate by voice from one PC to another over the Internet or with specialized telephone equipment using an ordinary-looking telephone on one or both ends.

`volatile` *res.* A C keyword that should be used to warn your compiler (particularly the optimizer) about any pointers that point to registers with volatile values. This will ensure that the actual value is reread each time the data is used.

volatile *adj.* Said of a value that can change without the intervention of software. For example, values within the registers of some I/O devices might change in response to external events. Similarly, the contents of global variables that are shared by two or more tasks or a task and an ISR can be considered volatile. *See also* `volatile`.

FURTHER READING: Jones, Nigel. "Introduction to Volatile," *Embedded Systems Programming*, July 2001.

volt *n.* A standard unit of electromotive force. Abbreviated V. One volt is the electrical force between two points for which 1 ampere of current will do 1 joule of work.

HISTORY: Named for Alessandro Giuseppe Anastasio Volta (1745–1827).

volt-ohm meter *n.* A piece of electrical test equipment that measures voltage and resistance. Abbreviated VOM.

voltage *n.* The amount of electromotive force between charges measured in volts.

voltage divider *n.* A circuit of two or more resistors that reduces an input voltage to some lower value.

EXAMPLE: In the circuit shown, R1 and R2 form a voltage divider. If R1 is 100 Ω, R2 is 200 Ω, and the battery is 10 V, then

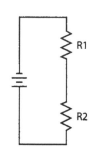

$$I = \frac{10}{100 + 200} = 33\,mA$$

and

$$V_{R2} = 0.033 \times 200 = 6.66\,V,$$

where I is current flow in the circuit and V_{R2} is voltage across R2.

voltage drop *n.* A decrease in voltage as a signal propagates down a conductor, caused by resistance in the conductor. The voltage drop is given by Ohm's law. Voltage drop is a headache for systems sending lots of current a long distance.

EXAMPLE: Voltage drop is the reason AC transmission lines operate at very high voltages. The goal of such lines is to send lots of power to end users. Power is measured in watts (voltage times current); yet, loss in a transmission line is also measured in power: $P = I^2 \times R$. Because the resistance of a particular line is constant, one can minimize power loss by reducing the amount of current transmitted. To keep the total power sent the same, the voltage is increased.

voltage island *n.* An area of an ASIC that is isolated from others for purposes of power management. Each voltage island can operate at a different voltage level and can be independently turned on and off.

voltage regulator *n.* A semiconductor that converts a DC input voltage in a supported range to a certain DC output voltage.

voltage-controlled oscillator *n.* An oscillator with an output frequency that is a function of an input voltage. Abbreviated VCO. VCOs are very useful for transforming analog data to digital and then transmitting the signal over a single wire.

voltmeter *n.* A piece of electrical test equipment that measures voltage.

VOM (as letters) *abbr. See* volt-ohm meter.

von Neumann architecture *n.* A processor structure based on a basic theory of operation that intermixes data and instructions so that any value in memory can be executed or interpreted as data. With the exception of some supercomputers and most DSPs, the von Neumann architecture is predominant.

HISTORY: Named after its inventor, John von Neumann (1903–1957).

VPN (as letters) *abbr.* A secure virtual TCP/IP network existing over the Internet or some other communications medium. Short for Virtual Private Network. VPN client software running on a laptop or home computer is often used to authenticate legitimate users of resources on a corporate intranet.

VRTX (virtex) *N.* A once-popular commercial RTOS developed at Ready Systems and now sold by Mentor Graphics.

VxWorks (vee ex works) *N.* A commercial real-time operating system from Wind River Systems. *See also* Tornado.

HISTORY: The "Vx" in VxWorks is short for VRTX. The product was originally a set of add-ons for the then-popular VRTX RTOS, rather than a direct competitor. A business dispute later caused Wind River Systems to write its own kernel and discontinue its previous practice of bundling the VRTX code and license.

wafer *n.* The nearly round disk of silicon onto which semiconductor vendors create many ICs. Chips are made by depositing chemicals on silicon wafers using photomasks in a process reminiscent of silkscreening but on an almost atomic scale. Each wafer contains hundreds or thousands of individual chips (usually all of the same design). A dicing operation cuts the wafer into the individual chips, which are then packaged.

Today's manufacturing processes use 200-mm-diameter wafers on the older technology fab lines and 300 mm on newer ones. It's pretty astonishing to consider that across that huge 300-mm (12-inch) disk, line widths are controlled to better than 90 nm (1000 atoms).

wait *n.* A microprocessor input that indicates the memory or I/O addressed in the current cycle needs more time to finish returning the requested data. Wait is generally active low on most processors. *See also* ready.

wait state *n.* An idle cycle used to give memory or I/O more time to respond. Wait states can be requested by memory systems or I/O devices or (as is more common in embedded systems) created by the processor's own wait state circuits. When the processor services a wait state request, it idles, issuing no bus activity for the entire cycle.

walking 0s test *n.* A memory test that involves moving a 0 bit through a byte or word to systematically confirm that each bit can hold a 0 value. All of the other bits are set to 1 during the test. A walking 0s or walking 1s test is effective in finding data bus pins that are wired improperly, shorted to other data bus pins, or not connected to the memory chip. Such tests should be used in conjunction with separate tests of the address bus and of the memory device itself.

walking 1s test *n.* A memory test that involves moving a 1 bit through a byte or word to systematically confirm each bit can hold a 1 value. All of the other bits are set to 0 during the test. *See also* checkerboard test.

EXAMPLE: An 8-bit walking 1s test begins by writing 00000001b to the test memory location, then reading it back. If the same value was read back successfully, then 00000010b is written and confirmed via a subsequent read. Then 00000100b, 00001000b, ... , and 10000000b are each tested. If all values are read back properly, then the data bus passes the test.

WAN (rhymes with man) *abbr. See* wide area network.

warm boot *n.* A system restart that does not go through a power-down cycle. Warm boots come from watchdog timeouts (which drive reset), smart switches (where the "off" switch puts the system into an alive but hibernating mode), or software trickery that causes a system restart.

It's common to stash a variable in volatile RAM that indicates the system has been through a cold boot at least once; this is a hint to the firmware that the current reset did not come from a power-down, but from a warm boot, so that (as one example) memory need not be tested again.

watch variable *n.* A piece of data that is being observed in a debugger. Whenever the running program breaks, the value in that memory location is read and the new value displayed.

watchdog timer *n.* A fail-safe mechanism that intervenes if a system stops functioning. Abbreviated WDT. A hardware timer that is periodically reset by software. If the software crashes or hangs, the watchdog timer will expire, and the entire system will be reset automatically.

watchpoint *n.* Like a breakpoint, but in the data area of memory rather than the code area. Any access to this location with the specified access type (read, write, read/write) stops execution and switches control to the debugger. Hardware support is required for realization of watchpoints. Watchpoints are not supported by all debugging tools.

waterfall development model *n.* The classic model of Big Up-Front Design, the waterfall development model separates each development activity into distinct parts, each of which is completed before moving on to the next.

The following steps are suggested:

- Requirements analysis
- Specification
- Architectural design
- Detailed design
- Coding
- Debugging
- Integration test

The difficulty of getting accurate requirements makes the waterfall model problematic. Modern methods stress a more iterative approach. *See also* agile development.

watt *n.* A standard unit of measure for power. Abbreviated W. One watt of power is 1 joule of work per second of time. This unit is used both in mechanics and in electricity, so it links the mechanical and electrical units to one another. In mechanical terms, 746 watts is about one horsepower. In electrical terms, 1 watt is the power produced by a current of 1 ampere flowing through an electric potential of 1 volt.

HISTORY: Named for James Watt (1736–1819).

wavelength *n.* The distance, in meters, between crests of an AC signal's waveform. Abbreviated ω.

$$\omega = \frac{c}{f}$$

where *c* is the speed of light and *f* is the frequency (Hz).

wchar_t *n.* C99's wide character type, which is large enough to hold a 16-bit Unicode character.

WDT (as letters) *abbr. See* watchdog timer.

web server *n.* A piece of software that operates over TCP/IP, to serve up HTML and other web pages. The client–server protocol standard recognized by web servers is called HTTP.

well-known port numbers *n.* TCP and UDP port numbers 0 through 1023, which are reserved for standardized protocols, such as FTP, telnet, HTTP, and others.

FURTHER READING: http://www.iana.org/assignments/port-numbers

Whetstone (wet stone) *n.* A Dhrystone-like benchmark suite for floating-point processors.

white noise *n.* A type of background noise that is present everywhere and can be characterized as having the same amount of energy at every individual frequency. It is not possible to use a lowpass, highpass, or any other filter to remove white noise, since there will still be noise components remaining in the passband of interest. By definition, the correlation between white noise and any other signal is 0. *See also* pink noise.

white paper *n.* A technical article that is either self-published or has not been peer reviewed.

USAGE: The term "white paper" is in some sense derogatory, since it is used most often to describe technical articles from vendors, which are mostly marketing pieces with a technical veneer. However, those who write white papers often call them by that very name; and we hope it stays that way. The mere fact that a technical article has been self-published without outside review does not make it invalid. The point is only that *caveat emptor* should be the norm when reading white papers; or as Ronald Reagan put it, "Trust, but verify."

white space *n.* The (hopefully) many spaces, tabs, and empty lines in a code listing. One goal of software engineering is to produce code that is easy to read and maintain. Judicious and consistent use of white space (and comments) is essential to achieving that goal.

wide area network *n.* A network that connects local area networks in distinct buildings, cities, or countries. Abbreviated WAN. Most large companies operate a WAN in addition to many LANs. The network technology of the WAN may be different from that of the LANs it interconnects. For a while, X.25 and, later, ATM were standard. Increasingly, though, corporations are getting out of the WAN management business by simplifying connecting their LANs via Internet-based virtual private networks.

wiggle *v.* To change the value of an electrical signal under software control, typically so that it can be observed on an oscilloscope.

WinCE (wince) *abbr. See* Windows CE.

Wind River Systems *N.* The company that developed the VxWorks real-time operating system. Sometimes just Wind River or abbreviated WRS. Since its acquisition of competitor Integrated Systems (developers of pSOS) in 2000, Wind River has been the dominant player in the RTOS marketplace. In a 2002 survey of *Embedded Systems Programming* subscribers, about 60% of those reporting they used a commercial RTOS in the past year had used one of Wind River's products.

window *n.* A transparent quartz portal into a ceramic IC's innards, generally to allow UV light in to erase its contents. A standard feature of EPROMs.

Windows *N.* The dominant family of operating systems for PCs. If you haven't heard of it, you've been living in a prison in a third world country for most of the last two decades.

Windows CE *n.* An embeddable variant of Microsoft's Windows operating systems. Abbreviated WinCE. Originally lacking real-time capabilities and still quite large (8 MB flash, minimum), WinCE has not yet taken off in the embedded space as Microsoft had hoped (and many RTOS vendors feared).

wire wrap *n.* A way of connecting components by tightly winding wire around a square post, creating mechanically and electrically tight connections. Wire wrap has traditionally been an inexpensive and quick way to create a prototype of a circuit. Used much more for logic than analog circuits. Properly done, it's highly reliable and was approved by NASA for ground support equipment. However, high-speed signals propagate poorly though wire wrap, and today's quick-turn PCBs are often cheaper than wire wrap.

wire wrap gun *n.* An electrically powered tool that wraps a wire around a square wire wrap post. Wire wrap guns give consistently high-quality wraps quickly and with minimal training. In the heyday of wire wrapping, the half-second "pzzzt" sound of these guns permeated prototyping labs. *See also* wire wrap.

wire wrap tool *n.* A pencil-shaped tool used to manually create a wire wrap joint. Used for rework or engineering changes only, it's very slow and inefficient, but most self-respecting digital engineers in the wire wrap days had one in their pocket protector. *See also* wire wrap.

wired-OR *adj.* An obsolete way of expanding OR gates to handle more inputs by paralleling the gates' outputs. Wired-OR devices have open-collector outputs. It's possible to connect these outputs together because there's no active pullup to create electrical problems and because any one gate driving low drives all outputs low.

Lacking an active pullup, wired-OR circuits are very slow, so they have mostly died out. They are more properly called wired-NOR, though that term is seldom heard.

wireless *n.* Sans physical connection. A la AM/FM radio, Bluetooth, 802.11, and a number of other technologies.

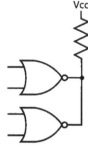

A wired-OR configuration. If any input goes to a 1, the NOR gate goes low, dragging both outputs low (because they are open-collector outputs). The resistor provides a logic 1 signal when all inputs are 0.

WLAN (W. LAN) *abbr.* A generic abbreviation for a wireless local area network of any sort.

WML (as letters) *abbr.* A variant of HTML for resource-constrained devices like cell phones. Short for Wireless Markup Language.

WOM (rhymes with ROM) *abbr. See* write-only memory.

word *n.* The "natural" width of integer data manipulated by a particular processor. On a 16-bit processor, a word is a 16-bit value. *See also* dword.

working set *n.* In a virtual memory environment, the set of pages for a particular process that are currently in physical memory. Pages outside the working set are in virtual memory (on disk) and will cause page faults if referenced.

write cycle *n.* A memory or I/O bus cycle used for writing data.

write protect *v.* To interlock a storage medium, preventing stored data from being changed. Floppy disks have a notch or switch to prevent writes. Some embedded nonvolatile memories are write protected by extra protection circuits, so errant programs cannot corrupt critical data. *See also* boot-block flash.

write() *n.* A common name for a system call that writes data from a specified memory buffer to an open file. A part of the standard Unix API for files and I/O devices. Once a file has been open()ed successfully, it can be written via the file descriptor held by the caller. *See also* read(), seek().

write-only memory *n.* A memory device that can be written, but never read. Think of it as the /dev/null of memory devices. In 1972, Signetics recognized April Fools Day by printing a datasheet for a new "Fully Encoded 9046 × N Random Access Write-Only Memory" device. Suggested uses included a datalogger for bombs.

FURTHER READING: The datasheet can be found at http://www.ganssle.com/misc/wom.html.

write-only register *n.* A peripheral control register that can be written but never read. Although write-only memory devices are merely humorous fictions, write-only registers actually do exist. They're very easy for hardware designers to create but extremely frustrating for software developers to use. The contents of such registers usually must be mirrored in memory so that the software will know what value the register holds.

write-through *See* cache, write-through.

X

X-Acto knife (ex act toe) *N.* A small, razor-sharp knife with a disposable blade used (in electronics) to remove solder bridges between IC pins, clean up PCB tracks, and trim fingernails. The X-Acto knife is part of the universal troubleshooting kit needed by every developer. Other components include duct tape, 10-kΩ resistors, and Super Glue.

x86 (ex eighty-six) *abbr. See* 80x86.

xcvr *See* transceiver.

Xilinx *N.* The world's leading provider of programmable logic devices, with 50% of the market in 2002. Founded in 1984, Xilinx pioneered the

X-acto knife The indispensable X-Acto knife, with the usual hint of blood on its tip.

FPGA and now also sells a line of CPLDs. Listed by Fortune Magazine in 2001 and 2002 as one of the best 100 companies to work for.

XIP (as letters) *abbr. See* execute-in-place.

XML (as letters) *abbr.* A language for the creation of customized markup languages. In that sense, a metalanguage. Short for eXtensible Markup Language. Unlike HTML, which has a fixed format, its cousin XML—both are defined in Standardized General Markup Language (SGML)—is flexible and extensible. It can be used to describe the content of any document or database.

XOFF (ex off) *n.* A special character transmitted in-band to request a resumption of a previously paused flow of incoming data. ASCII 0x13. *See also* XON, software flow control.

XON (ex on) *n.* A special character transmitted in-band to request a pause in the flow of incoming data. ASCII 0x11.

Note that because the XON character is sent in the communications channel, binary data sent across the channel must be stripped of all 0x11s. This is typically done by inserting an escape code before the binary data's 0x11 is sent so that the device on the other end will know not to inter-pret that next byte as an XON. *See also* XOFF, software flow control.

XOR (ex-or) *n.* A two-input Boolean operator that returns true if the inputs are different. Symbolically, $\oplus$.

$$A \oplus B = /AB + /BA$$

XOR is useful in circuits that compare quantities, in feedback shift registers, and in code converters. *See also* Boolean algebra.

XOR gate *n.* A logic circuit that computes the XOR function.

The schematic symbol of an XOR gate.

XP (as letters) *abbr. See* eXtreme Programming.

xtalk *See* crosstalk.

xtUML (as letters) *abbr.* A technique for separating design from implementation, yet using the same UML notations to facilitate each. Short for eXecutable and Translatable UML.

Y

Y2K (as letters) *abbr.* A predicted dramatic global embedded systems failure that never materialized. Short for Year 2000. Most embedded systems programmers correctly understood that the designers of elevators and sewer level monitors do not go to the trouble of including a calendar or of comparing dates and that, if they do, this date information is typically used only for event logging and not actual decision making.

Many Chicken Little outsiders, however, correctly grokking both the Y2K database problem linger-ing in legacy COBOL programs run by large private and government institutions and the increasing ubiquity of processors at the heart of almost everything that plugs into the wall or eats batteries, predicted a virtual doomsday, bought gold ingots or generators, and filled their bathtubs with water in anticipation of the nonevent of the century.

yacc (yak) *N.* A tool for generating C or C++ code for a parser. Short for Yet Another Compiler

Compiler. Once an stream of data has been converted into tokens by a lexical scanner, such as lex, the relationship between those tokens needs to be established. The possible token orders for a language is called its grammar. Yacc is a command-line tool that accepts a grammar description (in a text file) as input and generates the code for a parser for that grammar as output. Parsers are useful in many systems other than just compilers, such as for reading the contents of a configuration file stored in a system's flash memory.

yield 1. *v.* To offer use of the CPU to another task that is ready to run.

2. *n.* The percentage of good die on a wafer. IC vendors test each die, with the sure knowledge that some percentage of them will not pass. Mature manufacturing processes with smaller chips give high yields; very dense parts or those made with new processes could result in yields less than 50%.

Z

zero 1. *See* logic 0.

2. *n.* A processor flag indicating whether the previous instruction resulted in a zero result.

3. *v.* To set something (a bit or signal) to 0.

ZIF socket (like riff) *n.* An IC socket that is designed for ease of chip insertion and removal. Short for Zero Insertion Force.

ASCII Character Chart

The ASCII character set, complete with its original Teletype control characters.

Decimal	Hex	ASCII	Decimal	Hex	ASCII	Decimal	Hex	ASCII	Decimal	Hex	ASCII
0	00	NUL	32	20	Space	64	40	@	96	60	`
1	01	SOH	33	21	!	65	41	A	97	61	a
2	02	STX	34	22	"	66	42	B	98	62	b
3	03	ETX	35	23	#	67	43	C	99	63	c
4	04	EOT	36	24	$	68	44	D	100	64	d
5	05	ENQ	37	25	%	69	45	E	101	65	e
6	06	ACK	38	26	&	70	46	F	102	66	f
7	07	BEL	39	27	'	71	47	G	103	67	g
8	08	BS	40	28	(	72	48	H	104	68	h
9	09	TAB	41	29	)	73	49	I	105	69	i
10	0A	LF	42	2A	*	74	4A	J	106	6A	j
11	0B	VT	43	2B	+	75	4B	K	107	6B	k
12	0C	FF	44	2C	,	76	4C	L	108	6C	l
13	0D	CR	45	2D	-	77	4D	M	109	6D	m
14	0E	SO	46	2E	.	78	4E	N	110	6E	n
15	0F	SI	47	2F	/	79	4F	O	111	6F	o
16	10	DLE	48	30	0	80	50	P	112	70	p
17	11	DC1	49	31	1	81	51	Q	113	71	q
18	12	DC2	50	32	2	82	52	R	114	72	r
19	13	DC3	51	33	3	83	53	S	115	73	s
20	14	DC4	52	34	4	84	54	T	116	74	t
21	15	NAK	53	35	5	85	55	U	117	75	u
22	16	SYN	54	36	6	86	56	V	118	76	v
23	17	ETB	55	37	7	87	57	W	119	77	w
24	18	CAN	56	38	8	88	58	X	120	78	x
25	19	EM	57	39	9	89	59	Y	121	79	y
26	1A	SUB	58	3A	:	90	5A	Z	122	7A	z
27	1B	ESC	59	3B	;	91	5B	[	123	7B	{
28	1C	FS	60	3C	<	92	5C	\	124	7C		
29	1D	GS	61	3D	=	93	5D	]	125	7D	}
30	1E	RS	62	3E	>	94	5E	^	126	7E	~
31	1F	US	63	3F	?	95	5F	_	127	7F	DEL

Decimal Prefixes

Prefix	Symbol	Multiplier
exa-	E	10^{18}
peta-	P	10^{15}
tera-	T	10^{12}
giga-	G	10^{9}
mega-	M	10^{6}
kilo-	k	10^{3}
hecta-	h	10^{2}
deca-	da	10^{1}
deci-	d	10^{-1}
centi-	c	10^{-2}
milli-	m	10^{-3}
micro-	µ	10^{-6}
nano-	n	10^{-9}
pico-	p	10^{-12}
femto-	f	10^{-15}
atto-	a	10^{-18}

Binary Prefixes

kibi-	Ki	2^{10}
mebi-	Mi	2^{20}
gibi-	Gi	2^{30}
tebi-	Ti	2^{40}
pebi-	Pi	2^{50}
exbi-	Ei	2^{60}

Resistor Color Code

Color	Significant Figure	Multiplier	Tolerance
Black	0	1	-
Brown	1	10	-
Red	2	100	-
Orange	3	1,000	-
Yellow	4	10,000	-
Green	5	100,000	-
Blue	6	1,000,000	-
Violet	7	10,000,000	-
Gray	8	100,000,000	-
White	9	1,000,000,000	-
Gold	-	0.1	5%
Silver	-	0.01	10%
No color	-	-	20%

Author Biographies

Jack Ganssle

Jack Ganssle has been writing the Break Points column for *Embedded Systems Programming* for more than a dozen years, and is that magazine's technical editor. He has written two books on electronics—*The Art of Programming Embedded Systems* and *The Art of Designing Embedded Systems*—and another about his sailing exploits (*Go West: The 1992 Singlehanded Transatlantic Race*).

Jack started developing embedded systems in the early 1970s using the now-antique 8008 processor. Since then he's started and sold three electronics companies. He has developed or managed the development of over a hundred products, including in-circuit emulators, underwater navigation equipment, steel thickness gauges, agricultural measurement instruments, the White House security system, cross compilers, and numerous classified Government systems. He lectures internationally.

Michael Barr

Michael Barr has been an editor of *Embedded Systems Programming* since 1999 and a contributor since 1997; he is currently its editor-in-chief. His book about embedded software development—*Programming Embedded Systems in C and C++*—has taught tens of thousands of engineers the subject and been translated into several languages.

Michael is a lecturer at the University of Maryland and an Embedded Systems Conference instructor and advisor. Software he wrote helps run millions of systems around the world, ranging from satellite base stations to physical therapy equipment. Through the Netrino Consultants Network, Michael provides design advice and training. He holds MS and BS degrees in electrical engineering.

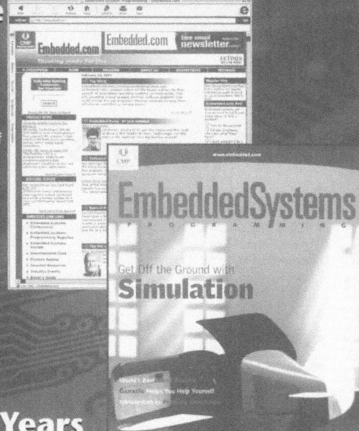

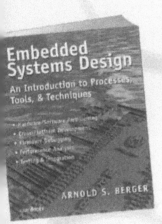